Memoirs of a
Wartime Interpreter

Memoirs of a Wartime Interpreter

From the Battle for Moscow to Hitler's Bunker

Yelena Rzhevskaya

Translated by
Arch Tait

Foreword by
Roger Moorhouse

Greenhill Books

Memoirs of a Wartime Interpreter
This edition first published in 2018 by
Greenhill Books,
c/o Pen & Sword Books Ltd,
47 Church Street, Barnsley,
S. Yorkshire, S70 2AS

www.greenhillbooks.com
contact@greenhillbooks.com

ISBN: 978–1–78438–281–0

CIP data records for this title are available from the British Library

Designed and typeset by Donald Sommerville
Printed and bound in the UK by TJ International Ltd, Padstow

Typeset in ITC Usherwood Book and Medium

Published by arrangement with
ELKOST International literary agency, Barcelona, Spain

The publication was effected under the auspices of the
Mikhail Prokhorov Foundation TRANSCRIPT Programme
to Support Translations of Russian Literature

Contents

Acknowledgements

This is the story of the war as I saw it, from the battle for Moscow to the last days in Hitler's bunker, and Stalin's efforts to rewrite history to his own ends.

I am profoundly grateful to Yelena Kostyukovich, who took this book to an Italian publisher and kept an eye on how it was faring, just when her own amazing book, *Food: Italian Happiness*, was being published to international acclaim (and meeting with great success in Moscow). She continued with unflagging attentiveness to advise and comment on my book during its final stages.

Thank you also for help and support as I worked on the book to my friend and discussant, my granddaughter Lyuba.

Plates

All images © the estate of Yelena Rzhevskaya.

Foreword

When Yelena Rzhevskaya joined up in the autumn of 1941, she could have had little inkling of the role that she would eventually play in the history of the twentieth century. A young literature student, studying at Moscow State University, she initially worked in an armament factory, then trained as a nurse, before her knowledge of German caused her to be sent for instruction as a Red Army interpreter. A couple of months later, armed with a pocket dictionary and a notebook, she was dispatched to the front.

The world into which she was sent was almost completely alien to her: a dystopia of murderous combat, destitute refugees and seemingly endless ruins, in which she had not even been trained to use a gun. Her journey took her westwards through Rzhev – the infamous 'meat-grinder', west of Moscow, which was finally liberated in March 1943, and in whose honour she took her *nom de plume* – via Warsaw and on to Poznań, where she arrived in the opening months of 1945.

Her primary task throughout was the interrogation of prisoners; often of 'squealers' – German sentries snatched from their posts by Red Army patrols, to be pressed for information. Most of them, she said, were little more than frightened boys. Her account, which brims with contemporary material – from captured German 'field-post' letters to official documents and extracts from her own diary – is beautifully and engagingly written, and full of wonderful vignettes of those caught up in the fighting or in the chaos of its aftermath. Throughout, Rzhevskaya's humanity, her sympathy for the ordinary people thrown into the maelstrom of war, stands out.

This human sympathy, coupled with Rzhevskaya's elegance as a writer, would have made her account memorable even without her participation in world-changing events. But, participate in them she did. In April 1945, she was transferred to the Soviet 3rd Shock Army, then poised for the final assault on Berlin. After fighting through the northern suburbs of the German capital, on 28th April units of the 3rd Shock Army crossed the Moltke Bridge in central Berlin, and began storming the Reichstag, decreed by Moscow to be the symbol of Nazi German power. The real seat of Nazi power; the Reich Chancellery, was barely 200 metres distant, and Soviet forces – with Rzhevskaya in their train – arrived there on 2 May. There – in what remained of the Reich Chancellery garden – she would be one of only a handful of people to see the corpses of both Josef Goebbels and Adolf Hitler. It would become the defining experience of her life.

Brought in to interpret for the small team trying to establish the identity of the charred corpses that were found in the Chancellery garden, and by extension investigating the circumstances of Hitler's death, Rzhevskaya found herself – for a few days at least – at the very epicentre of events. While the world pondered Hitler's fate, she was busy collecting and translating documents that had been taken from Hitler's bunker and interviewing those who had witnessed his final days. She was even put in charge of the remains of Hitler's teeth – rescued from his shell-hole grave – which were placed in a lined jewellery box for safe keeping. They were entrusted to her, it is thought, because she was considered less likely than her male counterparts to get drunk and mislay them.

Those teeth would prove decisive in identifying the corpse as Hitler's. Heavily dentured – having suffered from poor teeth for most of his life – Hitler had very extensive and distinctive dentistry; consisting of dentures, bridges and crowns, as well as his own few remaining teeth. A priority for the investigators, therefore, was to find Hitler's dentist – Hugo Blaschke – or any of the team that had worked with him, to aid the identification. Though Blaschke himself had fled to Bavaria, Rzhevskaya and her group of investigators tracked down his assistant, Käthe Heusermann, in Berlin, who confirmed that she had indeed worked on Hitler's teeth many times. She sketched his bridges and crowns from memory, matching perfectly the teeth in Rzhevskaya's jewellery box. And, when she was finally shown them, Heusermann confirmed: 'These are the teeth of Adolf Hitler.'

Yet, just as Rzhevskaya was expecting the crowning evidence of the identification – from the post mortem – word arrived that the Soviet press in Moscow was already reporting that Hitler might have escaped to Spain or South America. 'Our troops', she said 'were suddenly being urged to "Hunt for Hitler" . . . It was a deceitful charade, a weird attempt to disguise the fact that his body had been found.' She did not yet know it, but she had fallen foul of Stalin's mendacious desire to use the spectre of Hitler's survival as a stick with which to beat his erstwhile allies. With that, she wrote, 'Hitler was no longer an emblem of the war, he became an emblem of the kind of peace that was to follow.' Her investigation would thereby be rendered null and void. And all those witnesses who had assisted her, including Heusermann, were consigned to the prisons of the Soviet secret police, where they would be endlessly interrogated in an attempt to persuade them to collude in the lie of Hitler's supposed survival and escape. It was all part of a colossal task of deception and disinformation that would even be given its own title: 'Operation Myth'.

Returning to the Soviet Union after the war, Rzhevskaya shared the disappointments of many former soldiers: the dashed hope that victory might presage a loosening of the iron grip of Stalinism, and the wistful yearning for the excitement and sense of meaning that military life had brought with it. In her case, however, her frustrations were amplified by her enforced silence on the most important event of her life; a mere interpreter would have been profoundly unwise to have contradicted Comrade Stalin, especially on a matter as important as the death of Hitler. Consequently, it was not until the 1960s, more than a decade after Stalin's death, and two decades after Hitler's, that the first edition of her memoir – *Berlin, May 1945* – appeared in Russian.

Those memoirs were augmented and republished in a number of volumes over the years that followed, yet – oddly – have never appeared in English, until now. This new edition has *Berlin, May 1945* at its core, but also incorporates material predating that, as well as later additions, such as her account of a meeting with Georgiy Zhukov in 1965. It is worth mentioning perhaps that, while her account of the identification of Hitler's corpse has been shown to be incontrovertible, a few ancillary aspects of her narrative – such as her discussion of the precise circumstances of Hitler's suicide – are very much coloured by the Soviet assumptions of the 1960s, and therefore appear rather anachronistic by the standards of modern scholarship. To be fair to Rzhevskaya, she cannot have known this aspect for sure, and as she said, what really mattered – and what she could personally vouchsafe – was that Hitler was dead. Nonetheless, on this point, readers wishing to know more might want to refer to more recent works, such as the Hitler biographies by Ian Kershaw or Volker Ullrich.

Yelena Rzhevskaya wrote with deftness and no little poignancy. Despite the undoubted horrors of her wartime experience, she was a sympathetic guide through that Hades. She had an eye for the telling anecdote, certainly, but she also possessed the sensitivity and lyrical guile to remind her readers of the human bond that they shared with all those that she encountered, whether they be blustering Red Army captains, terrified German 'squealers', or forlorn prostitutes. Throughout, she is both thoughtful and thought-provoking, philosophical about mankind's frailties and foibles, and optimistic about its chances. It is a vision that is as seductive as it is enlightening.

Foreword

With its elegant prose, its memorable vignettes and its profound humanity, Yelena Rzhevskaya's memoir would be remarkable even without the headline act of her involvement in the identification of Hitler's corpse. The addition of that material, however, makes this book – quite simply – one of the most important memoirs to emerge from the Second World War.

Roger Moorhouse

Memoirs of a
Wartime Interpreter

Introduction:
The Documents Speak

This is a book about things I experienced personally. As a Red Army interpreter advancing with the front line of our army the whole way from Moscow in 1941 to Berlin in May 1945, I found myself at the epicentre of historic events that brought the Second World War to a close. As an interpreter at an army staff headquarters, I was a member of a counterintelligence group whose mission was to hunt down Adolf Hitler. I was present as we found his charred body and set about establishing the truth of how he met his end and identifying his remains. It was my task to sort through the documents we found in the underground complex of the Reich Chancellery and the Führerbunker, where Hitler spent his last days.

In the Chancellery I discovered files containing Martin Bormann's papers – radio-telegrams from his adjutant in Obersalzberg, Dr Helmut von Hummel, and copies of the telegrams he had sent. These confirmed there had been plans in the second half of April 1945 to move Hitler's general headquarters to Berchtesgaden, and also that Hitler had eventually refused to go. He decided to remain in the Führerbunker after an offensive he had ordered failed, but also because the Allies had entered Munich, which was no distance from Berchtesgaden. There were files of reports to Bormann from the *Kreisleiter,* heads of Nazi Party districts in Berlin, about the critical situation.

I sorted through those of Hitler's papers that remained in the bunker, including a file with monitored radio announcements, one of which reported that Mussolini, after being shot by partisans, had been strung upside down by his heels in a square in Milan alongside his mistress, Clara Petacci. Hitler had underlined that in blue pencil and I guessed (correctly) that this was what prompted him to have his own body destroyed. Here, too, we found drafts of letters Hitler wrote more than a decade previously to his sister, to President Hindenburg and to Franz von Papen.

In Goebbels' office we found two suitcases with documents, including a find of major importance for future historians: the ten or so notebooks of Goebbels' handwritten diary, begun before the Nazis came to power and breaking off on 8 July 1941. Here also was the minister of propaganda's official correspondence, and Magda Goebbels' files with detailed inventories of their family's personal property. There were family photographs of Magda and the children, the whole family with Goebbels, and also a portrait photograph of Magda I kept as a souvenir.

We were engaged in a feverish search for Hitler, dead or alive. I had time only to note the contents of the documents passing through my hands and add an explanatory note before sending them off to front headquarters. These brief notes were to come in very useful later when I was working in a secret Soviet archive and could immediately be reminded of the origin and context of each of them.

During the night of 5 May the remains of Adolf Hitler and Eva Braun were brought in from the Reich Chancellery garden. An autopsy was performed and on 8 May I was entrusted with a burgundy-coloured box containing Hitler's lower jaw and dentures, which were crucial for identifying his body. In that macabre manner I impinged on German history.

I now became involved in seeking out the people best placed to identify Hitler's body: his dentists. My signature, as interpreter, is appended to our records of their interrogation and to their identification of Hitler.

For the three months before I was demobilized, our army headquarters was in a small town called Stendal. There I was able to pore over the documents from the Reich Chancellery, from ministries and the apartments of the Nazi leaders. Already, though, interest in such documents was waning, the war was over, we ourselves had become history and nobody, except me, was much interested in them.

I am no professional historian or researcher, I am a writer. I cannot picture myself researching historical events or studying sociological matters unconnected with my own life, so this is a personal memoir backed up by documents. The facts and events it relates are true, and the theme holding everything together is a view of the war from the Soviet side, of the search for Hitler and discovery of his body, of how he was identified and the circumstances of his suicide investigated. In all of that I was personally involved as an interpreter and translator.

What matters most in a book of this kind is veracity. The biggest sensation is true information. The fact that Hitler's body had been found and identified by the Red Army was hushed up. I wrote about his death in *Znamya*, No. 2, 1955, but the part dealing with finding the body, the investigation and identification was censored. I was first able to reveal that state secret only in 1961 in my book, *Spring in an Army Greatcoat*, long after Stalin's death.

In order to give readers a full picture of these events and to document my eyewitness account, I long fought for access to Soviet archives. The response to all my appeals was, 'No, and we make no exceptions.' I even phoned the Communist Party Central Committee, but in the course of a lacklustre conversation was offered no encouragement. On the advice of V. Ilyin I wrote another letter, this time to Mikhail Suslov, a member of the Central Committee Praesidium. I recently came upon a copy of that letter, dated 6 August 1964, among my own papers. It evidently did the trick because, in late September 1964, the doors of a secret archive were opened to me.

A captain in the uniform of the tank corps was assigned to keep an eye on things. He belonged to a 'Group Studying Experience from the Patriotic War', and introduced himself as Vladimir Ivanovich. He took his obligation to provide me with the documents I needed very seriously.

Many years later, Vladimir Ivanovich phoned and spoke appreciatively about my latest book (about Rzhev during the war). 'This is lyrical documentary prose!' he exclaimed. I asked him for the name of the archive I had worked in, which had been kept secret. 'The Council of Ministers Archive,' he said, confirming a guess by Marshal Zhukov. Vladimir Ivanovich also told me I had been admitted on instructions from the Central Committee.

The approaching twentieth anniversary of the victory prompted people to think back to the war, and that included Vladimir Ivanovich. I could see he was not used to the watchdog role assigned to him and that, as I sat there working alone in a bare office with a portrait of Khrushchev on the wall, I really was an 'exception'. Vladimir Ivanovich did not keep to his brief of issuing only documents I was able to name. He would have been hard pressed to identify and extract them from the general heap of files, and instead let me see for myself everything that was brought. At the end of each working day I was required to hand in the notebook into which I had copied text and the thoughts that had occurred to me in the process. I had no technology to help me. Each morning the notebook was returned, presumably after being scrutinized. When one was full I was allowed to take it home, and in all I filled up five thick notebooks.

I was again encountering documents from May 1945, many of which bore my signature. They had lain untouched for twenty years and it was a very emotional experience.

Bolstered by these classified documents, the first edition of my book, *Berlin, May 1945*, was published in Russia in 1965, following an abridged publication in *Znamya*, No. 5, May 1965. Retitled *The End of Hitler, Without Myth or Mystification*, the book was translated into Italian, German, Hungarian, Finnish, Japanese and many other languages.

Since then, *Berlin, May 1945* has been republished twelve times in Russia, with over 1,500,000 copies sold, and each successive edition has been substantially revised and supplemented. The present volume is an updated version of that text, incorporating all the later additions.

As you look back over the years, what you experienced is not erased from memory: rather, certain aspects, certain facets become all the more visible. Your memory, appealed to yet again, takes you back to those days, and for me the story of the historic events at the end of the war would be incomplete without the pages describing its first days, the training course for military interpreters, my almost four years of active service and all the things I witnessed during them. I believe my reader will be interested to know the baggage I brought with me to Berlin.

A military interpreter is in a unique position during the cataclysm of war. He or she is in constant contact with the belligerents on both sides. Through my hands passed documents of every description, from some that were of great importance, to instructions to German soldiers on how to keep themselves warm; from orders and propaganda leaflets, to private letters home. As I was translating these documents, I would note down extracts to remember.

The notebooks I brought home from the front, dog-eared, with pages missing or untidily inserted, with barely legible entries written in the back of a jolting truck, were the raw material of my later tales about the war. Even now I return to them as I reconstruct my journey from Moscow to Berlin.

When my book was finally published it began to snowball, as new revelations came my way. One of the most important contacts coming out of it led to a conversation with Marshal Georgiy Zhukov. I received letters from other participants in the search for Hitler and the discovery and identification of his body, not least Dr Faust Shkaravsky, the pathologist in charge of the autopsy. They contributed new details from their specialist fields, and their letters, along with many others, make up my personal archive. The present edition has greatly benefited from them.

And finally, there are the documents themselves. In that first edition back in 1965 I wrote, 'The documents in these notes (testimony, papers, diaries, correspondence and so on) are being published for the first time by the present author.' In order to stick to that principle I only mentioned in passing such previously published documents as Hitler's personal will and his political testament. The only documents included were those I had sorted through early in May 1945 in the Reich Chancellery and later at army headquarters, as well, of course, as those unearthed in twenty hectic days in the archive in September 1964.

Many valuable discoveries I made in the archive found their way into the book. I published for the first time excerpts from the testimony of Hans Rattenhuber, the head of Hitler's bodyguard, and parts of the first interrogations at Soviet General Headquarters of Hitler's adjutant, Otto Günsche, and his valet, Heinz Linge. I published for the first time reports of the interrogation of the doctors who poisoned Goebbels' children, documents about the discovery of the bodies of Hitler and Eva Braun, of Goebbels and his wife, and the official reports of the autopsies.

The Council of Ministers Archive also held such important evidence as the diary of Martin Bormann in an official, typescript translation into Russian (the original having been found in early May lying in a Berlin street), and more detailed reminiscences from Hans Rattenhuber.

One of my most important revelations was the publication of excerpts from Goebbels' diary, which led to research by German historians who later published his notebooks in numerous volumes from microfilms provided by the archive.

Nowadays texts that I unearthed only after doggedly fighting my way through the obstacles of state secrecy and censorship are widely available and have been translated into many languages, so there is no longer any point in adhering rigidly to the principle of quoting only previously unpublished documents. It seems common sense to draw also on documents already known or published by others.

Authentic documents, especially when we look back at them from a distance, have a special aura, and the very fact that they are documents can lead to giving them more than their due and accepting them uncritically. We need to resist the temptation to consider every document tantamount to fact. They are not all factually true, and even a fact when out of context may not be the whole truth. Context matters. Information can conflict with, contradict, or even invalidate other information. When documents conflict with each other I have sometimes found myself having to referee on the basis of what I know about their background.

1 Into the Unknown: Moscow, 1941

When we sit down to write about past experience, we often force memory to be logical, but that goes against its nature. Memory is alive as moments, associations, ricochets, smells, and pain.

From my front-line diary:

The autumn twilight and the wind were cold, the sky black with dismaying grey flecks of impending dawn.

A god-forsaken road awash with mud, a straggling column of soldiers wandering towards the front line, in silence. No bawling out, no commands, no sound of voices. For a moment a German rocket flaring over the front lights up the indistinct faces of men no longer young. This will have been a company of reinforcements, put together from a regiment of reserves, of wounded soldiers patched up in hospitals or by the medical battalions.

I walk along the roadside on my way back to Staff Headquarters.

Muffled thunder in the silence, like the distant echo of a cannonade from the day before. The squelching of boots stumbling through the morass.

'Hey, sister!' an old timer detaches himself from the column. 'Got a smoke?'

'Sorry.'

He trudges on, out of luck, an old timer I will not forget.

Protected by a leaden sky lit up occasionally by a blinding enemy flare, the soldiers shamble on into the dank, inhospitable night towards the coming morning's battle.

I cannot explain even to myself why, down all the years and again today, that question gives me no peace, and why the memory of it so jars me and moves me to tears.

'Hey, sister! Got a smoke?'

*

They brought in a squealer, snatched from a forward lookout trench. He was perishing with the cold, swaddled in a woman's woollen shawl, a forage cap perched on his head. On his feet were thin leather boots no match for the frost, inserted in an apology for overshoes woven from straw. The scout escorting him was very publicly prodding the German in the back with the barrel of his rifle, encouraging him to look lively. In his straw overshoes he could barely drag himself along the slippery, churned-up road. Onlookers –two or three soldiers and a similar number of villagers – brought up the rear, curious to see what was going to happen. They halted at headquarters and the scout, leaving the soldiers to guard his prisoner, went into the hut to report.

Everyone surrounded the German, nobody speaking. An ill-defined tension. From autumn until December the village had been occupied by Germans, but they had looked nothing like this one. The villagers glanced awkwardly, furtively at him.

'War's over for you, Fritz,' remarked one battle-hardened soldier. 'You'll live, you scumbag.'

The German's eyes peered dimly out of the slits between frost-covered eyelashes, as dull and inanimate as the eyes of a water-sprite. He was not a happy Fritz and nobody else was sure quite how to behave, but a young soldier who had never seen a German before could not contain himself and burst out laughing. The German had icicles coming out of his nose and even out of his mouth, above the frost-covered shawl. They looked like a beard. You could hardly feel too hostile towards someone who looked so comical; besides, it was flattering to see the enemy reduced to such a state.

'You wouldn't even make much of a scarecrow,' the battle-hardened soldier said, and patted the German patronizingly on the shoulder. The young one joined in, tugging at one of the icicles for fun. It did not break off, and he, too, laid a mitt on the prisoner's shoulder.

The German, realizing what a sight he was, covered in icicles, and that this might be the saving of him, that he might not after all be killed, stretched his hands out of the long sleeves of his greatcoat and raised them to reveal a pair of thick socks pulled absurdly over them. He was rewarded with approving laughter.

The scout returned to take him in. On the porch, the German hastily took off his sock-gloves and stuffed them in his greatcoat pockets, shed the straw overshoes, and went inside. He clicked his heels, stood to attention, and gasped with the heat. It was very warm in the hut. He noticed that the commanding officer, looking him over, could barely conceal a smile. Name? Unit? Rank? The frozen German soldier pulled the shawl away from his wooden lips and replied, hardly aware of what he was saying, gulping the heat in greedily and, suddenly fearful, started to claw at his face.

Remembering himself, he put his arms back down smartly at his sides. Icicles slid down his face, over the shawl and greatcoat, and clattered to the floor.

A seasoned soldier remembers an incident last year:

I was given a mission to tow fake tanks to near Bely and Kholm. The sappers had knocked dummies together out of plywood and timber. I had six of them attached by tow-rope to my tank and I pulled them thirty or forty kilometres along main roads. I got fired at by one of the Germans' 'frame' spotter planes, which was furiously taking photographs.

The next day the roads were littered with leaflets reading, 'Russe, you tow plywood! Guderian's tanks are before Moscow.'

Roads. Engines labour and strain, wheels get stuck in deep ruts. Tanks, trucks on the move, horse-drawn artillery.

A column of infantry. A rucksack on someone's back with a swaying, sooty billy-can attached. A face, young or old, ear flaps lowered and tied tightly under the chin. A horse quivering with the strain. A hut emerges suddenly out of the screen of snow. A peasant woman, a shawl pulled down to her eyes, watches us pass, her gaze intent, thoughtful. I feel such a heartrending sense of involvement with everything and everyone there, which, at that time, it would have been difficult, odd, impossible to put into words.

A fork in the road, and a girl from Yelnya disappearing inside her huge sheepskin coat, a rifle on her back, waving a flag with one hand while holding a hurricane lamp in the other. She stops the vehicles and meticulously checks their documentation and what they are carrying. She arranges a lift for a wounded soldier trying to get to the field hospital. Some drivers joke with her, others curse her roundly. They drive on.

It is snowing. Mist shrouds the fields and the road. There is gunfire nearby. The front line is overextended, the line of defence compromised. You imagine you see Germans. The girl stands at her checkpoint and all the roughness, the daring, the hopes, the elation and anguish of the war flow past her.

'Soldiers! Moscow Lies Before You'

From the diary of Lieutenant Kurt Grumann of the 185th Infantry Regiment of 87th Division:

Our regiment greeted the morning of 22 June on the front lines. At 03:05 our first grenades were hurled across the border.

After the first battles all the way to Białystok I was awarded the Iron Cross Second Class. After that we languished in the rear. We think back now nostalgically to those carefree days in the territory of former Poland and remember the varied dishes on the Polish field menu. It was then I received the momentous news of my brother Hans' heroic death.

Sorting through my archive from the war, I came across this diary, and could not immediately think why I had kept it when I was ridding myself of so many materials, trying to retain only what was most important. As I browsed through the diary, though, I found it mentioned Rzhev and could see what had saved it.

Grumann's diary begins with the German Army already at the gates of Moscow. The fate of the beleaguered capital was closely linked to the cruel drama of the long, self-sacrificing struggle of the defenders on its near approaches, the bridgehead of Rzhev. Rzhev was to play a big part in my own destiny.

Five months of terrible bloodshed were coming to an end. Marshal Zhukov considered November 1941 the most threatening and critical month for Moscow, when its fate was decided in battle. Grumann's diary covers the way events then unfolded, when in December the apparently crushed Red Army went on the offensive and, for the first time in the war, the Germans suffered a devastating defeat. Grumann describes the confusion, the abandoned armaments, and chaos the like of which he had seen before only when French troops were in retreat. These honestly described scenes give us a rare opportunity to see the situation through enemy eyes at a time when victory seemed to be within the grasp of the Germans, but which ended in their precipitate withdrawal.

17 November 1941. I would like to go back in my mind to a time of which I have only the best of memories – the fruitful period of my training, the beauty of the countryside in Versailles. I so enjoy thinking back to those comradely evenings in the officers' mess with its deep armchairs, drinking a glass of sparkling absinthe or a bottle with those renowned labels: Martell, Hennessy or Monmousseau. My commissioning as an officer fulfilled a long-standing dream of my youth. The next outstanding event was my visit to a Paris awakened to new life, whose intoxicating brilliance it was my privilege to see. Then began the rumble and clattering of railway trains, and I, too, found myself on a train speeding us on, the officers of a newly formed company of bicycle troops.

We had again to fight in battle. After a long railway journey we arrived in Smolensk. I shall never forget the bitterly fought battles that resulted in heavy losses on both sides.

On 18 October my commanding officer awarded me the Iron Cross, First Class. After that I had to endure the season of impassable mud, and during this time I learned to ride a horse. I especially remember the Khloshchevka Stadium deep in mud. We crossed the field of Borodino, where Napoleon fought a battle, of which there are still reminders in the form of numerous obelisks on soldiers' graves. We waded across the Moscow River, then marched to Vishenki. We repulsed an enemy attack. Our first acquaintance with Siberian divisions. Beginning of the advance on Moscow.

In early October I was still in Moscow. Columns of volunteers – students, workers, academics – streamed along Leningrad Highway (now Leningrad Prospekt) on their way to the front to defend Moscow. The Moscow Conservatory marched past, our famous musicians. Everybody was marching out to defend Moscow. On the other side of the highway the No. 12 trolleybus (which today still follows the same route) was bringing back the wounded from the front line to the trolleybus terminal on Volokolamsk Highway; that is how close the front line was. By now long-distance trains were departing from just three railway stations; from the others local trains travelled only to suburban stops. At Byelorussia Station, near my house, there were anti-tank stakes and 'hedgehogs', and barricades on the Garden Ring Road. Shop windows were bricked up, with gun slits left in them. Moscow was preparing for fighting in the streets.

When war comes, you defend your home. My duty was to keep watch from the roof of a high neighbouring building and put out incendiary bombs. I had a supply of sand, but had not yet been told what to do with it. There I was, however, alone, looking out over the city, part of the war effort.

There is an explosion as a bomb drops nearby. An anti-aircraft gun opens up from an adjacent roof, giving away our whereabouts. A blacked-out city, everything swallowed up in darkness, lit only by the snaking of tracer bullets. It is all so peculiar, so unfathomable, so monstrously beautiful and breathtaking.

In those early weeks of intensive mobilization, when the recruitment offices were working flat out, it was impossible, and would have been point-less, for a girl not liable for conscription and devoid of useful qualifications to push her way into the enlistment centre.

My friend Vika Malt and I were sent to work at No. 2 Moscow Clock Factory in a workshop that, under the mobilization plan, had been switched to producing cartridge cases. Vika and I had no intention, however, of sitting out the war in a factory and enrolled, while continuing our contribution to producing military supplies, on an intensive evening course in nursing.

It was a course of no fixed abode and shifted up and down deserted Malaya Bronnaya Street. Our fellow nomad was a cumbersome visual aid, a large skeleton whose ribs rattled but who stood on his own two firmly fixed feet, and who had an inventory tag with the number '4417' attached to his pubic bone. He migrated with us to the food hall of a grocer's shop, then to a school gymnasium, and even on to the stage of the Malaya Bronnaya Jewish Theatre, behind a partition: 'Shhh! There's a rehearsal going on!' The theatre was preparing for the start of the season.

We received certificates testifying to our completion of an intensive nursing course, but then discovered nobody had any intention of sending us to the front: hospitals were being set up in the east of the country. Our thoughts, however, were only of going to the front line. I heard there was an urgent campaign to enlist students on military translation courses. Interpreters were in desperately short supply: this was not the First World War, when the officers themselves were fluent in the language of the enemy. The situation now was very different.

In those days there were no special schools teaching a foreign language, but almost all schools taught German at some level. How well it was taught, and what we thought of it, is conveyed by a verse that did the rounds in our school:

> German I'm not going to learn
> Learning German I will spurn.
> Why in the USSR
> Waste our time on *nein und ja*?

At the front, then, there was an acute shortage of interpreters, and it transpired that without them it was impossible to wage war at all competently. That eventually sank in, and, by order of General Headquarters, courses for military translators were hastily set up at the Army Faculty of Western Languages.

The entrance exam was laughable, and entirely appropriate to the level of our competence. Some of us, though, including me, had been learning the language since childhood, and I found my name on the lists of those who had passed. For the moment, however, I was on a waiting list because only boys were being enrolled; there was a rumour the interpreters would also be given parachute training.

Days passed. There was fighting on the approaches to Kalinin. Oryol had fallen. Finally, on 9 October, I went to ask when I would be able to join the course. 'You haven't taken the oath yet,' the major said. 'It's for you to decide. You can see for yourself what the situation is. But if you haven't changed your mind . . .' He named a time and place for me to present myself the next day.

Packing did not take long. I had done a lot of laundry the day before but the sheets and pillowcases just would not dry in my cold apartment, so I left them hanging on lines in the kitchen. I packed an old blanket in my suitcase; it had long been serving as an underlay for ironing and was covered in scorch marks, but it was to accompany me everywhere for the duration of the war. I could hardly take a quilt.

What else I packed I do not remember, because I even forgot to take a towel. I was sure that, like the volunteers, we would be sent to the nearest sector of the front to defend Moscow. In the army, I was also sure, we would be issued everything we needed. The reality was different.

A steamer was moored waiting for us, and we sailed out along the Moscow–Volga canal. There was already fighting on the approaches to Moscow. It was 10 October and the journey was long and slow. Aggravation, unease, but also curiosity: might something happen to us? We were hungry, we had a sense of foreboding, and we did not know where we were being taken because that was a military secret. The steamer finally tied up at a little town called Stavropol-on-Volga.

Later, at the front at Rzhev, I was to translate a captured document dated October 1941:

To the Soldiers of Germany: A Proclamation

Soldiers! Before you lies Moscow! In two years of warfare all the capitals of the continent have bowed before you; you have marched through the streets of the finest cities. That leaves Moscow. Force her to bow, show her the power of your weapons, stroll through her squares. Moscow is the end of the war!

High Command of the Wehrmacht

From the diary of Lieutenant Kurt Grumann:

18 November 1941. The day has come. We are to take part in the encirclement of Moscow.

The 3rd Battalion swiftly breaks enemy resistance at the edge of a forest. We are making for Petrovo. There, according to the testimony of prisoners, there will be field fortifications. Our neighbour lost his way on a snow-covered forest road. The maps are so inaccurate as to be almost unusable.

20 November. Increasing use of a Russian volley-firing weapon, which the soldiers have nicknamed the Stalin Organ. We have not yet come under fire from it. They say that the demoralizing effect of the exploding missiles is even greater than their destructive power.

21 November. Shells exploding in the middle of the village. Everyone lies flat. Outside, screams and groaning of the severely wounded . . . Our anti-tank guns are powerless against their heavy tanks. We demand reinforcement with an anti-aircraft unit.

November 22. The enemy attacks 173rd Regiment. A forceful blow and the enemy is defeated. Sixty dead Russians are left on the battlefield, one hundred are taken prisoner.

Our advance is an inspiring sight. The entire regiment mounts a frontal attack out of the forest at the village. Suddenly a T-34 tank is sent from behind the houses and turns round spewing fire. Anti-tank guns of every calibre and anti-aircraft guns are turned on it. The monster's turret evidently jams: at all events, it is firing only its machine gun. A shell goes into the exhaust pipe. Flames burst out. The engine is smoking, but the tank rushes on at high speed. Eventually, a chain comes off the drive mechanism. The tank spins round on one spot. The next shell tears off the second caterpillar. The T-34 is finally halted.

At the front I was instructed as an interpreter to ask officers taken prisoner what the Germans saw as the strengths of our army. They would mention the T-34, the stoicism of our soldiers, and Zhukov. I told Marshal Zhukov that when we met.

25–29 November 1941. We have failed to break the enemy's resistance. SS units and tanks have occupied Istra and are advancing to the east. For now they are depriving us of the glory of being the first to reach Moscow. We bury our regiment's dead at Surmino. Our hopes are resting on Guderian's tanks, which are punching through towards Moscow from the south-west.

5 December 1941. No indication of when we will be relieved. We are beginning to calculate when the last of us will be put out of action and there will be nobody left to hold the weapons. There are so few people left who are capable of manning the heavy machine guns and heavy mortars that, if we lose any more, we will be unable to continue using these armaments. Some of them, along with their means of transport, were left behind when we entered Ruza owing to shortage of personnel.

7 December 1941. We realize it is impossible to hold the line of defence. Together with the commanding officer, examine the locality for a new position. Organize a dressing station in an orphanage. Eighty people brought in, forty of them with second- and third-degree frostbite.

What comes next? What is the point of all this?

11 December 1941. Rear units pull out in accordance with orders and set fire to the villages. The flames from the fire light up the night sky.

At 15:00 we listen closely to the Führer's speech in the Reichstag and are pleased to hear of the declaration of war on the United States. Our naval forces will give a fitting response to Roosevelt's insolent challenge.

16 December 1941. I travel through Ruza, abandoned, almost completely deserted. Wooden huts burning here and there. These torches light up the town. It is as light as day. During the night comes the order: prepare for defensive action. At last, the Führer's masterful command. We may retreat no further, we must hold the Ruza line of defence to the last. Ruza itself is to become a bridgehead.

Field Marshal Walther von Brauchitsch, commander-in-chief of the Army, seeing the failure of the *Blitzkrieg*, considered the retreat from Moscow a catastrophe and a signal that the war had been lost. He and his generals demanded that their troops be withdrawn right back to the borders of the Reich. Hitler dismissed Brauchitsch and, himself already supreme commander-in-chief, appointed himself simultaneously commander-in-chief of the Army.

The war continued. The German front commands requested warm clothing for the soldiers from the quartermaster-general. The latter had supposed that, as the lightning war would be over during the summer months, none would be needed.

Under the Barbarossa Plan, an attack on the USSR had been timed for 15 May 1941. If it had begun then, the Germans would have had a significant advantage with an additional month before the coming of winter, but the plan was disrupted by the campaign in Greece. Working on Josef Goebbels' diaries in the Council of Ministers Archive, I came across an entry recording a very important discussion he had with Hitler on the eve of war against the USSR. Drawing up his plans for a *Blitzkrieg* to defeat Russia almost instantly, the Führer admitted, 'The campaign in Greece has severely weakened us in terms of materiel, so this matter is dragging on somewhat. Fortunately, the weather has been fairly bad and the harvest has not yet ripened in Ukraine' (*16 June 1941*).

In spring 1941 Hitler had declared war on Greece after it rejected an ultimatum from his Italian ally. An unequal struggle began between little Greece and the bloated military might of Nazi Germany, which by then had subjugated almost the whole of continental Europe. This heroic, steadfast, but tragically doomed struggle nevertheless tied up the German Army in a protracted war in the Balkans.

In the 1980s I found myself in Greece on Okhi Day, a national holiday celebrated on 28 October, when the Greeks said '*Okhi*', 'No', to that enemy ultimatum. Greece's very youngest citizens marched in holiday procession, very touching in their little white blouses, and each bearing a small Greek flag.

I felt very emotional as I reflected how profoundly Greece's Okhi Day is relevant to us Russians: it was a day that influenced the entire course of the war.

21 December 1941. At first we could help ourselves to a lot in the areas we occupied, where we were left to forage for ourselves. Now we are back in the same locality and it *seems to me we have almost nothing and nowhere to take anything from.*

28 December 1941. Everyone is suffering terribly from insects. Unfortunately, the bread ration is being reduced.

People have had no opportunity to change their clothes for several months now; dirty underwear has been in their satchels since the summer. To wash it you need more than soap and water, you need the confidence that there will be time for your washing to dry. In our present circumstances, every sick soldier remains on active service.

29 December 1941. The lack of winter clothing! It would have been so much simpler in the autumn to prepare for winter. It was already known that there would be a shortage of the uniforms essential for further advances owing to deliveries not having arrived in good time.

The Red High Command need harbour no false hopes and imagine they are going to win a brilliant victory. Their success for the moment is due to our mistakes. There can be no doubt that the Bolsheviks will again feel our force come the summer.

In North Africa it seems that the British have managed to rally their forces and are on the offensive. In Libya we have insufficient troops because, destined for that sector of the front, they have been brought into the fighting in the east. We place all our hopes on Rommel.

30 December 1941. The local people who had fled the villages and hamlets are returning in great numbers, looking for food, but we must be merciless. We cannot squander our modest stocks. Let famine finish the job where lead has not succeeded!

This phrase is taken almost literally from Hitler's directives, propounding his policy of using famine as another means of exterminating the Slavs in what he described as race war. This is the first mention in Grumann's diary of the local people, and he notices them only to leave them to face death.

31 December 1941. In a warm room the Christmas tree is brightly lit with candles for one last time. The sky is clear and starry, and it is very cold.
11 January 1942. Rzhev and Kaluga are now the sites of ferocious fighting . . . We are digging in. For our 185th Infantry Regiment there will be no retreat. We shall hold out or perish.
20 January 1942. Minus 40°. Tank traps, a barbed wire entanglement. What's it all for? It is a pity to leave this place to these dirty, ragged people. Most of the regiments in our division are retreating. Once more, several men suffering from frostbite. In many villages the wells have already been blown up.

The evening sky is blood-red in many places. Torched villages go up in flames. Tongues of flame greedily lick the squalid huts. War is merciless, and that means it's them or us . . .

On that note the diary ends.

In the towns and villages around Moscow from which the Germans had fled, I kept seeing a poster reading, '*Der Russe muß sterben, damit wir leben.*' The Russian must die so we may live.

'Your Weapon in this War is the German Language'

During the days in January of which a German lieutenant writes in his diary, we first graduates of the army translation course left Stavropol-on-Volga with two lieutenant's pips on our collar tabs. A quiet, small provincial town, little more than a village, it shared its name with the much larger Stavropol in the North Caucasus. The translation course had been set up there in the proximity of General Staff Headquarters, which had moved from Moscow to Kuibyshev. From Stavropol to Kuibyshev was over 100 km down the Volga. There was no railway, no road, and when the Volga froze over we were cut off from the rest of the world until a sledge track along the river could be established.

In this nondescript town with its mysterious hills beyond the Volga, with flickering lights burning in its low, iced-up windows, in the faint swish of sledge runners fading away in fluffy snow, in this ultimate stillness there was none of the thunder of war. Even here, however, the war signalled its presence: refugees, 'vacuees', heart-rending scenes at the flea market where poverty met profiteering. In the canteen the new waitresses were all evacuated pregnant women, the town council having decreed that they should receive 'humanitarian aid' by being allowed to work at the only catering institution in town operated by the state.

We were cut off from Moscow. How were things going there? We were in a state of constant anxiety. One winter's day an army division passed through the town, or rather, what remained of it. Down the main street, past the windows of the district land department where we were studying, they came from far away, from the war, Red Army men, limping, dragging their feet in boots and footcloths, frozen, exhausted.

In our lesson that day we were reciting paragraphs from the Wehrmacht's charter, which had to be learnt by heart: 'The aggressive spirit of the German infantry . . .' Taking in the sight of those trudging past, we fell silent, crowded round the windows and, stricken, could not tear ourselves away. A broken division was being led from the front to somewhere deep in the Russian hinterland to be reconstituted. In the ranks there were flashes of white: an arm in a sling, frostbitten on the way, bandaged ears under a summer forage cap. Some were being hauled along on sledges.

Still they came, more and more of them, exhausted, frozen. The column seemed endless. Darkness fell. They would evidently be coming through all night. A chilling presentiment of defeat crept over us. And that was the moment we took the oath.

The head of the army faculty running our course, handsome Lieutenant General Nikolai Biyazi, had until recently been the Soviet military attaché in Italy. He arrived in a low, wide sleigh from a requisitioned sanatorium. Stepping gingerly in black felt boots he had yet to wear in, he entered the room at the district land office, where our first platoon was lined up ready to take the oath. He warmed his hands at the round stove in the middle of the room and said simply, 'The future of our Motherland is at stake.'

We came forward one at a time and read out the text: 'If I break this, my solemn oath, may I be subject to the severity of Soviet law and to the general hatred and contempt of the workers.' We appended our signatures.

Our classes continue. Today's lesson is on 'The Organization of the German Army', and is being conducted by a captain with a razor-sharp parting in his abundant auburn hair, a rather good-looking man of thirty or so.

We are not paying proper attention. We are in two places at once. Our soul has already winged away and only our body is present here and now, in this room at the land office which looks out to the main road, a snowy white street leading down to the Volga and, beyond that, to the front.

How many howitzers are there in a German artillery regiment, and how much ammunition do they have? What are the calibres of the Germans' guns? What types of aircraft do they have? (The Henschel 126, the Junkers 88, the Messerschmitt 109.) It is all just too difficult to remember. When we get to the front no doubt we'll sort all that out, but here and now we do not take it too seriously.

The lessons given by Auerbach, a civilian teacher, are livelier. We do role-play. 'You are the prisoner: I am the interpreter. I am the prisoner: you are the interpreter. Let's talk serious interrogation.'

Civilian Comrade Auerbach is not like the other teachers, who are all captains with emphatically parted hair. He is rather small and wears a dark blue Boston suit you might not expect to see outside Moscow. It seems out of place among all the army tunics and grey greatcoats. He was born in Switzerland but has lived most of his life in Russia, and appears intensely committed to his work. Perhaps work is his homeland and he is cultivating its soil. Our course has just been set up and the teaching methodology is not yet set in stone, so he is his own master, free to do things his own way. He imparts useful knowledge to us.

In order to get used to the military cadence of the enemy's language, we translate newly captured documents, dated December and sent up the Volga from General Headquarters.

Reminder About Extreme Cold
1. Emergency Methods for Protection Against Cold
Insert felt under the helmet, a handkerchief, crumpled newspaper or a forage cap, with a balaclava. Makeshift balaclavas and oversleeves can be made from foot wrappings. Oversleeves can also be made from old socks
It is better to wear two shirts (even if thin) rather than one thick shirt. (The layer of air between two thin shirts provides excellent protection from cold.)
Particular care should be taken to protect the lower abdomen from cold. Use a lining of newspaper between undershirt and overshirt, or wrappings made from old clothes.
For legs and knees: newspaper between long johns and trousers; the slit in underpants should be sewn up; wear an extra pair of tracksuit bottoms under trousers . . .

That made us laugh. The enemy had been brought low. It cheered us to think that those swine were feeling cold and wrapping newspapers round their thighs. But on the other hand, there was something incongruous about the enemy feeling the cold, just like us, something perplexing.

While we were talking howitzers, the Hs 126, the Ju 88, paragraphs of their regulations, everything seemed more or less in its right place: tidy, alien, intangible and menacing; but that memorandum suddenly gave us a vivid insight into what these people were going through. They were suffering from the cold. They were, damn their eyes, animate beings.

The iced-over Volga cut us off from the outside world, but late one evening the news broke in those muffled, snowbound streets: the Germans were being driven back from Moscow! We could not sit still at school and rushed back to the hostel to the boys, hugging them and singing. Next I received a letter from my brother, a cavalry scout in a Moscow volunteer regiment: 'Where we are, the Germans are on the run!' What could be better?

14 December 1941. Enemy broke through to behind our lines. Unable to destroy them . . . Risk being cut off. Immediate retreat essential. Encounter other retreating regiments creating first bottlenecks, but complete chaos in next village, Likhovo: numerous units pouring in as divisions roll back.

15 December 1941. On the road I travel on, boxes of ammunition and shells abandoned everywhere, mountains of them. Gridlock. Can't go backwards or forwards.

16 December 1941. I think the only time I saw anything like this was during the campaign in the West, when the French troops were retreating.

I remember last summer. We were at war now. We had been told, 'The Soviet people will defend the Fatherland, honour and freedom.' Moscow: already cars with foreign flags were dashing through the streets, rescuing embassy families from our disaster. I stood in a silent crowd by a loud-speaker at Nikita Gate. The announcer warned that the situation was menacing. Across the road, the classic films cinema was advertising *When the Dead Awaken*.

I remember, too, on the very first day of the war, blackout 'curtains' were being issued to everyone. They were made of strong, heavy paper no one had ever seen before. We tacked them up, adjusted them, curtained the windows, masking the lights. They were to be in place 'for the duration of the war'. Now everything imaginable, everything you had to do had just one measure of time: 'for the duration'. If I was ironing a pair of trousers: 'Here, now you can wear them for the duration.'

It was a new concept of time: not present, not future, but a present extending into the future; not even into the future but into an invocation of a future when the war would be over. The invocation, though, was half-hearted. Yes, we were agitated, taken aback, bemused by the new ways. 'Oh, so this is it, the war we've had hanging over us for so long.' But everyone was still fine, still alive, not yet affected.

Now Churchill had said, 'We shall bomb Berlin night and day.'

Now the first bombs had fallen on Moscow.

Now ration cards had been introduced.

The city had shortages, but it also revealed to us unsuspected dimensions and hitherto unseen surfaces. We had 'our' roofs, on which, high above the ground, we did our stint, looking out for incendiary bombs. People had 'their' cellars, to which indestructible men and women with gas masks over their shoulders directed panicky citizens; from where explosions in the streets above could be heard; where children cried and women sobbed; where a boy of six, standing beside his mother who was sitting on the floor rocking a child wrapped in a blanket, held on to her shoulder and reassured her, pouting his lips: 'They won't get us.'

Moscow was not so easy to destroy, not so easy to crush by war. The city had many levels and was inseparable from the recent past, hence not wholly immersed in the war, but even its ordinary aspects came now to seem unusual. The scent of the nicotiana flowers in the courtyard of our block, the shooting stars falling on the city from a now very deep sky. It was August, so there were shooting stars. I noted in my diary then, in August 1941, 'Remember this is how it all really was: the nicotiana, Soviet power, shooting stars.' The mailbox by the entrance door had a postcard announcing classes would begin at college on 1 September, as usual. The routes of the trams and trolleybuses had not changed since I was at school. There was the little restaurant on Tverskoy Boulevard where I had to shelter from the rain, and found the throaty voices of the gypsies as impassioned as ever. The war had not stopped the town clock on Pushkin Square, the beacon for all our rendezvous.

Only we would not be going to college on 1 September. We would be saying goodbye to Moscow, never to return, because when we did return it would be to an entirely different city.

Our course, and a semblance of examinations, went on for about another week. On our way to the canteen we sang our customary ditty one last time.

> He is marching out the gate a
> military translator.
> But though he strained and strained,
> He is far from being trained.
> A maiden, like his shadow . . .

Actually, we had received some training, but suddenly realized (Auerbach raised the alarm) that we had not learned any German swear words. What if an officer needed to swear at a prisoner and the interpreter did not have the vocabulary? Consternation. The command instructed Auerbach to compile, as a matter of extreme urgency, a dictionary of German swear words. He would appear of an evening in the propaganda room, where we were preparing for the exams in the bright light of the topped up oil lamps. '"Beanpole", is that a very serious insult?' he enquired (he knew German much better than Russian). Suddenly melancholy, he gazed at a girl from the Moscow Institute of Philosophy, Literature and History [IPLH] for whom he had a weakness and told her gallantly, 'Your appearance at the front would cause the moral disintegration of a full-strength Bavarian division.'

In the final lessons he is teaching us hastily: 'You are being parachuted in behind enemy lines. You land. Suddenly out of the bushes – a Nazi! Imagine yourself for a moment . . .' Personally, I cannot imagine it, but nod affirmatively.

'You shout, "Halt!" But that is not enough. To crush his morale you must swear very hard!' Towering on tiptoe, he exclaims threateningly, 'In a minute I am going to hit you so hard that your head will crash into the wall and your brains will have to be scooped up with spoons!'

'*Genosse* [Comrade] Auerbach, do they not have any more succinct ways of swearing?'

The dictionary of German swearing was sent after us to the front but never reached headquarters. Although this particular reference work proved unnecessary, I was sad not to be in possession of such a unique publication. Learning this, one of my readers – by now in the 1990s – kindly donated me hers. It was a more than generous gift because, judging from the inscription, its author's relationship with her had been more than is customary between teacher and student.

As I browsed through the pages I immediately noticed 'beanpole', sometimes alternating with 'hatrack', again and again in different pejorative phrases. Auerbach's favourite term of abuse was perhaps not unrelated to the complexes of a man of diminutive stature. 'Swindler', 'cunning thief', 'cannibal', 'milksop', 'coffee grinder' (chatterbox), 'illegitimate person', 'cutthroat', 'clapped-out nag', 'obscurantist', 'Hitler dog', 'bumhole'. A member of the SS, the dictionary advises, should be called a 'lacquered turd'. Auerbach achieved the feat of getting past the military censor several words that at that time were considered totally unprintable, and beneath the dedication signed himself, 'Author of the world's only dictionary of swearing, Theo Auerbach'.

It strikes me as I write this that his time at Stavropol, the era of his dictionary, was probably Auerbach's finest hour. That makes me a little wistful.

New Year, 1942

At a New Year party, which doubled as our farewell party and was arranged by our superiors for us at the fermented mare's milk sanatorium, Lieutenant General Biyazi told us, 'Your weapon in this war is the German language. You can be taught to shoot once you get to the front line.'

With that, we departed, hustled through the German language in a rushed two and a half months because there really was an urgent need for military interpreters at the front.

'*Genossen*,' said Auerbach, his voice today rather solemn, 'This will be our last lesson.' He paused and we waited patiently, trying not to fidget, not to breathe too loudly. Standing on tiptoe, he began suddenly to recite:

> *Kein Wesen kann zu Nichts zerfallen!*
> *Das Ew'ge regt sich fort in allen.*
> *Am Sein erhalte dich beglückt!*

> No living atom comes at last to naught!
> Active in each is still the eternal Thought:
> Hold fast to Being if thou wouldst be blest.[1]

For a time we are confused, not understanding what is going on. '*Das Ew'ge regt sich fort in allen.*' Goethe put that well. Auerbach stops, and then says in an uncharacteristically stern tone, 'I would ask you, *Genossen*, to remember that the author of this poem was a German. When we win and fascism has finally been done away with in Germany, we shall have the right to tell ourselves that never, even during the years of war and brutality, did we cease to love this beautiful language.'

As far as we were concerned, our relations with the German language had not recovered from our experiences at school, but that was now beside the point. We were touched by the solemnity with which he addressed us. We were issued with hats with earflaps, and the girls finally had their canvas boots replaced with leather boots. So, now it really was time for us to leave. Farewell, Stavropol! We were the course's first cohort.

We had not yet lived there for four months, despite our diplomas certifying we had graduated from a four-month course, rather than the two-and-a-half months we had actually studied. It seemed like a whole epoch, lived in a lyrical whirl of imminent departure.

---

1. Johann Wolfgang von Goethe, *Vermächtnis* (1829), tr. Mildred Fish-Harnack (1902–43).

The Journey

'Ey, hey! Mother Volga!'

We had before us a hundred *versts* [1 *verst* is approx. 1.07 km] of the ancient sledge track down the Volga to Kuibyshev. A taciturn old man in a sheepskin coat, with a wispy beard the wind blew to one side, was answerable for our safe arrival. He was accompanied by young lads to handle the collective farm horses.

We took our places in the sledges, buried our feet in straw, and moved off. Our groom, a boy of fifteen or so, ran alongside, never letting go of the reins. Following the front runner, our sledge turned, creaking and swaying, and friskily picked up speed across the empty market square, tossing up bits of straw and sending lumps of frozen horse dung flying over the snow. And then, downhill to the Volga following a broad, well-travelled path and catching up with the other sledges. Our driver jumped into the sledge, whipped up the horse and yelled at the top of his voice, 'Hey! Mother Volga!'

And so began our nostalgic journey to war. More than thirty years ago I described that journey along the Volga. I am anxious now about repeating myself, but when, year after year, you are writing what, in truth, is the story of your life, you can hardly avoid (and does it matter?) repetition, if that is what you yourself need to achieve a new understanding of both life and yourself. I hope that in my case such rumination may be judged at least partly justifiable.

So, on we go. The horse pulling us along, the sledge swaying, the snow a light grey blanket. The white, frozen Volga slips past beneath us and its white, snowy banks have branches of scrub scrabbling out everywhere from under the snow. Beyond the sloping bank is a white expanse where earth meets sky, and when the bank falls away the infinitely receding white distance beckons enticingly. Suddenly a little house appears in the snow. Who can be living there? We speed on by, plucked now from our routine of German lessons, venturing into the unknown.

As I look back, I can say we had never before been so lighthearted and carefree, and never would be again. In the dusk the horses hauled themselves over to the bank and up to a village. We got out of the sledges and scrambled after them, sinking into the snow.

Dogs barked gruffly. Above the roofs the smoke stood in a motionless column. Now it was no longer snow underfoot but floorboards. The muggy, musty warmth of a hut, a baby crying, the sound of boots and bustle in the courtyard on the other side of the log cabin wall; grey eyes looking silently out from under a headscarf, patiently taking note of us, one by one, our whole posse; and a hand lit by a russet glow stirring red embers with a poker.

Frozen bread that had been thawed, a cauldron of steaming porridge, conversation in the evening with the master of the house beside a dented brass samovar. A night sleeping under greatcoats on a floor spread with straw.

'Arise, Monsieur le Comte, you have great things to accomplish!' Such was the wake-up call in our student hostel. It is supposedly how his servant would waken Saint-Simon. And again we take to the road. Low snow drifting. Blurred figures ahead. We catch up with them. Women wrapped in shawls are walking in single file a little to the side of us, on a footpath trodden in the snow. They are on their way to Kuibyshev to see for the last time their husbands, who have been taken for the war.

We continue in our sledges, and encounter another dark file of women. Women are on the move the whole length of the Volga: some will not have held back on abuse for their drunkard husbands; what names will they not have called them? But now they stumble, stooped and freezing, their felt boots sinking into the snow. They have no orders, no time by which they must arrive, no package sealed with wax, but carry a gift warmed by their bosom – some last farewell, some last token of love from home.

We, state officials with provisions and horses, we who are so necessary for the accomplishment of great things, go very quiet. Only one voice from among us sings uncertainly,

> Hey, machine gun, Rostovchanka,
> You are all our pride and joy . . .

A snowstorm blows up. We run behind the sledges to get warm. Suddenly, out of the blizzard, a dog is sitting alert in the snow, its jaw silvered with grey hoarfrost. A man sees us and stops shovelling and throwing snow to one side. He is a strange man, appearing out of nowhere, in a long black coat. His face is not old. He looks educated. He peers at us quizzically, quietly, intelligently . . . Suddenly someone yells, 'Move on!' That is addressed to us. 'Nothing to look at here!' The barrel of a rifle shows from behind the shoulder of a sheepskin coat. Somewhere nearby there will be a watchtower. We guess uneasily that we are in the vicinity of a forced labour camp, and feel bad.

We look around. The whirling snow blanks out this vision. There is no sign now of the man in black, or the dog, or the barrel of a rifle. We relapse into the cheery inebriation of new recruits.

> Hey, machine gun, our machine gun
> All our enemies destroy . . .

'All In? Anyone Out?'

From Kuibyshev to Moscow. GHQ on Gogol Boulevard. Some thirty of us are assembled there. A pleasant looking major with a shock of blond hair comes out to us, a folder with dangling laces pressed against his thigh. He informs us that, by order of Comrade Stalin, an Airborne Forces Directorate is being set up to strike at the enemy behind the front line in the territory temporarily occupied. 'Interpreters are needed and we have decided to pass you over to the AFD. Any questions?'

No one has any questions, but the major himself, after a pause, adds, 'Right, so you will be transferred. Only if you are willing, of course. All in? Anyone out, speak up now.'

That is all there is to it, this charged moment. Two refuse. One girl says she cannot stand heights; and one boy asks to stay grounded. We are embarrassed for them, and that is the end of the matter.

As for the rest of us? The folder with the laces is taken up a floor, delivering our personal files to the AFD. None of us pose a problem, in fact everything is splendid. We have been found worthy.

On the first floor the new directorate is taking shape before our eyes. A lieutenant colonel is pulling a chair somewhere, a wastepaper basket is being moved, someone else is doing something else.

The next day we are all in the corridor, waiting. Except for the two dropouts, of course. We are trying to look smart, feeling tense. We are called in individually. Finally, as if from far away, I hear my own name. I go in and identify myself, as trained in Stavropol. In the depths of the room two lieutenant colonels are sitting opposite each other at a table, half-turned towards the door. Towards me.

'Comrade technician-quartermaster second class, do you play sport?'

'I used to play volleyball.' (Our girls' team won the grade eight championship for Krasnaya Presnya District, but I had later given up volleyball. I forget why.)

'Good, good. And are you a good skier?' 'Not brilliant, but I'll do my best.' 'Good.'

'Yes, but actually how good is your skiing? How many kilometres could you manage?' I wonder frantically what reply to give. Five? They'll say that's not enough. Thirty? They won't believe me.

'She'll manage!' says the first lieutenant colonel, giving me a smile. 'She'll do what needs to be done!'

I feel a sense of tremendous relief, as if I have already jumped and am now dangling from a parachute. I can see we have only been going through the motions and that the whole thing is not as serious as it seemed. Their questions, my answers are neither here nor there.

'And how about walking? Have you got good, strong pins? Stamina?' That is the second one asking.

'Last year when we were hiking in Svanetia . . . I kept up fine.' They nod – good, good – a little conspiratorially. Then the lieutenant colonels exchange a glance and narrow their eyes as if to warn me that the next question is less straightforward and I should be ready for it. 'How would you feel about jumping out of a plane?' I have my answer ready. 'I suppose it's, well, just another form of transport.' They laugh loudly, encouragingly, stand up and shake my hand.

'All in? Anyone out?' 'To be or not to be?' There can be no hesitation. What you fear is not what is impending, what is coming after you leave this office. What you fear is messing up here, at this fateful moment, dropping out like those other two who were not up to it, the disgrace of letting down the others. You are all in this together.

The only thing that was truthful about that interview was that, on a tourist trip to Svanetia, I had indeed trekked along no worse than the rest. (We had donkeys to carry our rucksacks through the pass in the mountains.) All the rest was total nonsense. Skiing? So-so. Volleyball? I packed that in when I was fourteen. So why did I not just say so? But no, it was nothing to do with physical fitness, it was about a state of mind. How could you not play along with their brazenness? 'She'll do what needs to be done!' As to whether someone might be scared to jump out of a plane, you might have had an idea if you had at least jumped from the tower in Gorky Park! But in any case if, when you were already airborne, you panicked at the last moment, you would be shoved out anyway, like it or not, into thin air.

I knew perfectly well the questions were a formality, and they were already answering affirmatively on our behalf. It was yesterday's major who had been checking us out for resolve with his 'All in? Anyone out?' Today they were just beefing up parachute brigades with the requisite number of interpreters. And there was I with my half-baked answer, ready to respond to that tricky question – 'I suppose it's, well, just another means of transport' – and rewarded with approving laughter. But why was I conniving with these lieutenant colonels whose job was to turn me into a tick in a box on a larger list of brigades being brought up to strength? Why, when I still had a choice, was I being drawn with so little resistance into the maw of war?

My dear friend Yury Dikov told me, 'There always remains the desire, the attempt to clarify that about yourself, but you will never be able to reproduce exactly what it was that made you leap into the maw. There will always be more puzzles than you can find an answer to.'

It would seem we will never break through to the truth about ourselves even if we try for a lifetime.

Active Service

The train was for Tula. Through the blackness of the night, without headlights, without warning signals, it hurtled on, hoping for the best, jolting over places where the track had been patched up. Mysterious stations, fleeting in the dark. Sudden stops in open, snowbound, January countryside.

I had the top shelf, the one for luggage. Neither the blissful hardness of the planks, nor hitting my head on the low ceiling while clumsily trying to change position, seemed to involve me in the slightest, any more than the fug from cheap tobacco, the rustling in the dim light down below, the occasional sob, the snoring, the laughter and swearing, the clinking of kettles.

The person occupying the top baggage shelf was not really me. Within the familiar shell of my muscles and joints, my incorporeal spirit was being borne towards its destination, a parachute unit. That probably sounds pretentious, but how else can I describe the peculiar sense of weightlessness and uncertainty of a body destined to parachute to earth with no knowledge of how to do so, behind enemy lines, moreover, where it will combat the enemy in a firefight without a clue about how to shoot.

Tula was as far as the train could take us. The five of us, three boys, myself and Lyudmila, spent the night in a house by the station, in the train crews' recreation room. In this room lined with metal bunks, the washstand clattered early in the morning as the male railway workers and our paratroop lads queued up to wash, stripped to the waist and with towels over their shoulders.

In the dimly lit room their sculpted torsos and biceps seemed unbelievably strong. I was numbed by a sense of our physical inadequacy for the demands shortly to be made of us. But that was only for a moment. We moved on and everything again seemed bearable, no longer beyond our strength.

Our group of interpreters was to report to 8th Airborne Brigade under the command of Major General Levashov. The brigade was being formed as a matter of urgency, on Stalin's orders, in newly liberated Kaluga. Also on Stalin's orders, all freight for the brigade was to be forwarded by rail with absolutely top priority. The railway tracks, however, had been restored only on certain stretches. At crippled stations, halts and sidings, a hoarse commandant, besieged by soldiers and civilians, would glance at our orders and hastily push us on to the first train that arrived. We were on Kremlin business, we were urgently needed to accomplish great deeds. The train would move out to a barrage of furious abuse from soldiers and the wailing of hapless women left behind, burdened with their bundles, their churns and sacks.

Beyond Plekhanovo we came to a stop. Ryurikovo. From here we would be walking along the track. White, white, frozen vistas, sometimes obscured by the gloom of a blizzard but then, when the weather cleared, still there, unchanged. Snow-covered burnt-out huts, whole villages of them. Exposed chimneys of stoves like black obelisks plastered with layers of snow.

What lies ahead? The lack of fear is almost puzzling. The unprecedented nature of everything grips you and roils your stomach. You have set out and already there is no turning back. Already that vista, the snow, and those burnt-out remains like black, uprooted trees are doing something to you, drawing you into their world. Already you are committed to that far distance, as if you have already drowned and dissolved in its boundlessness. For some reason you feel a little sad, but also touched.

Only it is so cold. Today, as I write, I can check that with what our German lieutenant had to say:

14 December 1942. –21°.
20 January 1942. Temperature fallen to –40°. Impossible to describe how wooden your face becomes from the cold. Frost even penetrates your greatcoat.

Well, it is no easier for us. Admittedly, I have felt boots. In Stavropol, when I was issued a greatcoat, I sold my civilian coat and bought a pair of second-hand, mended felt boots at the bazaar with the money. Under my greatcoat I have a sleeveless flannelette pullover. My face suffers most, like the German's, and there is the danger of frostbite in your hands. Is it really only a few days since we were sliding in our sledges down from the bank onto the Volga at Stavropol? 'Ey, hey! Mother Volga!' I can't believe it.

We bypassed a blown-up bridge and got on to the Moscow–Tula–Kaluga highway. There was almost no traffic; trucks hooted occasionally as they passed. To either side of the highway were abandoned tanks and pieces of enemy hardware covered in snow. There had been a bloody battle on the highway a few days earlier. The all-conquering Second Panzer Army of General Guderian, the father of tank warfare and ideologist of *Blitzkrieg* who had never known defeat, had been tearing towards Moscow, before being stopped. And defeated.

GHQ sent a captured book by Guderian to us in Stavropol to learn specialized military terminology and the technical specifications of the enemy's tanks. The book's jubilant title, *Achtung – Panzer!* and the spirit in which it was written proclaimed that conquered lands would soon be squirming beneath the caterpillar tracks of his tanks.

'Our hopes rest on Guderian's tanks, which have punched through towards Moscow from the south-west,' Lieutenant Kurt Grumann had written in late November. But Colonel General Guderian, who had crushed the rest of Europe beneath the tracks of his tanks, had met his first defeat. It had been here, so close to Moscow, the capital which he was in such a hurry to 'punch through' to. It was here, too, that he had taken the decision, on his own initiative, to retreat, which was unheard of! An enraged Hitler retaliated by dismissing him and leaving him to languish in disgrace for many months. He was rehabilitated only in 1943 when he was appointed inspector general of armoured troops to rebuild the shattered tank forces after the defeat at Stalingrad, and in 1944 he was appointed chief of staff of the German Army. But once again, in spring 1945, he was dismissed when a battle on the Oder, against my 3rd Shock Army and others, was lost. He was relieved of all duties by Hitler and sent off on 'sick leave'. This mitigated his fate after the war when the Allies came to dealing with Hitler's generals.

But all that was later. Right then, on that highway, moving over to the shoulder, you wanted to sweep the snow off a tank lying on its side and, just for a moment, so as not to freeze to it, touch its armour with your mittened hand. In far-off Stavropol we had so feared for Moscow, knowing that these tanks of Guderian's were already on the approaches to the capital.

The cold kept us moving. We left the highway and turned onto a sledge track. Towards us came low sledges transporting the wounded, covered with straw to give them some warmth. A lanky soldier came running in their wake. He was wearing a short coat whose broad flaps slapped against his thighs as he ran by, pressing a bandaged hand to his chest. From beneath a grey helmet, exhausted child-like blue eyes looked out at us, but only for a moment, and then he was past and all we could see were his legs in their black wrappings, as stiff as the legs of a compass.

We walked on in silence, not talking, numb with cold. The entry in my diary about those hours of our journey is almost delirious. That is sometimes true of Kurt Grumann's diary, too. I volunteer this unedited excerpt from my diary:

January 1942. From Ryurikovo to Alexino is about 12 km. Roads destroyed. Route through open country. Treading in the footsteps of war. Dead chimneys sticking out of the snow, nothing else. Nowhere to live. Scarf breathed over, burns face with ice. My God, Russia is so big. Hands so painfully cold you could cry. Start of Alexino there somewhere. A little further, further . . .

Evening. We arrived. There was no smoke anywhere. Only chimneys, no houses. How come? There was supposed to be a station somewhere, a proper station. Okay, no station, but there should be a commandant. We bumped into each other in the dark, wandered apart. There was a small hut. I felt a door and pushed it. It opened from the street outside straight into a room. A woman was leaning protectively over a table which had children on it.

'Let no one in without firewood!' she shouted. 'It's a woman,' someone replied. She turned round. 'Hello.' I could barely move my lips and with wooden fingers could not pull the prickly scarf away from my face. 'Let no one in without firewood! I've got sick children here!'

The window was curtained with German packaging material, hessian with a huge black swastika in the middle. It was the first time I had seen a swastika.

Later, having found the commandant, we say, 'We are looking for staff headquarters and have to report to Major General Levashov.' 'Yes, yes, sit down. He passed through only yesterday.'

The commandant gets us a place in a heated cattle truck which, we discover, belongs to staff headquarters and is the battalion's command post. A Siberian division has arrived at the front. Lieutenant Kurt Grumann dated his 'first acquaintance with Siberian divisions' from November. For us, too, it is all new: the white half-length fur coats, the submachine guns and short skis. We sit by an iron stove in the middle of the wagon, supping hot buckwheat gruel with pork fat and listening to tales about Siberia and Siberian girls. For these lieutenants, as for Kurt Grumann, the war means separation from their sweethearts. Grumann wrote about that in his diary also.

The young battalion commander, the same age as us, is giving orders by telephone, and his voice is relayed by wires the length of the train. The clerk licks his pencil and writes pensively in a notebook headed *History of the Battalion* about their combat-readiness. I, too, when the stove has thawed me out, am moved to get out my diary and write about this headquarters on wheels, the hot gruel with fat, the soldier in his ankle boots and black leg wrappings running after the sledges, pressing his wounded arm to his chest, and about that huge black swastika.

Everything is in a state of readiness here in the wagon, and yet at the same time the atmosphere is straightforward, calm and hospitable, as if this were a scheduled train in peacetime rather than one heading to battle. Yet tomorrow these young lieutenants will perhaps be fighting the Germans.

At a junction we say goodbye and get out. Dark, unfathomable night. We walk for a while along the track and then, for the last stretch of our journey to Kaluga, travel in a train crammed with Red Army soldiers. For what remains of the night in our wagon, the bolt is being pulled back, the sliding door clattering, the cold blowing in until, in the opening, above the dark back of a soldier, a subdued light glimmers as morning approaches.

'Don't piss into the wind!' someone shouts jocularly, and yet again I am troubled by a sense of woman's less than perfect physiological adaptation to the vexing exigencies of army life. It is only for a moment. Chided by my soul, I speed incorporeally on.

Kaluga is a district centre and lies on the River Oka. It had been under occupation for two and a half months and suffered the usual fate of front-line towns. The last battles to retake it were particularly bitter. On 13 December our troops broke into the outskirts but were cut off and surrounded. There was desperate street fighting. On 30 December Kaluga was recaptured.

The entry in my diary reads:

Kaluga. January 1942. On the railway track there is a sign: an arrow plus the French word 'Latrine', written in charcoal by a German hand. In the wrecked latrine, a privy of long standing, a mountain of frozen mixed German and Russian muck. It is cold. A train on the tracks, '*Nach Plechanovo*' chalked on the wagons. If writing isn't in the Russian alphabet it doesn't count.

By the central station there is a pile of enemy vehicles. The station building has been smashed: shell holes in the walls, collapsed ceilings, wiring ripped out. And so cold! Nowhere to warm up. On the first floor – no floor, only bare joists. A door, still supported by a single nail: the political lectures room. We open the door slightly. What is this, a sickbay? Then why is everyone wearing white? They are preparing for take-off. These are the paratroopers, in white camouflage.

There is a floor here but no space, nowhere to put a foot down. Heating! A metal keg, a chimney formed from a piece of pipe and tin cans. The fumes go out the window via a frame with no glass in it. They let Lyudmila and me go under the table but won't let the boys in. There's no room. They go off to look for brigade headquarters.

The table is massive. No drawers – they've been burned for fuel. We sleep under it, others on ammunition boxes or on the floor. Everyone is asleep, some standing, leaning against the wall, sliding down on top of each other. They wake up, shove each other, pull a shoulder free, stir their neighbours up and extract their legs from underneath them. Cross, sleepy swearing before they fall asleep again. What plaster remains on the walls thaws out, crumbles, trickles dirty stripes over their white camouflage smocks. They are tired after seven days on the road and this is not much of a rest, but they have their orders. They will fly out on their mission tonight, after giving their smocks a good shake and drinking the entire alcohol ration allocated for the journey.

What happened after that I noted shortly afterwards:

Hunched up under the table, warming up, I look at the crushed, crumpled figures of the paratroopers, with their sheath knives on their belts and the flask of vodka they have been issued at the side, cursing and swearing in their sleep. What on earth use am I supposed to be to them? They do not know me. I will be in the way. None of them will take any notice of me. They will dump me.

A young lieutenant squeezes his way through to us over the legs and heads of his subordinates. Perhaps he really has previous experience, or is he just putting on a show? The ordinary soldiers clearly have no experience at all. He mentions 'the azimuth'. After we have parachuted down, we will all need to take our bearings and come together. How do we do that? How are we supposed to fold and bury our parachutes so as not to betray our presence to the Germans? On the way back, he says, we will have to ski 300 km to the front line and then, when we find somewhere not well guarded, we'll be able to slip back across to our own side.

So simple, so straightforward, so implausible. In fact, so totally absurd. What bearings! What 300 km? It is brainless. We are obviously going to be separated, with one interpreter to each battalion and each battalion acting in isolation. We will have no chance of supporting each other, when that is the whole point, crucial to success.

My mind is taking everything in clearly and I am not overwhelmed by fear; in fact I feel no emotion. Lyudmila is dozing but I am just feeling resigned. I do, however, write a letter home to Moscow, to my friend, with my most important last wishes.

The door opened slightly. The boys had returned and called me and Lyudmila to come out. They had found the headquarters of 8th Airborne Brigade in a little wooden hut that was still standing but the commanding officer, General Levashov, was not there. They waited for him, warming up in the well-heated room. One of the boys said he was thirsty and was pointed in the direction of various full carafes and a teapot. He poured himself a glass, and found it was vodka.

The brigade commander returned, the boys jumped up, introduced themselves and presented our joint warrant. 'How many training jumps?'

the general demanded, coming over to the table. Hearing we had never undergone any training jumps, he placed the warrant on the table, angrily crossed it through, and wrote, 'Send me no more untrained personnel. This is the front line. I have no facilities and no time to train people.' 'We are flying out tonight,' he said. Our leader objected that the soldiers too had never had any training jumps: they had told us so. To this the general replied, 'They are ordinary soldiers, but you have had money spent on you.' He pointed to the boy's collar tabs. That made all the difference. We had two lieutenant's pips on our collars.

We returned to General Headquarters. There had evidently been some changes in the Airborne Forces Directorate: either the plan to provide the parachute units with interpreters had now been fulfilled, or General Levashov's obstruction had made an impression. At all events, the boys were sent to a training brigade for paratroopers near Moscow, and Lyudmila and I were sent back to the infantry. I was temporarily seconded to the Intelligence Directorate.

There was a report shortly afterwards that Major General Levashov had died doing his duty. He had saved our lives, but had himself been doomed to die leading his untrained parachutists on the mission they had so blithely been assigned.

Recalling my sojourn under that table in Kaluga, I realized just how much idiocy there is in war. Working at GHQ, where they already had more than enough translators without me and seemed to have rather few captured documents to translate, began to rankle, and the thought that this might be how, day after day, my life would drag pointlessly on until the war ended, provoked me to rebellion. I went to the personnel department and asked to be sent to the front with ground troops. They brushed that aside, and my temporary situation showed every sign of becoming permanent, not least because at that very moment, by order of Stalin, all the directorates at General Headquarters were reclassified as *main* directorates. An order to this effect, in respect also of the Intelligence Directorate, was duly pinned up with a list of the established personnel. It included my name, as an interpreter; it was the last on the list, the only name below it being the signature of Stalin. Just then, however, a major arrived at GHQ from the front with instructions from General Lelyushenko not to come back without an interpreter. They could hardly refuse the general, who had covered himself in glory during the December offensive, and unloaded me on to him, evidently unaware that Lelyushenko could not stand women in the army.

2 The Paths of War: Russia, 1942–3

My First German

Thank God there was a blizzard, concealing us from aircraft, but the field we had to cross seemed endless. The distant grey dots of huts disappeared in the darkness even as we were moving towards them. By now, though, they must be nearby, those havens, not burned down, remote beacons among the hummocks of snow.

We finally reached the village street in Voskresenskoye and immediately were caught up in a commotion. There were voices. 'We need an interpreter!'

I imagine there were other calls, but that was the one I heard.

Seventeen Germans! Seventeen prisoners! Seventeen Fritzes under the command of a senior lieutenant had surrendered. The news swept down the street together with the snow.

Someone, scattering light to right and left with a torch, cleaving the slanting flurries of snow with the flaps of his billowing camouflage smock, was heading towards us, substantial and authoritative. He confronted us point blank: 'We need an interpreter!'

My escort rushed over. 'Comrade Regimental Commissar!' He saluted, and reported my availability as if he had just captured me personally and was delivering me with perfect timing. 'This way!' That was addressed to me by the regimental commissar, who flashed his torch in my direction.

The snow stops, the wind now levelling out the crunching banks of snow. We come to an outhouse. The sentry steps aside. The light from the regimental commissar's torch glides over the snow and suddenly, in the wide open doors of the outhouse, picks out alien, foreign, freezing soldiers huddled in a heap on rotten straw, clad in greatcoats, helmets and forage caps, and thin boots.

'Ask who's in charge.' That I can manage. That I have learned. I say painstakingly, 'Who is the senior person here?' Stirring, swarming, consternation.

'I am.' A man comes to the open door, his greatcoat covered in wisps of straw.

'Identify yourself! Rank? Name?'

'Lance Corporal . . .'

He has been left in charge because the commanding officer, the senior lieutenant, has already been taken away. 'He's been taken for interrogation, to the chief of staff,' the sentry reports.

'This way!' the regimental commissar strode off briskly to wherever we were to go. We followed, I and the German, stooped, his arms listlessly by his sides. We crunched across the snow, both of us cold, but he desperately cold.

A vehicle serving as an office, its bodywork covered with plywood. Felled spruce firs were leaned up against it for camouflage and in there, behind the plywood, like in a proper building, was a blazing hot stove. It was blissfully warm inside.

I pulled off a striped woollen scarf and put it in my greatcoat pocket. The German, stooping even more, sat down as indicated by the regimental commissar on the edge of a trestle bed. He was not young, forty or more, and had a haggard, greenish face. I would have been embarrassed to look at him too closely, and in any case had other things on my mind. I was trembling as if about to take an exam.

Did I have a pencil and paper? Only a German–Russian dictionary in my satchel, otherwise nothing. My rucksack had been left in a village on the far side of that field. Commissar Bachurin put a pencil on the table and tore a couple of sheets out of a notebook. 'Let's make a start! Ask him his name, age, where he comes from. And so on.'

I knew these questions in German by heart and, feeling a surge of confidence, turned to the German. The oil lamp on the table illuminated him clearly, and as I pronounced the question I saw his wrinkled, green-tinged face and his ears tucked under a cloth forage cap. It was the worn-out face of a working man whose best years are behind him. All that, however, was of secondary importance. If there was one virtue I was desperately hoping to find in the captive German facing me, it was clear diction and nothing remotely resembling a Bavarian accent. '*Bitte, sprechen Sie langsam und deutlich,*' I said. Speak slowly and clearly.

'Write!' the regimental commissar instructed me. I elicited the prisoner's first name and surname. He was born in 1896, so was seven years younger than my father. He pronounced numbers rather oddly, 'ayn, tsvay, dray', although I could guess what he meant.

The burden of anxiety that I would be unable to ask him questions or understand his answers gradually lifted. There remained, however, the burden of being in contact with him, with his ordinary little eyes and irredeemably foreign, disagreeable greatcoat. There sat Karl Steiger – I think that was his name – haggard, middle-aged, wearing his enemy greatcoat and representing something frightful and baffling: a prisoner. We were sitting close together, peacefully, but seeing each other through the inexorable distancing effect of our enmity.

'*Mällen*,' Steiger enunciated with some effort. I had never heard that word before. What could it mean? '*Mällen*,' the prisoner repeated, showing black teeth when he smiled. '*Raschen Mällen*.'

During the First World War he and his family – who were living in Lithuania – had been interned deep in the Russian heartland, in Central Asia. 'Mällen' was evidently a word he was recalling from that time.

'Melon,' Commissar Bachurin responded unsmilingly. 'Melon. Very good.' '*Jawohl!*' the prisoner agreed. '*Mällen ist gut, sehr gut!*' 'And war?' the commissar asked pointedly.

'*Mällen*,' the prisoner persisted, evidently seeing his one word of Russian as a bridge between us. '*Mällen ist gut.*' He lifted one foot, exhibiting a battered boot with a short, misshapen top. 'War . . .' Confidingly, smiling again, he said, 'Please give me a blanket. In the shed it is so terribly cold. Brr!' he added expressively, so that he should be understood by the regimental commissar without the need for translation. The commissar did not respond positively. 'Ask him whether a Russian who gets captured also asks for a blanket?'

I translated and the conversation was over. Bachurin stood up. I and the German also stood up and waited for him to put his coat on. He went down the steps attached to the vehicle, folding the camouflage smock over his arm. I followed. The sentry saluted. The guard got out of the driver's cab and stood next to the German.

'Go to that hut,' Bachurin instructed me. 'Ask for Kondratiev, the cryptographer. He has German documents. Proceed to translate them immediately.'

In the hut the commissar had directed me to everyone was sound asleep on the floor. That struck me as odd. Wasn't this the front line? Had I imagined that soldiers at the front stayed awake for nights on end? The truth was that, having only just arrived, I would not have minded lying down somewhere myself, but the commissar had ordered me to start translating a backlog of captured documents no one had even sorted through. The only person awake in the hut, the duty telephonist, opened a filing cabinet and took out the documents. In great agitation, I sat down by a lamp, anticipating that

I was about to discover something of great importance. It was, however, only instructions on how to deal with lubricating oil at low temperatures, and I had translated something almost identical at GHQ. The other papers were of no greater significance. The cryptographer, Lieutenant Kondratiev, was a clever, ironical and independent-minded young man, something I appreciated only later. He gathered up all the papers and nodded at a chest. It was small, but something to sleep on nevertheless. Pulling off my felt boots, I thought about the Germans in that shed. 'Please give me a blanket. In the shed it is so terribly cold.' Oh God, how awful. 'You're not allowed to take your footwear off at night,' the duty officer told the rookie scornfully.

I put my feet back in my boots. Fitting on top of the chest, no matter how I contorted my legs, proved even more difficult in felt boots. My legs hung over the edge, my greatcoat fell off, my hat and the bag with my dictionary, serving as a pillow, slipped from under my head.

In general, I never slept more soundly anywhere than at the front, no matter what the situation and in any position: on a bare trestle bed, on a bench, on the floor, propped up on my fists with my elbows resting on a table, standing, standing propped up by a wall. It did not matter how, just as long as I could sleep. That first night, however, it took me some time.

The phone rang and I heard the duty officer say briskly, 'Stay alert. Yes, sir!' Seeing I was not yet sleeping, when he had hung up he grinned at me and said, 'Who was going to take her boots off? German tanks have broken through at Nozhkino-Kokoshkino. That's 4 km from here.' Having learned a few things about German tanks in Stavropol, I anxiously calculated that they could appear at any moment, but everyone carried on sleeping. Shortly afterwards, I fell asleep myself.

In the morning the village was bombed mercilessly. The Germans had worked out that our army headquarters was located here, although the command post had already moved to the forest. With only brief pauses, they were circling above the village all day.

The ghastly shrieking of planes circling lower and lower, their shadows speeding over the snow: the unendurable whistling of a released bomb eats into your spine. Then the roar as it explodes. Above us, whether we are dead or alive, a snowy tornado whirls. Suddenly, very close, there comes the harsh rattling of a machine gun. More fountains. We, dark, motionless marks on the snow, wait, quaking. How easy it would be, right here, right now, to cease to be. Then, at last, he is leaving, wagging his tail with its black German cross.

And we are still alive! We rush onwards, somersaulting in the snow, throwing back our heads to gaze up into the sky and its unbounded openness. Sky and snow, and ahead of us the black edge of the forest beyond the snow-covered field. Safety! Just get there, hide out until dark. But before we can reach the forest God knows how much more snow we have to wade through, perhaps almost a kilometre. In the air, from afar, still weak, but . . . a droning. The droning of an aircraft!

Those who are strong and further ahead, closer to the forest, may get there in time but we will not. We are not going to make it. We turn off on to a hardened, icy strip of snow towards a shed we see not too far away. When we reach it, the commander of the anti-aircraft gunners, a round-faced, placid, neat man appears on its icy threshold. He tells us the political instructor has been killed; he had just finished handing out parcels to the soldiers.

'His stomach was turned inside out. We are sad!' he said and went back to his post at the gun.

Until the end of that day we were shifting around, trying to dodge the bombing. The places we found! Vegetable plots in someone's snow-covered trenches, potato clamps, a dugout occupied by a family whose hut had burned down. It was the kind of day that might have been described in official German reports in language along the lines of, 'Engaged in fighting of local significance. Air power used for targeted bombing to harass enemy forces.'

My own forces were well and truly harassed by the time it started snowing, darkness fell, and it was finally possible to get back home.

The prisoners were being led through the village towards us. They were not marching but straggling, bent over against the cold. I stopped to see whether yesterday's Karl Steiger was among them, a man who knew the Russian for 'melon' and wanted a blanket. In the darkness all the Germans looked alike. I managed only to count them. There were seventeen, so he must have been. They were being taken off somewhere. Well, good luck to them. No business of mine.

Ginger-Haired Charon

When it was dark, all those with whom I had shared my first day at the front being bombed were taken out of the village and into the forest where they would be safer. I was not.

Holding a sooty cooking pot at a distance in order not to mark my greatcoat, and clutching the German papers I had been given, I entered the hut to which I had been ordered to report. The first thing I saw was my rucksack, tied with the twisted blue cord from my mother's curtain, which had evidently been delivered from the village where our truck got stuck yesterday as we were on our way here with our escort. I introduced myself.

'Excellent!' said a hefty, red-haired man, a captain by the name of Kasko, who was sitting on a wooden bench by a desk and, with the aid of a thick book which served as a ruler, drawing a table on a sheet of paper. 'Where did you disappear to for twenty-four hours?' 'I was translating this,' I said, waving my pathetic bundle of papers.

'We're really suffering from a shortage of translators.' That was rather pleasing to hear. Evidently great things had just been waiting for me to come and accomplish them. 'Get your ID ready for me to inspect.'

For some reason this is always the way: you are getting along fine, feeling relaxed, when someone suddenly demands, 'ID!' and you practically choke. Cooking pot down on the floor, hasty delving into the field case at my side, and all it is about is your travel orders, your food ration entitlement, and your graduation certificate from the army translation course.

'What a shower! They didn't even ask to see your food ration entitlement? They fed you anyway?' 'Yes.' 'They feed just anyone. Have they no shame?' He pushed my documents to the end of the table and invited me to take off my greatcoat and sit down. 'We'll get round to you in a moment.' It was at least warm in here and I was perfectly happy to wait.

Kasko carried on busily plotting his table. The edge of the book he was using as a ruler was uneven, and he would sit down, then get up, move the oil lamp around on the table examining his work and, when he found a less than straight line, erase it and return to his drawing.

It was already night but he was evidently still not ready for the couriers. They arrived nevertheless, and came in one by one, dusted with snow, frozen stiff, from various sectors of the front. They sat down at the table, lit up a cigarette avidly, talked excitedly about how the fighting had gone, who had prevailed over whom and, out of the chaos of battle, the incoherence of war, emerged the names of those who had died. Some had gone over the top, crawling out into the snow to suppress a firing point and never returning; some had been covering the withdrawal of a raiding patrol; or been cut down by enemy fire, a hail of bullets, raking fire, crossfire . . .

Captain Kasko heard the couriers out amiably enough, then stood up from behind the table. He was a big man, his ginger hair cropped short up the back of his head. He stretched, shifted from one foot to the other in his felt boots, and in a far from nocturnal, indeed brusque morning tone, slapped one hand upwards against the other and barked, 'Details of location (slap), time (another slap). Proof of death?'

The person reporting was not, however, a professional messenger of death and could not fit the tale he had to tell to the three points demanded.

He had made his way through the icy cold, the snow, the darkness to bring to this place his last farewell to the dead and to register their heroism for posterity. He became even more heated. There was only one person listening to him: me, and even I was less than reliable. I was dog tired, half-asleep, and had swimming around in my head, 'ID!' 'Proof of death!' and suddenly, 'We are sad!'

'Bed down here to sleep tonight,' the captain said, indicating the wooden bench he was sitting on. So my first day at the front was not yet over. Was this how I had imagined it back there on the army translation course? 'Air attack!' 'Don't give your position away!' 'Get down!' There had been only the rap of these commands, and fear, and nothing heroic. Perhaps there was something different, right up at the front where the couriers were coming from, not just the freezing cold and death. Perhaps there death could not be fitted into such dull headings as 'at his post', 'while on a military mission'. The messengers, however, went back, and the dead were left in the hands of Captain Kasko. If only this ginger-mopped Charon would get his butt off that bench and move to the stool, but it did not occur to him to let me sleep in the place he had indicated; he was too busy casting spells over his chart, preparing his report, his summary for this day of war.

'Right then,' said Captain Kasko. 'Now for some information about you.' He took a blank sheet of paper and dipped his pen in the spill-proof inkwell. 'So, born in Byelorussia, nationality Jewish, resident of Moscow, student.' He then informed me, 'In the morning you are being sent to Captain Borisov in an intelligence section group.'

He clattered about, pushing stools out of the way, gathering up his papers, moved the lamp to the stove, seized the desk and, pressing it to his stomach, humped it over to the wall.

He undid a cape groundsheet, took out his bedding and spread it on the table in a neat, housewifely manner, showing not the slightest concern about German tanks and bombs and, turning down the wick in the lamp, lay down and slept the sleep of the just.

Zaimishche

The night passed. Before dawn I was again in the plywood-faced vehicle I had visited with the commissar and the prisoner. We were on the move to a new destination, but where we were or what sights we might be driving past there was no telling from inside this plywood hut on wheels. They set me down at the entrance to the village. 'Look for a hut opposite the well; that's where the intelligence unit is, and get to work.'

I walked along, keeping to the huts on the side they had indicated. There the houses were intact, but opposite several in a row had been destroyed. Through a gaping hole I could see a stove, but anything that had been destroyed by a bomb or a shell was either covered with snow or had been dismantled for firewood. A cat darted out and stood waiting, motionless, hungry, her eye glinting peevishly. She vanished through the gap, leaving her dainty, despairing pawprints in the snow.

A Red Army soldier was bowling along in an empty sleigh. In the distance a soldier with a rifle was walking to and fro outside a log hut. There was no one else, no sign of villagers. The village seemed extinct.

The well – my landmark – was very visible, with the long arm of the well sweep upraised. Opposite was a house with three windows. I turned the latch and the door opened. Little did I know as I went in how firmly that house would remain lodged in my memory and my heart.

I climbed stairs to the landing, where there were two doors: one leading to a covered courtyard and the other, to the right and insulated, leading into the hut itself. I discovered that later, but back then I just pushed one open at random and found myself in a smoky kitchen full of children. It was so unexpected that I was completely thrown and did not know what to do when Nyurka, the five-year-old ataman of this nursery, came dancing over to greet me with a German ramrod in her hands.

The extinct village in the crossfire of the battle for Moscow was decidedly alive.

The German was sitting in a corner by the table. The children shied away to a different corner and stared at him. It was impossible to compare him with those seventeen phantoms writhing with cold in that barn. He was handsome and young, and somehow fresh.

'What is your name?' I asked woodenly as I sat down on the edge of the bench.

'Hans. Hans Thiel.'

The baby in a wicker basket whimpered and the eldest boy, barefoot and wearing a cap that had slid over his ears, began furiously rocking the cradle. The rod from which it was suspended swayed and creaked above us.

What else should I ask him? The blue light of his Aryan eyes was dazzling and I looked around for something else to focus on, deciding on the wall clock above the table. Green kittens frolicked on its dial, the hands indicated twenty-four minutes to ten, and a rusty padlock on a chain stood in for the clock's weight.

'Hans Thiel, do you have a profession or are you a professional soldier?'

'I was training to become a naturalist.'

'And what exactly were you intending to study?' That was really the best

I could do, and I could not shake off a strange feeling that I had known this German for ages.

The baby was still crying, and her brother bent over her, clutching the edges of the basket: 'Shush, Shurka, that's enough!' He began singing in a thin, girlish voice, nodding his head up and down in the big cap. 'There now, Shurushochki, shush Shurushochki!'

'The topic of my dissertation,' the senior lieutenant said loudly over the crying and the lullaby, 'was Papilio.' 'What is that?' 'Or more precisely, the butterfly's proboscis.' Oh, a butterfly. *Der Schmetterling*. The very sound was musical. 'Der Schmetterling'.

What is happening? I am six and my brother is a little older. We are lying under the bed waiting for our German teacher, Luiza Ivanovna. Her skirt rustles and smells of liquorice. '*Guten Tag*.' We stay silent, pretending not to be there. She does not poke around the room, does not pull us out from under the bed, but sits down at the table, opens her extraordinary book published in Berlin and reads aloud, enticing us into the open like the Pied Piper.

Greta, Hans and Peter are three German children. They are keeping a diary, each for one week at a time. In Luiza Ivanovna's voice they tell how they caught butterflies, and how frightened they were by a grass snake. They like brooks, and sunsets, and surprises on Christmas Eve.

A calf stirred itself and tried to get up. It stood for a moment on wobbly outspread legs before collapsing back on to the straw. A little barefoot boy with no trousers on, probably about two years old, peed on the floor. Captain Borisov returned from the communications point and commenced the interrogation. Lieutenant Thiel replied succinctly, making no attempt to be evasive.

The lady of the house arrived back wearing a dark sheepskin, and gasped, 'Oh, my God, a German!' She stood dumbfounded at the door. The German stood up, very straight, in a double-breasted greatcoat buttoned up high to a black cloth collar. The dark face of St Nicholas the Wonderworker peered from an icon in the corner behind his blond head. The clear, regular face of the German, in contrast, looked so much like one in a glossy picture in *Fifty-Two Weeks*, that old picture book in which sensible, storybook children lived long, long before two world wars in their musical German childhood. *Schmet-ter-ling*.

The woman moved away from the door. Senior Lieutenant Thiel turned abruptly in the doorway, stood motionlessly to attention, and threw back his bare, handsome head in an act of formal leave-taking. 'Weirdo,' said his hostess, but without malice. He strode through the doorway, past the home-made millstones in the passage, and down the steps with Savelov close on his heels, holding a rifle.

Zaimishche village. The Finns had already visited. Our hostess, Matryona Nilovna, told us they were even more vicious than the Germans. She had hidden their life-giving cow and five children in the forest from the Germans and waited for them to be gone. God alone knows how they survived and did not freeze to death. Now she had us in her house. Would we be staying long 'or will you be running off again?' she asked despondently. Her face was dark with soot from the stove and all her worries. About her husband she knew 'nothing you can count on'; he had disappeared somewhere without trace in the war. She would sit down for a moment on the bench, her hands heavy in her lap until it was time to lift Shurka from her cradle and breastfeed her; or get to work washing at the trough; or perhaps it would be 'time to feed the cow'.

We, the army, were in the guest half of the hut, and the entire family was in the kitchen. It was crowded there. In a cradle suspended over straw Shurka was lying on rags. Kostya, the eldest son, wearing his father's cap over his ears, would lean his elbows on the table, talk to our guard and, without looking, rock the cradle with his bare foot. He was in charge of everything. Genka, a bit younger, rushed around all day and would stray away from the house. Nyurka fidgeted with her twisted German ramrod. Two-year-old Minka, barefoot, with a hole torn in his pants, felt the cold and periodically peed on the floor, tried to get the ramrod off Nyurka, and whined. 'Shush!' said his mother and, to Nyurka, 'Don't be mean, let him play with the chain.' A loud bang, very close. Nyurka jumped and whimpered. 'Shush, little one. The good Lord will protect us,' Matryona Nilovna reminded her quietly.

The sound of those homemade millstones grinding came from the passage from early morning – Kostya was already hard at work. A knock on the kitchen window frame was the collective farm team leader calling Matryona Nilovna to come and clear the roads of snow. The pole holding up the cradle creaked. Minka waddled over, barefoot, dully took Shurka's foot in his mouth and started sucking. Nyurka chose a log from the pile by the stove, deftly tucked it up in a shawl and nursed it like a doll.

She, the ataman, has been told not to bring the neighbour's little girl in any more, one of the children I had found here when I first arrived. Now it is prisoners who are brought in, to the kitchen, for interrogation, and after a day or two I am trusted to talk to them alone. My questions and the answers of the German are lost in that quiet 'There now, Shurushochki, shush Shurushochki!' as Kostya rocks Shurka, and in the kerfuffle caused by the calf trying to stand up in its enclosure on its weak legs.

The calf annoys Captain Borisov, and as he passes through the kitchen he wrinkles his nose to indicate he can hardly breathe because of it. He has a thing about clean air, as if he thinks we were made to live life, not to wage war.

Zaimishche has changed hands more than once. Matryona Nilovna's house has remained unscathed up till now, but will it survive under fire from planes and shelling from heavy artillery? Her supplies, if they have not been stolen, are running low, and when they come to an end there will be no way to replenish them. She has to see to everything: what to feed the children on, how to keep them safe. In war there is no heavier burden at the front line than that of a mother, especially if she has many children. She is expected also to do her bit for the war effort, as that knock at the window, reminding her to come and clear the roads of snow for the army, testifies. Even so, she shares the last of her flaxseed cakes with us army people.

Next to her, I feel the chaos of war all the more keenly, and the poignant fragility of life itself. The innate resilience with which Matryona Nilovna protects it in these inhuman conditions, her simple-heartedness and gracious acceptance of her fate, affect me greatly.

Although I told her I had volunteered for the front, that did not register with her. She sees me as caught in military servitude, and pities me. That is not at all how I see myself, although at first it was not easy to be the only woman among men. They, too, were, as people might say nowadays, weirded out after becoming so used to an all-male environment. It inhibited them when they felt like letting off steam, when they wanted to turn the air blue and simply could not say what they really meant. At that time it was not done to swear in the presence of the opposite sex. One night, supposing I must already be asleep behind the partition wall, which had an opening draped with a cape groundsheet, they embarked on some salacious discussion. In the end I could stand it no longer, got up and went out to them. 'Why did you do that?' Matryona asked me from the stove. 'I'm tired of listening to their foul language.' 'But they need to talk like that, to get things off their chest,' she said matter-of-factly. She taught me to put up with it.

It did not happen again. They showed considerable tact, although it was clearly a strain. They treated me well, although we did not see eye to eye about everything. These men had retreated all the way from the USSR border, they had taken a lot from the Germans, become a real team, and now along comes someone new who does not know the score, feels sorry for the prisoners, and tries to divide Germans into those on the other side of the front line, who are enemies, and those on this side of it, in captivity, who are victims. It was indisputable, however, that an intelligence outfit with no translator would be blind, so they put up with me. What did disturb them was that I was periodically writing things in my notebook. Keeping a diary or any kind of record was for us, unlike the Germans, strictly prohibited. I guessed they would look in my diary, so I wrote in it in large letters, 'Comrade Captain Borisov, are you not ashamed to read other people's diaries?' One day, when I opened it, I saw underneath my question, also in large letters, 'Should I be?' There it stands in my diary, which has survived to this day. They got used to me, though, and to the fact that in my field case I carried, not only a German–Russian dictionary, but also a thick notebook.

From My Front-Line Notebook

A clear-eyed, talkative, disciplined German soldier. 'Are you going to shoot me now?' I translated.

'Just go to hell, will you?' the captain told him.

'You ought not to kill me. Please.'

In his soldier's booklet he has inserted the *Reminder for the German Soldier*. 'The Führer has said: "The Army made us men, the Army will conquer the world . . . The world belongs to the strong, the weak must be destroyed."'

The wounded were staggering back from the front, stumbling, supporting each other, dragging their rifles along with them. An old woman who saw them stopped in her tracks. She was bent under a bundle of firewood she carried on her back, watching the wounded with tears in her eyes, and suddenly said, so emphatically, so sadly, 'Who will come to help these lads?'

The time the Germans were here, before they were driven out in our winter offensive, is over and done with in the minds of the local people. It was like a war within the war, the war they suffered within the endless stream of the larger war that is still going on. 'Everything imaginable happened,' they say about that past war. 'Fire, suffering.' Someone said, it was bad for everyone. A human squeak in the midst of a raging war, a reminder that every living thing suffers. 'What time has anyone for love?' the young woman said with never a care. 'You snatch what you can in the moment.' You could see she liked that.

It is amazing the way any headscarf, any chipped saucer, any little pot, shawl, inkwell, poker, any object no matter how worn has become unimaginably special, with its unique identity, its individuality, its personal charm; and everything here is imbued with that now, because it is irreplaceable. Even the most ordinary pre-war items seem magical and extraordinary.

There are times in history when the best members of the younger generation are enthralled by the current of the times – all the most active, the most steadfast young people. That current is carrying them not towards personal gain or material benefit, but into battle, into mortal combat in which the stream will dwindle almost away. But to drop out of it is to be a traitor to your generation's cause.

Misha Molochko used to say in the IPLH, 'Our romantic destiny is the coming war against fascism, which we will win.' It was a faith we all shared.

I thought: *war*. But it is roads and sky, children, peasants, people in towns, and death.

A tin with a wick, a lamp.
   'The German anti-aircraft gunners left it behind. It's really clever.'
   'How long will it last?'
   'A long time, a long time. Obviously.'

I was not prepared practically for the war at all, only emotionally, but we went to war believing it would be the most important thing we did in our lives. It would seem we were not mistaken. And something else: emotions have proved more durable than many practical things, certainly than my leaky boots.

People shoot, kill, bury, rush into the attack, go out on reconnaissance, and that is war. But the starving women with their bags, without proper boots, wandering God knows where with their hungry children, the old people, the refugees, the people burned out of their homes – they are the real horror of war.

We think it is right that the part of the people fighting the war should have everything; for us nothing is too much in comparison with the peaceful civilian population. But what kind of peaceful civilians are these people who have borne a heavier burden of war than many a soldier?

German soldiers, every last one of them, have packs of photographs of identical format, six by nine, with those pinked edges. *Mutti*, *Vati*, the much-loved sister. The righteous family having breakfast, the bike ride, the meal in the garden, the fat uncle with his big-boned wife and diminutive children, the tiled roof, the solidly built house covered with ivy. What an unimaginable level of comfort! Contentment, smugness, but above all – comfort. Why have they all come piling in here? Why have they been in such a rush to leave all that comfort behind?

My last entry in Zaimishche:

Genka jumps on to the running board of the truck and laughs with his mouth closed. I am already in the back. Matryona Nilovna comes running with Shura, wrapped in a cloth shawl. Nyurka is clinging to her skirt and hiding her face. Kostya stands to one side. I catch an expression in their eyes that makes my nose tingle. Or perhaps I'm imagining it. (In the margin of the diary I have written, 'Perhaps I'm just making this up.') The truck moves off. It is sunny, there is so much air. Goodbye, Zaimishche.

'What Is That Old Woman Crying About?'

We get shaken about in the back of the truck after leaving the village limit of Zaimishche as the truck strains to climb a slope over snow compacted by wheels. We have hardly come any distance, but already the routine that was beginning to make sense of our life in Zaimishche has been broken and fallen away. There are six of us in the back of the truck, including Senior Lieutenant Thiel. Our group is holding on to him for now. He is deemed useful.

Two weeks ago our troops were ordered to complete the encirclement of the German Ninth Army but considerable enemy forces were moved towards Limestone Mountain and, from the north, blocked our breakthrough, in the process cutting off units of the army adjacent to us. The Germans are now furiously taking revenge. I translated an intercepted order from Hitler, which instructed that it was to be 'communicated immediately to all units'.

Soldiers of the Ninth Army!
The breach on your sector of the front to the north-west of Rzhev has been closed. As a result, the enemy who had broken through in this direction are no longer able to communicate with their logistical base. If you continue in the coming days to do your duty as you have been, many Russian divisions will be destroyed.

The army next to us had been surrounded. Only a few troops had managed to break out. The army fought on in an encirclement about which there is not a word in the *History of the Second World War*, the official line being that there were no encirclements after 1941. This army, that perished or was taken prisoner in the forests of Rzhev, gave the lie to that line so no one mentioned it subsequently. Through to our sector, in random groups or individually, came soldiers traumatized by the suffering they had endured. They were very few. In our sector the fighting continued.

Our truck was following behind Commissar Bachurin's Molotov saloon car. The sky darkened and it began to snow. That was all to the good; it made everything safer. From time to time we would get stuck. Soldiers passed by, their greatcoats rubbing the side of our truck. 'Hey, would you believe that?' They had noticed our Fritz and looked over as they passed, the steam of their breath hanging by the side of the truck. 'What a scarecrow. Only fit to keep sparrows off the hemp.'

We drove into the village of Lyskovo in accordance with orders, on the first day of our 'march'. We went into a log hut, where an oil lamp was flickering in the kitchen. The old woman who lived in the hut was stoking the stove. 'Saints preserve us!' she gasped at the sight of the German. She was old, poor and unkempt. 'Why would you bring him in here?' 'Not up to us,' Savelov said and, having worked out how to communicate without the need for an interpreter, gave Thiel's shoulder a shove to move him away from the door. 'Shift!'

Savelov propped his rifle up in a corner of the kitchen, hunched squarely over the table, spread out his elbows and ate. The old woman took her bowl of porridge off behind the stove, came back and walked over to the bench where the German was sitting. She leaned over to check whether he was really eating. 'Eat, since you're being fed, you parasite, while you're alive. Hunger hollows out the soul.' 'You mean, they've got a soul?' Savelov enquired with his mouth full. 'Well, no,' the old woman nodded. 'Maybe they haven't, you're right.'

Captain Borisov came back from Commissar Bachurin and, passing through the kitchen, remarked, 'Mind you remember which bowl that German ate from.' It was true, no one was squeamish about sharing plates with someone else, but no one would want to drink out of a mug the Fritz had used.

I went through to the living room and pulled off my felt boots. Even if the chief of staff had forbidden taking them off at night, we did anyway. I put them by the bed and lay down, loosened my belt, pulled my greatcoat over myself, and was about to fall sleep when I heard Thiel sounding alarmed. What was going on? I went back to the kitchen.

The old lady was sitting quietly opposite the German in her tatty jacket, her arms folded, peering at him. She had pulled in her scrawny shoulders and was rocking to and fro, sighing and sniffling. Thiel, anxious, repeated his question straight to her face: '*Mütterchen, was ist los*? Fräulein Lieutenant, please be so kind, what is this woman saying?' 'Oh dear, oh dear, oh dear,' the old woman lamented. 'Oh, holy Mother of God.' She went behind the stove, brought out her bowl of millet porridge that had long ago gone cold, put it on the table and moved it towards the German. 'Here, take it, eat this,' and, crumpling her fingers up against her mouth, she began to cry.

'Listen,' Thiel said, 'Why is this old woman crying?' 'I have no idea.' What was I to make of her? Heaven knows what she was thinking as she looked at our prisoner. Perhaps someone in her family was a prisoner too.

He ate a little. 'If you may,' he said in some agitation, running a hand over that wavy hair with the parting, then, manfully, continued, 'If it is permissible, I would prefer to know the truth. Am I to be shot?' 'What are you doing, auntie. Here you are crying because you're sorry for the German and you've scared him to death.'

The old woman sobbed, and blew her nose on the end of her headscarf. 'It's not him. No-o. I feel sorry for his ma. She gave birth to him. She nursed and raised him, such a young prince, and sent him out into the world, only to be a scourge to other people and himself.'

A dark column of people is coming our way along a country track at an angle to our main road. These are our soldiers who broke out of the encirclement. Some, using their rifles as crutches, hobble on frostbitten feet; others are supporting an exhausted comrade. They are escaping along a corridor our army has hewn out for them. Their sparse numbers soon pass. Is that all of them? Why so few? Have they been cut down by gunfire? Have they died of cold in the forest? Are there other tracks they are stumbling along?

'*Fräulein, bitte.*' Something in our German is irreparably broken. 'What was the name of that village where we stayed the night before yesterday? I would like to remember that village. That old Russian mother . . .'

Artillery fire, the rattle of machine guns, and shooting too. The incessant din of battle. The wounded are being brought towards us in ambulances, in the back of trucks carpeted with straw, on sledges. Our truck moves aside to let them pass and we look silently on.

The cold is merciless. We shelter from the wind in a shed and, from somewhere back when all this began I recollect a beseeching smile, black teeth: 'Please give me a blanket. In the shed it is so terribly cold.' Get lost. It is unbearably cold for us as well, even if I do have a blanket, the one I brought from home.

The door of the shed creaks open and even colder air billows in. A crowd of unfamiliar soldiers enters. They switch on a torch. 'Oh, shit!' They have spotted the German. 'Give 'im a sniff of your rifle butt,' someone says lazily. Then, more ominously, vindictively, 'Pull 'im out into the snow.' 'Get 'is legs!'

'Stop it!' I shout shakily, jumping up. A torch probes me at close range. 'There's a lieutenant here, my fellow boyars.' Someone else swears in the dark. 'What you being so nice to a German for? You'd do better being nice to us lads . . .'

Now they're joking. They calm down, settle in. Savelov does not wake up. Thiel, our German, is restive, probably with fear. I hear him sit up. *'Verflucht! Damn!'* I mutter. Damn Germans, damn the war and all the violence, damn this cold.

War Is War

Everything that came after that was just war, only here, perhaps, so close to the capital, it was bloodier and more brutal. The endless battle for Moscow. It was a long war and I was in the thick of it. Zaimishche was the last glimmer of light, of human warmth. Mutilated, scorched earth, cruelty and pity, dark chasms and a soaring of the spirit. War embraced so much that was contradictory, conflicting, and primal.

Somewhere, lost in the abyss of bygone centuries, is this city's beginning – Rzhevka, Rzhova, Rzhev-Volodimerov; some passing mention of it in a Novgorod statute on pavements dating from 1010. Was that an omen? Everything is still obscure, and the territory that now lies beneath the city and district of Rzhev was disputed, it is surmised, and fought over by the feudal princes, but more often it was conquered by Novgorod. Whether that was really so remains uncertain – hypotheses, speculation, arguments between researchers: to this day the outlines of the territory seem blurred.

But then the chronicle does unambiguously note that the city was besieged during a war between Prince Svyatoslav Vsevolodovich and the Prince of Toropets in 1216. That is incontrovertible evidence of the existence of a city, the progenitor of modern Rzhev. Those are the circumstances in which history succeeds in retrieving Rzhev from the depths of centuries past. A siege! And in the ever-rolling stream of time – stop! An event has piqued the curiosity of history and makes us aware of the founding of this city!

Right now Rzhev, captured by the Germans and besieged by our troops, is the focus of everyone's attention and history, we imagine, will not overlook it. This is, after all, the price to be paid.

16 April 1942. You manage not to lose your balance; swollen felt boots, the 'great water' where the level of the swamps has risen, flooding trenches, dugouts and bunkers. The roads are impassable and there is no bread, fresh or dried. People are desperately hungry, and what seems somehow particularly woeful is the mute starvation of the horses. Cavalry horses are being taken back for veterinary treatment, but they stop at a gully, retreat a little and then, lacking the strength to cross it, lie down to die in the roadside mud.

The Germans had driven the villagers away but not had time to set fire to the village. They were expelled without warning. There had been a German baling machine at work here but they took it with them. All that remained was the compressed bales of hay they had been preparing to send back to Germany.

We are in a shed and those bales are serving as our table and chairs. There are two of us: me and the prisoner, a strapping young German. I ask him the usual questions: where are the firing points, where does one unit's sector end and another's begin, about the bringing in of fresh troops and such like. As always, though, although I know it is beside the point, I ask about more than that: for example, why he came here?

He suddenly stands up, blocking the doorway so that it becomes almost dark in the shed. With solemn dutifulness he intones that this has been commanded by the Führer. 'Russia must be defeated so that we can destroy our main enemy, England.'

I suddenly feel how, at moments like this, reality and fantasy fuse. I will never forget the smell of the hay, the neat yellow bales, the macabre combination of bloody slaughter and brisk, economical business efficiency; the deserted street and delicate sky, and the trial of being in such close contact with this captive enemy, his black silhouette in the doorway of a shed where the two of us are bound together in such a diabolically unnatural relationship.

In my head I hear the tinkling tune of one of their army songs: 'With war we sail to Engel-land, and speed out to the East.'

A top secret German document dated 20 April 1942: Programme of the Chief Commissioner for Utilization of the Labour Force (circulated by our front headquarters for information):

In order significantly to relieve the burden of work on the extremely busy German peasant woman, the Führer has instructed me to deliver to Germany from the eastern regions 400,000–500,000 selected healthy and robust young women.

Sauckel.

I turn on the radio during the night to hear the emotionless voice of a female announcer intoning: 'Bloo-dy bat-tle in south. Stop. Our Mo-ther-land in danger. Stop. I repeat. Our Mo-ther-land in danger. Stop.'

This extract from the newspapers is right now being received by the partisans' radio operators in the forests. The mechanical, colourless radio voice mercilessly hammers nails into your heart: 'The fate of our coun-try is be-ing deci-ded in bat-tles in the south. Stop. I repeat, the fate . . .'

Outside the tent there is stillness, the scraping sound of tree branches, the challenges of sentries.

The door of the dugout is torn off its hinges and no longer fits into the door frame. It has been knocked off its bearings and so have I, a bit. There is such a ringing in my ears that I am unsure what is going on around me. If I fall asleep, I hear someone breathing in my ears. I drank vodka and suddenly felt warm. What next?

War whirls you round and grinds you down, and frees you from everything. All that is indestructible is the hearts of the village women.

During the offensive by units of the Red Army, German soldiers in the village of Podorki set fire to thirty-five houses . . . they did not allow people to rescue their property; they locked the houses and shot at anyone trying to do so . . . they shot Lavrentievna, an old woman . . . they also machine-gunned Citizen Braushkin, a collective farmer who was moving away hay that was next to his barn. (*Report on the village of Podorki*)

Between two juggernauts, two belligerent armies, people are crushed. Civilians not at war but in the war.

The old saying goes, 'God is not in power, but in truth,' and all the truth is on our side: it was they who invaded and trampled on everything. Truth alone, however, will not deter or overcome them. Or is God, perhaps, now on the side of power?

To start with, the whole calamity of the war was blamed on Hitler, the evil-doer, the mass murderer, the accursed Herod. He alone had caused all the misery. As the war has gone on, though, and spread, the German soldiers, their death-dealing army, their tanks and motorcycles, their swastika-bearing planes, their seizure of our lands, the brutality, everything and everyone German that now fills our hearts with hatred has become united with Hitler, has become Hitler. He is now the collective image of the Nazis.

An order issued in Yelnya: 'All Jews, of both sexes, are to wear a six-pointed star of David on their right and left sleeves.'

Another 'reminder' for the German soldier:

'You have no heart, no nerves, they are not needed in war. Kill any Russian, any Soviet. Do not stop if before you is an old man or a woman, a young girl or boy. Kill them.'

You have only to become the slightest bit detached from your routine, walking by yourself along a road, or given a lift by a truck driver or on a cart, to be suddenly aware of how unusual everything is, how new, and you try to write something down. Being shaken about means much of it is almost illegible, the letters jumping all over the place, the words piling up on each other. Afterwards you can hardly decipher it.

The Germans are banging on again about 'The Führer's invincible line'. They mean our poor, suffering Rzhev.

He was sitting hunched on a tree stump with his arms around his rifle, completely exhausted.
   'Time to stop roosting,' his comrade prompted him, getting up.
   They staggered off to the front line.

We have been forced to become warlike,' the girl sniper tells me. She is wearing a quilted jumpsuit. When she is going out on ambush she also wears a white sheepskin jacket and white camouflage smock with a hood. She lies in the snow with her sights trained on a German bunker they have found, or think they have found, just waiting for one of the enemy to stick his head out. She lies there all the daylight hours, with unbelievable female patience. With all due respect, I cannot help feeling her work is more like hunting than warfare.
   She studied at an economic planning college and sounds bookish when she speaks, tense but truthful. She worries that she may get too cold, lying there in the snow, and then find herself unable to have children.

War opens wounds, it injects something into your soul that was not there before it . . . Everything is 'seen from the viewpoint of war', 'from the standpoint of war'. It takes over everything. What else is there besides its cruel dictates. Even the ability to feel pity can be remade into something more attuned to war. I am no better, no wiser, no more contemptible or purer than war. I, too, belong to it.

An evil-smelling aspen grove swimming in autumn mist; the invasive, inky smell of wet boughs beginning to sprout. The squelch of marsh mud beneath boots. The pealing thunder of battle. In this grove are several Germans we have already interrogated, no longer squealers, just prisoners, but we cannot spare anyone to escort them to the rear: everyone fit for combat is fighting, so for now we have to keep these prisoners within our headquarters compound. They have made themselves a lean-to and sleep in that, then spend the day outside awaiting whatever fate has in store for them. In the light of dawn, when everything is spectral in that dank aspen grove, the moment I emerge from the bunker the Germans, waiting and raring to go, start their comedy jazz routine. These ghostly, chilled Germans alongside their lean-to, their jazz antics to greet me in the morning, making fun of themselves and me, their efforts to attract my attention, to incline fate more kindly towards them, and simply to warm themselves up: that too is something that will stay with me now and give me no peace.

'Here We Are in Rzhev'

The prisoner was brought to headquarters blindfolded in accordance with the regulations, although this was the first time I had seen them observed. The new commander of our army interrogated him personally, with me interpreting.

The questioning left us none the wiser: the prisoner had arrived in this sector two days previously and knew nothing about anything. Suddenly, right at the end, he dropped in passing the fact that yesterday they had been ordered to hand in their second blanket to the baggage train, keeping just one for themselves. From my experience as an interpreter I recognized that this was of major significance: soldiers usually surrendered surplus items to the baggage train immediately before a move, so it was true: the Germans were preparing to retreat before the ring of encirclement closed around Rzhev.

In the bunker of the divisional chief of staff, Lieutenant Colonel Rodionov. The regimental commander's courier brought a first report from Rzhev. I asked permission to copy it into my diary: 'We are clearing the city of snipers. The Regimental Headquarters is located at 128 Kalinin Street.'

A second courier: '1,000 wagons of captured goods. The population has been driven into the church. It has been boarded up and mines laid round it.'

How poignant, solemn and simple these moments are. We are in Rzhev. 3 March 1943.

The bullet-riddled water tower sticks up bizarrely over everything. Black ruins of buildings blanketed in snow. That is all there is. Can this be what remains of Rzhev?

It is getting dark. An armoured train steams down the track.

This time there were no great battles, no tank engagements. The enemy surrendered the city without a fight, withdrew, using rearguard units to cover the main forces' retreat. But what of it, when the seventeen months it has taken to get back here into Rzhev, every metre we advanced or even just managed to hold, has been paid for by the crucifixion of the Red Army?

But now I am writing in my diary, 'I am in Rzhev' and, having written it, I am awestruck. I have been advancing towards this turning point for years, losing one after another of those with whom I should have been sharing these emotions and the sense of responsibility imposed by this return to Rzhev.

Seventeen peaceful years after the end of the war in 1945 I returned to Rzhev, following the same route I had taken to the front in February 1942, freezing in the back of a truck with my warrant of assignment. It had been a dog-legged route via recently liberated Kalinin, because the direct road to Rzhev at that time was the front line.

This time when I reached Kalinin I went to visit the local history museum. There was a special exhibition on 'The Patriotic War of 1812', the war with Napoleon, because that year we were separated from it by a full 150 years. About 'The Second Patriotic War', also known as 'The Second World War', there was nothing, and by the time they get round to mounting an exhibition on it in connection with some suitably round number of elapsed years, the memory will have faded away, the would-be exhibits will be buried in the earth, and it will be just as dull, official and devoid of human reality as the exhibition presented here for a 150th anniversary.

Where are our banners riddled with bullet holes, discoloured by the rain, shredded by the wind? Our soot-covered mess tins, cape groundsheets, and soldiers' foot wrappings a *verst* long? Where are our 1891-vintage rifles, the local kilometre-to-the-centimetre maps, the morse code telegraph keys, the dried bread you softened in a puddle? Where are the dog tags that identified dead soldiers?

In a small volunteer-run museum in a small, remote town in this province I saw a pair of straw overshoes. That was just one detail of the enemy's day-to-day life, but what a lot it tells us. I have a small museum of my own, more precisely, an archive. It preserves my wartime diary entries, written on the move; later sketches written from memory; stories of local people that I noted down; letters, diaries and documents.

After I adopted the name of this city as my pen name, and after publishing some writing, I started to receive letters from correspondents I had never met, telling me about the far-off days of their childhood in Rzhev, or when they were fighting in the battles for the city, or about what went on while Rzhev was under occupation. I received over forty letters about that from a man who had been a boy at the time of the war. The city museum, the staff at the local newspaper and radio station, and workers at the 'tourism headquarters' sent me materials donated to them by people who did not want the wartime voices, events and fate of the city to be forgotten.

So I continue to tell the story whose main character is the shambles of a war I too lived through, and now find myself the archivist of my own archive.

A. S. Andrievskaya:

When they descended on us they first ate, they feasted, so well groomed, playing their mouth organs, having a fine time: they had opened the gateway to Moscow!

But then next there was the commandant's office, taking a census of the population. The firing squads appeared, the gallows. We went to the slaughter-house for bones and offal we would have fed to the pigs before that. We went out to the villages to barter it. The Germans confiscated things, sent them away back to their homes. They dug up the pits where townspeople had tried to hide at least some of their property.

In the summer and spring we ate goosefoot and nettles, dug out the tubers of frozen potatoes left over from the autumn of '41. The number of people left in the city went down and down, dying of starvation and typhus they were. And then the real calamity began when they started taking people and sending them west. Trainloads of us. They took us under guard to Rzhev station, issued us one loaf of bread with sawdust per family, put us in goods wagons, locked them and took us off to who knows where. It was dark in the wagons, people, shouting and groaning, crying . . .

Faina Krochak:

The Germans are not all the same sort. There was some humanity. And one or two of our own troops, there's no denying, were just brutes. Take Lena, my daughter, she was twelve then, had a fever; she was dying. I went to Chachkino to see the doctor. Fifteen kilograms of grain he wanted before he would even look at her. Anyway, in the city they had a clinic at the school. The German doctor came, and he said, 'She needs to go to hospital at once.'

'They took me on a sledge,' Lena adds. 'He came with us. A German orderly carried me. He came to see me after the operation and bandaged me up.'

The worst thing was the hunger. And also, out of all the other things, the sorting. On Commune Street, opposite the commandant's office. Masses of people. The Germans forced everyone to go there, they shot people who did not go to the sorting. That was the most horrible of all the things that happened. People clinging to each other, wailing, crying. They tore a mother away from her sick child. They were deporting people.

The Germans, when they first came piling into the city, strutted around like they owned the place. One German came in to us with an interpreter and went to see Masha, who was in charge:

'Tell me, will you, where the Jews are here.'

'Never had any Jews here,' Masha told them, quick as a flash.

'Well, Communists then?'

'They've all run away.'

On the school gate, people saw a teacher hanging. Hanged by the Germans. They said he was a Communist. Even before that they'd seized other Communists. Paraded them through the town and shot them by the Volga, on the far bank and on ours. For three days they wouldn't let anyone take the bodies.

Every day the headman for our district came round. 'Any Jews here, Communists?'

'Why, do you think we're breeding them?'

Two men were sawing in the street, Jews. 'No more sawing for you,' the headman told them. He betrayed them, and the same night they were taken away.

He came to see us again. 'Faina, where were you yesterday?'

'At home.'

'I came round yesterday with the gendarmes and you weren't in. I've registered you.'

'What the hell's it got to do with you?'

'Me, I'm the Russian people. Who are you then?'

He took me to the police station. The mayor of the city, what they call the Burgomeister, Kuzmin, says, 'Why aren't you wearing an armband?'

'What armband, for heaven's sake?'

'It's obvious from your accent what armband.'

I wasn't afraid of their bullets. I was afraid they might bury me alive. But he let me go.

All the time they were driving residents from that side of the Volga to this one, to get everyone in one place. And after that they started deporting people.

Lena's legs were all swollen. She had something growing on her face from the starvation.

Along comes the headman with the gendarme. The gendarme has this shiny badge on his chest, spurs clattering. 'Well, young ladies are you ready?' asks the headman.

'We've no intention of being ready,' Taisiya Strunina tells him. She was living with us at the time.

I started crying. 'Are you a father?' That's what I said to the German. 'I pulled back the blanket and showed her legs. 'How can I go?' He shook his head and left.

'We'll shoot her. You don't have to worry.' That was the headman. 'And you will come with us.'

How many more days we had like that.

Lena:

The Germans came charging in. About ten in the morning on 1 March. Beside themselves, they were. Retreating. Surrendering the city. Scouring the place to find anyone who was hiding. The last ones. They herded us into the church. Our windows had the curtains closed. They smashed the glass with their rifle butts. They didn't care if people were sick, or dead. They were crazy. I couldn't stand. They put me on a sledge, tied me on with sackcloth.

Anna Grigorievna Kuzmina:

They packed the church full of people. It was cold. All the windows in the church were broken. I gave my husband one of my shawls. 'A granny with a beard,' the children in the church laughed. And then we heard, they were boarding the doors up from the outside.

Faina Krochak:

'Give us water! Give us water! 'A sentry threw a snowball in the window. Everybody wanted to suck it.

The gendarmes came twice, looking for some woman. They said, 'Tomorrow it's the end.'

Anna Grigorievna Kuzmina:

There were explosions, explosions everywhere. The people in the church groaned, screamed. Some people embraced. 'It's time to say goodbye! It's time to say goodbye!'

It became very, very quiet. For three hours, it must have been. We look out the windows and see people in white smocks. With red stars.

This was resurrection. We hugged and kissed each other. Tears and weeping. A solemn moment. We had risen from the dead. It was a resurrection.

And then one old woman, whose name I don't know, said, 'Russians! Real Russians! They're outside . . . their greatcoats are frozen hard as boards. Their boots are covered in ice. Everything on them is covered in ice. Can you believe it?'

The last people in Rzhev were supposed to suffer a cruel martyrdom in that church, for not abandoning their city. Their saviours appeared in white smocks, wearing a red star, in frozen greatcoats.

A Letter from Munich

I received a letter, together with a bouquet of white roses, from Otto Spranger, a person in Munich I did not know. Here is how he explains what prompted him to write to me.

He saw a documentary film by Renata Stegmüller and Raimund Koplin about three women whose destinies were bound up with the war: a Norwegian woman; the famous Italian writer, Luce d'Eramo; and me.

As soon as the footage of Rzhev appeared on the screen, I was electrified. I realized that the Russian woman featured in the film had been a participant in the confrontation at Rzhev, had obviously chosen her pen name with reference to that city and, like a flash of lightning I remembered a close relative who, under particular circumstances, had also received a name in connection with Rzhev. With embarrassment I learnt that at that time Yelena Rzhevskaya was involved in the struggle against my uncle, Colonel Hans Beckmann, my mother's elder brother: Beckmann von Rzhev, as he was called by his fellow officers.

As a seven-year-old boy, my correspondent had heard the news in his home that Uncle Hans had been awarded the Knight's Cross, a very high award, for successfully repulsing a massive offensive by Soviet troops attempting to retake Rzhev.

He also recalled that in April 1945 his parents read in the newspaper that their brother Hans, by now no longer a colonel but a lieutenant general, had been awarded an even higher honour, the Order of the Knight's Cross with Oak Leaves, and his mother said ruefully, 'That means he will soon be hanged!' Otto Spranger thinks there was an element of condemnation in his mother's comment about her brother: why serve in such a way as to be awarded military laurels at a time when everyone knew the war had been lost?

Uncle Hans did not have long to enjoy his military successes: as the war was ending he was arrested by Czech partisans, and on the very last day of the war, 9 May, found himself a prisoner of the Russians.

For a long time the family had no news of him, but in 1947 or so, one of his soldiers who had been released brought the news that Lieutenant General Hans Beckmann had been sentenced by a Soviet court as a war criminal to twenty-five years in forced labour camps. The sentence related to a charge that the population of Rzhev had been herded into the church for deportation to Germany.

This was a blow for our whole family. How was that possible? Was it imaginable that a member of a decent, educated family that was no supporter of Nazism could have violated human rights, international law and the moral laws of humane waging of war? I remember very exactly that my mother said at the time her brother had nothing to do with deportation, that was dealt with by the occupying commandant. We cursed Soviet, Stalinist, vengeful, terrorist justice.

There was no prospect of seeing Uncle Hans in twenty-five years' time: he was already over fifty, but then a diplomatic initiative by Chancellor Konrad Adenauer was successful and German prisoners of war were released. In 1955 General Beckmann returned to Germany and lived for a time with the family of my correspondent. Beckmann's relatives treated him with kid gloves. As soon as the conversation turned to anything painful, tears would come to his eyes. Eventually, when it had become possible to talk to him about the trial and the sentence, he said he had been slandered by false witnesses.

Hans Beckmann moved with his wife to an old university town where his daughter and her family lived. He celebrated his seventieth birthday there, and died a year later. Someone in the Spranger family continued, however, to enquire into the circumstances of his career during the war.

I once asked my mother: 'What did Uncle Hans say about the *Kristallnacht* pogrom?' My mother replied that he said at the time, 'I think this is a complete disgrace.' I asked her, 'Uncle Hans, as a senior army officer and an educated man, must surely have understood what a completely criminal regime was at the helm. Why did not he resign from the Wehrmacht, which was there to fight for that regime? Perhaps that is why he was sentenced to twenty-five years' hard labour, and not only because he was falsely accused. Perhaps that is another way of looking at it.

The jogging of Otto Spranger's memory and conscience after seeing the film led him to the military archives in Potsdam. He found a document signed by Colonel General Walter Model, commander of the Ninth Army, which said, 'Colonel Beckmann was not at that time in command of his regiment but had been appointed commander of the Rzhev garrison. By his resolute action on 17 August 1942 he managed to avoid surrendering the city.'

Accordingly, deportation of the population was carried out with the full knowledge of Colonel Beckmann, and perhaps on his orders. Otto Spranger visited his uncle's grave.

I told Uncle Hans I would go to Rzhev. I wished the trip to be a sign of penitence and hoped it would lay the foundation for reconciliation with the people of Rzhev. At his grave I expressed all my troubling thoughts because, as a Christian, I know that he has life after death. I know he is not against my intention and has no objections to it. I believe that he also does not object today, dear Mme Rzhevskaya, that I am sending you, as someone who took part in the Russian resistance to Nazi aggression, this letter and a bouquet of flowers to ask forgiveness for the guilt of my uncle who, like thousands of other top German officers, incurred it by following the orders of his supreme commander-in-chief, the Führer of the regime, even after that regime's criminal deeds in Germany had been known for some time, especially to the 'educated elite', to which my family was always so proud to belong.

I have asked that, together with this letter, you should receive white roses. They were the symbol of the renowned student resistance movement in Munich which called itself The White Rose.

I received the letter and flowers in 1996.

More Memory-Jogging

By the time Rzhev was retaken I was the only translator at our army head-quarters. Another had gone home to Siberia to have a baby. The need for translation, however, increased. There was a mountain of German bureaucratic documentation: papers of the municipal administration, the city commandant's office, residents' personal certificates. Much of it was not strictly relevant to military priorities.

When we had moved on much further to the west, Stalin visited Rzhev. This was his only excursion in the direction of the front. The house where he slept is still standing. He summoned General Yeremenko there and took the decision to celebrate victorious battles with artillery cannonades.

Those whole seventeen months of battles for Rzhev, all that cost in terms of mental anguish and blood, all the orderliness and chaos of war and its daily routines were in pursuit of one great goal: to drive the enemy out of our land, and for us that meant retaking Rzhev. We were in a hurry to get back into the crucified city we had forced the enemy to surrender.

The war is an inexhaustible topic. No matter how much I have written about it, I cannot free myself of the feeling that there are important things yet to be said, things not yet fully revealed. Rzhev today and Rzhev back then are still very much a part of my life; I am tied to the city by painful memories that trouble me still in a way very similar to love.

More than twenty years were to pass before I set out to find Zaimishche again. It was very odd: neither on the map of the district, nor in the district executive Party committee was there any mention of Zaimishche, either among the ninety-two villages in the district that the war had wiped from the face of the earth, or among those still in existence. I set out on a quest to find it. A young lad who delivered movies round the villages drove me. His name was Sasha and he was keen to help. The two of us travelled the country roads, driving into villages, collecting films in metal cans that had been projected and leaving new ones, and each time asking people about Zaimishche.

Everybody still remembered everything. Nothing had yet been trampled underfoot by tourists or those groups of young admirers of our military glory, and everything was mixed up together: the mossy headstone of Count Seslavin, a hero of the First World War, and the legend of Dunka, the local Robin Hood, a woman who robbed rich citizens of Tver on the highways, and the River Dunka, which had invariably featured in our daily situation reports during the war. It was the front line between us and the Germans, where, it seems the valiant female ataman had finally been caught by the prince's guards. Here the dead are still waiting for the living to bury them. Sasha related what his mother had told him: she and some other women had been going to scythe remote meadows. Suddenly, in an overgrown trench, they saw a soldier sitting wearing his greatcoat and helmet. The women were stunned. They wept and rushed to him, but the moment they touched him he crumbled to dust.

There were still landmines buried everywhere. Where a village had been burned down there was now a forest, creeping towards the boundary fence of other villages in decline. We finally drove into Zaimishche. The village street was noticeably shorter. I later discovered there had been seventy houses, but now only twenty-five remained. I remembered the village as it was in winter, and now, in autumn, it seemed unrecognizable. But it was still alive. The log huts stood in a row: one in good order, with a new roof of black roofing felt; another leaning to one side; another again newly refurbished and full of life. I remembered the well sweep in front of the house but the well had changed. It had had to be altered three years previously because the sweep was in the way when the village finally got electricity (something else I only found out later).

I got out of the car and asked two schoolgirls going by with their school bags if they could tell me where Matryona Nilovna lived. They thought hard, and then it dawned on one: Auntie Matryosha? She pointed out her house to me.

I pushed the gate, as people here call the outer door of a hut, and went in on tenterhooks. In the passage, lit by a tiny window, a few steps higher up on the platform where Kostya, the eldest son, used to grind grain between the millstones, stood an iron bed. Leaning over it, taking something off the bed, was a woman. She straightened up and turned round at the sound of the door opening.

I asked if Matryona Nilovna live here. She replied, 'Yes.'

I took a step up on the mat covering the stairs.

'Is that you . . .?'

'Me,' she said, peering down at me.

'We were billeted here with you during the war.'

'Are you Lena?' she asked. I felt my heart leap. I gasped with emotion.

'Why did you not come back?' she asked in such a slow, calm way. 'You promised.' I could not say a word. I just silently hugged her.

'Come on in. I'll put the samovar on.'

I followed her in, half blinded by tears, and stubbed my toe in the kitchen on the ring on the hatch down to the cellar. When the bombs were falling I had passed the younger children down there to her (the boys, Kostya and Genka, had rushed out into the street), and climbed down myself to join them. Soldiers running past shouted to us that this was a deadly place to stay, but there was nowhere else to take cover. And, as if the veil of time had been drawn back, I again saw a calf in the enclosure, exactly like the one that had so annoyed Captain Borisov.

Looking at me, Matryona Nilovna shook her head. In all those years her face had not lost that trustful expression. She was not at all taken aback that I had reappeared: I had promised, and had just taken rather a long time to keep my promise. She said sadly, 'Out working there in the field you do wonder, is she still alive? She did promise . . .' Lord, what did we not promise all sorts of people if we came through the war alive.

A short fellow came in, and looked at me in amazement. 'You never got to meet her,' Matryona Nilovna said regretfully. And how could he have, missing at the front and in captivity? 'Nothing you can count on,' Matryona Nilovna used to say when asked what she knew of her husband's whereabouts. Thinking how he should react to my appearance, he began shaving, looking me over, this stranger. I felt awkward. After all, I meant nothing to him.

Sasha, waiting outside by the car, hearing what was embarrassing me and that I did not know what to do, said firmly, 'In your place, I would stay.' And that being so, he did not deny me one last favour, turned the car round, and we bumped off over the potholes to the next village. There a show trial was being held at the clubhouse, and during the proceedings the sale of vodka was prohibited. One or two men were hanging around on the porch of the village store, visibly wilting as they waited for the resumption of business. The assistant, learning why we needed vodka, sympathized with my predicament and, laden with purchases, we made our way back out past the parched would-be drinkers.

Vasiliy Mikhailovich, as Matryona's husband was called, brightened up considerably at the sight of our party preparations. 'One for the road!' he urged Sasha, who was in a hurry to be on his way. Vasiliy had a drink with him and went off to check whether the flax was to be raised. Sasha took his farewells.

In the kitchen nothing had changed, only now a bare electric light bulb was hanging from the ceiling on its flex, and on the slanting shelf over the table, next to St Nicholas the Wonderworker, there was a small box and the football was being broadcast on the radio.

Little Shurka had not lived long after we left. In the autumn the fighting was again moving towards Zaimishche and everyone was hastily evacuated. 'We kicked up a fuss and did not want any of their evacuation. Then an officer said, "We just have to wait and see what comes next. We don't know for sure whether we'll lick them or maybe they'll lick us." Well, then we stopped yelling. That wasn't going to help, we had to get out, from what he said. We packed our things. Left. Stopped where they told us to. No gate on the house. The officers safe in their bunker. Everything was wide open and it was such a cold day. She fell sick. The children had run off somewhere. I swore at them for leaving Shurka. But what could we do for her? Where could we take her? There was no hospital.'

I remembered her in that cradle, her hungry crying, her toothless, old woman's smile that went straight to your heart, her quick little legs, pounding the damp straw. And Kostya's 'There now, Shurushochki, shush Shurushochki!'

Matryona Nilovna asked about my family. 'You said after the war you'd come back here for a holiday.' Did I really say that, about coming for a holiday? But if that was what she remembered, then, fool that I was, I must have said it. 'And do you remember Jesus saving your life?' I did not understand what she was talking about.

By now the village women had come to see what was going on. 'Look, I've got a visitor!' Matryona could scarcely conceal her sense of triumph. Vasiliy Mikhailovich returned. Two young men came in, 'Look at them now!' Matryona said. They were her sons, Genka, now Genya, and Shura. A girl of around thirteen came rushing home from school after hearing that someone had come to visit. This was Valya. 'After Valya I had a little boy, stillborn, and that was that. I was an old woman.'

Everyone began sitting round the table, the women shuffling about hesitantly at the door. Matryona, after a suitable pause, called to them, 'Come on in, uninvited guests. We'll spare you a glass, one, and if we get drunk, maybe two.' Unhurriedly, primly, they came in and sat down. They drank, and became lost in their own thoughts: 'If it had been shorter, the war, at least one of my sons might have come back, even wounded . . . But I have no one.'

'You just grabbed your kiddies under your arm and headed for Mikitka's vegetable plot and into the little ditch he'd dug. We had such a fright! We sat there all night. And he kept flying around. And then, away over on Yegorka's, he dropped the bomb. What a fright . . .' says Matryona. 'They're coming, do you hear? They're coming, hear that creaking. Oh, are they really Russians? It's Russians coming. Stop whining, Nyurka, I say. Oh, what's going on over there. The Germans are on the run. Oh, daughter. Light the *pegaska* the German anti-aircraft gunners left.' 'Germans? It's how it is. They took them off to fight a war, so fight they did. It's not for us to judge.'

Vasiliy Mikhailovich filled the glasses and added his voice to the conversation, all about today's farming worries. The women couldn't wait to tell their stories about how it had been in the past. 'It was time for the sowing, we had no horses, nothing. Just the women on their own. We hitched five of us to the harrow.' 'Well, now we're getting a life again. Especially anyone whose got some men.' 'Just as long as we don't have another war. Now, God have mercy on us if we have to.' And then Matryona's voice, tenderly: 'And I was wondering, who can that be? The schoolmistress? Now I'll recognize her anywhere.' That was about me.

I kept quiet. I could not contain my emotion. The war really had passed through the door of this house. Just about everybody had been billeted here: Finns, Germans (more than once), the German anti-aircraft gunners with their '*pegaskas*', as Matryona called their lamps, and we Russians, repeatedly being driven from the village, then retaking it. In a large picture frame on the wall, among the family photos, are some girls in hats with earflaps and forage caps who stayed here after us. There is no photo of me: I did not have one with me. But now I find that all along I have been hovering here, those long years during which she was seeing children laid in their graves, giving birth to others, then seeing the children she already had grown up, bidding them farewell as they moved far away.

'She sent me dried bread with a soldier once,' she kept repeating, and to me, 'Do you remember?' To my shame, I had not the wits to say I did. Of course I would have, at the first opportunity, as soon as I found someone coming this way, only I did not remember doing it. 'And I wanted to pour him some milk to take back to you,' she said, suddenly deflated. 'But he said, no way! "She has plenty to eat! She's well fed!"' That memory about the bread was so important to her, so treasured; to this day I cannot forgive myself for not immediately confirming it.

Vasiliy Mikhailovich went out and returned with a lantern, having done the rounds of the houses. He was the night watchman. Everybody went home. Vasiliy and the boys settled down to sleep; they would all be up in the morning and off to harvest the potatoes. Matryona and I talked as we cleared the table and washed the dishes. 'Do you remember,' she asked, 'that last night before you were travelling on, and we had the bombing?' I remembered it only too well. The Germans were rarely flying nights at that time: they had pretty much a free hand even during the day. Matryona had been generous with heating the hut, so that we should be well warmed up before going on our way. The house was positively hot and the bedbugs crawled out in droves. To get away from them, I moved out of my corner to the bench by the wall opposite, with my head to the icon corner. I was wakened by a loud explosion and the whistling of shards of glass from the windows flying through the air.

'They riddled the house,' someone said. Matryona, protecting the flickering light of the *pegaska* with her hand, looked around and said, 'He hit our holy Saviour.' If I had woken up a moment sooner and sat up, I would have had my brains blown out. Matryona decided it was the Saviour who had saved me, and been wounded himself.

'And now, if you please, I have my daughter Valya coming home from the school and saying, "Mummy, you have to get rid of the boards."' Their teacher had been asking them to get the icons taken down. I said, 'While we have breath in our bodies they're doing no harm.' 'Well then, Mum, at least give me the cloths from them.'

The schoolmistress is very respected in the village. Before she came nobody grew flowers in Zaimishche. She was very persistent, showed how to grow them, and now people have lilac planted, flowers growing under their windows, and they sow them in their vegetable plots. Everybody is very pleased, but there is Valya saying, 'Mum, we need to throw the icons out.'

In the morning I found myself alone in the house. Matryona and her entire family had got on a cart and gone off to dig up the potatoes. I went out to the passage and opened the door to the yard. Just as then, there were the birch-twig brushes ready for use in the bathhouse. Sawn logs were piled up by the wall. The salted cabbage was being pressed by a weight in the keg. Chickens dozed on their perch. That smell was just the same. Nothing, I suppose, stirs our emotions and reawakens our memories like smells.

I went back to the kitchen and there too, in my solitude, I was pursued by smells. There was a smell of calf, tobacco, sheepskin, and leather. The smell of our nomadic army life seemed to have suffused this peasant lodging ineradicably.

I remembered the icon. In the 'clean', living half of the hut, where it used to hang, there was nothing. What had become of it?

From the low ceiling there hung paper crackers for the New Year tree, each containing some little treat. They alternated with embroidered towels folded in half and pinned to the ceiling. That continued right through the room, and the closer you came to the corner, the more dense were the colourful crackers, and the towels from the trunk for Valya's dowry were lowered full length, blocking any view of the corner.

I parted the towels, disrupting Valya's little masquerade. The icon she had 'masked' was in its place. I looked at it again and gasped. The Saviour was holding an open book on which was inscribed:

> A new commandment
> I give unto you,
> That ye love one another

A jagged wound had pierced the old dark wood and damaged the words 'That ye love'. To anyone who did not see it with their own eyes this will seem far fetched, and that is why I never mentioned it. 'That ye love one another'. It continued in Church Slavonic, 'as I . . .' That was all: there was no room for more on the open page of the book.

Matryona and Vasiliy Mikhailovich wrote to me, sharing their worries and urging me to visit them. Two years later I was again in Rzhev, and again went to Zaimishche to see them. We were sitting at the table when I suddenly noticed that the icon, that very icon, was now, for some reason, leaning on the kitchen windowsill. I asked why it was in such an unbecoming place. Vasiliy Mikhailovich answered animatedly, 'Well, the next time you come it will have been chopped up for firewood.'

I was horrified. What was he saying? This was a historic icon. They needed to take such good care of it. 'Would you?' he asked. 'Of course I would.' 'Then you take it.' 'But it's not my icon. You should put it back in the icon corner. Why did you move it? That was its place. After all, that is where it was hit.'

Matryona, who had said nothing up till now, said, 'Take it.' 'Only I'm telling you,' Vasiliy Mikhailovich said, 'you'll get woodworm in all your furniture.' He turned the icon round and showed where the wood had been eaten away on the back.

On my last visit Matryona had said of the icons, 'While we have breath in our bodies they're doing no harm.' Evidently, however, her husband had sided with the children against her. On my last morning, when I came into the kitchen I saw Matryona washing the icon, preparing it for its journey and talking to it. 'Now, don't be upset, Lord Jesus. You'll be better off there.' She wrapped the icon in an old apron and put it into a bag along with a pair of woollen socks she had knitted for me.

We hugged and took a long time saying goodbye. I assured her I would come again and invited her to come and stay with me. 'My sister Katya keeps inviting me to stay with her and Nyura. "What are you doing pottering about there? Come to us and have a holiday." Well, one of these days I will, I'll come and visit you all.' It did not happen.

We corresponded until the day she died, and after that I corresponded with Valya, the daughter born just after the war. And later, in February 2006, just as I was working on this book, there was one of those small miracles my life has been so full of. I had a letter from Valya's daughter, who by then was about thirty. She wrote to say they had seen me in a television programme and been remembering me. All her family were living well and sent greetings. She was not herself planning to have any children yet because, as young people do nowadays, she thought it was still a bit early.

Onwards

It is pouring with rain in the Smolensk region and in the swampy woodlands there is no shelter. My tunic is soaked, my underwear damp, my boots squelch. In this place at this time the rain never stops.

I might have expected the historic events in Berlin in which I was involved during the last days of the war would have erased many other things from memory. In fact, though, what has left the deepest impression are those days of incessant rain in the environs of Rzhev when the efforts of an army at war and the lives of the population in that frontal zone created a tremendous sense of a whole people at war.

In the initial dismaying succession of defeats, the war gave us back a sense of our value, of human solidarity, and often also of human dignity. After the terrible delusions of the late 1930s, we had a clear, righteous aim to strive for: to defend our Motherland and vanquish a terrible foe that had almost all the rest of Europe under its heel.

Now, as the tide of war changed in the direction of victory, something supremely important was being taken away again.

Our army newspaper, *Boevoye Znamya*, The Battle Standard: 'Yesterday at dawn our units re-entered the territory of Soviet Byelorussia.' There is a hill in front of me. The sun is setting and the sky becomes as golden as pie crust. On the horizon, outlined against what will be tomorrow's frost, horses, people on foot, and laden trucks are on the move.

General Kutuzov before the Battle of the Berezina: 'God is with us, we have a broken enemy before us, let there be stillness and peace behind us.'

3 A Distant Thunder: Europe, 1945

Vergangenes steht noch bevor[1] – Warsaw

It is said with resignation, 'Our earthly life is but a little time.' Have we still future enough to get to the root of everything, to the core of life? What is certain is how long the past has been. Reverse the future and the past and there will be an infinity of days that seem sometimes a hazy succession, sometimes an elusive delight, and sometimes have such density and fullness that the thunder reaching you from that chasm pounds against your transient being.

Warsaw has a suburb called Praga. It had long been taken back from the Germans. Fate had been kind to us, not compelling us to languish here, on this side of the Vistula, while the Warsaw Uprising flared tragically on the other. We had not, thank God, been here at that time but were deployed to Poland from our Motherland just before Christmas. Almost immediately the Wojsko Polskie and our troops moved on Warsaw.

Now Warsaw is liberated and we are in its suburbs, in Praga, in the midst of jubilant red-and-white Polish flags. Somewhere a small orchestra flares up briefly and goes out. There is broken stone and shattered glass underfoot, the walls have breaches in them. Front-line vehicles and the infantry are on the move. A houseowner in warm earmuffs waves a small red flag and stands there in the street, loudly welcoming our unit as it passes through, eager to shake every hand.

Here is where we will stop for the night. A steep climb up a dark, frail, creaking staircase to the second floor where we are to sleep in empty, freezing rooms abandoned by their occupants. We find a lonely old woman,

---

1. 'The past is yet to come,' Rainer Maria Rilke, *Das Stundenbuch*, Book II (1901), p. 308. The verse continues, '*Und in der Zukunft liegen Leichen.*' 'And in the future corpses lie.'

the one remaining, longstanding resident. Hearing our heavy footsteps coming up the stairs, she waits warily in the corridor.

She has a worn, black velvet coat and a felt hat that must once have been fashionable, with the snouts of two small, unidentifiable animals artfully attached to it. Her gaze is detached, unfocused, and she seems to be looking past us. She greets us courteously and in slow motion. Her delicate hand, removed from a velvet muff, indicates the doors of the rooms that are empty, '*Proszę panowie* [Gentlemen, please],' before it is replaced in the muff. In her high laced boots she minces back down the corridor to her own apartment.

In the morning she is waiting for me in the corridor, wearing an old shapeless dress that looks like a mantle, and long, elegant black earrings. Her grey hair is carefully divided into small tresses. She takes me to her room. A pair of men's worn-out shoes serve as her indoor footwear and clatter on the worn, black parquet. Pieces of cotton wool are sticking out of the backs of the shoes, pushed in for warmth or, more probably, to keep them from falling off as she is walking. Her heels do, nevertheless, pop out and holes gleam all the way through several layers of stockings. At the door of her room she introduces herself: Madame Maria, a music teacher.

A big room, a divan, an open harmonium. Freezing cold. A baby grand piano, 'Becker. St Petersburg', covered in pillows, blankets, pieces of soft cloth to keep it from getting too cold. It seems to be the only thing here with any life. In a notebook I got hold of back in Latvia, inside a hard dark blue cover with light blue marbling, I write that day, 'From somewhere, a wave of depressing weariness and pain.' It must be because, having glimpsed someone else's life, shot to pieces by the war and the German occupation, I was suddenly shaken by her rugged, uncomplaining solitariness. Perhaps it was an austere reward for my own nomadic, homeless destiny at the front. The entry is dated 19 January 1945, two days after Warsaw was liberated.

Madame Maria says she wants to celebrate it somehow, and touches one of her long black earrings. It is the first time in over five years she has worn them. She invites me to be seated and, looking a little absently in my direction, begins removing the pillows and blankets from the piano and putting them on the divan. Yes, yes, something to celebrate it, she says, mixing Russian and Polish words together. If Maria can be permitted, she would like to play something for me. She loves Bach, but after the Germans declared him an Aryan she stopped playing him.

She extracts sheet music from the pile on the piano and sets it on the music rack. She sits down on the rotating music stool, adjusts her hair, raises a hand to her mouth, breathes on her fingers and rubs them, then runs them over the keys.

She plays and her earrings sway. The pedal is operated by a foot wearing a man's worn-out shoe. I do not listen very attentively but, as tends to happen when you hear music played, something inside you seems to fill with a sense of participation in living, perturbs you with an unfocused joy or hope of life, and carries you away from the limitations of war. My feet feel cold.

Maria finishes with a cascade of chords, looks across to me and says, with perhaps a hint of irritation, that she would, of course, have preferred to play something more serious but it would be difficult to do that from memory nowadays, and her finest music has long ago been taken to the bomb shelter for safekeeping. What she has here – she indicates the pile – is just what she is practising with her pupils, easy pieces.

Her pupils? Here in a suburb which has been on the front line for months and which only the Vistula separated from all the fighting and destruction in Warsaw? She evidently notices my puzzlement and tells me with quiet dignity that her son is *over there*, by which she clearly means on the other side of the front line, where the Germans are. He is in the underground. She reaches for her late husband's warm dressing gown, thrown on the divan. Rising slightly, she wraps it around herself. Yes, yes, she still has two pupils. Their parents are not so rich, she tells me with an increasingly evident, and evidently defensive, haughtiness, as to be able to throw away all they have already spent on their daughters' musical education. Quite possibly the ability to entertain a party with light music will be the only dowry they get. Just recently, though, she has taken on another student, a strange man, Pan Wojciech. His villa, requisitioned by the Germans, has been returned to him and he is intending to sit out the remainder of the war alone, minding his own business, whatever happens outside the walls of his home. That is why he has taken to learning the piano. He is fifty-four and his hands are completely unsuitable. 'You need to be playing while your hands are growing to fit the keyboard!' she says rather intensely, and it is evident from the way she says it that she disapproves of Pan Wojciech. She should have declined taking him on but now only has two other pupils – not enough to survive on.

It is time for her to get ready to give him his lesson, and our truck is already snorting down in the street. I run downstairs, pulling on my outdoor clothes as I go. The engine is being warmed up and the truck is juddering.

When Madame Maria emerges through the front door, I am sitting in the back of the truck. She comes over and, in the unforgiving light of a clear winter's day, it is only too obvious how bloodless her aristocratic face, criss-crossed with wrinkles, is. A purple vein twitches under one eye. How old and scrawny the snouts of those little animals on her hat are. She is looking distractedly, perhaps at me or somewhere above my head, pressing her muff high up on her chest. There is something she is hesitating to say.

'Warsaw,' she quavers but breaks off. Pulling herself together, she says simply, 'Give Bach back to us. How can anyone play the piano without Bach?' She could equally well have said, bring my son back to me but she does not. She hurries off to give her lesson, teetering in her high lace-up boots over the frozen cobbles.

I wrote at the time in my diary, 'She has lived her life and has no future, but she is giving music lessons in a town which for a long time was the front line, her hair carefully divided into little tresses. This is not senile affectation, it is her way of life.' And with that way of life she is retaining her sense of self-respect, discipline, nobility and femininity in spite of her age and the sad losses she has suffered.

She goes off to give her lesson, and the brittle clacking of her heels gradually dies away. As I look after her, I am painfully aware how vulnerable Maria is amidst the collapsing masonry of war, how homeless, as if it is she rather than I who has no roof over her head. And in fact, that really is the situation: the war is my home. The war takes some account of me, I have business with it, while Maria, a private person, has none. It is up to her to survive as best she can.

The agony of Warsaw stares out at us, the blackened gaps between the buildings, the jagged fragments of walls, the spectral skeletons of houses stripped bare by the avalanche of shells and fire, the silent testimony of its ruins.

These ruins are a tragic monument to the spirit: its torment, its doomed passion, its inspiration and its horror. They are an emblem of something that cannot be gauged against earlier knowledge or experience. What these ruins encapsulate cannot be articulated or sculpted. Only the ruins all the way from Vyazma to Warsaw speak the language of what has transpired here.

The open road. The snow on the ground is drifting, the tall, thin Catholic crosses by the roadside with the figure of the crucified Christ flash by. Beyond the boundary of the road is open country and woodland shrouded in mist. What is it about this land that so clutches at your heart, so unsettles and bewitches you? You cannot pin it down. Only many years later did I see surviving newsreel footage of the Polish cavalry, with sabres drawn, charging German tanks. In that chivalrous, warrior-like outburst of valour there is such love and beauty and vulnerability that you are transfixed. I thought when I saw that sight that this gesture was the very embodiment of a Poland that had languished for so long under the yoke of tyranny; it was all in that gesture – the boundless devotion of spirit, imprisoned in mortal flesh, raising its immortal arm against soulless, invincible brute force.

We drive through some ruined town. The townspeople are ceremonially bearing two Polish soldiers shoulder-high through the streets. We have not been issued felt boots. The quartermasters withheld them on the grounds that winter in Europe does not compare with winter in Russia. In the back of our truck, however, our legs are frozen in our thin boots. We have no option but to stop at a village to warm ourselves. Our hosts cannot do enough for us. Before I can pull off my boots myself they rush to help. The mother shouts and a young lad grabs a basin, skips outside to collect snow, comes back, sits down on the floor beside me and starts rubbing my numb legs with snow.

Two little urchins wake up, escape from under the quilt and start jumping up and down on the bed. The only person in the house not involved in all the turmoil and excitement around us is an orphaned girl from Warsaw whom they have taken in. Kneeling by the stove, she is constantly, unsmilingly topping up the fire. It is her job to keep the stove fuelled. She half turns round and I see sunken, deeply melancholy eyes not at all like those of a child. She does not belong here. 'Girl by the fire in the stove, her narrow little back wrapped crosswise in a grey shawl, saving something up, hiding it against . . .' Against whom? I did not finish the sentence on the scrap of paper that has survived. Against the people who had given her shelter, against all of us for her orphaned life that can never be put right again.

A modest, subdued far horizon, a low sky, a snowstorm is trying to tear a poster down, flapping it above the road with one end still clinging to the post. 'Brother Slavs!' 'Brothers . . .'

Bydgoszcz

The war lumbered onwards, and brought us to the Polish city of Bydgoszcz, which the Germans called Bromberg, alien, not demolished, not devastated, as if the war, having passed it by, had now been pushed aside. The enemy had been forced out at dawn, or rather, obliged to depart, leaving no sign of having put up a fight. The tanks and infantry did not pause to fortify the position but rushed straight on. It was they who rightly enjoyed the enthusiastic welcome of the local Polish population.

The blizzard was dying down, but it was still snowing and foggy. Our truck was following the car with the chief of staff, drawn increasingly into the straight, narrow streets of the outskirts. From the back I could see the stone walls of prim grey houses, the pavements empty. Only on one corner, a collection of strange, stunted creatures, enveloped in what looked like dark flannel soldiers' blankets, were shifting from one foot to the other to keep warm. We drove on towards the city centre and again saw, swarming on the corners, more of these indefinite, small, lumpish people. As the mist cleared you could just glimpse, if someone peeped out from a blanket, a woman's face, dark, angular, with a vacant, unseeing gaze. There was something deeply disturbing about their unfathomable swarming, their incoherence, their disconnectedness from their surroundings. We learned later that they were Hungarian Jewesses who had walked out of a concentration camp abandoned by fleeing guards.

Our truck was already entering the town centre, where a confusion of vehicles had created a traffic jam. The place was full of people out in the street enjoying the tumult of victory. There were Polish girls, soldiers with dapper Polish caps, tomfoolery going on, boys jubilantly shouting threats to the Germans, and townspeople carrying armfuls of goods looted from the German depots and shops. We heard the order 'Back to your vehicles!', and the vehicles, extricating themselves, slowly moved off to their destinations around the city.

I finally jump down from the back of the truck and, on feet stiff with cold, advance through an echoing main entrance, crushing fallen plaster under my boots, and go upstairs to an apartment abandoned by its occupants. In the semi-darkness of the hallway someone comes towards me. I step back, alarmed, not immediately accepting that this is me, my own dim reflection in a dark mirror. Not half turned towards me, not in a shard of mirror glass, but straight ahead, full length. Had I ever experienced that before? Perhaps years ago, but I had forgotten it.

Antlers on the wall. A round wooden stand on the floor with the knobs of walking sticks and umbrellas sticking out. On a pier glass commode are a clothes brush and the stump of a candle that has run. I inspect and take all this in, and enough light is coming from the vestibule through the open front door to make out the dark depths of a corridor. The toe of my boot makes contact with displaced blocks of parquet in the doorway of a room.

The room is home to a sideboard too massive to be carried off by people fleeing in panic, its cut-glass panes sparkling. Outside the window a ragged bluish twilight is descending. The dense stone houses are bespattered with slithering snow. It is fast becoming dark in the room. Something darts across the floor and rustles in one corner, perhaps a mouse, perhaps some malevolent Germanic spirit. I come out of my reverie, pull off my mittens and grope in the already dark hallway for what remains of the candle. I pull it off the commode where at the last moment it has been blown out as those who had lived here retreated in haste from the apartment with their suitcases, bearing all the bundles of belongings they could carry and more, and now their ghosts are haunting the nooks and crannies, colliding with the ghosts of the Poles heaved out of their family home five years ago. All their other property became the spoils of war for the German family that invaded their apartment. Now a German catastrophe totters on top of that of the Poles.

I went back to the room and remembered about the window. From high up by the ceiling there hung a twined cord which I pulled and heavy curtains floated towards each other and fitted snugly together. For me it was an unfamiliar blackout method, but it was good not to have to fix a groundsheet or a blanket over a window. Now I could allow myself to light the candle. I struck a match, acutely aware, and later when recalling that evening, even more acutely aware, of the incongruity of how this half-burned candle had passed from one set of owners to another, and on from them to me.

I stood there, clutching what remained of the candle, looking round at the imperturbable sideboard and the magnificent curtains with their fringe and pompoms, so treacherously willing to serve new masters. I heard heavy footsteps on the stairs – one thing you don't enjoy in war is privacy – and along the corridor, flashing his torch, came our Major Bystrov.

'Cold enough to freeze hell over, Lelchen! *Kalt! Sehr kalt! Warum kalt?* Why is it cold when we've got a stove here?' As indeed we had, only I had no idea how to get it going. I had never seen one like it before: low, small, square. It looked more like a locker, a smooth-faced stove with no chimney. Where was the smoke supposed to go? On the floor beside it was a wicker basket with neat briquettes of brown coal.

Bystrov had nothing against a degree of female incompetence, and may even have felt it displayed him to advantage. With speed and efficiency he worked out how to operate the stove and dealt with the perplexing fastenings on its door. (I held the candle.) The stove opened and the acrid smell of cold ash wafted out, a memory of the life lived here before we came, its last residue of expiring warmth.

A house that until recently had belonged to someone else was now abandoned. A candle. A few curious moments of a serenity rare in war, when everything is up in the air, still being made sense of by administrations, but when one thing at least is clear: the enemy has been pushed out and our orders are to stop here for now, in this city. Did something happen at that moment? It seemed at the time that nothing had, but looking back now it is clear that something did, at least as far as Major Bystrov was concerned.

I was used to his intimate German nickname for me ('Lelchen') and took it in my stride. I was used to his laborious efforts to piece phrases together from what he remembered of his school German. I had got used to his secret, passionate decision in respect of Klava – Klavochka! That brought us together, too. Even before then he had been happy to share confidences with me, but now, because Klavochka was my friend, I was positively his confidante. This time it was quite some confidence he shared.

Bystrov got the stove going and gave me instructions on how to keep it alight. Tonight, when people billeted here arrived, they would have somewhere to warm up. He was in a hurry to return to headquarters and prepare a reconnaissance report from intelligence coming in from the division, but paused for a moment and suddenly told me, as if it were obvious, 'Here is what I have decided, Lelchen – or rather, this is the task I have set myself: when we enter Germany I am going to capture Goebbels.' He might even have come specially looking for me to tell me that.

He had told me before that he could not be satisfied with a life without a specific task to accomplish in each phase of it, but then he had been speaking about before the war. At the front his job was to implement aims and plans that had been decided for him. In that respect, the war had clipped his wings. Now, however, it seemed he was on the brink of acquiring a clear mission of his own.

Who in their right mind would come up with an idea like that? But then again, Bystrov was not a loudmouth, not immature, not a fantasist. You could never have accused him of that, and now, somehow, he was growing rapidly. Those relentless days that fused into one long day left no time to delve into what might be going on in his mind, and in any case I had no inclination to try. We were in thrall to just one, overarching goal that was common to all of us, and that was to win the war.

It is only now, from a distance of many years, that I am trying to understand the meaning of the changes in him then, when victory was imminent. The blurred shadow from a guttering candle flame, its light glinting in the glass of that portly sideboard, the pretentious pompoms, the chimneyless stove, the obscure nooks populated by the town's undead, the rustling . . . And in this weird setting, unflappably real, Major Bystrov. For a moment I see that calm expression on his yellow-tinted face but then, elusive, he dissolves in the candlelight and is gone.

Bystrov at the mature age of thirty-eight had a successful life behind him, and was still focused on it. In that life he had a candidate's degree in biological science and was passionately devoted to the theories of Lysenko and the notion of being able to predetermine the sex of calves, bull or heifer, at will. He believed he was close to obtaining practical results when the war, temporarily, intervened. The war had also interrupted his work on a second dissertation, in philosophy. This, for some reason, I found incredible. Even though life at the front so discouraged speculative thinking, simplified matters and left no time for disconsolate navel-gazing, there were apparently highbrow individuals who still thought differently and devoted themselves to philosophical studies.

But what did I really know about Bystrov? I only imagined at that time that I knew him. He seemed just a level-headed, unassuming sort of fellow, until he emphatically made his mark. His slightly yellowed face was impassive but there was something in his movements, in the way he seemed always to be leaning forwards, as if preparing to jump; he seemed impulsive, focused, with a secret inner spring waiting to be released. It seems to me now that he was not really as immersed as the rest of us in the flow of the war.

In Omsk, in a comfortable apartment that had become chilly only as a result of the war, his wife, a chemist, would sit down at the piano late at night, after work, wearing a pair of warm boots and warmly wrapped up. He asked her to do that, and he would read us the letters she wrote him. So what was she playing back there? Scriabin, as I recall. How stable life was there, even now, safe, far away from the front! His only sadness was that they had no children. Others had far greater problems, their homes reduced to a heap of ashes, their relatives suffering in occupied territory, missing, or refugees barely alive, perhaps not all that far from his home in Omsk.

The keeper of the hearth was his wife, in the homely comfort of his mother-in-law's apartment. Although that lady had died before the war, he cherished the memory of a representative of the 'former people', the *ci-devants*, with her sagacity and kindly benevolence towards him. The lynchpin of Bystrov's life at the front was the dream he and his wife shared of the day when the war would be over, he would come back home and they would be reunited. But then, like a bolt from the blue, there was Klavochka! Who could have seen that coming? This is what happened.

We had reached the Baltic coast and, on our front, the war was over. For the time being, however, only our army was withdrawn and redeployed to Poland. The officers of the adjacent army, 'my' Guards army from which I had been transferred six months previously, came to our farewell party, and my friend, the headquarters clerk, Klavochka, asked to be allowed to come along. Out of a military tunic for the first time, she was wearing a neat suit made up from hessian of some sort, but skilfully tailored in the military mobile store. How deplorable that for so many years a tunic, so absurd and constricting on voluptuous Klavochka, should have masked her feminine deportment, the lightness of her vivacious shoulders. Her small head, crowned with billowing, self-styled curls, no longer seemed at all small above Bystrov's shoulder as he whirled her round in a waltz. He had once mentioned having won a prize at an evening of ballroom dancing in Omsk, and that he had also come first in a motor race.

All this dated, 1930s, superman tinsel seemed thoroughly improbable in the charred setting of Byelorussia, which is where we were talking about it, but perhaps no more improbable than the cows that were going produce male or female calves on Lysenko's say-so. There was, however, evidence to back up his claims, and when the time came for Bystrov to take his place at the wheel of a patched-up captured Opel, he proved an outstanding driver. Even before that, at our farewell party, he showed himself to be an outstanding dancer.

Klavochka danced tirelessly, heart and soul for the first time since the outbreak of war, with an outstanding dance partner! And she sang. She had a powerful, beautiful voice, and took her place, big and sumptuous, in the centre of the hall, eclipsing all other puny attempts by homegrown army entertainers. Her audience clapped and begged for encores, which she gladly provided. There was jubilation in her singing, and that evening Klavochka won every heart. Our colonel, unable to take his eyes off the pair of them, exclaimed, 'Go for it, Klavochka! Klavdia the Great!'

Bystrov did not leave her side for an instant, and when she sang he stood close by. Again and again he whirled her round and, when he took her back to her seat he ardently, tenderly kissed her plump hands. He would have been the last person anyone would have expected so to lose his heart on the dance floor, in front of everyone. Bystrov was not, of course, so much captivated by the resemblance the colonel's sportive eye had detected of Klavochka to Catherine the Great as she sang centre-stage in such grandeur. No, as he danced with her in his arms, whispering in her ear, kissing her hands, he was bewitched by her lightness, her warmth and gaiety.

The next morning Bystrov summoned a soldier and instructed him, 'Right now, lad, take yourself off straight away ...' He sent by special courier to the headquarters of our neighbouring army a fervent declaration of love asking Klavochka to marry him. For the few days remaining before we were on our way again, the same scene was repeated every morning: 'Right now, lad . . .' and letter after letter winged its way to Klavochka.

He was entranced and wondrous to behold in those days, but what had brought this about? What sudden squall had so blown him off his steady course that he could, without a second thought of Omsk, surrender to this enchantment? Was it Klavochka? Yes, of course, partly; but something in Bystrov himself had been quietly ripening and just waiting to be detonated. The squall was that period of time itself, as victory beckoned. In a mere two weeks' time we would be seeing in the New Year of 1945.

Bystrov had been changing. Close up it had been less visible than it is now, from afar, as I write these lines. He was already looking back less to his old life than to the new life incontrovertibly approaching as victory came nearer. Its contours were as yet obscure but already exhilarating. He was on tenterhooks, and suddenly there was Klavochka. Perhaps it was a personality change, a revelation.

He had served in the Army unassumingly, unhurriedly, not making himself unduly conspicuous, but now he was in a hurry. Eager for risk, he assigned himself a mission and went behind German lines, something his rank officially precluded. He did that not to gain recognition but because he needed to, in a hurry to compensate for things he had not found time for, had not made the effort for, despite being aware of inexhaustible reserves of strength within himself. Now he wanted everything: Klavochka, personal renown and, apparently, the scalp of Josef Goebbels.

Although I had great faith in him, not least because he succeeded at everything he undertook, his determination to capture Goebbels struck me as hare-brained. That sort of exploit was the last thing in my own mind. It seemed the purest vanity project. For a start, we did not know what route our army would be taking, where we would be when victory came, or where Goebbels might be hiding by then.

There was nothing hare-brained about the way Bystrov achieved a goal he had set himself, and the time was to come when not only was he moving in on his quarry, but his quarry was itself moving towards him. Perhaps it was the excitement of a researcher that motivated his pursuit of such a prize specimen. I do not know. Just as I do not know whether it was chance or predestination that made what he announced by the light of that candle beside that stove, which seemed a mere ridiculous whim, come true. I was to find myself drawn into the thick of events beyond even the dreams of Major Bystrov, and certainly of anything I myself could have imagined in our billet in Bydgoszcz.

All night Studebakers with doused headlights were rumbling through the city.[1] By dawn the sound of their labouring engines had ceased and the front seemed to have moved on. I was sent from headquarters to support the commandant appointed for the city because the garrison had no other interpreter. I was walking through the city to the outskirts. The liveliness in the streets had subsided; everything seemed quiet and empty. There was a slight frost in the air, and suddenly the sun peeped out, almost spring-like in its brightness.

Then I noticed that to one side and slightly behind, my shadow was following me like a compacted version of myself. It had never seemed to be there at the front, or perhaps I had not noticed it. I felt suddenly uneasy, as if I, and my shadow following me like a pet dog, in this unfamiliar city were separate from everything of which I had been so much a part all these years at the front: as if now I was on my own, no longer belonging. It was a weird, even alarming sensation. It gradually faded as I walked on, but perhaps it was a portent of a new dimension my life was about to take on. I don't know.

Neither do I quite remember how I came to be talking to Marianna, but it happened when I reached the city prison. The massive, brown, five-storey prison was empty, all the prisoners having been freed. Through the open gate of the prison yard and visible from the street, the former Polish warders were pacing around. They had suffered under the Germans and were ready now to go back to their old jobs. All were wearing their uniform caps and old heavy blue greatcoats, which in itself testified to their patriotism, since retaining any Polish uniform had been severely punishable under the Germans. This crowd of blue greatcoats seen through a prison gateway was a token in the winter sun of a resurgent nation.

A small person in grey, perhaps a young girl perhaps an old lady, tightly wrapped in a raincoat, was scurrying to and fro by the prison perimeter. This was Marianna K__skaya, a prostitute. Her shoulders were hunched, her collar pulled up to her ears. The ends of a light headscarf were firmly tied under her chin. Her face was blue with cold but her prominent green eyes looked up at me trustingly. She had been freed from prison by the Red Army but had not gone away. She was waiting for someone she was sure would be coming back for her and whom she called Alfred. There was something touchingly vulnerable about her.

I cannot recall which of us spoke first or why, but we got talking and she must have led me to the commandant's office and gone back to the

1. The reference is to Studebaker US6 trucks, made in the USA during the Second World War for use by the American forces and, from 1942, also by those of the USSR.

prison. Yes, that must have been how it was, or she would not have known to find me there the next day, which she did. She was already changed out of all recognition. A kind friend had not only given her somewhere to sleep but also clothes from her own wardrobe. She was wearing a mauve hat with the brim lowered over her face and a narrow-waisted, flared coat with a fluffy boa. To me, someone who had lived for over three years surrounded exclusively by greatcoats, winter jackets and padded body warmers, and who had worn nothing different myself all these years, she seemed decidedly elegant. She had a pleasant face, but it was faded and could hardly be called pretty.

Tucked between the pages of my notebook are two photographs she gave me when we parted: Marianna on her own, and Marianna with Alfred R___d. He was a regular client at an establishment in Pflünderstrasse, a second-class brothel for foreign workers brought by force to Bromberg to build a defensive rampart. There Marianna had caught his eye. It is difficult to tell what so attracted him to the faded creature in the photograph taken before she met him, with her sunken cheeks, her bulging eyes peering intently and anxiously upwards, with a bow on her sailcloth hat and with prim, unsmiling lips. In spite of everything, he fell in love and demanded that she immediately leave her place of work and become his wife. The German law on total mobilization stipulated, however, that no one might leave their post until the war was over, so the malnourished Belgian, spending such savings as he had brought from home, ransomed her anew every day.

The front line was approaching Bromberg, however, and the unfinished rampart was no guarantee the Germans would be able to defend the city. They began clearing it of the foreign workers, who were seen as a potential threat. As the contingent of Belgians was being marched out of Bromberg, Marianna ran after them. The German guards chased her away, throwing stones at her, calling her filthy names and menacing her with their assault rifles. In the end they seized her, handcuffed her, dragged her back into the city and threw her into prison as a Pole whose intimate relations with a foreign worker had far exceeded her job specification.

Now she was waiting for Alfred to come back to Bromberg for her, without giving a thought to the practicalities of how, under guard, he was going to do that. She trusted him implicitly, although what certainty could anyone have of anything in this world at war? She was, nevertheless, naively, calmly convinced that she needed only to wait patiently there at the prison for him to return. He had seen her being handcuffed, so he would come to the prison. Where else could she be, when even that other establishment, to which she would not dream of returning, had been closed? All along

Pflünderstrasse the brothels, the better class ones for Germans and the lesser ones for poorer people, had been closed, and any young ladies who had not managed to run away in time were behind bars. Where would they be going now? Perhaps even to Siberia.

The sky above the city cleared to a bare, cold blue that might betoken bombing by Junkers. The uncleared snow crunched under the heavy marching of our patrol along the roadway.

Until now we had only entered major cities, like Smolensk, Minsk or Riga. There had been no question of stopping there, but now, in the ceaseless flow of the war, there came a new development. Bromberg was different: the first big city in our path to have survived a long occupation relatively unscathed, and which we were to occupy. This was a completely different, incomprehensible, unfamiliar kind of warfare, and created all manner of unforeseen problems for us to solve.

Alfred R___d did come back. He escaped by lagging behind the column of Belgians, at the risk of being shot in the back by a guard. I do not know what he looked like at the moment of his reunion outside the prison with Marianna, having made his way back to the city through the obstacles of warring front lines. The unspeaking man to whom I was introduced was clean-shaven, with a dark bar of a moustache: upright, broad-shouldered, stocky, bespectacled; with a high forehead, hatless, dark-haired, looking through his glasses with a rather glum but steady gaze. I remember it with painful clarity, but mostly for the dramatic days that followed. Now, when I look at the snapshot taken back then, I see how young this thirty-year old teacher from Liège still was. At the time he seemed to me a very mature man.

That first time we were photographed, the three of us just stood there, dazed. Marianna did not say a word. Her lips seemed puffed up with excitement and intoxication, and just as in the photograph of the two of them together (with its edges pinked in that German fashion), she stands there so puny, her shoulder pressed against Alfred, her gaze intense, trusting, looking out to somewhere far beyond us. The hollows in her cheeks have disappeared, the oval of her face is softly outlined, and she looks nothing like that fright in the sailcloth hat with a bow. He, though, looks out from the photo with the same firm, reserved, adamant, steady gaze as he had back then. The two of them. It seems as if only the two of them are in their right minds while everything around has gone mad, and war has no dominion over them.

Dear God, what high hopes! Years later I heard a saying in Alfred's homeland that a Belgian is born with a brick in his belly, either in self-deprecation or proud assertion of the national obsession with building a house of one's own. A Belgian in Nazi captivity had chanced upon the most humiliated, pathetic, crushed creature, had raised her up, taken her under his protection, and defiantly chucked his brick at the forces of chaos.

There was, though, something unresolved, something still bubbling away under the surface in the city. The countenance of victory can change in an instant when people remember the disproportionate sacrifices that had to be made to achieve it. What mattered most had come to pass: Poland had risen again and this city, seized by the Germans and called by them Bromberg, was once again Bydgoszcz.

But now what? Nothing had yet been definitively proclaimed. There had been no announcements. No notices had been pasted up on walls and columns. A Polish municipal magistracy had been hastily organized and was in session, but what was to be done about people who were starving? It was essential to establish immediately which Germans were still in the city and where, and how they were to be treated. What punishment should be visited on them, what reparation demanded for their seizure of Poland, the crucifixion of Warsaw, for the slavery, the inexcusable humiliations and plundering? There was a grimness in the city as it grappled with immediate and long-term issues.

The former Polish warders and prison officials were still hanging around at the prison without a job to do. All I can find about this in my diary is an entry consisting of a single sentence, which I had forgotten but now, as I am browsing, jumps out at me. 'The magistracy has decided not to feed Germans.' Many years later that still makes me shudder. Next to it I drew a swastika. I did not immediately remember why I had done that.

I heard footsteps. Someone with a brisk, confident manner, crossing the vast entrance hall of the commandant's office, stopped in the doorway and saluted. It does not often happen that you meet someone to whom you immediately, at first sight, take a liking, but that is how I reacted to this person wearing an unfamiliar military uniform and a beret. He introduced himself as an officer of the French Army. He had fought in Africa and been taken prisoner by the Germans. He had been the adjutant of General Henri Giraud and had come as a delegate from an internment camp for French prisoners of war which was 10 km outside the city. The German guards had fled. The French had elected a camp council, made an inventory of all the remaining food, and sent him to report their presence to the Soviet command and ask how they should proceed.

While we waited for the commandant to return, I invited my French visitor to take a seat and offered him some high-energy cola chocolate we had lying on the windowsill. It was made to a special recipe designed to give a boost to the spirits of Luftwaffe pilots.

It seemed extraordinary to be meeting here in Bydgoszcz a man who had fought in Africa as the adjutant of the famous French general. Everything about the newcomer was very correct. He had not been robbed in the camp and still had his broad army belt, his sword belt, his insignia of rank, and a shock of wavy hair projecting from under his beret. There was no sign of recent captivity to be detected in his free and easy bearing and ready smile, but the conditions of captivity for French officers bore little similarity to those experienced by Russians and Poles. The French were allowed to correspond with their families and receive parcels from home and from the Red Cross. They enlivened their time in captivity with amateur dramatics, and General Giraud's adjutant produced photographs to prove it (all with that crenellated border.) He handed me one depicting a scene from a play in which he featured. He was sitting in his officer's uniform in the corner of a soft sofa. Sitting on his lap was a frisky, well-built blonde with a high bust, wearing a spotted dress, above knee-length and revealing unattractive legs without shapely calves and feet shod with plimsolls. She was embracing him with bare arms.

The role of the mademoiselle was also being taken by a captive French officer, wearing a dress belonging to one of the camp's waitresses and a wig. This scene had evidently evoked much laughter and applause. Noticing that I was rather taken with the photograph, the Frenchman took out a pen with a fine nib and inscribed on the back of it, '*Un souvenir à l'armée russe qui est venue nous délivrer du joug hitlérien.*' A souvenir for the Russian army that has come to liberate us from the yoke of Hitler. '*Un soldat français d'Afrique en captivité à l'armée victorieuse. Amicalement.*' From a French soldier of the African army in captivity to the victorious army. In amity. I cannot read the signature. The date is '1 February 1945'.

The absent military commandant came back, a morose young major wearing a white Kuban Cossack hat, a winter jacket, and with eyebrows trimmed with a razor. He was the commander of an infantry regiment, and when I told him who this foreign officer was, looked him straight in the eye, enthusiastically lumbered over and with his great paws clutched him firmly by the shoulders. He did not, however, go so far as to kiss him. When I think back to that day, I see the moment as a pendant to the famous photograph of the Allies meeting at the Elbe. This 'soldier of the French army in captivity' was the first Allied soldier we had encountered on our long journey.

Looking much more cheerful than usual, casting aside for a moment all the attendant concerns of a city commandant and the need for diplomacy that did not come naturally to a regimental commander, he exclaimed in an outburst of cordiality, 'Move them all here!', emphasizing the order with a sweeping gesture that said, 'Let the whole lot come piling into the city!'

Meanwhile, from all directions prisoners of war were already flooding in from the outskirts, abandoning their camps. Without receiving permission or thinking to ask for it, they came into what was again Bydgoszcz, marching in columns under their national flags, which they had stitched together out of scraps of material. And what a sight that was! Again, as on the day of liberation, the entire Polish population poured out of their houses, every one of them with a scrap of cloth, a miniature red-and-white Polish flag, pinned to their chest. Again the city exploded in a burst of exultation, tears and hugging. Soviet soldiers were in the middle of a whirlpool of people. Polish soldiers, identifying who was French, walked arm in arm with them two at a time. A huge liberated American pilot without a hat, in a khaki jumpsuit, was yelling, laughing happily, waving his arms about and grabbing everyone he met by the sleeve. Everything was in tumult and a spontaneous, unbelievable procession marched down the main street of the city: our soldiers and Polish soldiers with their arms round tall Englishmen in khaki, Frenchmen in forage caps and berets, Irishmen in green hats, and Polish girls.

At one point, an emotional Bystrov caught sight of me. Very excited and, unusually, with his fur hat pushed dashingly back on his head, he shouted, 'Lelchen, look, it's the second front!' He shouted something else but his voice was drowned out by the happy hubbub in the street. We were carried off in different directions, but I took his paradoxical exclamation to mean that, even if this was not the second front we had so been anticipating during the fighting at Rzhev, when we had cursed our laggard allies, even if it was not the second front that had landed on continental Europe in Normandy and which we were advancing to support, these soldiers who had fought and been captured in Africa, these pilots who had bombed Nazi Germany, were they not a second front? And now they had joined forces with us here in Bydgoszcz, the 'Russian Army that has come to liberate us', as General Giraud's adjutant had written. My God, I too was part of that army of liberation.

Everyone was singing, each in their own language, in splendid disunity. Somehow, magically, the songs all merged, a discordant, colourful, celebratory hymn to freedom. It was so uplifting, so joyful; it seemed that surely this was how we would all live together in peace when the war was over, in one great brotherhood of man. Italian soldiers, now also freed from their prison camp, clustered together on the pavements, staying close to the buildings. Until recently allies of the Germans and fighting against us, since Italy withdrew from the war they had been herded behind barbed wire by the Germans and were now thoroughly confused: who were they in our eyes, enemies or captives of the Germans? But the holiday atmosphere was contagious, and in the end they too joined in, bringing up the procession, raggedly wandering along together, not mixing with the others.

When the procession had moved on a little, we began to hear the squeals and shrieks of children in the streets. A whole generation of little Polish kids had been brought up having to keep their voices down. Poles were forbidden to talk loudly, and could be punished for doing so. Now the children had just discovered shouting, and were ecstatically yelling at the tops of their voices, revelling in the newly revealed power of their lungs. The children's shrieks of emancipation reverberated through the city.

While this diverse, multilingual carnival was pulsating so vibrantly on the main street two quite different things were happening. Firstly, the Germans were preparing a major offensive to retake Bromberg–Bydgoszcz, something that for the present was known only to those privy to such matters, of whom I was not one. But the second thing was happening in full view of me in a quiet side street adjacent to the main road.

Here there was a straggling line of people with their belongings loaded on carts, sledges and on their backs. They were German smallholders, driven off their farms by the Poles, from villages where they had been settled for centuries, now wandering with only a few possessions to heaven knows where, but westwards. A posse of Polish teenagers were skating around them, whooping. Their ringleader broke away, skated ahead, and completely blocked the refugees' way. An elderly German woman, with a coarse, heavy blanket on top of her coat, which our own village women, too, were wearing at that time and calling a shawl, tried to explain something to him, but he was not listening and frenziedly beat her bundle of possessions with a stick and shouted furiously, 'Why you not speak Polish? Why you can't speak Polish?' I took him by the shoulder and said, 'What are you doing? Leave them alone!' He looked up, his face full of anger and with tears in his eyes. He stared at me, or rather, at my army jacket and the red star on my hat, and skated to one side. But I saw him watching bewildered from a distance. He found it unbearable that today Germans were being allowed to walk away freely after all they had done.

Beneath this festival of brotherhood there was an undertow of fury and violence that had been building up under the yoke of brutality and was ready to break out and rage.

It was frosty, and fine, prickly snow was falling. Where on earth were these people headed? Who was likely to give them shelter, where, on which remote country track would they finally perish? Far from the great highways of history, from the global cataclysms and satanic dreams of world domination, these people who had known only the hard toil of a peasant life had been driven into a trap by the play of diabolical forces and now were being held responsible for everything that had happened. Neither the heavens under which they were born, nor the land they had cultivated for centuries, nor the ancient roots their families had put down in this soil counted for anything. Everything had receded, repudiating them. People are judged, brought together, or sundered by blood. It was Germans who had caused such suffering here, and now these pariahs were cut off by a front line from those with whom they had blood ties. What did they face? Where was the refuge that would take them in? For hatred and vengefulness these were irrelevancies. Who would argue their case?

Everything was a mess: the jubilant spirit of universal brotherhood, and this dark murderousness – these persecuted German peasants and the fury of the young boys pursuing them. People herded here, to 'Bromberg', to build a rampart against the Red Army, who, under the yoke of the enemy had lost their ties with the outside world, had so jubilantly, so inspiringly found them again, here, now. But if you can cut someone else off, expel them, is this not the beginning of a road that leads over the cliff edge? 'If at one end of the world you cause harm, the effect will be felt at the other.'

At the entry to the commandant's office, seated on a very serviceable stallion, the commandant, without dismounting, was issuing urgent orders in the light of the military emergency threatening the city. Along the highway a column was approaching, and the commandant peered impatiently at it, his horse pacing restlessly beneath him.

We could already make out a flag, the tricolour of France, but these people were not marching like soldiers but spread out across the highway like an odd crowd of private citizens. The French came closer and stopped, and from among the ranks of the soldiers, grey, dishevelled figures separated and grouped together to one side of the road. The commandant, high up in his saddle, was the first to notice, and was aghast.

'Whatever next!' he muttered angrily, leaping down from his horse, pointing with his chin and raising his stubbly eyebrows, signalling to me to follow. He walked quickly to the main road. The French greeted us as soldiers but the commandant appeared not to notice. He walked a little to one side of them where those strange, grey creatures were huddled, clinging to each other and, from a distance, looking like a ghostly, dust-laden grey cloud. It was difficult to recognize them as women.

The commandant addressed them loudly. 'Hello!' I translated into German. 'Once again, hello!' he repeated furiously and with strained courtesy. The cloud stirred, and a yellow star was briefly seen on one woman's back. That was the first time I had seen the yellow, six-pointed star, one of several the commandant had been shocked by when he saw them in the distance. Before that we had only heard about them.

These were Jewish women from a concentration camp, in sackcloth, with a blanket over their shoulders or a piece of hessian hiding those stars. Some had already cut the stars off, but those that remained were more than enough to leave you feeling pierced by an unbearable emotion. 'Tell them they are free. You are free!' the commandant said, beating me to it.

One woman in the crowd asked in Polish in a low, hoarse voice where they would now be sent. 'Nowhere, of course! You are free!' the commandant said, bestowing upon them all the conquered kingdoms of the earth. 'See those buildings over there? There are empty apartments in them. The Germans have run away and abandoned them. Go and take them over, and everything that has been left there, all the property is yours. Take it! Did they understand you?' he asked. I nodded.

The French soldiers, exhausted, in worn-out greatcoats, looked at us tentatively and smiled. General Giraud's adjutant was not among them. These were rank-and-file soldiers, probably from a different camp. They went over and again mingled with the grey mass, giving the women back their small bundles and sacks. Their belongings were very basic but nevertheless a burden. The Frenchmen had carried them the ten kilometres, and lent a shoulder to those of the women who were too desperately weak. Now they bade them farewell with great warmth.

'*Vive la France!*' I said quietly and very sincerely. That was the extent of my knowledge of French, but they responded enthusiastically, joyfully.

'Listen here!' the major shouted. 'French comrades . . .' Not understanding what was being said to them, they rapidly fell back into line. 'First of all, I sincerely welcome you.' 'Please, does anybody understand German?' I asked. 'Please tell the French soldiers that the major welcomes you warmly.' There was silence. 'I must apologize on behalf of all of us,' someone in the ranks said in good German. 'But we hope our contacts with Russians can take place without our having to use the language of the Germans.'

'What's the problem?' the commandant asked impatiently. He was in a hurry. 'They don't want to use the enemy's language for talking to us.' The commandant grunted approvingly. 'Do you know French? No? Well, where does that leave us?' He looked round anxiously at his horse, which a courier had just brought up. 'Well, that's for them to sort out.' 'I can translate for you.' A woman emerged from the grey mass of women. She moved her hessian head-covering down to her shoulders, revealing a head of blond hair and a young, enchanting face.

'Well, fine. Comrade Frenchmen! On behalf of the Red Army I am fraternally glad that we have liberated you . . . This girl will now translate that for you.' Now we could communicate effectively, by mediated translation, and the French cheered up instantly. A soldier came out of the ranks, took off his forage cap and placed it on the interpreter's fair hair.

Watching this, the commandant had lost his thread but now resumed. 'There is an order in respect of yourselves. Right, then, you are immediately to proceed to the city centre and join up there with the French contingent. I don't know whether they are from your camp or some other, but so what, you are compatriots. So stick with them. So you are all in one place. No one is to wander off. Observe that order strictly. Understood?'

As I listened to the commandant's order, I could immediately tell that something had happened, something had changed, something had ended. The free-and-easy atmosphere of even a few hours ago was over. The commandant adroitly mounted his horse and galloped off to his regiment.

One of our soldiers, perhaps, the commandant's courier, took the liberty of shouting, 'Long live free France!' and was understood by the French soldiers, who clustered around him and responded, *'Vive la Russie!'* The French marched off in free formation, waving encouragingly to the women as they departed.

The women remained hesitantly in the road. The sky was still calm.

About three days after our troops liberated Bydgoszcz and drove the enemy further west, with only a few of our units remaining in the city, a message was received that German troops to the north were preparing a counter-attack on the city. You can imagine the unenviable situation in which the small Bydgoszcz–Bromberg garrison found itself as it faced a targeted blow from German troops desperately attempting to break out of encirclement. Everywhere in the city, hackles rose. The sense of community all had shared, the fervent friendship, the multi-ethnic unity was disrupted by this new reminder of the war. An augmented patrol was combing the city, looking for German spies who might have infiltrated during those hours of jubilation.

A very thin woman, a German refugee, ran in the entrance of the commandant's office. She was looking for her five-year-old son, whom she had lost the day before at the station. I appealed to a Polish administrator, who was sympathetic and phoned round the local commandant's departments, while the woman sat on a bench anxiously clasping her hands together.

The telephone enquiries yielded no results . The woman got up, as if she had never supposed they would – she was so slim and so very young, just a girl. You could see she was reluctant to leave, how afraid she was to go out of the building, to be on her own again, running God knows where in her desperation. 'Oh Lord, how cold it is!' she exclaimed. How could she be expected to bear this monstrous burden the war had imposed on her?

I am still terribly pained by the memory of that woman. What became of her? Of her son? Was he ever found?

The prisoners of war who had left their camps, and the forced labourers brought here by the Germans to build their defensive rampart, were ordered to stay together in national groupings. They were lodged, some here, some there, in very varied accommodation. Where the French went I do not know, but I was sent off to the jail to smooth relations with our British allies, who had been allocated this cavernous, deserted residence. They would at least have a roof over their heads until morning, when everything could be sorted out. But was it really hospitable to put our allies in a jail, even if was not functioning as such? In wartime such niceties have to go by the board, and we were facing a military emergency. It was left to me to sort out this delicate situation.

The prison gates were still open. At the entrance the sentry shouldered his rifle and let me through. The interior was dark. Upstairs, on a broad landing lit by barred windows, the Italians were lying around in their baggy clothes, desperately cold and dejected. 'Hello. How are you?' I asked awkwardly in German. They did not reply. Perhaps they had not understood. Someone sighed and groaned, 'Oh, Madonna!' Others joined in, sighing loudly, stirring about. They were demonstratively unhappy and, as only people from the south and children can, communicated this by their downcast mien and the inconsolable mournfulness in their eyes.

Someone sitting with his back to me turned his head, said wearily, '*Salve, signorina!*' '*Signorina russa!*' a resonant young voice sang out. An older man raised his narrow, almost truncated-looking face, drew back the scarf from his long, veiny neck, rose to his knees and gently spread his arms as if to say, see for yourself how we are. Carefully selecting the German words, he said hoarsely, 'War is *Scheisse!*' '*Scheisse! Scheisse!*' the others joined in.

The only German they knew, apart from commands, were curses, and they tried to outdo each other, shouting, becoming animated, gesticulating, appealing to heaven: '*O cielo, perché?*' Oh, heavens, why? '*Krieg finito,*' I said, mixing German with Latin which, I felt, as Romans they ought to understand. War finito! For the Italians, at least, it was.

'*È finita. Basta! Santo Dio . . .*' 'So, *bene,*' I said. '*Che bello!*' the man with a narrow face repeated. They were, however, in a desperately bad situation, having been dragged all this way from their sunny Italy to the misery of this war. '*Adieu!*' '*Addio, signorina!*'

The British were in prison cells. I knocked. The door was opened from the inside and I was let in, with courtesy and British reserve. There was an amazingly pleasant scent in the cell: of soap, eau-de-cologne. Aromatic refreshing tissues dispelled the odour of prison. A large table in the middle of the cell had a tartan blanket on it and the British were sitting there playing cards. They desisted and stood up – lanky men in long greatcoats, very proper. Our allies.

Politely addressing me as 'Miss Lieutenant', they inspected me with curiosity, supposing I must be a representative of the Red Cross. 'No, no. From headquarters.' 'Would you have some news for us?' I shook my head. No. 'What then?' Indeed – what now?

How was I supposed to smooth over the obvious difficulty? The commandant had told me to paper over it somehow, but just turning up was not enough to cheer them, or reconcile them to their present anomalous and unwelcome situation. In fact, it had the opposite effect, because now they had someone on whom to vent their frustration, which only became the greater the longer I stood there.

'What are we doing in here?' What could I say? I certainly could not tell them about the parlous situation the city was in, which had obliged the command to separate everyone by nationality, to keep them under control and make preparations for their speedy repatriation. In any case, what language were we supposed to speak? As with the French, it seemed that German was taboo. I could more or less understand what they were saying, but could pronounce only a very few words of English myself. During the years of war, German had displaced from memory the little I had learned at the institute.

'One day here, tomorrow not here,' I somehow scraped together. 'War.' These were people who had experienced disaster at Dunkirk, on Crete and who knows where else. They had been held in captivity for four, even five years. Perhaps they could have been more tolerant, more amenable because, after all, it was only for 'one day' and we were, after all, in a 'war', but there were already British troops fighting the war in the Ardennes, and this evidently stiffened the sense of self-worth and pride of my British allies here in their prison cell. They were insistent, demanding. How and when would they be given transport? Did the Soviet command at least have a plan of action? I knew nothing about that, but suddenly, from my student past, an old British soldier's song we had sung many times came to my aid. I said, 'It's a long way to Tipperary . . .'

All of them laughed approvingly. Several voices began singing,

> It's a long way to Tipperary,
> It's a long way to go.
> It's a long way to little Mary,
> And the sweetest girl I know . . .

When the British were marching the next day to their repatriation point, they sang this contagious song as a joke, making fun of themselves.

Then, that evening, we were brought a contingent of captured German soldiers. They were held in a dark warehouse. Bystrov and I went in. There were a lot of them, lying about on the ground or sitting. 'Are there any officers?' There were none. 'Perhaps somebody has something important they want to tell the Soviet command?' 'I have something to say.' Major Bystrov directed his torch beam towards the voice. This caused a stir among the Germans, who looked across. Voice: 'I am Private Schulenburg, the nephew of Count Schulenburg.'

The Germans' attempted counter-attack came to nothing and prisoners were arriving for the rest of the night. The usual interrogations were carried out. Count Schulenburg's nephew had nothing important to contribute to the standard intelligence report and remained in the warehouse. We accumulated enemy documents: reports, orders, letters, and a leaflet from the German command, addressed to the surrounded units:

Soldiers! The current situation in the east is only a temporary state of affairs in the gigantic manoeuvres of the war. It is too soon to expect significant changes in the situation after such an unprecedented onslaught by the enemy, but the initiative will come back into our hands!

Each of us must learn the lesson of this war that, where spearheads of enemy tanks have reached certain points, no tightly consolidated Bolshevik front ever forms, and the districts to the rear of these points are never cleared of German troops. All the time our westward moving 'mobile cauldrons', these mighty combat groupings, succeed in meeting up with our front-line units.

This leaflet was calling on German soldiers to break out of their encirclement towards Bromberg. It went on to remind them that,

The Führer has ordered that all servicemen who break through from cut-off front-line units to the German line, alone or in groups, should receive special recognition. The Führer wishes all such soldiers to be given an award as well as a medal for distinction in close combat.

During the night we heard the distant rumble of approaching vehicles and the clanking of tank caterpillar tracks. The commander of the front's reserve was being brought into battle to counter and repulse the German onslaught. Tanks continued to arrive, and rumbled through the city streets heading for the front line.

In the morning, while I was at headquarters, a representative of the newly appointed Repatriation Committee of the Council of People's Commissars flew in from Moscow. The representative, who had the rank of lieutenant colonel, was a middle-aged, ill-looking man, tall, very thin, with a hollow chest, abrupt gestures, and an unexpectedly powerful voice. To tell the truth, he looked as if he had just been discharged from hospital. Quite possibly he had and, after being treated for a wound, had been sent to the rear, back to Moscow.

In some inexplicable way he already had a detailed knowledge of the situation in the city. He was here to discuss with our command the plan for repatriating liberated allies and others, but roared in outrage with that powerful voice, as if banging his fist on the table: 'Are you aware that there are Poles who yesterday prevented Jewish women from taking refuge in buildings here?'

I was stirred to hear the wrathful voice of my nation speaking out in that manner at that fateful moment, but we also knew that other Poles had risked their lives to shelter Jews, whom they had regarded simply as their persecuted fellow citizens.

The yellow stars to identify Jews had been dreamed up by Goebbels. Very pleased with himself, he noted in his diary that the Führer had thought them a good idea. There had been a time when, for many years, Josef Goebbels had had a half-Jewish fiancée, to whom he had presented a volume of his favourite poet, Heinrich Heine. There had been a time when he was in raptures about a Jewish professor, under whose supervision he went on to defend a dissertation. Then, however, he threw in his lot with Hitler and all mention of his fiancée and the professor ceased. Heine's books went up in flames at the very first *auto-da-fé* Goebbels organized as minister of propaganda. The *Kristallnacht* pogroms, the burning down of the major synagogues, were more of his detestable gestures as he rushed to identify himself unambiguously with the ideology of the Führer.

Now we were encountering those yellow stars on prisoners coming in from the hinterland of Bromberg. By good luck I managed to evade the yellow star intended to blight my own destiny.

The blonde girl who translated from German for the Frenchmen gave the soldier his cap back and, again covering her head with hessian, became indistinguishable from a distance from the other Jewish prisoners. Seen close to, however, they were all so different you would have thought they belonged to many different nationalities. The Austrian Jewish women, like this Viennese girl, looked quite different from the Hungarians, and those in turn were quite unlike the Polish or Baltic women. They all spoke different languages, each the language of their homeland. Selecting women who could sew from the ghettoes of different countries, the Germans brought them to a concentration camp here, outside Bromberg. They were given a temporary extra lease of life while they could be of use to the German Army. There was no one from Russia among them.

I was able to talk briefly in the commandant's office to a woman from Vilnius. She was about thirty, short, with a dark, exhausted face and great inner composure. She was a dressmaker but told me that, no matter how events developed now, she would not return to her native city. She could never forget that, when the Germans invaded, students who were Nazi sympathizers burst into the apartments of Jews, created havoc, jeered and, when the Jews were herded off to concentration camp, derisively accompanied them with a jolly little amateur orchestra of their own.

I came out of the commandant's office with her. The women were still standing there in the road, unable to decide where they should go now. I repeated what the commandant had said about the large apartment buildings that were empty now the Germans had fled Bromberg – and felt how indifferent they were to their fate. They had lived too long with the belief that extermination was inevitable to spring back to life immediately. They had no choice, however, but to decide something, and they slowly made their way in that direction. The cold February sun lounged disinterestedly above them, picking out the yellow stars among their grey rags. I stood there feeling desolate, perhaps trying to comprehend something that was beyond comprehension, that could not be fitted into even the diabolical categories of this war, which I was incapable of looking beyond.

The liberated foreign soldiers and forced labourers marched with their heads held high towards the repatriation point. 'It's a long way to

Tipperary.' They, at least, were on their way home. The war once more invaded Bydgoszcz. The sky was rent by the roar of ground-attack aircraft. The singing stopped, the march halted and everyone looked skywards.

Meanwhile, back at the warehouse a group of prisoners of war in German uniform were lining up, eager also to head to the repatriation point, also breathing the air of freedom. 'We are Austrians!' they declared. 'Unfortunately, gentlemen,' I had to inform them, 'you are also soldiers of the enemy army.' The Austrians filed disconsolately back into the warehouse.

Marianna tracked me down. Alfred had been taken to the repatriation point and was forbidden to leave it. Her voice had lost its crispness, its intonations, and now her speech was colourless and halting. She asked me to pass him a note. She could not do it herself because the sentries were not letting anyone in.

It was very noisy at the repatriation point. The soldiers reacted enthusiastically to my appearance, and as I crossed the broad courtyard I was bombarded with witticisms that evoked an explosion of mirth, perhaps inoffensive, perhaps not. The Italians were looking a bit more cheerful than the previous day. They wanted to tell me something but I could not understand what. It seemed, though, to be friendly.

To one side, beside a post stuck in the melting snow and bearing the flag of Belgium to summon his compatriots, stood Alfred. Alas, the Belgians who had been herded out of Bromberg were by now being marched by German guards far from this place. He was the only one in that column to have escaped. He stood there hatless, his dark coat unbuttoned, inscrutable.

I don't remember now what language they communicated in, but I brought Alfred's note back to Marianna. When she had been scurrying around by the prison waiting for him she had seemed much more confident that they would be reunited than she was now. She was baffled by the new circumstances that had so pitilessly parted them. Her face grew long, her cheeks were sunken, her lips tightly pursed together. She seemed stunned, but from beneath those downcast eyelids her bulging grey-green eyes were feverish with hope. I found some pretext to visit the repatriation point one more time.

In the courtyard soldiers of different nations were clowning around, energetically playing soldier games. I found Alfred still in the same place at the back of the courtyard, as if he could not move away from the pole with the Belgian flag. He was a lonely man. He took the note silently, quickly read it, undid and moved aside the flap of his open coat, and hid the note in the inside pocket of his jacket. Hurriedly, as if afraid of running out of time, he painstakingly outlined the letters of his answer, very large, as if he were writing to a child. His hand was trembling with tension. When he had filled the sheet of paper, he tore it out of his notebook, folded the little page in four and handed it to me. He watched silently, making sure I put it safely in the breast pocket of my tunic. He did not speak, but his face said it all, expressing the pain, the rage, the powerlessness. Or did it? That is how I remember it now but he was stony-faced. That made me even more afraid to look straight at him, to meet that unwavering gaze through his glasses.

Outside the gates tanks were passing, infantry were being deployed to Bydgoszcz in trucks. At any moment a battle might break out on the approaches to the city. The outskirts were being fortified, artillery brought in. The war was approaching again. A strict regime was enforced. That is how it was and, probably, the only way it could be in the avalanche of war, that victories crushed personal destinies. It seems it is easier to defend a city than to protect your feelings and the one person you love.

An early winter's morning and the light is still dim. The church roofs are black and we are driving through this city for the last time. Trucks manoeuvre through narrow streets lined by buildings.

Leaving Bydgoszcz. Grey houses built long ago; narrow, hospitable streets. Two little three-year-old Polish citizens, in long trousers but without hats on their heads, are shrieking by a gate. A blind old man with a bicolour scrap of cloth on his tall astrakhan hat is feeling his way along the pavement.

(An entry in my diary)

We overtake the prison officials in their blue uniform, walking to work: the prison is back in business. Ahead we see some male civilians sweeping the last of the snow off the pavements. We catch up and I see a swastika chalked on the lapels of their coats. And that explains the Nazi emblem I drew next to my copy of the magistracy's decree not to feed Germans. I was not expecting what I saw. In fact I was dumbstruck. The magistracy had also decided that the remaining Germans in Bydgoszcz must go out to clear the streets. Not having to hand anything more suitable, a swastika had been chalked on their clothes. I cannot describe the wave of revulsion that swept over me. Everything seemed catastrophically turned upside down. *Eine verkehrte Welt.* A world capsized. Something irreparable had surged up from the dregs of the war on the very road to victory. How deadly this enemy was proving: you could kill him, but that did not free you from him.

Neither before nor after that day did I see anyone marked with a swastika. In Bydgoszcz it probably lasted only a single day, but on that morning there they were, those dark, grim figures, those identification marks chalked on human beings, those people cast out from the protection of the law, or even of common human decency.

We drove out of the city, leaving behind us the solid phalanx of our troops, and again saw at the roadside those tall, slender crosses bearing Christ crucified. Trees flanked the road, the lower part of their trunks whitewashed.

For some reason in the land around Rzhev while the fighting was going on every cell of life was eternal, in every physical detail, down to the most fragmentary, minute, tremulous particle. Everything was part of you. There, the road leading you to face danger and uncertainty kept you alert. Here, on the path of invasion, something was different. You could feel something was being pulled tight into an inextricable knot. At Rzhev there had been pain, but for that only the enemy was to blame. Here, an indefinable anxiety was wearing me down. I could not yet tell what was burdening me with a troubling sense of responsibility far too great for me to bear, and far above my authority to deal with in terms of rank. It was pursuing me, but why me? How could I put things right? Who was I to assume the responsibility?

We drove away from Bromberg–Bydgoszcz, having stayed there only a few days. So why do I find my thoughts returning so relentlessly, again and again to that city? Why are my memories of it still so sharp? Why do they still smart so? Why is it those particular faces and those particular episodes that so upset me?

I know nothing of what happened after that. Were Alfred and Marianna ever reunited, or were they inexorably separated by the state borders imposed by the victory and so pitiless towards an alliance of love? If they waited and met again many years later, had that sublime emotion they had shared survived, or had it withered and lost its amazing potency?

Did the Jewish women find refuge in that city liberated from a shared deadly enemy? Or were they doomed to stand around in the cold on street corners, like the Hungarian Jewesses on the day we drove into Bydgoszcz? 'You are free!' But what sort of freedom can there be in wartime? The idea was absurd. Captivity had provided a roof over their heads, and freedom none.

Where did those German peasants find respite, who had been torn from their native land? Where could they rest when Germany was beyond their reach, on the far side of an impassable front line?

And what of the nephew of Count Schulenburg, the German ambassador to Moscow who had warned of the German attack and was executed for complicity in the plot to assassinate Hitler? Perhaps he really could have been shown a little more sympathy, or at least interest? Nobody had any time for him, so there he stayed, in the darkness of that warehouse.

What became of the town's German citizens, who were not expelled from Bydgoszcz but whom it was resolved not to feed? What did that mean anyway? I should have jumped down then from the back of that truck and rubbed off those swastikas chalked on human beings, but that was possible only in my dreams in later years. The war did not understand or tolerate such feeble acts of protest, manifestly inappropriate to your rank. And in any case, I did not have the bottle to do it.

Among the throng of faces and the ferment of events, how poignant is that skinny, very young German refugee woman in the doorway of the commandant's office, who had lost her five-year-old at the station twenty-four hours previously. Even today I shudder to remember her, to think of the horror of that mother, and the horror for her child of being lost in the madness of war.

That is the way things were. There is no changing the course of those events now, but neither can I resign myself to accepting them. It is a torment.

At a fork in the road the traffic ground to a halt and re-formed itself into two streams. Our headquarters unit was going with the troops to the west. I found myself detached from people I knew and assigned to a Smersh group subordinate to the commander of the front and attached to the units storming Poznań. With one foot on the step of a truck cabin, Major Bystrov, bade me farewell. 'We'll meet again, Lelchen, if we survive!' He rapturously exclaimed, in an outburst of emotion, 'Our tanks roar forward and our infantry advance, in trucks not even on foot, in Studebakers and Donnerwetters . . . Hurrah!'

We were to meet again, in just over two months' time.

Poznań

The highway to Poznań. A plain without snow; a dead, barefoot German soldier frozen to the ground; slain horses; the white leaf-fall of leaflets we had dropped before the attack; soldiers' helmets as dark as crows on the battlefield. Columns of prisoners. The intensifying rumble of artillery. The second, third echelons of our troops advancing. Banners being carried in their covers, trucks, horse-drawn carts, carriages and people on foot, on foot, on foot . . . Everything is on the move, wandering the roads of Poland. In the back of a truck an old man sitting on a chair is shaken about. Two nuns wearing huge white starched wimples are stubbornly marching in step. A woman in widow's weeds is pulling a boy along by the hand. Only here and there is there any snow. It is cold. The roads are flanked by trees with whitewashed trunks.

I was shown a letter by the family of an electrician in Gniezno. It had been smuggled from Breslau–Wrocław: '*Czy idą Rosjanie? Bo my tu umieramy.*' Are the Russians coming? Because we are dying here. The Red Army is on the march and, together with the Wojsko Polskie, is scouring Poland clean of the Nazi occupation.

On 9 February, our army newspaper comes out with the headline, 'Be afraid, Germany! Russia is coming to Berlin.'

The Nazi armed forces invaded Poland before dawn on 1 September 1939. Having carried out their first *Blitzkrieg* ('lightning war'), the Germans annexed a large part of its territory to the Reich. There remained a small region that the Germans declared to be a 'General Government'.

Sovereignty over this territory is held by the Führer of the Greater German Reich and exercised on his behalf by the Governor General.

About a year later, Governor General Hans Frank said,

If I came to the Führer and told him, 'My Führer, I have to report that I have again exterminated 150,000 Poles,' he would say, 'Fine, if that was necessary.' The Führer stressed yet again that the Poles should have only one lord, the German: two lords, one next to the other, cannot and should not exist; accordingly, all representatives of the Polish intelligentsia must be exterminated. That sounds cruel, but such is the law of life.

The General Government is a Polish reserve, a large Polish work camp . . . If the Poles rise to a higher level of development, they will cease to be the workforce that we need.

'It is our duty to eradicate the population; that is part of our mission to protect the German population,' Hitler instructed his accomplices. 'We will have to develop the technology for eradicating the population. If I am asked what I mean by eradicating the population, I shall reply that I mean the extermination of entire racial categories. That is exactly what I am preparing to implement. To put it bluntly, that is my mission.'

In the path of our troops lay the hell, revealed to the world at this time, of the Treblinka, Majdanek, Auschwitz, and other death camps. The soldiers broke down the gates and cut the cable providing power for the electrified barbed wire. What was exposed through the gates of the concentration camps seemed beyond human comprehension. Hundreds of thousands of people murdered, asphyxiated or tortured to death. Those still breathing had been left to die of starvation or from their physical and moral torments.

Near Poznań we stayed in an empty house. In a polished frame on a bedside table was a photograph of a boy with his arms folded, frozen in motionless delight. His father, Paul von Heydenreich, a Baltic German, read the New Testament and Schiller's plays. In a large desk was a copy of a document which, after bursting into this well appointed home in October 1939 with an escort of German policemen, Heydenreich presented to its owner. In it the owner read that, in accordance with an order of the German Burgomeister, he, the Polish architect Bolesław Matuszewski, owner of the house at No. 4, former Mickiewicz Street, must without delay leave the house together with his family. He was permitted to take with him two changes of underwear and a raincoat. He had twenty-five minutes to pack . . . *Heil Führer!* (I copied the document into my diary).

We had now long been advancing through the part of Poland the Nazis had annexed to their Reich and attempted to Germanize forcibly. After a crossing of the Rivers Warta and Noteć, General Vasiliy Chuikov's troops surrounded Poznań. The approaches to the outskirts were blocked by a powerful defensive ring of forts, which withstood attack. They had to be besieged and taken by storm.

Here, in Poznań, on 4 October 1943, Himmler had declared,

How well the Russians live, how well the Czechs live is of no interest to me. What there is among these peoples of good blood of our sort, we shall take to ourselves and, if need be, select children and bring them up ourselves. Whether other peoples live in prosperity or die of hunger interests me only to the extent that our culture needs them as slaves. This is of no interest to me in any other sense.

Poznań was one of the first Polish cities to be captured by the Germans. In 1939, hot on the heels of the German divisions, thousands of German businessmen and Nazi Party officials came running to assimilate the 'Province of Wartheland'. The Poles were expelled from all even half-decent apartments. They no longer had any factories, department stores, schools or personal belongings. Their streets were renamed, their language banned, their monuments vandalized and churches desecrated.

Focke-Wulf workshops were moved from Bremen into the fortresses. Poles were deported to provide forced labour in Germany. The Jewish population was shot on the outskirts of the city. Such was the triumph here of the spirit of National Socialism.

Stalingrad assault detachments experienced in street fighting battled in Poznań for every street, building and stairwell. The artillery helped, but every time the outcome was decided by assaults that sometimes came to hand-to-hand fighting. The sky above the city was aglow, lit by the flames as, losing block after block, the Germans burned and blew up buildings in the centre. Now all they still held was the citadel of Poznań, an ancient stronghold designed to withstand attack for a long time. It towers over the city and occupies a large area, two square kilometres as I recall. The ground on the approaches to the citadel was lined with trenches, behind which were the fortress' embankment and massive wall.

On the day I arrived, the greater part of the city was already in our hands but fighting was continuing in the north-eastern outskirts. The Germans were retreating, after dogged skirmishes, into the protection of the citadel they still held.

From its commanding height, and with a still powerful enemy ensconced in it, the fortress was a threat to the city. Shells periodically exploded as artillery fired from the fortress, but there was no stopping the great, solemn procession of the Polish population, who had come out in large numbers to commemorate the victims of the occupation. They were carrying wreaths to lay at a symbolic mass grave within the cathedral grounds. How touching it was to see among the ranks of the marchers children in school blazers they had so outgrown they looked quite strange, but which their parents had kept as a sign of patriotism and despite the strict orders of the German regime that every reminder of the old Poland should be destroyed. The Poznań tradespeople, butchers and tailors, bakers and furriers, came out to greet the Red Army with the banners of their guilds, which they had secretly preserved at the risk of their lives.

The stream of people stretched the length of the street, all the way from the railway station. Over five years ago, when the Germans overran Poznań and annexed it to the Reich, Alfred Rosenberg, the ideologist of their racism, arrived from Berlin, got off the train and promptly gave a speech. *'Posen ist der Exerzierplatz des Nazionalsozialismus.'* Poznań is the training ground of National Socialism. What that meant was closing Polish schools, banning the Polish language and publications in Polish, and banning the performance of Polish music or songs, not only in public but even at home. The Poles were to be crushed by every manner of humiliation, like not being allowed to sit in the front tramcar, only in the one drawn behind it. I saw a notice to that effect on one tramcar.

On the day I am describing, amateur bands came out of hiding, and the Polish tunes they played in the streets were met with gratitude and much jubilation. Joy at being liberated mingled with sorrow at so many losses, in a united spirit of thanksgiving.

Bombardment of the city from the fortress had almost ceased. Evidently our forces had managed to suppress the guns or the enemy were running low on shells. The army assigned units to storm the citadel and then moved further westwards. Troops of our 1st Byelorussian Front had crossed the German border on 29 January.

No order came, however, to storm the citadel. It really was all but impregnable and the cost would have been too high. The situation of the troops holed up in the besieged fortress was in any case hopeless: capitulation was only a matter of time.

In my first days in Poznań German aircraft were busily dropping supplies to the besieged. There was no sign of our own fighter planes. We had no anti-aircraft guns here and, although we shot at the planes, they were fairly free to fly in and back at will. Periodically leaflets were dropped over the citadel, which rotated slowly in the air before landing in the fortress. Some of them blew our way.

1945 will bring us victory and our reward. Of this our soldiers are profoundly sure, their faith is rock hard. Our valorous homeland expects feats of unexampled heroism from us this year. Loyalty and fortitude in the name of our Führer and Fatherland – let that be our watchword in 1945. *Heil Führer!*

There were other leaflets along much the same lines, and one that was not quite what we might have expected:

To German soldiers on the front line!
    The Modern History Publishing House announces that the High Command has published the following booklets for 1945:
    Victory over France, 4 marks 80 pfennigs; *1939: Against England*, 3 marks 75 pfennigs; *Victory in Poland*, 3 marks 75 pfennigs. Orders taken.

Such persistent marketing! 'Orders taken', so everything is hunky-dory in the Fatherland. Right then, back to more victories! This primitive drivel, designed to flatter the soldiers' vanity by playing up earlier battles, was now being dropped, with a remarkable lack of tact, on troops irremediably holed up in the Poznań citadel. It was the height of absurdity, not immediately distinguishable from an act of derision.

Initially the aircraft were also dropping mail, to judge by the postbag sealed with wax and packed with letters that was misdelivered to our sector. It contained letters dating from the autumn. Our surmise, subsequently confirmed, was that the unit to which they were addressed had been straying about for months in one of the 'mobile cauldrons' before breaking out of encirclement and joining up with the German troops in Poznań. There it was finally located by the German forces' post office and its correspondence forwarded when the opportunity arose, albeit with a substantial delay.

We greatly valued enemy correspondence at the front, because letters often contained significant information, sometimes unexpectedly important, and this all contributed to our intelligence effort. Letters also contained information about morale, facts, the climate, events, hopes, circumstances, anxieties, threats, hardship and changes – everything, in fact, that constituted our adversary's world at the front and at home. They were studied at the level of the front headquarters, in whose operational section I was temporarily working in Poznań. I was instructed to compile a summary of these letters.

Most of them were from relatives in the western regions of Germany. That told us where the main contingent of soldiers in the unit had been recruited: on the territorial principle, as was often the case. Also that later, having suffered losses, the unit had been reinforced with soldiers from other regions.

During those months the western regions of Germany were being mercilessly bombed by the British Royal Air Force. Tales of intolerable suffering and despair were raining down from home on these front-line soldiers. But letters from the front, as we read in the soldiers' answering correspondence, also conveyed the soldiers' despair. Family members wrote very openly, not sparing each other, or perhaps their sufferings were already such that they were beyond being able to conceal them. Or it may be that a merciless lack of empathy was part of the way the Germans viewed the world during the war.

I still have some of the letters from that sack. Here are some excerpts:

Uncle Otto writes from Berlin to private soldier Gerhard:

September 1944
Much has happened during this time. On 20 July our Führer nearly departed this life. Then Romania deserted and Finland followed. Bulgaria is looking much the same. You poor soldiers at the front are suffering more as a result, I do not doubt for a moment, though, that in the end, in spite of everything, we will cope with all this, because the German soldier is the best in the world. We believe that after the counter-attack victory will be ours. We have nine girl soldiers quartered in our extension near Berlin. People here call them no-knapsack soldiers.

'My dear René,' his wife writes to Grenadier Renatus Coulognie,

I can't possibly ask for you to come on leave, telegraphing that I'm in bed and about to give birth when it simply isn't true. You are being completely crazy, because no leave has been given for ages, let alone to Alsace-Lorraine when they're already so near. I only wish myself that you could be here instead of stuck out there. If only it could all be over. It's enough to drive a person out of their mind. The fighting is going on now on German territory and they still won't stop. 'To the last man!' Air raids day and night, and now we can even hear gunfire. They are advancing so quickly. They're already in Holland and Luxembourg. Another 2–3 days and they'll be here. We'll be all right, but what about you at the front?

To Lieutenant Spiller:

I am writing to you in the hope that you are alive. I spent a lot of time in hospital but still am not right after the last wound I got in Crimea. I have no idea where to look for my unit. We have left Crimea, but we will be back there again. That land, soaked with German blood, belongs to us Germans. If I am not able to return there, I lay the duty on my son to take it back and make it German once and for all, this land studded with our graves, made fertile with our blood. Crimea is ours! We have left it but we will return, and if not we, then our next generation. I swear it on my life!

Lieutenant Kurt Rollinger , Field Post No. 32906

To Senior Lance Corporal Ludwig Ruf, from his girlfriend:

Do not be angry about the long silence. I thought that after the assassination attempt on our beloved Führer he would bring the war to an end, but everything is going topsy-turvy. The Tommies fly here frequently. We have air raid alarms almost every night. Our dear, wonderful Munich – what have they done to it?

Your Friedl.

'Our Prince von Baruth is also behind bars in connection with the 20 July *Putsch*,' Sergeant Ernst Ditschke was informed in a letter from his sister in Halbe. Another correspondent wrote:

Dear Paul, That you are in hell out there we can well imagine. It is terrible, but it is no better for us here. And you have so much tobacco there, and here there is so little. And we cannot get a parcel from you! We can only wish and hope it will soon be over. The main thing is for you to stay healthy and stop being in such despair. Remember the song: 'Everything will pass away: after winter comes the May.' Day after day we wait for news of Kurt, but there is none. It is so dreadful.

Your sister.

Oh, Ludwig, Ludwig, your schoolfriend Delp has died, too, of wounds received in Russia. He was a sergeant major. Helmuth Bott lost an arm in Italy, and his brother Willi has been showing no signs of life for a long time. In Bensheim a lot of people have been arrested, why I do not know. Maybe something to do with 20 July. And Spranger's wife, too, you remember her, a fat woman. They had lost their son as well. Jürgen Hein has been killed, and so it will go on and on until there is no one left. It is so terrible.

To Senior Lance Corporal Hans Stressner from his wife in Hof on Saale:

I've just come back from church – today's sermon was very authoritarian. The basic message was that we live by the grace of the Lord and have absolutely no rights of our own. Just what I wanted to hear!

Only yesterday, when I read an article in the *Völkischer Beobachter* [People's Observer] and the war correspondent's final words were, 'Victory really is close at hand,' I was beginning to feel more cheerful.

To Lance Corporal Heinz Grumann from his father in Schönwiese:

You write that you do not want the Russians to get into East Prussia, but now we are being overwhelmed by aircraft. They have almost completely done Königsberg in, and after Königsberg it will be the turn of other cities.

To Lieutenant Willi Wüsthoff from a friend in Elbing-Danzig (East Prussia):

Just a little more and we will have won the war. We lost the 1914–18 war, and we will *also* win this one [*sic*], but perhaps our children will get to see at least something of the good times we were, and still are, being promised. I have no doubt we are yet going to endure times more cruel than Germany has ever known before. To be or not to be, that is the question.

It was at this time that Bertolt Brecht wrote:

These are the cities where we bawled our '*Heils*' in honour of the world's destroyers. And our cities are now just some of all the other cities we have destroyed.

In September, and later, people were still harbouring hopes of Hitler's promised 'miracle weapon', said to be all but ready for action, and set to turn the course of the war in Germany's favour.

'In the homeland everything is facing east and everyone is waiting to see if some decisive weapon will be put into action to stop the Russians' advance,' Senior Lance Corporal Damm writes from Küstrin to Sergeant Major Fritz Nowka.

To Lieutenant Willi Wüsthoff, from a friend in East Prussia:

The day is not far off when the Führer will press the button. For now we need only to play for time and soon the new weapon will do its job.

But there are already signs of mistrust and sarcasm. Senior Lance Corporal Karl Stein's wife writes to him from Munich-Kochel,

The enemy is advancing ever closer. In places they are already at the Rhine, but when that new weapon is launched everything will be fine. Have you heard what it is? It is a tank with a 53-man crew: one to steer, two to shoot, and fifty to push because we've run out of petrol. Today's jokes are absolutely terrifying.

'What do you think about our new amateur militia, the Volkssturm?' a soldier's father asks. 'Great idea, isn't it? They say that is the new weapon.' 'I just want to see how this will all finish,' his mother writes. 'A horrible end or horror without end. Our thoughts are always with you all, there in the trenches. Our only prayer is that God protects you.'

As I worked through that sack, reading the letters, that abstract concept 'the enemy', stuck in there behind the walls of the besieged fortress, began under the pressure of the different voices in these letters to separate out into the blurred figures of all these Ludwigs and Willis, Karls and Hanses. Meanwhile, the German front was retreating ever further to the west, and the transport planes were seen less and less frequently above the citadel.

An order was issued to the Wehrmacht from its commander-in-chief, A. Hitler, that soldiers who were captured, 'if they had not been wounded or in the absence of evidence that they fought to the last,' were to be executed and their relatives arrested.

My work on the letters was drawing to a close. I had got to the end of those dated September. Although they had not been delivered to their addressees, they had been written in response to news received from the front, with which there had still been a live connection. Increasingly, however, the western regions of Germany were being occupied by British and American troops. The names of certain cities disappear and the stream of letters becomes a trickle. Some time in October, the reciprocal contact ends, presumably because the unit is surrounded. They are getting no news from their loved ones at the front but parents, fiancées and girlfriends continue hopefully to write, perhaps from superstition, sharing their woes.

To Lance Corporal Fritz Karpanyk from his mother in Hindenburg:

15 October. I can find no respite from the sorrow and torment, and your lives are a path of martyrdom that you must travel. I am alone, and repeat to myself, 'God, just let me have my children back!'

Everyone must buckle down because enemies have crossed the German border, the newspaper says . . . The house is full of Russians but nobody is getting down to work, nothing is being done. God is nowhere to be found in a house where there is no master, and that is how it is now in our house. I can't believe you have as much to put up with as I do.

There were no letters dated December, but there is one, just one, dated January. This solitary letter, written as if into the void ('I do not know if this will reach you'), is addressed to a son with a disillusioned final injunction.

Jacob Paur from Rosenheim (near Munich) is writing in the evening of 8 January 1945 to his son, Senior Lance Corporal Lothar Paur:

I got up today at 5.00, and by 6.00 was already on my way to Munich. I was there at 14.00 but there was nothing I could do. I pulled a bicycle from the rubble of our stockroom . . . From the East Station I headed over Ludwigsbrücke to the Stock Exchange . . . This route to the city centre passes through ruins . . . A bulletin from the command reports that the Royal Court Theatre and the Maximilianeum etc. have been destroyed, but these buildings were already so badly damaged that there was virtually nothing left to destroy. The chamber of the Regional Economic Administration is on fire, the Exchange has been razed to the ground by direct hits, the upper part of the city is burning, the Regina is ablaze, the Continental having already been burnt down. The Hotel Leinfelder has collapsed, but one wall of the Bitzig banking house has miraculously survived. The Nuncio's House no longer exists, the Central Credit Bank is in flames, the Turkish Barracks are in flames . . . The Chinese Tower has vanished and the nearby buildings are burning, and the railway line has been blown up as far as Pasing Station . . . Everything is very disheartening and sad, especially when you look at the people who have been subjected to this cruel ordeal. I saw many houses in flames. Many streets are impassable for vehicles and you can make your way along them only through narrow paths. In all parts of the city and its environs a terrible number of blockbuster mines have been dropped and everywhere the destruction is immense. I do not want to look any more. I have seen quite enough in the places I am obliged to visit.

I am insisting that your mother should go to Mellek. I will then lead a vagrant lifestyle, or rather, the life of a gypsy. At all events, as soon as the roads allow it, I will cycle off. I have already written so much to you about all this, although there is nothing we can change. Enough. We are allowed only to remain silent, but you can still think what you please. For that reason I cannot answer your question about the end. But again I say to you – remain patient and calm and try to get out of all this horror alive. Dear Lothar, there is much more that should be written and said, but we will leave it at that and take ourselves patiently in hand. I will run my business for as long as circumstances allow, and you do what you are instructed to do, and that will be right because then you will have nothing to reproach yourself with. If I, too, am personally complicit in disaster and grief, I regret it with all my heart, even if my guilt is only that, like the rest of us, I did not rise up against everything, and allowed it to go the way it went, and has rebounded.

I wish you luck so far away. Perhaps your years will pass less disturbingly than they began in your first decades.

Your father.

The Polish population of Poznań resurrected its city, its laws and dignity with extraordinary vitality and resilience, somehow managing to disregard the citadel, although there were feverish rumours the Germans were sneaking out through underground passages, murdering whoever they come across for their civilian clothes and then, disguised, melting away in the streets with plans for murder and sabotage. There was a more straightforward version that had the same underground passages, only the Germans materialized in the streets already disguised and Poles were capturing them and taking them to military headquarters. Perhaps that was so, but none were brought to our headquarters.

For a time I was staying overnight in the apartment of the Buziński family, and made friends with the mother, Wiktoria. The head of the family, Stefan Buziński, went out early in the morning to his job at the railway depot wearing trousers too tight for him and a patched donkey jacket. His wife, *pani* Wiktoria, was a dressmaker by profession and had just acquired some new customers – our traffic-control girls, who were living on the ground floor of the same house. Standing that spring in full view of the whole of Europe, they naturally found it essential to have their tunics neatly altered to fit their figures. To the delight of hospitable and sociable Wiktoria, the girls pestered her from morning till night.

The housework in the family was done mainly by Alka, Wiktoria's daughter. Slow-moving but pretty, she casually shifted the crude, ancient chairs around and would suddenly freeze, deep in thought, with a duster in her hands. If you happened to look at such a moment into her wonderful blue eyes, the contrast was very striking between her phlegmatic outward appearance and the hidden temperament her eyes betrayed. Passionate forces seemed to be slumbering in her soul, awaiting their hour. Where would Alka direct them?

Wiktoria's son, a chubby adolescent with curly hair, was his mother's darling. Every day he would retire behind a partition to play the violin. He was considered musically gifted and, before the war, a teacher at the conservatory gave him lessons, in return for which Mrs Buzińska did the teacher's laundry and cleaned her apartment. During the years of occupation, the boy could play the violin only in secret, away from the eyes and ears of the German police. One time Mrs Buzińska confided to me she was hoping that her son would be admitted now to a music school.

Standing back a little from her tailor's dummy, short-sightedly peering with her tired, light blue eyes, which had probably once been the same colour as Alka's, she carefully examined the darts marked on the waist and shoulders of the tunic.

All those years, 'the German period', her children had had no schooling. I asked in surprise if there had been no schools in Poznań. I even noted down our conversation afterwards in my diary.

There were German-language schools for Polish children, but I certainly did not want my children learning German.

But they would have been taught other subjects than just German.

Oh, no, miss! In those schools Polish children were taught only German, and how to count. The Germans said Poles should only be labourers and *Knechte* – servants; they had no use for educated Poles.

The 'German period' was truly a time of dark and wasted years. I suppose I already knew all this, because I had translated German orders and Hitler's views on the uses of Poles and Russians, but I was astounded every time I came across them in action.

The street in the suburbs was so peaceful, so unscathed. There was no sign of bitter fighting, of people running away, of devastation. The last train to Berlin, on which the fleeing Germans departed, left when there was already heavy fighting in the city. All four apartments in the villa where our operational group was working on the ground floor, were empty. Their previous, Polish, owners had not reappeared. Were they alive? After waiting for a time, I was allocated a room on the first floor, and said farewell to Wiktoria. For the first time during the war and, to tell the truth, in my entire life, I had, if only for a time, a room of my own. It was small, came with a sofa, an SS uniform on the back of a chair, an open writing pad on the table, and a cigarette butt in the ashtray. Also a framed exhortation on the wall from Hitler:

'*Sichere Nerven und eiserne Zähigkeit sind die besten Garanten für die Erfolge auf dieser Welt.*'

'Strong nerves and iron tenacity are the best guarantees for succeeding in this world.' On a shelf with illustrated magazines there was a plastic puppy with its paw raised in something approximating to a '*Heil!*' Posters with similar puppies hailing Hitler were to be seen on the walls of houses and in shop windows.

Not far from us was an airfield that provided our communications link with Moscow. The planes of Front Commander Marshal Zhukov were always parked there at the ready. From time to time senior figures on their way to the airfield to fly to Moscow would drop in on us, as, indeed, did emissaries of Moscow arriving at the front. On one occasion we had a phone call from front headquarters to warn us that a Yugoslav general on his way to see Stalin would stop with us for a time before leaving for Moscow.[1]

We were all feeling a sense of great responsibility. I was entrusted with receiving the general, that is, giving him lunch and looking after him because it was believed that, as a Muscovite, I would know about that sort of thing.

Cooking a respectable meal with the assistance of our neighbour, Ewa, who looked after the kitchen for us, was not a problem. Serving it properly was more challenging. We Muscovite children of the first five-year plans, of the rolling five-day working week when not everybody had the same day off, barely knew what a family meal was. When the seven-day week was restored, with Sundays off for everyone, our fathers got home from work, as was expected, after midnight, devotedly giving their all to their jobs. It was a rare Sunday when they were to be found at home. As for the war . . . barely a month had passed since everyone had their personal spoon tucked into the top of their boot.

In short, I had scant knowledge of how to serve a meal properly. I was also bewildered by the abundance in the sideboard of our 'working apartment'

1. Naturally nobody told us his name at the time. In writings about the war it is sometimes given as Stefanović.

of knives and forks of varying calibre and shape, and all manner of smaller items of unknown purpose. Zhenya Gavrilov, a bright-eyed headquarters messenger, walked behind me, dragging a rigidly starched bedsheet along the floor and rigorously polishing with it the wine and vodka glasses and anything else I found in the dining room and kitchen that we could use. For better or worse the table was laid, my superiors inspected it and found my improvisations convincing.

The Yugoslav general was a big man of indeterminate age, in a baggy, tawdry uniform, with a straight parting in his barely greying dark hair. He seemed not to notice the elaborate setting of the table in his honour. His manner was very formal, either because that was natural to him or because he had got into the habit of being reserved. He unintentionally mortified me when, taking his napkin out of its silver ring, he stopped short and looked closely at the German monogram on it. I do not know what he was thinking, but I scolded myself. To hell with all their napkins and napkin rings, their monograms and all their other flim-flam.

The general seemed to be eating and drinking more out of politeness than because he was hungry, although he had only just got out of a German concentration camp where he would have known all about hunger. In addition, he was distracted from eating by the conversation. There was none of the usual military spiritedness in the gaze of his light grey eyes, which was slow and gentle, at times alert, at times remote. Our common language was German. As I translated what he was telling us, he looked silently and in a friendly way at everybody sitting at the table, nodding slightly. In part he knew individual words in Russian, and there were also many that were cognate with his language.

As a Yugoslav general, our guest had long been held in a special concentration camp for prominent military and political figures captured by the Germans. René Blum, the son of the sometime French Prime Minister, Léon Blum, was there, as was Yakov Dzhugashvili, Stalin's son. The Yugoslav general spoke very warmly about him and how he had comported himself in the camp. The Germans gave Yakov no peace, constantly threatening him, trying to get something from him, to get him to do something, but he behaved impeccably and with dignity. The general was transferred to a different camp, and there heard the news that the Germans had dealt with Yakov Dzhugashvili and he was no longer alive.[1] This was reported to Stalin and he ordered the Yugoslav general to be brought to him.

1. Yakov was shot at the Sachsenhausen concentration camp. Stalin refused a German proposal to exchange him for Field Marshal Paulus, taken captive at Stalingrad, remarking that 'You do not exchange a marshal for a soldier.' Yakov was particularly

A general in a tattered uniform, liberated from a concentration camp; his closeness to the captured Yakov Dzhugashvili; the fact that Stalin wanted to see him and would perhaps that very evening hear from him what he was telling us now, could not but excite his listeners' curiosity. We bade him a warm goodbye when he and the individuals accompanying him got into a car to be driven to the airfield.

I never heard another word about him and know nothing of his fate. Stalin tended to be hard on witnesses. I was left with a liking for the general, and remember his eyes, the eyes of a man who had been through a lot, spent a lot of time thinking, and who had perhaps already resigned himself to something.

From the day the Yugoslav general appeared there began an increasing number of incidents, circumstances and events that reached all the way to Stalin. Marshal Zhukov's pilots dropped in on us for tea and to kill time. They were so good looking, each more handsome than the one before, and they brought news of Moscow, the city so dear to us. Hearing that I lived in Moscow on Leningrad Highway, they volunteered to look up my family. 'We'll be going past your door,' they said. Planes were landing at that time on the Leningrad Highway, where the air terminal is now. But I no longer had any family for them to look up: my father had left my mother, and guests would not be welcome. 'Okay, then, let's grab Ewa and take her for a spin round Moscow. We'll bring her back tomorrow.' They would have, too. They were very dashing.

All the time at the front people had joked and got up to pranks with great gusto. They had been scathing, cheery, flamboyant. Here, though, everything was different. We were hanging about as if we were less involved with the war. It really was difficult to know whether we were fighting or not. Now and again our lads would loose off some shots, but in an offhand sort of way. The citadel did not snarl back. Were the Germans all dead? Were they hiding? Or were they saving their shells to fight back when our troops mounted their assault? All was quiet. It was a long time since any German planes had come to drop supplies.

The workplaces of our cryptographer and myself, with their associated equipment, were in the third room of the apartment, a pink bedroom.

---

depressed by Stalin's statement, broadcast over the camp radio, that 'there are no Russian prisoners of war, only traitors to the Motherland'. He effectively committed suicide in 1943 by refusing to return to his hut and running into the camp's death strip, where he was shot by a guard. Website Khronos, quoted in 'Dzhugashvili (Stalin) Yakov Iosifovich 1908–1943', *Semeinye istorii*. http://www.famhist.ru/famhist/elag/00033f25.htm. Accessed 20 October 2017. Tr.

We had pink wallpaper and a fluffy pink double bedspread, rolled up but abandoned at the last moment. The cryptographer now slept in the double bed. In place of a chandelier, an open, upside-down pink umbrella was playfully attached by its handle to the ceiling. In this spacious room with two windows, the cryptographer and I were allocated our separate spaces on opposite walls: the man was after all working with codes that had to be kept secret from everyone. I, far more modestly, was working with a dictionary, sifting through that postbag of German letters or newly acquired documents, and a typewriter. The cryptographer did not say much: he was always wearing a headset and always had a cigarette in his lips, the ash from which he periodically tapped off on to the carpet. He and his secrets were not, however, so hermetically sealed off from me that I did not know a coded message had been sent 'upstairs' to the effect that the gold in the German bank had been found not to have been evacuated.

Each of the apartment's three rooms was kitsch in its own way. Either that, or its German cosiness only seemed obnoxious and vulgar to us in our state of homelessness. You tried not to look in the corner where scattered children's toys had been swept off the pink carpet. You tried not to, but you did peep, and might even find yourself looking rather closely and working out from the toys what the age of their owner must have been: just over one year old, probably. The, probably folding, cot that had stood there – there was nowhere else for it – had been taken with them. There were no other clues. But those colourful toys: the blow-up animals and wooden blocks, the plastic rings and rattles . . . but that's enough of that, because first, before this baby was born, its parents had kicked a Polish family out of their own apartment. In the apartment opposite, across the landing, where other staff members now worked and slept, there had also been Polish people living before the Germans arrived.

But later, dating the entry 'late March 1945', when I had taken in many more impressions, I wrote in the diary again, 'Poznań, misery here in archaeological layers: first, five years ago, Polish; now German.'

A bulky, reinforced coffer was brought from the bank and dragged up to my 'attic' bedroom on the first floor. This no longer boasted the SS uniform or Hitler's helpful framed advice on the need for strong nerves but only a table and a sofa bed, and the funny little plastic puppy which, after all, could hardly be blamed for the Hitler salute imputed to it.

The top of the sofa was raised, the lower compartment where the bedding was stored was cleared, and sundry gold items emptied into it. Inventories were stacked on top of them. The mattress was lowered, entombing the contents beneath it. The reinforced coffer was removed from the premises in order not to attract attention. This was all done with great excitement, in the certain belief that precious possessions of the Soviet state had been recovered, which the Germans had stolen and exported to their Reich.

To mount a 24-hour guard with changes of sentries would have tied up too many resources, and we were short of armed soldiers. It was thought that the gold would in any case be safest in my sofa bed. I was trusted. So in Poznań I slept on a hoard of gold. Nothing special about that, eh? It was only later, after the war, when I graduated and could not get a job because of 'Point Five', as people said at the time (Point Five in a personnel questionnaire enquired after your 'nationality', which I gave as 'Jewish'), and as I spent years in straitened personal circumstances, that I sometimes smiled wryly at myself and the twists and turns of destiny as I recalled that sofa.

One or two days later, maybe three, encrypted instructions came back from Moscow. The gold, along with the inventories, was scooped out from under me and despatched in sealed bags to the address of the government department indicated in the secret message.

'Right, let's go!' said Colonel Latyshev. A wounded lieutenant general had been captured in the Frankfurt-on-Oder area. Our saloon car roared off at full speed, as it usually did when the colonel was being taken anywhere. Out in the country, indistinguishable villages flashed by, some of their dwellings destroyed, others intact. Polish men and women were pushing wheelbarrows and prams with whatever of their possessions had survived.

I glimpsed the threatening German notices with whose colour and design I was so familiar. Pasted up on ruined walls and posts, whole or in tatters, they flew by: 'Show light – you die!' Or 'Light means death!' Or 'Pssst! Shhh! The enemy is listening! Keep quiet or die!' Death, death, death . . . But everything became a blur and was left behind as the car sped on at reckless speed, as if in search of the risk and danger without which life would now have seemed bland to us.

A Polish soldier rushed to open the camp gates. The depressing, numbingly regular rows of huts stretched far inside. They had been built by Russian prisoners of war herded here to do German forced labour. They themselves had surrounded the camp with six rows of barbed wire, and then lived behind it.

The colonel disappeared through the door of the Polish commandant's office. The prisoners of war in the camp were now Germans. A miserable, straggly tree still retained frozen leaves here and there. On the inside of the gate a German warning in Russian had not yet been torn down: 'If passing the barbed-wire perimeter of the camp unescorted by German guards, you will be shot.'

In the nearest hut, in a partitioned-off compartment, the general was lying face upwards on an iron bed. He was covered to his neck by an army blanket and had a young adjutant attending him. They had been captured on a stretch of the railway line, in the track inspector's lodge. As the German troops were scrambling to get away, the general had suffered a serious wound and had to be left behind. His field tunic, as if crucified on a piece of wood, hung from a nail on the wall. His toiletries – shaving kit, hairbrush, soap – were laid out on a stool.

Our colonel, stocky, burly, wearing a high grey astrakhan hat, took up a considerable proportion of the available space. The adjutant gave him a chair and quickly cleared the stool for me, sweeping everything into a field case. He looked at me in puzzlement, wondering who I was. A representative of the Red Cross, perhaps?

From the other side of the partition came the subdued buzz of conversation of the other German officers. In here was relatively quieter, and the general's pale face was similarly at peace. Looking at him, you might have imagined the two sides in the war had been engaged in chivalrous combat and that there were no grounds for anxiety that that would not continue.

'How do you assess Germany's military position?' the colonel asked. 'The situation is extremely serious.' He did not move: his head remained motionless, and only the bags under his eyes seemed to tense. 'Your forecast for the immediate future?' 'I cannot say it is optimistic, but while the war continues anything remains possible.'

I translated and made notes, but something was troubling me. The colonel hesitated for a moment, and I suddenly asked, 'I believe you were at Vyazma.' Our colonel gave me a disapproving look. 'I asked if he was at Vyazma,' I explained. 'I have one other question. May I ask it?' 'Go ahead.' 'Was the track inspector not anxious about you staying in his lodge?' 'He was German. And there are circumstances in which fear has no place,' he said almost didactically and slightly more animatedly. He brought his white-sleeved arm out of the blanket and smoothed his hair. 'Although I do not think I brought any additional sanctions down on him.'

I remembered the orders pasted up in the villages around Vyazma: 'Anyone who conceals or provides lodging or food to a Soviet soldier or commander . . . will be hanged.' There he was, lying in his underwear with a blanket up to his chin, and now was not the time to start enquiring whether he had been at Vyazma and whether that order was over his signature Should I continue? I let it drop.

The colonel asked if the general knew about the predicament of the garrison in Poznań citadel. He did. The colonel told him – and this was the whole point of his visit – that the general should send them a message, calling on them to lay down their arms.

The wounded man stirred. His adjutant bent forward to assist him, but was frozen with a look. He laboriously shifted his shoulder and head, turning his pale, puffy face to the colonel. He found it a considerable strain, and sweat trickled from his scalp. 'Are you proposing to force me to do this as a prisoner?' 'It is your duty in the present situation. People are starving to death there now. Your compatriots. Why create needless losses on both sides when it is clear what the only outcome can be?'

'Call on them to surrender?' he said. 'Impossible. That is impossible,' he repeated after a moment's reflection. 'In my place would you really behave differently?' Now it was the colonel's turn to reflect. Getting up from his seat, he asked whether the general had any requests to the Soviet command. He had not.

'Let's go!' the colonel said.

During the night a herd of cows was being driven east along a dark road. Cars coming the other way, driving slowly without lights, turned on their headlights, startling the cows which, dazzled, bumped into each other and found themselves with no room to move. Among their black and white coats were flashes of ginger from Russian or Byelorussian cows that had been rustled by the Germans and brought back to their Reich. Cars hooted, the beams from their headlights sought a path through the panicking herd, a whip whistled, lights danced in the cows' huge eyes. For some reason it was frightening.

Soon people began to forget the enemy in the citadel; the liberated city had better things to think about. General Chuikov's army had allocated units to storm it and moved on. Red Army troops were already advancing beyond the borders of Brandenburg and Pomerania. At this time I was still assigned to a Smersh group subordinate to front headquarters that had remained in Poznań.

Forty kilometres from Poznań, to our rear, in a *shtetl* away from the highways of the war, there was, we learned, a camp for captured Italian generals. We went to take a look. The German guards had fled before the Red Army arrived, and 160 Italian generals, now unguarded by anyone, just carried on living in the camp. Not long ago they had been fighting us, but after the coup in Italy, the German command summoned them from the front for a supposed meeting and promptly declared them prisoners of war. In the changed situation, they found themselves as confused as the Italian soldiers we had liberated in Bydgoszcz. How would we regard them: as prisoners of the Germans or as our recent enemies?

We drove past the barbed wire. Emptiness. Several huts. Two men sawing a log. We approached and, when they saw us, they stopped sawing. Two weary, elderly men, two pairs of eyes looked gloomily and expectantly towards us. We said hello in German. One man, dark-skinned with heavy folds on his face, with a bright woollen scarf round his neck, nodded silently. He was in the uniform of an Italian general. The other talked to us. This was Specialist Leader Walther Treublut, a German interpreter and the only member of the German camp administration to have remained at his post. He was bareheaded, grey-haired, and had a pointed nose. His upper lip was drawn inwards.

Our colonel went round the huts, accompanied by Walther Treublut, and informed the Italians, with Sonderführer Treublut translating, that they were free and, as soon as the situation at the front allowed, would be assisted to return home.

Some time later, when the weather was warmer, when the food supplies in the camp ran out and the generals had set off back to Italy, I was to talk to Walther Treublut again, after he was arrested one night in the city park where he was sleeping on a bench.

Having bade farewell to the Italian generals and not knowing what to do, he headed for Poznań, went to the house where he had lived for several years, but found that it was once more occupied by the Polish family who had lived there before being expelled during the occupation. Not wanting to get on the wrong side of anybody, he lay down on a bench in the park, because he was very tired and hungry.

I asked him why he had not fled with the camp administration and guards. He shrugged and did not reply. Then he told me about himself. He was born and lived in Reval, now Tallinn. He owned a chemical laboratory that manufactured perfume products, which he sold through his father's chemist's shop.

He suffered from pulmonary disease and, travelling in Italy, met a girl in the village of Domaso on Lake Como. They had known each other for only five days, and the Italian girl knew not a word of German while Treublut knew barely five words in Italian. When he got home to Reval, he swotted up on Italian, sent a stream of postcards to Domaso, and finally offered his hand and his heart to the beautiful Nereida Betetti. Their wedding took place beside Lake Como, and Treublut took his Italian bride to Reval and Estonian citizenship.

'In German literature much was written about the faithfulness of German women and the frivolity and duplicity of French and Italian women, but I was very happy in my marriage.'

Soon the policy of 'repatriation' of Germans began, and he found himself in Poznań where, on this bridgehead, National Socialism blossomed in all its glory. The authorities would not register his daughter, because he had called her Fiametta.

He stopped. His eyes were dilated and motionless. He knew nothing about his family and was indifferent to what fate might hold in store for him now. He was infinitely tired of living in this world of Nazism and war.

The Poznań citadel was taken on the eve of 23 February, the twenty-seventh anniversary of the establishment of the Red Army. It seemed a significant gesture on the part of history, of which there were many on our path to victory. From the records of our interrogation of the German officers, I was able to piece together the last hours of the commander of the citadel, Major General Ernst Gonnel. He gave the order to surrender, arranged for it to be communicated to the troops, and spent the rest of the night in an armchair in the large vaulted underground hall of the citadel. He still had radio communication with the German high command, but was in no hurry to make his report.

When it was dawn, Gonnel went upstairs and headed to the southern gate, which had been designated in the capitulation terms as the point of surrender. Here, during the night, the soldiers under his command had been gathering, making no secret of wanting to get as close as possible to the gate. It was worse than he had imagined. They were no longer subject to his inexorable will and when, at the hour appointed, the gates were opened, they turned into a rabble as he watched, worn down by hunger and thirst, flinging their rifles in a heap, raising their hands above their heads, and rushed past, pushing Gonnel aside, taking no notice of him. It might have struck him that this was how he took the salute at the last parade of his troops. It lasted a long time, because the remnants of many other units had ended up in the citadel under his command. When the last stretchers with the wounded lurched through the gate, he hastily unfastened his holster, put the pistol to his temple and fired.

The surrendering troops, headed by the fortress commander, Major General Ernst Mattern, straggled in a long, glum column through the streets of Poznań. Among the ranks, tin trunks were visible above their heads where staff officers were carrying the papers of their headquarters. Those at the head of the column were already behind barbed wire, in a camp where only recently Russian prisoners of war had been confined, while those at its tail straggled through the city for a long time yet, exhausted and hungry.

Poznań Is Free

To this day I preserve three blue invitation cards: to a service of thanksgiving, a parade, and an evening of celebration.

The service took place on Wednesday 7 March 1945 in the market square. There, before an altar, shoulder to shoulder, were ranks of Polish soldiers. Closer to it were the Sisters of Mercy in their white headgear. Carpets hung from every balcony. Men and women came running up the street. The voices in the square were raised in unison, and high up to the lowering sky there rose a solemn hymn of praise, thanksgiving and faith. Women with babies in their arms came out onto the balconies to join their voices to the singing.

Later, also in the market square, there was a parade. The commander-in-chief, General Michał Rola-Żymierski, reviewed a march-past of troops on the paving in front of the tribune. Beside him stood his tall, lean chief of staff, General Władysław Korczyc. Banners fluttered. A dark red banner with a cow's head and crossed poleaxes was borne by a man with a ginger moustache and a kerchief round his neck, the standard-bearer of the Guild of Butchers. The banner of the Polish Workers' Party was carried by an old man in blue spectacles. Up there, by the tribune, a young man in a worn grey coat, raised a microphone to his lips and, removing his hat while the national anthem was played, gave a running commentary.

The tribune was covered in greenery. The safely preserved banner of the municipality was brought, escorted on both sides by women orderlies girdled with red and white brocade.

The infantry were wearing helmets, with the Polish bicolour on a Russian three-sided bayonet. Then a platoon of anti-tank gunners, a platoon with submachine guns, with girls in the front rank. Then machine-gun carriages. Then the cavalry, with bicoloured ribbons braided in their horses' manes. Public societies came to the tribune with their banners. Flags fluttered, red, and red and white.

'*Niech żyje Armia czerwona!*' Long live the Red Army.

'*Niech żyje!*' we heard from the tribune.

Children and adults climbed up telegraph poles and trees, and stood on the church wall.

'*Niech żyje bohaterski Poznań!*' Long live heroic Poznań.

Hats were thrown in the air, bouquets of greenhouse flowers were thrown to the soldiers. The last to clatter past the tribune were six tanks, and no sooner had their clamour died down than an astonished, joyful exclamation was heard and taken up by the crowd: 'Look! The cranes are flying back!'

Taking off their caps, their heads thrown back, the crowd gazed upwards to where, in a sky that had meanwhile cleared, cranes returning from the south soared over the city. A sign of spring!

Today in a newsreel I caught a glimpse of the snowbound Russian winter and samovars and felt unhelpfully homesick.

Here, spring is on its way, even though in places last year's leaves have not yet fallen from the trees. A long autumn passes into spring, almost omitting winter.

Imagine such a dull, monotonous life, not wakening to new excitement from autumn to spring.

In Russia every season is clearly marked, and with each new season you start your life afresh. *(My diary, 6 April 1945)*

Perhaps because there was a war on, I was still eager for challenges, but somehow no longer in the thick of the action. I was looking around to see if I could find something new and exciting.

Poznań stagnated, ever further from the front line of the advancing army, which had already forced a crossing of the River Oder. Troops of the 1st Byelorussian Front, under the command of Marshal Zhukov, had fought their way forward 400 km in two weeks.

The city was changing in front of our eyes, primarily by becoming spring-like. Although that was entirely natural, many people may remember the sense of solidarity of that spring of 1945 in the West, with gentle breezes wafting the aroma of fields ploughed, for the first time in freedom, by Polish peasants, with their green, tender shoots and hopes of peace and work.

The city was coming back to a life that was still austere but enlivened by the coming of spring. The plasterers and painters were suspended on the walls of buildings in their cradles. The chimney sweeps in black top hats and with all their appurtenances rode everywhere on bicycles. The schoolchildren of Poznań hurried to get to school in time for the bell, and any one of them, with their satchel bumping up and down on their back, was sure to say good day if they met me: '*Dzień dobry, panno* lieutenant!'

Wiktoria Buzińska sewed me a green dress from the lining of a coat, and ornamented it with a yoke from a piece of polka-dotted satin. How amazing that was, what luxury suddenly to be wearing, if only for a moment, a light, feminine dress with short sleeves, after three-and-a-half years of constantly wearing a tunic. What a delight to lock my door and secretly put it on. The SS man's room had no mirror, and I tried as best I could to make myself out in the glass of the windows when evening darkened them. There is no describing how enchanted I was by my own appearance.

Later, in May, I wore this dress when I was photographed in Berlin at the monument to Bismarck, at a hoarding with portraits of Roosevelt, Stalin and Churchill, and in various other temporary or permanent historic settings.

At New Year 1945, when our army was redeployed from the Baltic states to Poland and had its headquarters in Kałuszyn, something between a town and a shtetl, Major Bystrov had told me when no one was listening that he would try from now on to carve out a 'creative day' for me, because the war was coming to an end and I would find myself trying to get back into the Literary Institute with absolutely no new qualifications. Pulling my desk over to one corner and spreading out some unimportant German papers to make it look as if I were translating, I made a conspiratorial start under Bystrov's watchful eye. In a slim, blue Polish school notebook I wrote down the title of a story, 'The "Son-in-Law"'. I had had it in mind for a long time: there was something secretive about it that moved and excited me. I had been imagining everything that would go on in the story. All I needed was an opportunity to sit down and write it.

And now I had it. 'The "Son-in-Law"'. I wrote it once more, this time as part of the text. '. . . that was the name they gave to young Russian deserters in encirclement who shacked up with grass widows in nearby villages whose husbands were absent in the war.' Now what?

I decided the first sentence was not quite right. It sounded like a dictionary definition. I crossed it out. Something more 'literary' was needed. In the end I wrote down, 'A cow was pulling an oxcart,' then improved it to 'a spotted cow was pulling an oxcart.' And that was the fruit of a day's work.

Bystrov's sound pragmatism saw no signs of promise in this, and he said frankly that with such a woeful level of productivity he could not justify further diversion of the war effort. He stripped me of my creative day, and was right to do so. The notebook survives as testimony to my incompetence. I was able to write 'The "Son-in-Law"' as I had imagined it, about the tensions of life behind German lines, only after I got home when the war was over.

How easily and willingly I would jot down this and that as it happened (when, that is, I was allowed to), and how difficult it proved to sit down and just write.

Captured Germans were sent, over time, in echelons to the east. Fearing the hatred of the Poles, they always asked to be escorted by Russian soldiers.

Studying German staff headquarters documents from the captured citadel was becoming less operationally valuable, and had not yet become of historical interest. It was also thoroughly depressing. Our army was standing 80 km from Berlin, and here we still were putting on weight in Poznań where nothing serious was happening. Little did I know how merciful fate was being, holing me up in Poznań for the whole time the Red Army was advancing through Germany, right up until the assault on Berlin. But that is an aside.

Already in Poznań the war was covertly preparing to withdraw and allow the return of what is, perhaps, the truly dominant feature of human existence: love – personal, intimate feelings. There was danger in those, there was risk, but also all the radiant wonder of being alive. Since we were in Riga I had been collecting slim volumes of Ivan Bunin's poetry, and magazines with Marina Tsvetayeva's poems, whenever I came across them. I carried some with me wherever I went. They were pulsating with a life that had unfamiliar facets, a different sadness, different passions.

What a blow was coming my way! A famous writer flew in from Moscow and called on us when I was not there. He asked the colonel hospitably welcoming him whether, by chance, we had any emigré literature, because he would really like some to read. That was our visiting celebrity's only request to us.

I can imagine our Colonel Latyshev regretfully shrugging his shoulders as he explained he had nothing to offer. Being a generous man, he no doubt imagined others were equally generous. He called Zhenya Gavrilov in from the kitchen. Zhenya was always pottering around there, drying dishes with his bedsheet, because we never had any shortage of people looking for a meal, or of dishes to wash when they left. Zhenya, keen to make a good impression on Ewa, helped her out when he had time to spare, which was more or less all the time except, of course, when he was spending late evenings with Ewa's neighbour, young Zosia.

The colonel told Zhenya to go up to the translator's room and see if there was any literature there in Russian. The impatient writer followed him up the stairs, and there the literature lay, on the wide, deep sill of the window at which the SS officer used to sit.

My diary entry reads: 'On 28 March, visit from so and so, who helped himself to my Bunin and Tsvetayeva.'

My resentment and indignation were such that I could write nothing more. A few days later I again wrote in my diary, 'On 28 March, visit from so and so. . .': exactly the same entry.

I would probably not have felt so intensely about this if I had known that for me the war would not be ending in Poznań, and that destiny was about to move me to the very epicentre of events as it did.

Our troops, having overcome what the Germans had supposed to be their impregnable defences on the River Oder, were by this time already fighting on the plateau near Berlin. How eager we were to be there and not in Poznań! At last an order was received that we should all return to our units.

When I heard the news, I ran outside, round our house and turned in at the gate. It was late, but in the courtyard I could see the black silhouettes of our cars and, under one of them, the bright light of a torch shining on and off.

I called to Sergey. The hand holding the torch appeared from beneath the car, and then Sergey, our driver, emerged wearing the dark blue Gestapo uniform he used as his overalls. I advised him that we were leaving for Berlin, and that he was to have the cars ready for six in the morning. Sergey put out the torch and we stood silently in the dark.

Who in those days was not only too eager to get to Berlin? Of course, Sergey was too, but we had been stationed in Poznań for over two months, a lifetime during a war, and Sergey, after a whirlwind romance with a Poznań girl, had contrived to marry her secretly in church. Ever since there had been a slightly crazy, mischievous expression on his likeable, thoughtful face.

He wiped his hands on the Gestapo uniform, clicked his cigarette lighter – his broad, Slavic face paled, he frowned and said, lighting a cigarette: '*Ah, wszystko jedno – wojna!*' What can you do about it? That's war! It was something you often heard in Poznań at that time.

At dawn we prepared to leave and, just before we did, I observed the customary moment of reflection before setting out on a journey. I went to the front garden of our house and was suddenly transfixed by the sight of the apple tree, alive with white blossom, by a square of bare, damp earth through which, here and there, delicate young blades of grass were sprouting, and by the sight of last year's leaves decomposing underfoot. A gusting breeze brought such a sense of spring in the air.

Along the street on his bicycle, clad in black, came a chimney sweep, complete with his top hat, stepladder and brush slung over his back. The feeling of safety, which had been becoming oppressive with its overtone of stagnation and a kind of emotional turmoil, gave way to a sense of melancholy now at having to leave.

Sergey cast a farewell glance at the old Molotov saloon painted a ghastly, muddy, camouflage colour, with an unbroken red edging the length of its bodywork and on the wheel rims, which he had constantly retouched. He had driven this battered, bullet-scarred car for the first four years of the war. Now he drove out to the roadway in his new baby – a captured, high-powered Ford 8 he had rescued from a ditch near Poznań and lovingly repaired. His fresh black paint had run and grey showed through in places, but the bodywork and the wheel rims sported the same ostentatious red edging. He was incorrigible.

Next Vanya came out to the road, a taxi driver from Riga, brought against his will by the Germans to work in Poznań. He was shivering in a short, once dapper but now bedraggled, suede jacket, and inspected the Ford approvingly. Unfastening his shoulder strap, Sergey took a flask of vodka and presented it to him.

Sergey looked first at one then at the other side of the street A lone figure was conspicuous on the pavement, a girl in a short checked skirt, with large legs and a scarf on her head. She was watching tensely as we prepared to leave. The cars were already moving off. Sergey said quietly, 'Go home. Why do I have to say it. For heaven's sake, *idź do domu.*'

She turned and walked slowly away, turning to look back again and again. Sergey stood there, unable to move, then straightened the folds of his tunic under his belt and yanked the car door open.

With the flask tucked under one arm, Vanya the taxi driver smoothed his sparse fair hair with the other and waved us goodbye. The Ford's wheels screeched furiously, but the engine immediately settled down and we drove smoothly on our way. I was sitting behind Sergey. To either side of the street a white surf of apple trees in bloom was foaming. The city was waking. The girl directing traffic at the city gate gave a signal and the barrier floated up. A schoolboy with a satchel on his back came out of a house and politely took off his little kepi to wish us, '*Dzień dobry'*.

The car emerged onto the highway to Berlin. Sergey lowered the window and took off his cap.

4 Last Days: Berlin, May 1945

'*Deutschland liegt im Herzen Europas.*' Germany lies at the heart of Europe. So we had been informed with admirable accuracy yet, at the same time, poetically, by our school textbook.

Beyond Birnbaum there was a checkpoint with a large, hastily knocked-together archway and a sign reading, 'This was the German border.' Everyone passing along the highway to Berlin at that time read also a second inscription, scrawled in tar in huge, uneven letters by a soldier on the nearest ruined house: 'Take a good look: this is fucking Germany!'

That soldier had been marching towards this place for four years. Fires, ruins: the war had come back to haunt the land from which it had sallied forth. The wind ruffled sheets and towels on fences and trees, the white flags of surrender. Somewhere far beyond the uncultivated fields peaceful windmills rose like a mirage.

An old, small, half-ruined town. The war had moved on and here, muffled, barely audible, life was pulsating. At the crossroads, opposite the grey house of the *Dachdeckermeister* (roofer), a lad in a sheepskin jacket bawled from a large poster, 'Fire into the lair of the beast!'

Boys wearing white armbands were climbing over a wrecked Opel on the pavement, which had lost its wheels. They were evidently playing at war. There were many townspeople, burdened with bundles, pushing laden prams, and one and all, adults and children, were wearing white armbands on their left sleeves. It was completely unexpected for me that the whole country had put on white armbands to indicate surrender, and I do not recall reading about it anywhere else.

Beside the road on the outskirts of the town an elderly man was digging his garden. We stopped and went into his house. His wife, evidently accustomed by now to such guests, offered to warm coffee for us.

In this small house, perched by the roadside of war, the kitchen was cosy and dazzlingly clean. On the shelves there was a dauntless parade of beer mugs. The porcelain skirts of an artful-looking lady crouching on the sideboard billowed upwards. This merry little trinket was a wedding present given to our hostess thirty-two years before. Two terrible wars had raged, but the porcelain coquette had survived in one piece, along with the inscription on her apron: '*Kaffee und Bier, das lob' ich mir.*' Coffee and beer, I hold them dear.

We left the house. Our hostess's husband was planting flowers in the ground he had dug, as he did every year, to sell. Armoured personnel carriers trundled by, their caterpillar tracks clanking.

In the sky a German spy plane hovered above us, a Focke-Wulf 'frame', and where the road forked, the Military Roads Commission had an information kiosk for anyone driving in Germany, severely warning that 'Driving on the left will result in confiscation of the driver's licence.' The warning looked comically out of place, but also rather touching in the way that it hinted at a different way of life with sensible regulations, a different world without war.

People of many nationalities, newly liberated, streamed along the roads towards us: French, Russian, British, Polish, Italians, Belgians, Yugoslavs ... Prisoners of war, captives from concentration camps and torture chambers, slaves dragged here from the USSR, from all over Europe, to forced labour, starvation and death.

A few were riding in German vans or on purloined bicycles. More commonly, they were on foot, in groups, under a homemade flag of their own country. Some were in military uniform, some in civilian clothing, some in the striped jacket of a prisoner. Their exclamations of greeting, radiant with warmth, lit by a smile, the frank, open expression of emotion were heart-warming, profoundly touching encounters I will never forget.

Past a cavalry regiment stationed in a village adjacent to the highway, past a tank brigade of the commander of the front's reserve, past a roadside poster urging 'Forward, Victory is Near!', overtaking trucks heavy-laden with ammunition, we drove into Küstrin, a town on the Oder, deserted, ruined. 'The key to the gates of Berlin', the Germans called it.

The main square was now a graveyard of the buildings that had once looked on to it. They seemed to be advancing on it from all directions, reduced now to grim piles of rubble. Beams left suspended in mid-air groaned; stone dust poured down from the gaps in walls. In the middle of the square a monument with a bronze bird on top of it had miraculously survived. My God, how lonely this place felt, with that idiotic, vainglorious bird all on its own in a dreadful wasteland of stone.

Back on the highway. Again, fields and woodland, windmills looming on the horizon. Pigs, unfed, crazed, rushing around the fields.

The retreating enemy had blown up the bridges, the main roads had been wrecked and were littered with broken vehicles, but the trucks with their cargoes were getting through somehow, clocking up hundreds of kilometres on the difficult route into the heart of Germany. What hardships did these front-line drivers not endure, what trackless wastes did they not traverse with their loads, sinking down in river crossings, bogged down in swamps, dodging bombs and shells and mines in order to get here, in a truck riddled by bullets and shrapnel, to participate in the final battle!

Dusk fell, protecting us from attack by enemy aircraft, and the amount of traffic on the highway increased markedly. Tanks, trucks, self-propelled guns, armoured personnel carriers, amphibious tanks, horse carts. Infantry in Studebaker trucks and marching on foot. On rifle barrels, on tank turrets, on carts, everywhere you saw the slogan, 'Berlin, here we come!'

When it was completely dark the traffic only grew heavier. The night was short and you had to get into position while you could. People drove slowly, not turning on their headlights, getting snarled up in traffic jams. Anti-aircraft guns were firing. From village byroads artillery, tanks, and infantry were all drawn to the highway. Vehicles drove several abreast, peeled off and drove through land to the sides of the road. Everywhere there was rasping and clanking, furious honking, horses being whipped, everybody trying to overtake those ahead of them.

Night in Berlin

The centre of Berlin was ablaze, and huge tongues of fire leapt skywards. The multistorey buildings they lit up seemed very close, but were in reality kilometres away. Great beams of light from searchlights swept the sky. The dull rumble of never-ending artillery fire reached our ears. Here the suburbs were still bristling with enemy anti-tank traps, but our tanks were already thundering towards the centre.

And this very night, in the catacombs beneath the Reich Chancellery, Adolf Hitler married Eva Braun. When later I learned this, I recalled the collapsing walls of burnt-out buildings, the acrid smell of charred ruins, the grim tank traps no longer capable of protecting anyone from anything, and in the darkness the inexorable thunder of tanks rushing towards the centre of Berlin, to the Reichstag and the Reich Chancellery.

I sat on an abandoned empty oil drum in a suburban street outside a boarded-up shop window, under a signboard whose gold letters proclaimed it to be a patisserie, Franz Schulz Feinbäckerei, waiting to hear from headquarters where we were to go. That night the front line ran through the centre of Berlin. From time to time there were flashes of artillery fire.

I remembered our river crossings at Smolensk in 1943, when starved horses refused to pull the artillery pieces and exhausted people had finally to push the guns themselves, under a squall of shelling by the enemy. I recalled cameraman Ivan Sokolnikov, who risked his life to film there for the newsreels. In addition to providing footage for the next edition of the newsreel, Sokolnikov was charged with using a proportion of the film allocated to record for the so-called 'historical film library', which was to preserve for posterity the tragic face of war. And film he did: the crossing, the soldiers straining under the intolerable weight of the guns, dying in the bombing and under fire.

One sequence that lodged in my memory did not make it into the newsreel or the official historical record: that same spring, although somewhat earlier, when it was difficult but still possible to use sledges over the thawing snow, by the side of one such trail a transport soldier was sitting in his sledge. His horse had collapsed. The driver unharnessed her and, without looking at the horse, pushed the shaft to one side and hung a cooking pot on it filled with snow. He lit a small fire. There were strict orders to look after and protect the horses for as long as was conceivably possible. In this case, however, there seemed no likelihood the poor animal could be got back on its feet. The yellow water in the cooking pot came to the boil, but the doomed horse was still sorrowfully blinking. The driver waited grimly . . .

Did that soldier make it to Berlin? If only we could have brought to the place where we were all those who had endured the harshness of army life, who had suffered unbearably from hunger, from the bitter cold, from wounds and fear; if only we could have brought back to life those who had perished so that they could at least see what a formidable force their army was as it entered the lair of the beast.

The Ring Closes

For three days Berlin had been completely surrounded. In heavy fighting, breaking through the defence of one district of the city after another, the troops of the 3rd Shock Army of Colonel General Kuznetsov, the 5th Assault Army of Colonel General Berzarin, and the 8th Guards Army of Colonel General Chuikov advanced towards the city centre, towards the Tiergarten, towards Unter den Linden, towards the government district. The newly appointed Soviet commandant of Berlin, Colonel General Berzarin, had already issued an order dissolving the National Socialist Party and banning its activities.

The residents of Berlin cowered in basements beneath burning, collapsing buildings. The water situation was dire, and their meagre supplies of food were running low. On the surface there was non-stop gunfire, shells exploding, chunks of masonry flying through the air, the fumes and smoke from burning buildings, the air suffocating. The situation of the population was desperate.

In circumstances like these, when the outcome was so blindingly obvious, every hour this senseless fighting was prolonged was a crime. So what were the plans of the German side at this time? It was only later, when it was all over, that it was possible to dig down and answer that question.

Hitler's adjutant, SS Sturmbannführer Otto Günsche, captured on 2 May in the Schultheis Brewery and interrogated at the main Smersh intelligence directorate of the general staff, gave the following written answer.[1] On 22 April, as artillery shells were falling in central Berlin, a meeting of the supreme command, chaired by Hitler, was held at 16.30 hrs.

The Führer had in mind for the Ninth Army to attack in a northwesterly direction, and for the army group of SS General Steiner to attack in a southerly direction. He was counting on driving back the breakthrough by Russian forces, which he believed to be weak, and for our main forces to reach Berlin and thereby create a new front. The front would then run approximately from Stettin up the River Oder to Frankfurt-on-Oder, then in a westerly direction through Fürstenwalde, Zossen and Treuenbrietzen to the River Elbe.

The preconditions for this were:

1. To hold the front line on the lower reaches of the Oder at all costs.
2. For the Americans to remain on the west bank of the Elbe.
3. For the left flank of the Ninth Army, stationed on the Oder, to hold at all costs.

After Chief of the Army General Staff General Krebs reported a major breakthrough by Russian forces of the front to the south of Stettin, it must have been clear to the Führer that it was impossible to create the aforementioned front, and he expressed the opinion that in this connection Mecklenburg would also be besieged within a few days by Russian forces. Despite this, however, the Ninth and Twelfth Armies and Steiner's army group were ordered to mount an offensive towards Berlin.

---

1. I found Günsche's testimony in the archive, File 130: 'Testimony of Hitler's personal adjutant, SS Sturmbannführer Otto Günsche, 14 May 1945'. First published in my *Berlin, May 1945*.

Günsche wrote this six days after the surrender, hot on the heels of the events described, and with his memory still clear:

On 26 April 45, the last telephone communication lines connecting the city with the outside world ceased to operate. Communication was maintained only by means of radio. However, as a result of incessant bombardment the aerials were damaged, more exactly, they were totally out of action. Reports on the advance or progress of offensives of the above-mentioned three armies arrived in limited numbers. Most often they were delivered to Berlin by a roundabout route. On 28 April 45, Field Marshal Keitel reported the following:

1. The offensive of the Ninth and Twelfth armies had been halted by a strong counter-attack by Russian forces, rendering continuation of the offensive impossible.
2. The army group of SS General Steiner had still not yet arrived.

After that, it became clear to everyone that the fate of Berlin was sealed.

German soldiers were dying in the streets of Berlin. Their orders in these tragic days were to fight fanatically for the Third Reich and they would win! But the Reich already lay in ruins. It had been defeated. They were promised reinforcements, which did not in fact exist. If they were suspected of the least disloyalty or wavering, they were hanged or shot. But whether they were battle-hardened soldiers or ill-trained home guard *Volksstürmer*, they were mortal.

The German troops totally surrounded by the ring of encirclement continued to be thrown bales of Goebbels' newspaper, *Der Panzerbär* (*The Armoured Bear*, the bear being the coat of arms of Berlin) and 'newsletters', deceitful and inflammatory, flattering and threatening.

Here is one of the last, dated 27 April: Goebbels' *Berliner Frontblatt* (The Berlin Front Newssheet).

Bravo, Berliners!

Berlin will remain German! The Führer has announced this to the world, and you, the Berliners, will ensure that his word remains the truth. Bravo, Berliners! Your conduct is exemplary! Continue just as valorously, continue just as stubbornly, without mercy or leniency, and the waves of the Bolsheviks' assault will crash in vain against you . . . You will prevail, Berliners. Help is on its way!

This little flysheet reached us on 29 April when we were already near Potsdamer Platz.

The Government District

We were instructed to head for the area from which the troops of our 3rd Shock Army would attack in the direction of Potsdamer Platz. Early in the morning we proceeded in our adverse terrain vehicle over first one and then another barricade where they had been overturned and crushed by tanks, picking our way amidst mangled rails, timbers and guns. We passed over an anti-tank trench that had been filled in with shattered masonry and empty barrels. The buildings became more frequent, some docked by several storeys, others with only a charred wall remaining, as if it had forgotten to collapse. These were monuments to the fighting that had taken place two days earlier. In places, tanks had ploughed their way through the rubble, and vehicles, of which there were increasing numbers, were diverting on to the trails blazed by the tanks' caterpillar tracks.

The traffic in the streets of Berlin was being directed by lasses from Smolensk, Kalinin and Ryazan in well-fitting tunics that must surely have been altered by Mrs Buzińska in Poznań. The car came to a stop when the road ahead was impassable. We saw advancing towards us small groups of Frenchmen with their luggage trolleys with the French flag on the side, picking their way through the accumulations of crushed brick, scrap metal and rubble. We waved to each other.

The closer we came to the centre, the more unbreathable the air became. Anyone who was in Berlin in those days will remember that air, acrid and opaque from the fumes and stone dust, and the grittiness of sand in their teeth.

We made our way behind the walls of the ruined buildings. No one was trying to put the fires out. The walls were still smoking, and decorative creepers continued to cling to them with burned paws.

'*Unsere Mauern brachen, unsere Herzen nicht!*' Our walls have broken, but not our hearts, declared a poster above a door that had survived but now led only to darkness and devastation.

Diving out of one basement into another, we encountered German families. They all asked us the same thing: 'How soon will this nightmare end?' Hitler declared, 'If the war should be lost, the German nation must disappear.' But people, in defiance of the Führer's will, had no wish to disappear. White sheets and pillowcases were hung from windows.

'In any house hanging out a white flag, all the men are to be shot.' Such was Himmler's order.

It was very difficult to find your way through the city by map reading. We had run out of Russian signs and the German ones had mostly disappeared along with the walls. We resorted to asking directions from people we met in the streets, who were hauling their possessions somewhere.

The signallers could be glimpsed, pulling their cables along behind them. Hay was being transported on a cart, and a moustachioed driver from a Guards regiment was chewing a dry straw. Other straw was being lightly sprinkled over the cratered Berlin roadway. A group of soldiers with submachine guns marched by, one with a bandaged head taking care not to fall behind or become detached from the column.

The coat of a bareheaded elderly woman crossing the road displayed a white armband prominently. She was leading two young children by the hand, a boy and a girl. Both of them, with their hair neatly brushed, had white armbands sewn to their sleeves above the elbow. As she passed us she said loudly, not bothered whether we understood or not, 'These are orphans. Our house has been bombed. I am taking them to another place. These are orphans . . . Our house has been bombed . . .'

A man in a black hat came out of a gateway. He stopped when he saw us and held out a small package wrapped in greaseproof paper. He unwrapped it to reveal a yellowed box, which he opened. 'L'Origan Coty, *Fräulein Offizier*. I swap for a packet of tobacco.' He stood for a moment, then tucked his package away in the pocket of his long overcoat and wandered off.

After that the streets were completely deserted. I remember a pillar covered with posters, chiffon curtains reaching like outstretched white hands from a window, a bus with an advert on its roof, an enormous papier mâché shoe, which had crashed into a building. And Goebbels' categorical assurances on the walls that the Russians would never enter Berlin.

Now, increasingly, it was dead districts containing nothing but ruins. It became even harder to breathe. Dust and smoke obscured the way forward. At every step we were risking a bullet. A fierce battle was by now raging in the government district. The latest order from the Nazi leadership demanded that the capital should be defended to the last man. 'Men, women and boys stand side by side with the battle-tempered and stubbornly resisting Wehrmacht, which has been fighting the Bolshevik hordes for years and knows that this is a matter not of negotiations, but of life and death.'

Barricades, ditches, rubble, blocks and traps were to stop the advance of tanks. Concrete structures and major buildings had been turned into ramparts, their windows into gun embrasures. Damaged tanks that still had a functioning gun, and often undamaged tanks too, were dug into the ground, turning them into powerful firing points.

Goebbels' *Berliner Frontblatt* listed the directions of the main attacks that had been mounted to repel 'the Soviets' in the preceding twenty-four hours: between Grunewald and Siemensstadt, in the Tempelhof–Neukölln district and streets to the south of the Wedding railway station.

'Attack! On to complete and final victory, army comrades!' exclaimed the appeal of our military soviet of the 1st Byelorussian Front.

A huge, unfamiliar city. The smoke from burning buildings shrouded its outlines, whole districts of ruins gave it the appearance of fantasy. Just under six years before, an invasion of Europe, criminal and unprecedented in its brutality, was launched from here, and now to here it had returned.

The River Spree

How many times, in the darkest days of the war, our soldiers had repeated, 'We'll reach Berlin yet, we'll find out what that River Spree amounts to.' And now they had. The meandering, high-banked River Spree, like Berlin's other rivers, canals and lakes, complicated the advance of the attacking units. The haze from gunfire, smoke and dust hovered over the river like a dense pall, fancifully reflecting the light of burning buildings. Beyond the Spree was the government district, 'the 9th Special Defence District', where heavy fighting was in train.

On panels indicating the direction of traffic, on tanks, on shells being loaded into artillery, and on the barrels of rifles you saw the slogan, 'To the Reichstag!' It was on everyone's mind in those days in Berlin. On 29 April troops of our army arrived at Königsplatz, on to which the six-pillared façade of the Reichstag's grey hulk faced.

It was considered that once we took the Reichstag, once we raised the red flag above its cupola, the world would know that Hitler and fascism had been vanquished. The storming of the Reichstag riveted the attention of every journalist, whether newly arrived from Moscow or already with the front-line press. The honour of actually taking the building fell to our 3rd Shock Army under Colonel General Kuznetsov.

In 1933, after the ominous 'false flag' arson attack on the Reichstag, Hitler was able to force the aged President Hindenburg 'temporarily' to suspend civil liberties. They were never restored. This allowed Hitler to carry out a clampdown, with mass arrests of Communists and Social Democrats, giving the Nazis an absolute majority in the Reichstag. The burned-out building was not repaired and, under the Nazi regime, parliament ceased to be important. Its subsequent infrequent sessions were held elsewhere.

The principal building under the new regime was a new Reich Chancellery, built specially for Reich Chancellor Hitler by his favourite architect, Albert Speer (later Minister of Armaments and War Production). It was 500 metres from the Reichstag.

At that time we still had no firm intelligence to confirm that Hitler and his staff headquarters were in the shelter beneath the Reich Chancellery. Such information as the intelligence services had was scanty, inconsistent, unreliable and contradictory. Captured German soldiers had little to tell us. Some believed Hitler had flown to Bavaria or elsewhere, others were totally indifferent to everything, including the matter of where he might be. They were overwhelmed and burned out by what they had been through.

A squealer was captured, a boy of fifteen or so in the uniform of the Hitler Youth, his eyes reddened, his lips cracked. He had been shooting furiously but now just sat there, looking around puzzled but with evident curiosity, like any other young kid. These instant transformations in the war always amazed me. He told us that their division, commanded by Reichsjugendführer Artur Axmann, the national leader of the Hitler Youth, was protecting Hitler. He had heard that from their commanders. They had kept repeating it, and saying it was essential to hold out until General Wenck's army came to the rescue.

All day I had to interpret at the interrogation of prisoners in the basement of a house not far from Potsdamer Platz. It was occupied by a tailor's family, also by a woman and her son, and a girl in a ski outfit. The ceaseless thunder of battle was muffled in the basement. Sometimes we experienced what felt like earthquake tremors.

The tailor, an elderly man, hardly ever got up from his chair. He often took out his pocket watch and inspected it at length. Everyone involuntarily watched him doing so. His grown-up son was a cripple who had contracted polio as a child; he sat at the tailor's feet with his head on his father's lap. The elder daughter was either asleep or rushed round looking anxious. Her husband was in the Volkssturm and was outside somewhere in the streets of Berlin. Of all these bewildered, worn-out people, only the tailor's wife was busy with something all the time; her duties as a mother took priority over war or her fear of death. At the appropriate time, she would spread a napkin on her knees and lay out tiny pieces of bread and jam.

The young woman with the thin, serious boy and the girl in the ski suit, were 'refugees' from another basement. They tried to take up as little space as possible. The woman periodically talked loudly about herself: she was married to a firefighter who had been mobilized and sent to the front. She had been waiting two years for her husband to come home on leave, and had made a list of things he needed to do in the apartment: change a door handle, fix the window fastenings, etc., but now their house had burned down. The boy scowled, evidently tired of listening yet again to his mother's stories. The girl was wearing rough boots and had a pack on her back that she could not bring herself to take off. She was ugly and gawky and nobody asked her who she was or where she came from.

Prisoners waiting to be called for interrogation sat in there also. A not particularly young German lieutenant told me quietly, 'I've spent half the day sitting among civilians,' by which he meant the occupants of the basement. 'I'm not sure if you're aware of that.' 'What can we do?' 'No, by all means, if they are decent people I don't mind.'

We were interested in just one thing: where was Hitler? He did not have the answer to that, but wanted to speak his mind, and started in a roundabout way. He stood up and straightened himself before beginning. 'Our enemy No. 1 was England. Enemy No. 2 was Russia. In order to defeat England, we had first to finish off Russia . . . Oh God!' he said and covered his face with his hands.

A miner from Alsace who had surrendered asked darkly to be trusted with a rifle so he could fight against the Germans. 'Even at this last minute,' he said, 'for everything!' He turned up his sleeve to show the tattoo of a cross, which confirmed he came from Alsace.

Scant though the intelligence was that we obtained, putting everything together, getting an insight into the structure of the German defences around the Reich Chancellery, we felt able to conclude that, most likely, that is where Hitler was.

On the evening of 29 April a nurse was detained who had run through the line of fire to look for her mother. As she talked to us, she pulled a white headscarf from her coat pocket, either without thinking or seeking the protection of the red cross on its white background. Throughout the war that sign had afforded our wounded no protection. At first sight of it the Germans mercilessly targeted their bombing there.

The day before, the nurse had been accompanying the wounded from Vossstrasse to the only nearby place of safety, the bomb shelter of the Reich Chancellery. There she had heard from the soldiers and the staff of the building that Hitler was in the underground bunker.

White Flags

Dawn. Streets after fighting. A dead German soldier. Shop windows ripped apart by shells, holes in walls leading deep into the interior of a deserted house. The wind sweeping rubbish and crushed stone over a cobbled street. By a building, on the pavement, are our soldiers. One is sleeping on his side, his knees drawn up, using a piece of a door as a headrest. Another is rewinding his foot wrappings. The last long minutes before another day of assault . . .

Everywhere there are barricades, anti-tank barriers, ditches and piles of rubble. Labyrinthine streets. Chaotic ruins. Burning, collapsing buildings, and buildings from whose windows the enemy is firing. Our soldiers rose to face death with unforgettable courage and selflessness in those testing years when death was not rewarded with victory; but there is a particular grief when a soldier dies with only a few hours left before victory. The Russian soldiers who entered Berlin had been through everything: pain and hatred, the bitterness of defeat and self-sacrifice, the hopelessness of encirclement, the despair of captivity, the rage of attacking, and the surge of enthusiasm in victorious battles from the Volga to the Spree – only for many of them to be cut down at the last minute in the streets of Berlin.

The battle raged day and night, ever fiercer. The Berlin garrison, the SS regiments, the troops retreating from the Oder and Küstrin or redeployed from the Elbe, all those troops that managed to get through to Berlin before the ring of encirclement closed around the city, were concentrated here in the government district.

On 30 April at 11.30 hrs the order was given to the attacking troops: fire with all weaponry! The bombardment began, from heavy artillery, the self-propelled guns, tanks, fire from machine guns and submachine guns. Guns that had come all the way from the Volga fired for all the wrongs that had been done, for all the people who had been harmed. When the artillery fell silent, the soldiers attacked.

On the evening of that day, 30 April 1945, the red flag fluttered over the Reichstag. Fighting within the building itself continued throughout 1 May.

The Reichstag, a mighty building with a great dome visible from far and wide, was to go down in history as a symbol of victory. It was the heart of the 9th Special Defence District, and when it fell the Reich Chancellery could hold out no longer.

Berlin. The night before May Day 1945. A night of apocalypse. Blazing buildings grotesquely lighting up a crippled city sunk in darkness, the crash of collapsing masonry, the gunfire, the choking fumes of battle and conflagration. Searchlight beams probe the darkness of the night sky: not a single German aircraft is to cross the firmament over the ring encircling Berlin. No one and nothing can fly in, or escape from here by air.

In the centre of the German capital, in the government district, the German troops were trapped, surrounded. This was their hour of tragedy, of desperate persistence and self-immolation. Gunfire raked the dark street separating the enemies when suddenly (this came about in the sector of our neighbouring 8th Guards Army under General Chuikov) someone appeared from the enemy side. A flare picked him out from the chaos of war, waving a white flag. The first envoy in Berlin to parley about a truce, the first sign of recognition that the enemy's situation was hopeless. The firing ceased immediately.

The envoy walked, clinging to masonry and shattered concrete, crushing glass and rubble underfoot. As the soldiers watched him approach step by step, behind him a historic epoch was receding, drawing to a close.

The episode is described in his memoirs by Lieutenant General Illarion Tolkonyuk, chief of the operational department of Chuikov's headquarters. For the first time both sides stopped shooting at each other on a Berlin street. The envoy, Lieutenant Colonel Seifert, hastily reached the now silent Russian firing point in a grey corner building. Along the telephone wire the news of the envoy ran through the appropriate channels to Army Commander Chuikov. The envoy delivered a bilingual document in Russian and German, signed by Martin Bormann, to the effect that Lieutenant Colonel Seifert was authorized to negotiate with the Russian command. The purpose of the negotiation was to agree the matter of the crossing of the front line by the Chief of the General Staff of the German Army, General Hans Krebs, in view of the particular importance of the message he would bring.

Seifert returned across the street separating us from the enemy, and about an hour and a half later, as agreed, the Germans appeared in the same place, emerging from the fresh ruins. It was 3.00 a.m. Moscow time and, on the other side of the street, for the Germans, it was 1.00 a.m. Berlin time.

There was a fair amount of light, and the soldiers of the opposing sides watched tensely as General Krebs and his party, an orderly carrying his briefcase, an officer (Colonel Theodor von Dufving), and a soldier with a white flag, came forward in the early hours of a fateful new day.

Krebs was conveyed through the divisional headquarters to Chuikov's command post. It was 3.30 a.m. Moscow time. At 3.30 p.m. the previous day Hitler had committed suicide. Krebs brought with him this news from Bormann and Goebbels and told General Chuikov, whom he mistook for Marshal Zhukov, that he was the first non-German to be notified of this fact.

He brought with him a letter from Goebbels to 'the Leader of the Soviet people'. Marshal Zhukov gives the text of the letter in his book. The letter announced that, 'The Führer has today voluntarily passed away. On the basis of his lawful right, the Führer has, in the will he has left, transferred all power to Dönitz, myself and Bormann. I have authorized Bormann to establish contact with the Leader of the Soviet people. This contact is essential for peace negotiations between the powers that have suffered the greatest losses. Goebbels.'

The letter had appended to it a list of the members of the new government in accordance with Hitler's will. In this ephemeral government of the collapsed Third Reich, Goebbels was designated Reich Chancellor and Krebs Minister of War. A new post of Minister of the Party was invented for Bormann. Grand Admiral Dönitz was appointed Reich President and Commander of the Armed Forces.

Krebs was instructed to request a truce in Berlin so that the new government could reunite (Dönitz was at Flensburg) and, legally constituted, proceed to negotiations with the Soviet command. This was an obvious last effort to break out of encircled Berlin.

The substance of the discussions between Generals Chuikov and Sokolovsky and General Krebs is now public knowledge. At the time we heard only rumours about the arrival of Krebs, and the discussions immediately became secret.

Krebs was one of the victims of the last appointments and meteoric career promotions in the doomed Third Reich. He was elevated to the post of Chief of the General Staff of the Army only in late March or even in April 1945, to replace Guderian, whom Hitler had dismissed. Very upright, clean-shaven, with a pistol on his greatcoat belt, he maintained a military bearing. That is how he looks in a photograph taken at the conclusion of the failed negotiations. Krebs had served for a long time in Moscow as the military attaché of the German embassy. He spoke Russian, and understood the hard-line remarks Chuikov and his officers were exchanging: 'We'll have to finish them off!' and, into the telephone when talking to Marshal Zhukov: 'I wouldn't ponce around. Unconditional surrender and *basta!*'

The toughest, most implacable character present at the talks was, however, Vsevolod Vishnevsky, a former officer in the tsarist Life Guards, now wearing the epaulettes of a colonel, a famous Soviet writer who appeared in Berlin right at the end of the war.

Vishnevsky shrieked in fear and indignation, 'Take the pistol off that bandit!' They had some difficulty calming him down, owing to his inability to differentiate between an envoy and a prisoner. Another outburst came when he saw that, when Krebs handed the documents over to Chuikov, he kept some pages himself, and demanded that they be taken off him by force. This writer and socialist humanitarian was restrained with difficulty by soldiers who had been fighting throughout the war years and become toughened and embittered towards the enemy, but who nevertheless retained respect for military ethics and a sense of personal dignity.

For the German side, the negotiations were doomed to fail. Marshal Zhukov, to whom Chuikov was reporting by phone, emphasized that negotiations could be conducted only with the agreement of all the allies, who expected scrupulous observance of mutual obligations.

The documents presented by Krebs were delivered to Zhukov at the command point of front headquarters. It was obvious that the reply could only be a demand for unconditional surrender to all the Allies. Ultimately, however, it was for Stalin to decide, and he was asleep at his *dacha*, as Zhukov was informed over the telephone by the general on duty. This would delay the negotiations, and Zhukov was concerned that this might give the Allies grounds to blame the Soviet command for engaging in separate negotiations. He decided. 'I must ask you to wake him. The matter is urgent and cannot be left until morning.'

In a conversation I had with him years later, Georgiy Zhukov praised his memory as 'remarkable', but even people who did not have that distinction had no difficulty in retaining firmly in their minds the words they heard Stalin utter. We can rest assured that Zhukov's recollection of Stalin's reply was accurate. I quoted them when I wrote about my meeting with Zhukov, and I will repeat them here, with some additional comments.

Awakened by Zhukov's call, Stalin, perhaps still half asleep, reacted to the news of Hitler's suicide in less than his usual phlegmatic manner, and even with a degree of spontaneity:

'The game's up for the scum!' (as if he were talking about a partner in crime who had ratted on him. Hitler was, after all, the only person the mistrustful Stalin had ever trusted, only to be perfidiously fooled by him). 'Pity we couldn't have taken him alive. Where's Hitler's body?'

'As reported by General Krebs, Hitler's body was cremated on a bonfire.'

'Tell Sokolovsky,' the Supreme Commander said, 'to conduct no negotiations except on unconditional surrender, neither with Krebs nor with other Hitlerites. If nothing out of the ordinary happens, do not call until morning. I want to rest a bit before the [May Day] parade.' Stalin thus terminated his conversation with Zhukov on the most sensitive topic of the time.

Stalin was not given to trusting people, but gave no orders then or subsequently to confirm the veracity of the message about Hitler. 'Cremated on a bonfire.' One way or another, he had disappeared. This left room for speculation that Hitler was still alive and in hiding. Hitler was no longer an emblem of the war: he became an emblem of the kind of peace that was to follow.

Zhukov, with his forthrightness, which Stalin had probably valued in the war, was quite unsuitable for joining in the imminent political games and, if he personally verified Hitler's death, could even be dangerous. So he was abruptly sidelined and, we can imagine, must have been aware of it. Stalin never once asked him whether the search for Hitler's remains was continuing.

Our newspapers, from 2 May onwards, alarmed their readers with TASS reports that Hitler had managed to escape. *Pravda* declared on 2 May:

Yesterday evening, German radio was broadcasting an announcement by the so-called 'Führer's General Headquarters' to the effect that Hitler died on the afternoon of 1 May [*sic*]. The announcement continues that on 30 April Hitler appointed Admiral Dönitz as his successor . . . These German radio announcements are evidently a new Nazi trick. By spreading the claim that Hitler is dead, the German Fascists are clearly hoping to enable him to leave the stage and go underground.

So Hitler was alive and hiding somewhere? The question of whether he was alive or had committed suicide, and even more, the question of whether he had been found, moved from being an army matter into the sphere of international politics, so Zhukov may have deliberately moved aside on the grounds that this was not his province. A new day had dawned, with complex new problems and concerns, and the toppled dictator was demoted to yesterday's news.

In my talk with Marshal Zhukov I mentioned that at that time we had the feeling that the front command was taking little interest in the search. Zhukov did not deny it. For some reason he had not insisted on receiving reports with all the details. He had ignored the issue. Why? Was it solely because of Stalin's disinterest? I can come up with no convincing answer.

As for Stalin, he was not interested in seeing a search conducted, Hitler's dead body discovered and the matter closed. That much is clear from how events were to develop.

The negotiations, which were now being conducted by Colonel General Sokolovsky, ended. The request for a truce was categorically rejected. Krebs was told that, as agreed with the three other Allies, only unconditional surrender could be discussed. Krebs was not authorized to accept that, and the talks ended with his return to the Reich Chancellery with that uncomfortable news. Colonel von Dufving was sent to Goebbels with a demand that he should surrender in order to avoid senseless bloodshed on both sides. Our command decided at the same time to set up a direct telephone line to Goebbels.

The signaller ordered to follow in Colonel von Dufving's footsteps reached his destination safely, unwinding cable all the way and, with the assistance of German signallers, connected himself to their wire, plugged in his telephone equipment and let our side know that he was at the bottom of a crater, sheltering from any gunfire that might come from our side, in the amicable company of Fritzes, and having a smoke.

For the first time a direct telephone line connected the command posts of the opposing sides, but this entirely operational line was never used. The German side, which was expected to respond to the Soviet conditions, did not negotiate. While waiting for their decision, combat operations on our side were halted. Only at 18.00 hrs did an SS lieutenant colonel sent by Goebbels deliver, across the front line, the Germans' written refusal to accept our conditions.

For Goebbels and Bormann personally, surrender had little to commend it. For them, capitulating to the Soviet side was tantamount to something worse than death. Saving the lives of German soldiers and of the German population was evidently not a priority. At 18.30 the Red Army, on the orders of Marshal Zhukov, resumed the assault. The unused hotline connecting the opposing sides was destroyed.

I often wondered what had happened to our signaller on the other side of the front line, lying in that crater with his German colleagues, alone in the enemy camp as the Red Army resumed its furious assault. Did the Nazi soldiers take their desperation and anger out on him in their darkest hour?

It was only in 1985, after being forgotten for so many years, that the heroic signaller resurfaced. I was so delighted to learn from a newspaper report that a Kazakh film about him had won an award at an international festival of documentary short films. All these years he had been living in Alma-Ata in obscurity.

Late in the evening of 1 May, the Hamburg radio station broadcast an announcement 'from the Führer's Headquarters' that, 'This afternoon, continuing the fight against Bolshevism to his last breath, our Führer, Adolf Hitler, fell in the battle for Germany at his command post in the Reich Chancellery.' The announcement was broadcast a second time, accompanied by Wagnerian music. The circumstances had changed, but our task remained the same: to find Hitler, dead or alive.

The Führerbunker

Hitler's headquarters was located in a bomb shelter under the Reich Chancellery. It had more than fifty rooms (most of them no bigger than a boxroom). It also housed a powerful communications centre, had food supplies and a kitchen. An underground garage was connected to it. There were two ways into the underground complex: from the internal garden of the Reich Chancellery, and from the Chancellery's vestibule, from which a fairly broad and gentle staircase led downwards. Descending the stairs, you immediately came to a long corridor with numerous doors opening off it. The route to Hitler's bunker was rather long and complicated. An entrance from the enclosed garden led directly to the *Führerbunker*, as those inhabiting this underworld called it.

The two-storey Führerbunker was much deeper down than the bomb shelter under the Reich Chancellery and its reinforced concrete ceiling much thicker. The head of Hitler's bodyguard, Hans Rattenhuber, in his memoirs, *Hitler, As I Knew Him*,[1] describes it: 'Hitler's new bomb shelter was the most solid of any built in Germany. The reinforced concrete ceiling of the bunker was eight metres thick.'

There was a concrete mixer near the garden entrance to the bunker: work had recently been carried out to strengthen the concrete roof, probably after it suffered a direct hit from artillery shells.

Russian assault detachments broke through the final defensive ring and burst into the Reich Chancellery on the morning of 2 May.

There was a firefight in the vestibule with the remnants of the guard, most of whom, however, had fled. Next came the descent. Military and civilian staff began coming out of the corridors, the boxrooms and the rest of the complex with their hands up. The wounded were sitting or lying on the floor. There was groaning. In the underground complex and in the storeys of the Reich Chancellery shooting broke out repeatedly.

We needed to get our bearings immediately, to locate all the exits and block them, get the lie of the land and start searching. In the very mixed collection of people occupying the complex it was no simple matter to identify those who could be helpful, people who would know more than others about Hitler's fate and could guide us through the labyrinthine complex. We conducted a first sketchy enquiry.

Down there we found a portly forty-year old, Karl Schneider, one of the Chancellery's garage mechanics. He testified that on 28 or 29 April, he could not remember which exactly, the telephone operator on duty in Hitler's secretariat gave him an order to deliver all the petrol he had to the Führer's bunker. Schneider sent eight cans, each containing twenty litres of petrol. Later the same day, he received a further order from the operator to send firelighters. He had eight and sent them all.

---

1. There are two typescript texts translated into Russian in the archive: Testimony of Hans Rattenhuber (file 132, pp. 63–91, titled 'The Truth about the Death of Hitler'; also more detailed memoirs titled 'Hitler As I Knew Him' (file 131).

Yelena Rzhevskaya, photographed at GHQ on 29 January 1942.

Yelena Rzhevskaya in 1943.

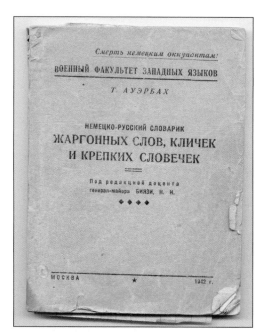

Theo Auerbach's German–Russian
'dictionary of swearing', published by
the Army Faculty of Western Languages,
Moscow, 1942.

Rzhevskaya and comrades enjoying a lighthearted moment during the winter of 1943.

The best-known photograph of Yelena Rzhevskaya in uniform, dated 30 May 1943.

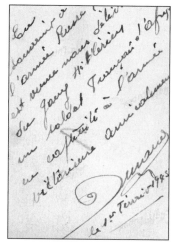

Amateur dramatics in the French POW camp near Bydgoszcz, seen in the photo given to Rzhevskaya: 'The role of the mademoiselle was also being taken by a captive French officer.' With its inscription: 'From a French soldier of the African army in captivity to the victorious army.'

Marianna and Alfred in Bydgoszcz. 'Now . . . I see how young this thirty-year old teacher from Liége still was.'

'I did manage to tear myself away from the documents for a short while, and walk round the city in the company of our driver, Sergey, and several officers . . . the Reichstag, not yet cool after the fire, was still smoking.'

Above & top: In front of the temporary monument built by the Russians to celebrate the Allied victory, decorated with portraits of Truman, Stalin and Churchill.

Rzhevskaya with a pair of traffic cops, German and Russian, large and small: 'The girls directing traffic . . . were . . . enlivening Berlin's crossroads.'

8 May 1945. The post-mortem examination of the body of Josef Goebbels. Dr Faust Shkaravsky, principal forensic medicine specialist of the 1st Byelorussian Front, is third from the left.

Dental assistant Käthe Heusermann's diagram of Hitler's teeth, crucial to identification of the body. Heusermann and her colleague Echtmann were later harshly treated in Soviet captivity.

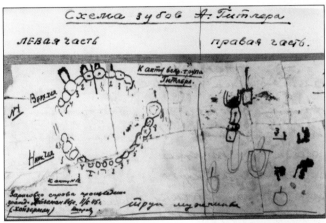

Käthe Heusermann and dental technician Fritz Echtmann with two Russian officers.

In the Tiergarten with a German sFH 15 cm gun (*left, top*); in the government district (*far left, below*); at the Bismarck memorial in the Tiergarten (*left*). 'Wyktoria Buzińska sewed me a green dress from the lining of a coat, and ornamented it with . . . a piece of polka-dotted satin . . . Later, in May, I wore this dress when I was photographed in Berlin at . . . various . . . historic settings.'

Yelena Rzhevskaya at Finow, where the remains of Hitler and Goebbels were re-examined by Stalin's special emissary, an unnamed general.

Yelena Rzhevskaya at a 1986 conference in memory of Marshal Georgiy Zhukov. His driver, Alexander Buchin, is on the right .

Schneider had not himself seen Hitler and did not know whether he was in Berlin, but on 1 May he was told by the head of the garage and by Hitler's chauffeur, Erich Kempka, that the Führer was dead. Rumours were circulating among the security soldiers that he had committed suicide and that his body had been burnt. Putting these rumours together with the orders he had received, Schneider concluded that the petrol he had sent had been used to burn the Führer's body.

Then, on the evening of 1 May, he had another call from the duty telephonist, again demanding that all available petrol should be sent to the Führer's bunker. Schneider siphoned petrol from the fuel tanks of the cars and sent another four cans.

What had that call been about? Who had the petrol been meant for this time? Together with Karl Schneider and Wilhelm Lange (a cook), Major Bystrov, Lieutenant Colonel Klimenko[1] and Major Khazin went out into the garden. The ground had been churned up by shells, the trees mutilated, and their charred branches were strewn underfoot. The lawns were blackened by fire and soot, and there was broken glass and piles of bricks everywhere. How were they to determine where the bodies had been burned?

They began an inspection of the garden and, three metres from the garden exit of the Führerbunker, found the half-burnt bodies of Goebbels and his wife. So that was what the second supply of petrol had been for. 'The German found them first,' Ivan Klimenko wrote to me in a letter dated 9 February 1965, referring to Schneider. If it had been any later, the torrent of Red Army soldiers pouring into the Reich Chancellery would have trampled the bodies to pieces without even noticing what was under their feet.

The sky over Berlin had not yet ceased to glow; the Reich Chancellery was still smoking. It was dark in the underground complex, and with the ventilation not working it was stuffy, dank and gloomy. In those days, down in the Chancellery's shelter, I had to sort through a vast number of papers and documents by the light of humble oil lamps. There were on-the-spot accounts of street fighting in Bormann's files, reports from the Berlin Nazi Party leadership about the hopelessness of the situation, their lack of ammunition, the demoralized state of the soldiers. There was Bormann's correspondence, and Hitler's personal papers.

My priority in searching through these papers was to find anything that would shed some light at least on what had been happening there in the last

---

1. Ivan Klimenko was head of the Smersh counterintelligence department of the 79th Infantry Corps, 3rd Shock Army, 1st Byelorussian Front. Vadim J. Birstein, SMERSH: *Stalin's Secret Weapon*, London: Biteback, 2013, p. 303.

few days, that would add a brush stroke or give a clue as to how everything had ended.

Here was Bormann sending telegram after telegram to his adjutant, Hummel, in Obersalzberg, all bearing the red stamp *'Geheim'*, Secret! From the nature of his instructions it was clear they were preparing to move Hitler's headquarters to Berchtesgaden. They had been planning to get out of Berlin.

Here was a folder containing information from their enemy's sources, radio intercepts from the last days of April: Reuters news agency reports from Allied headquarters, broadcasts from Moscow about combat operations on the fronts, telegrams about events in the rest of the world, from London, Rome, San Francisco, Washington and Zurich. These sources were used at Hitler's headquarters to gain a sense of what was happening on other sectors of the front, and in Berlin itself, in the last days of April. By this time, direct contact with the troops had been finally lost.

All the papers in the folder were typewritten in huge letters. I had never before come across such a strange font: it was as if you were reading through a magnifying glass. What was that for? Later I learned that Hitler's secretary, Gertraud Junge, retyped all the papers on a special typewriter. For reasons of image, Hitler did not want to wear spectacles.

Here was a report from a foreign radio station about the execution of Mussolini and his mistress, Clara Petacci. With a blue pencil, Hitler had underlined the words 'Mussolini' and 'hung upside down'. This discovery seemed to me to be significant: the news of Mussolini's fate made it clear to Hitler that he needed to avoid discovery of his body after his death. That was my conclusion at the time, and I later found it confirmed in the Council of Ministers Archive, in the memoirs of Rattenhuber, and in the conclusions of the Control Commission for Germany (British element) of 1 November 1945. We searched for documents and, having familiarized myself with them, I annotated them. They were then forwarded, as already mentioned, to front headquarters, as were our own papers, interrogation reports and all other documentation.

Goebbels' Diary

One of our major finds at the time was Goebbels' diary. It was found in the underground complex where Goebbels lived with his family, in one of two suitcases of documents. There were ten or so thick notebooks from different years, covered in closely written, heavy handwriting in straight lines. The letters had a barely noticeable slant to the left and were tightly squeezed together. The first books of the diary dated from 1932, before the

Nazis came to power, and the last ended on 8 July 1941. We discovered later that this was only the date on which the handwritten diary ends. From the following day, 9 July 1941, and almost to the end, he dictated his entries each day to two shorthand typists.

I greatly regretted not being able to sit down and study this diary, which it was not easy to decipher. It would have needed many days of diligent work, and we were having to count the minutes. Our immediate task was to establish what had happened to Hitler and where we could find him. I had no option but to forward the diaries to front headquarters. With the war at an end, such documents were of purely historical interest and considered to be of no value. They suffered a major devaluation.

In the years that followed, when I recalled Goebbels' diary I feared the notebooks had been lost along with a host of other documents, but a time came when I had the opportunity to read very carefully a part of this diary, to whose discovery I had contributed and which had been preserved in the archive. It was the last handwritten notebook dating from May, June and early July 1941. Realizing that this diary was a tremendously valuable historical document, I quoted abundantly from it in my book (translated, naturally, into Russian). I thus presided over the first publication from this body of handwritten diaries, revealing their whereabouts to the world. Nobody, of course, had any intention of making the original of the diary available for a foreign edition, and accordingly this chapter is all but missing in the [East] German edition of my book that was edited in the USSR.[1]

However, the mere mention of the existence of this notebook and the exact date on which it ended, 8 July 1941, proved to be enough. [West] German historians already had Goebbels' typewritten diaries at their disposal, which began from the following day, 9 July 1941, and now they knew that the manuscript diary was extant and preserved in an archive in Moscow. They began seeking access to it, and in 1969 microfilm copies were conveyed to the German side. In 1987 all the surviving pages of the manuscript diary were published.

The last notebook of that diary is uniquely interesting historical testimony, reflecting as it does the facts and atmosphere of preparations for the attack on the USSR. It discloses the nature of the provocations and the methods of disinformation undertaken at the time by Nazi Germany.

Goebbels' diary introduces us to the routine day-to-day activities of the Third Reich's minister of propaganda. In May–June 1941, these activities are preparing for the attack on the USSR which, for us, marked the beginning

1. Jelena Rshewskaja, *Hitlers Ende ohne Mythos*, tr. Werner Hantke, Berlin: Deutscher Militärverlag, 1967.

of the war. The first references to the impending attack appear in the diary on 24 May. Goebbels sent his representative to Alfred Rosenberg, who was to become minister for the occupied eastern territories, to coordinate their activities in the impending operation. 'R. must be broken down into component parts . . . the existence of such a colossal state in the east cannot be tolerated.'

Goebbels was busy with active disinformation, spreading false rumours about a supposedly imminent invasion of Britain in order to mask Germany's true intentions. 'The rumours we have sown about the invasion are working. There is a climate of exceptional nervousness in England.'

29 May 1941. In Moscow they are busy solving puzzles. Stalin is apparently beginning little by little, to get the knack. But for the rest, he is still entranced . . . A heavenly summer! Quiet, a beautiful evening. But you do not enjoy it.

31 May. Operation Barbarossa is developing. We are beginning the first big deception. The entire state and military machinery is being mobilized. Only a few individuals are informed about the true course of events. I am obliged to send the whole ministry off on a false trail, risking, in the event of failure, the loss of my prestige . . .

Little by little we are elaborating the theme of the invasion. I ordered a song to be composed about it, a new theme, increasing the use of broadcasts in English, training a propaganda company for England, etc. Two weeks allowed for everything . . . If nobody blabs and, given the small circle of initiates, one can count on that, the deception will succeed.

Forward march!

A busy time is beginning. We will prove that our propaganda is unrivalled. The civilian ministries suspect nothing. They are working in the direction set for them. It will be interesting when the balloon goes up.

Directives on propaganda against R.: no anti-socialism, no restoration of tsarism, no open talk of dismembering the Russian state (otherwise we will alienate the army with its Great Russian inclinations) . . . Retain the collective farms for the present in order to save the harvest.

Goebbels received a programme for the territorial partitioning of Russia from Hitler:

7 June. The Asian part of R. does not need to be discussed. The European part we shall assimilate. Stalin recently told Matsuoka he is Asian. He can hardly complain!

Goebbels put his back into preparing for the new war. He tightened the screws wherever he could, forbidding the showing of foreign films in the

Cabaret of Comedians where 'all the gripers go' to watch them; he 'prepared new measures against the Berlin Jews'. He castigated those sections of the press that failed sufficiently to extol the achievements of German arms, calling them the 'petty-bourgeois press'. He intervened in matters of ensuring military secrecy in all the Berlin ministries. 'We will even have to call on the services of the Gestapo.'

He kept Robert Ley of the Nazis' German Labour Front from promising new post-war social programmes, so as not to awaken an appetite for peace among the population. At the same time, he cancelled the existing ban on dances. 'That is necessary in order as far as possible to conceal our next operation. The people must believe that we are now "replete with victories" and no longer interested in anything beyond recreation and dancing' (*10 June*). Goebbels decided to go easy on anti-tobacco propaganda in order not to offend soldiers who smoked or introduce 'inflammable matter' among the populace. 'War already conceals within itself quite enough natural incendiary matter. Accordingly, I am ordering a toning down of excessively harsh anti-clerical propaganda. There will be time enough for that after the war' (*17 June*).

He rhapsodizes about his box of disinformation tricks:

11 June. Together with the High Command of the Wehrmacht and with the Führer's consent, I am elaborating my article about invasion. The topic is 'the island of Crete as an example'. It is fairly obvious. It should appear in the *Völkischer Beobachter* and the copies will then be confiscated. London will learn of this twenty-four hours later through the United States Embassy. This is the whole point of the manoeuvre. It should all serve to disguise the actions in the east. Now we need to use more powerful methods . . . I shall finish the article this afternoon. It will be magnificent, a masterpiece of deviousness.

The article was written, approved by the Führer, and 'is being sent with due ceremony to the *Völkischer Beobachter*. The issue will be confiscated during the night.'

The point of the trick is that the article, examining the operation to capture Crete, contained a clear hint that experience gained there contained lessons for the supposedly impending invasion of Britain. Having the issue confiscated would serve to show that Goebbels had inadvertently blurted out Germany's 'true' intentions.

14 June. The Russians seem not yet to have any presentiment. At all events, they are acting in a way that is fully consonant with our wishes: densely massed troops are an easy prey for taking prisoner.

There are other entries under the same date:

East Prussia is crammed so full of troops that the Russians could inflict great damage on us with pre-emptive strikes. But they will not do so . . .

I order lunatic rumours to be spread in Berlin: Stalin is supposedly coming to Berlin, the red banners are already being sewn, and so on. Dr Ley phones me, having fallen for it hook line and sinker. I leave him to his delusion. At this present moment it is all to the good.

Further:

15 June. From radio intercepts we for our part can conclude that Moscow is bringing the Russian fleet into a state of combat readiness. So they are no longer as unworried as they pretend to be. But their preparations are extraordinarily amateurish. Their actions cannot be taken seriously.

Goebbels also viewed the war as a source of abundant material for German newsreels: 'Inevitably, during such a relatively peaceful time it [the newsreel] cannot be as good as when there is fighting.'

Goebbels did not overlook his own self-interest: in Berlin, construction of a highly secure bomb shelter was commenced on Göringstrasse where he lived. It was going to be 'a colossal structure,' he noted with satisfaction.

In Schwanenwerder near Berlin, adding to the country houses he already possessed, construction of Goebbels' castle was coming to a conclusion. He thought the building itself was 'magnificent', and also the way his wife had furnished it. Here, in comfortable remoteness, against the backdrop of an idyllic landscape, Dr Goebbels was intending to operate even more productively to 'create general mayhem', not omitting, in the process, to help himself to some prize treasures: 'I bought a marvellous painting by Goya privately in France.'

Paintings from all over were being funnelled to the Ministry of Propaganda.

We have already brought together an amazing collection. The ministry will gradually be transformed into an art gallery. That is as it should be: after all this is where art is being managed from.

He intended to manage it on an international scale.

On Goebbels' instructions a plan was being developed to establish a Berlin Academy of Fashion under the direction of Benno von Arent, Führer at that time of Germany's artists. Here are the instructions Goebbels gave his subordinate as he sent him off to allied Italy as the representative of German cinematography.

Your mission is to bring back as much as possible that we can use. Keep smiling as you rip them off. Don't let Italian cinema develop too much. Germany must remain the leading power in terms of cinema and consolidate its dominant position even further.

The only kind of art Goebbels had mastered to perfection was the art of blackmail, deception and conspiracy.

15 June had been the last Sunday before a terrible war was unleashed in the east. As usual, Goebbels described the previous day's events in his diary. There had been a secret meeting of the conspirators.

16 June.

After lunch the Führer summons me to the Reich Chancellery. I am to enter through the back entrance so that no one will notice. Wilhelmstrasse is under constant surveillance by foreign journalists, so the precaution was necessary . . . The Führer explains the situation to me in detail: the offensive against Russia will begin as soon as deployment of our forces is completed. This will be in about one week's time. The campaign in Greece has severely weakened us in material terms, so the matter has been slightly delayed. Fortunately the weather is fairly bad and the harvest in Ukraine has not yet ripened.

We are thus hoping additionally to acquire a large proportion of that harvest. This will be a massed offensive on an extremely large scale. Probably the biggest history has ever known. There will be no repetition of Napoleon's predicament. On the very first morning a bombardment using 10,000 guns will begin. We will use the new, powerful artillery pieces that had been intended for use against the Maginot line but were not needed. The Russians have concentrated right on the border. The best situation we could have expected. If they were dispersed in the depths of the country, they would be a greater threat. They have at their disposal about 180–200 divisions, maybe a little less, but at all events about the same numbers as we have. In respect of the quality of the manpower and materiel, however, they bear no comparison at all with us. The attack will be spearheaded in different places. The Russians will be driven back without too much difficulty. The Führer expects this campaign to be completed within about four months. I believe it will be less. Bolshevism will collapse like a house of cards. An unexampled victory awaits us . . .

We need to attack Russia also in order to gain people. Undefeated, Russia ties up 150 of our divisions, a potential workforce we very much need for our arms industry. Our arms industry needs to work more intensively so that we can implement our programme for the production of weaponry, submarines and aircraft, then the United States, too, will be unable to harm us in any way. We have the resources, raw materials and machinery for three-shift working, but not enough people. When Russia is conquered we shall be able to demobilize several age cohorts, and then build, arm and prepare ourselves.

Only after that will we be able to begin the attack on England, from the air, on a large scale. Invading England by land is hardly going to be possible, ever. Accordingly, we must devise other ways of ensuring victory.

This time we are adopting a totally different approach from the usual, and are playing a new tune. We conduct no polemics in the press, maintain complete silence and then, one fine day, simply strike. I do my very best to persuade the Führer not to convene the Reichstag for that day. Otherwise, our entire system of deception will be vitiated. He accepts my proposal to read the proclamation over the radio . . .

The aim of the campaign is clear: Bolshevism must fall, and additionally England's last sword on the continent will be knocked out of its hands . . .

We may possibly request the German bishops of both denominations to bless this war as ordained by God. Tsarism will not be restored in Russia, but to counteract Bolshevism we shall implement real socialism. Every old Nazi will be extremely pleased to see this. Collaboration with Russia has been, to tell the truth, a rank stain on our honour. Now we shall also destroy what we have fought against all our lives. I say this to the Führer and he entirely agrees with me. I also put in a word for Rosenberg, whose purpose in life, thanks to this campaign, is once more justified.

The Führer says that, by fair means or foul, we must win. That is the only way, and it is right morally and from necessity. When we are the victors, who will question our methods? We already have so much on our conscience that we must win, otherwise our people, with us leading it, and everything that is dear to us will be wiped off the face of the earth. So, to work!

The Führer asks what the people think. The people think that we are acting in concert with Russia, but will conduct themselves just as bravely if we call on them to wage war against Russia . . .

The denial by TASS is, in the Führer's opinion, only a sign of fear. Stalin is trembling before the impending events. An end will be put to his false game. We will exploit the raw materials of this resource-rich country. The hope of the British to destroy us with a blockade will thereby be totally neutralized, and only after this will the real submarine war begin.

Italy and Japan will now receive messages that we are intending to present Russia with certain ultimatum demands in early July. They will blab about it everywhere. Then we will again have several days at our disposal. The Duce is not yet fully informed of the true extent of the planned operation. Antonescu knows a little more. Romania and Finland are joining forces with

146

us. So, forwards! The abundant fields of Ukraine are beckoning. Our military leaders, who saw the Führer on Saturday, have prepared everything in the best possible way. Our propaganda machinery is ready and waiting . . .

I must now prepare everything in the most meticulous manner. It is essential, no matter what, to continue to spread the rumours: peace with Moscow, Stalin coming to Berlin, the invasion of England in the near future, all in order to cover up every aspect of the situation as it actually is. We have to hope that succeeds for some time yet . . .

I drove through the park, through the rear portal where people were strolling carefree in the rain. Lucky people who know nothing of all our worries and live one day at a time. It is for the sake of all of them that we work and struggle and take upon ourselves such risk. In order that our people should thrive.

I oblige everybody to say nothing about my secret visit to the Führer.

And the Germans on this last Sunday 'stroll carefree in the rain', with no inkling of the catastrophe into which they are to be plunged in a few days' time by those whom they so recklessly entrusted with their destiny.

17 June.

All the preparations have been made. It is to begin in the early hours of Sunday. At 3.30 a.m. The Russians are still gathered on the border in a dense, massed formation. With their minimal transport capacity they will be unable to alter the situation in just a few days . . .

The US demanded that our consulates should close by 10 July and leave the country. The information library of our ministry in New York is also being closed. These are all petty pinpricks, not stabbing with a knife. We will have no problem coping with this.

As for the freezing of German deposits in the United States, Goebbels noted,

[Roosevelt] can do no more than tickle us.

18 June.

Our deception in respect of Russia has come to a climax. We have flooded the world with a torrent of rumours, until now it is difficult for us ourselves to know what is what . . . I have been trying out new fanfares. Still have not found the ideal one. At the same time, everything has to be disguised.

'Rumours are our daily bread,' Goebbels writes.

Apart from special 'spreaders', the world is flooded with rumours by the press of Germany's allies, notably the Italians. 'They blabber about everything they know and even about what they do not know. Their press is terribly frivolous,' Goebbels writes, quoting the opinions Hitler expressed in conversation with him.

Accordingly, they cannot be trusted with secrets, at least not with any it would be undesirable to have disclosed.

Worked until late at night. The question of Russia is becoming ever more impenetrable. Our rumour-mongers are doing an excellent job. With all this muddle we end up almost in the situation of a squirrel that has concealed its nest so well that in the end it cannot find it.

The entries during these days end in sighs:

The time until the dramatic hour drags by so slowly.

I am longing for it to be the end of the week. It frays your nerves. When it begins, you will feel, as always, as if a mountain has fallen from your shoulders.

19 June. We need for now to print 800,000 leaflets for our soldiers. I order this to be done with all necessary precautions. The printing company will be sealed by the Gestapo and the workers will not be allowed to leave until a particular day . . .

The issue of Russia is gradually becoming clear. It was impossible to avoid that. In Russia itself they are preparing to celebrate the Day of the Navy. It is not going to be a success.

20 June. See the Führer: the matter of Russia is now clear to everybody. The machine is gradually starting to move. Everything is going like clockwork. The Führer praises the superiority of our regime . . . We contain the people within a standardized world view. For that we use cinema, radio and the press, which the Führer described as the most important means of educating the populace. The state should never renounce them. The Führer also praises the good tactics of our journalism.

21 June. Yesterday: the dramatic hour is approaching. A very busy day. A mass of petty details still need to be resolved. So much work my head is splitting . . .

The question of Russia is becoming increasingly dramatic hour by hour . . .

In London they now have a correct understanding in respect of Moscow. They anticipate war any day . . .

The Führer is very pleased with our fanfares. He orders a few things to be added. From the Horst Wessel Anthem.

22 June. The day German troops crossed the border and attacked the USSR. Irrepressibly methodical, Goebbels first describes the day that has passed.

Even though, as he is writing, the world has been shaken by news of the invasion of Russia and new information is coming in from the Eastern Front, he rattles on at length in the diary about this and that: listening to new fanfares; a chat with an actress invited to appear in a new war film; a breakfast in honour of the Italian minister of popular culture, Alessandro Pavolini; a reception he arranged for the Italians in his castle at Schwanenwerder – before moving on to the main topic of the day.

At 3.30 a.m. the offensive will begin. One hundred and sixty fully manned divisions. A 3,000-kilometre-long front. Much debate about the weather. The biggest campaign in the history of the world. The nearer the time for the strike approaches, the faster the Führer's mood improves. That is how it always is with him. He just thaws out. All the weariness in him immediately vanishes. . . .

Our time of preparation is over. He [Hitler] has worked at it since July last year and now the decisive moment has arrived. Everything has been done that possibly could be done. Now everything hangs on the fortunes of war . . .

0300 hours. The artillery thunders.

God's blessing on our guns!

Outside the window on Wilhelmplatz all is quiet and empty. Berlin sleeps; the empire sleeps. I have half an hour to myself but cannot get to sleep. I pace restlessly round the room. I hear the breathing of history.

It is the grand, marvellous moment of the birth of a new empire. Overcoming the pains, it will see the light.

The new fanfare rings out, powerful, resounding, majestic. I proclaim over all the radio stations of Germany the Führer's call to the German people. It is a moment of great solemnity for me too . . .

There are still a few urgent matters. Then I drive to Schwanenwerder. A marvellous sun has risen high in the sky.

The birds are chirping in the garden.

I fall on my bed and sleep for two hours.

A deep, healthy sleep.

Goebbels entered the war, trusting in his belief that 'for the German soldier nothing is impossible,' and in the instinct of the Führer ('Once again the Führer's instinct has proved correct').

Hitler's wretched instinct was the last hope for his entourage in the underground complex of the Reich Chancellery during those fateful days when Berlin was surrounded by Soviet troops and inescapable catastrophe was imminent!

23 June. The Russians are deploying their forces the way the French did in 1870, and will suffer the same disaster. The Russians are currently defending themselves only moderately, but their air force has already suffered terrible losses . . . We will soon deal with them. We must. The mood among the people is slightly disconcerted. The people want peace, not a dishonourable peace, certainly, but every new theatre of military operations brings grief and anxieties.

24 June. There are mixed feelings among the people. The change of direction has been too sudden. The public needs time to get used to it. It will not last long (he notes cynically). Only until the first palpable victories.

'I am holding back on large-scale maps of Russia,' he writes the following day. 'The vast expanses will only frighten our people.'

In Germany, the food situation is very bad, Goebbels notes immediately before the attack on the USSR, and a further reduction in the meat ration is imminent. Italy presents 'a dismal spectacle'.

Everywhere there is a lack of organization and system. They have no system of ration cards, no decent food, and at the same time they have a great appetite for conquests. They want us, as far as possible, to fight the war, and themselves to reap the rewards. Fascism has not yet overcome its internal crisis. It is sick in body and soul. Too much corroded by corruption.

The war is to stifle all the inner contradictions. Military success is their only god. Goebbels himself, and with the Führer's assistance, bans Christian publications for soldiers in the Wehrmacht. 'Right now the soldiers have better things to do than read these wretched tracts . . . This cissy, spineless doctrine could have a very damaging effect on the soldiers.'

The notion of a 'crusade' against the USSR, at least for external consumption, is greatly promoted.

It suits us entirely.

We can make good use of it.

So, forwards! The abundant fields of Ukraine are beckoning.

At the same time:

I will not allow discussion of the economic benefits that will result from the taking of Moscow. Our polemics are conducted exclusively in political terms.

25 June. I think that the war against Moscow will be psychologically, and perhaps militarily, a great success for us . . .

1 July. All countries greatly admire the power of our armed forces.

Finland is now officially entering the war. Sweden allows one German division through ... In Spain there are demonstrations directed against Moscow. Italy intends to send an expeditionary corps and only hopes it will not turn against them themselves. Creation of Europe's anti-Bolshevik front continues.

Turkey is moving ever more firmly to our side.

Mannerheim's group in Finland is ready for action.

Japan should be given a free hand in China so it can be included in our calculations.

Jews in Moldavia are shooting at German soldiers, but Antonescu is carrying out a purge. He is behaving magnificently in this war.

The Hungarians are advancing through the Carpathians. Tarnopol [in western Ukraine] has been occupied. An oil region has fallen almost intact into our hands.

The friends of England are at loggerheads with the Bolsheviks. Disunity in the enemy camp is getting ever more serious. We need to make the fullest possible use of this time. We may even be able to inflame this so much that the enemy's front will begin to wobble. (*28 June*)

This was an idea that, as we will see below, obsessed Hitler to the last.

Everybody was busy deciding when victory would be achieved. If Hitler said four months, voices from all directions were now predicting a victorious conclusion of the war within weeks or even days.

In the diary there is anticipation of imminent triumph. Goebbels' main concern is that that the triumph should not be overshadowed by unrealistic prophesying.

I strongly oppose the Foreign Ministry's foolish predictions of when victory will be achieved. If it is said it will be in four weeks when in fact it takes six, our amazing victory will ultimately be seen as a defeat. The Foreign Ministry is also not sufficiently respecting military secrets. I order the Gestapo to intervene against the loudmouths.

Goebbels instructs the poets to compose a song about the Russian campaign as a matter of urgency, but nothing satisfactory is forthcoming, to his annoyance and indignation. Finally, 'A new song about Russia is ready. The joint work of Anacker, Tieszler and Kolbe. I am now editing and reworking it. After that, it will be unrecognizable,' he writes with his usual complacency. 'A magnificent song.'

'Magnificent', now his standard category, he applies to the newsreel, to which he devotes a lot of attention.

26 June. Its subject matter is war.

30 June. Excellent filming from the East. The montage is breathtaking.

4 July. Every half hour there is more news. These are wild, exciting times. In the evening the newsreel is ready. A full-length piece, gripping music, shots and text. I am now completely satisfied. I managed another half-hour nap on the terrace.

The pace in Berlin is almost breathtaking. During these days I have positively to steal time for myself. But such is the kind of life I have wished for myself, and it truly is splendid.

No matter how Goebbels enthuses about the results of the surprise attack, we detect a new and unexpected tone in his notes. At first he sounds merely puzzled: 'The enemy is fighting well,' he records as early as 24 June (writing, as always, about the previous day).

He ponders how this new circumstance can be turned to advantage.

The Russians defend themselves courageously. There is no retreating. That is good. So much the faster will things go later. They are losing countless numbers of tanks and planes. This is a prerequisite for our victory.

The tone becomes increasingly uneasy: the Southern Front 'is resisting desperately and has a good command. The situation is not dangerous, but we have our hands full.'

The German doctrinaire insistence on the weakness of the Red Army has suffered a setback, and so does Goebbels' psychological state. Like a gambler he grows more arrogant with every win, and wilts and lapses into depression when he loses or encounters adversity. These are only the first days of the war in the east: the notebook ends with 8 July. The Nazi army has yet to experience its first defeats . . . and yet the spectre of failure is clearly haunting these entries:

Strong, desperate resistance by the enemy . . . Army Group South reports that an enemy attempt to break through near Dubnov has been repulsed . . . Desperate attempts at Białystok to break through . . . One red regiment broke through . . . The Russians have suffered enormous losses in tanks and aircraft, but they are still fighting well, and since Sunday have wised up a lot.
(*27 June*)

The Russians are desperately defending themselves. A Russian tank division breaks through our tank positions.

The Russians are resisting more strongly than initially expected. Our losses in people and materiel are significant.
(*1 July*)

He tries to find an explanation for this 'anomaly': 'For now their ally is still Slavic persistence, but that will one day disappear!'

He is buffeted from one conclusion to another, exactly opposite: 'In a single day we again destroy 235 Russian aircraft. If the Russians lose their air force, they are doomed. God willing!' (*2 July*).

But immediately afterwards:

There is altogether very fierce and heavy fighting. There is no question of this being a walkover. The red regime has mobilized the people. To this is added the legendary stubbornness of the Russians. Our soldiers are only just coping. But so far everything is going to plan. The situation is not critical, but serious, and we are going to have to put every effort into it. . . .

In the United States they are becoming increasingly insolent. Knox delivers an impudent speech demanding immediate entry into the war.   (*2 July*)

The functioning of our secret transmitters is a model of cunning and sophistication.   (*5 July*)

Soviet propaganda, however, is causing him grave concern: up till now, German soldiers have never been on the receiving end of enemy propaganda: 'The Bolsheviks are not the English. Moscow has more powerful radio stations.' (*27 June*)

Goebbels is having a lot of trouble in Germany itself, trying strictly to suppress listening-in to foreign broadcasts. With the help of the Führer, he attempts to impose a ban on all Russian writers and composers.

There is no peace among the Nazi leaders themselves. 'Rosenberg is intending to set up his very own little propaganda stall . . . Everyone wants to play at propaganda, and the less they understand it, the more they want to.' Thus ends his temporary alliance with Rosenberg. The more customary atmosphere of intrigue, poisonous jealousy and denunciation resumes.

The war with Russia has not resolved some burning issues, has not brought the expected relief: in the Balkans 'there is a real famine. Especially in Greece. Serious discontent is expressed in Italy. Mussolini is not acting energetically enough. In Romania, support for us has decreased noticeably. Worries wherever you look . . . In France and Belgium there is almost famine. That determines the mood there.'

Worries, wars, and hardships of the German people notwithstanding, nothing gets in the way of his personal wellbeing and enrichment. In addition to the newly built castle in Schwanenwerder, where Goebbels now often resides, a complex of houses at Krumme Lanke, which he also frequents from Berlin, and other country properties, he is also at this time building 'a new Norwegian cabin. It will be in the most idyllic location . . .

Inspected our new blockhouse, which is very pretty. It is located in the forest and adapted for peacetime, which will, of course, come.'

All that needed was a small matter of defeating the Russians: 'We must act quickly, and the operation on the Eastern Front must not go on too long. The Führer will take care of that.'

Goebbels writes, infuriated, at the end of this notebook,

The English are now trying everything they can to exploit this stay of their execution. But it will not, we must hope, be long in coming.

Smolensk is under heavy bombardment. Ever closer to Moscow.

Capitulation! That is the watchword. *(8 July 1941)*

Capitulation

It was the evening of 2 May 1945.

The war had come to Berlin. Capitulation was not a watchword but a lived reality, only not in the sense that Goebbels and Hitler had intended.

Several hours had passed since the Berlin garrison had given up resistance. The dumping of weapons, which had started at 3.00 p.m., was still going on. The square by the Town Hall was piled high with abandoned machine guns, assault and ordinary rifles. In the streets abandoned German artillery pieces had their barrels pointing at the ground. There was a drizzle.

Under the triumphal arch of the Brandenburg Gate, over which the red flag was flying, straggled German units that had been defeated at the Volga, the Dnieper, the Danube, the Vistula and the Oder. Many of the soldiers were wearing helmets that were now an absurdity. They walked by, exhausted, deceived, their faces blackened; some of them crushed and round-shouldered, some with obvious relief, but most in a state of abject depression and apathy.

The fires had not yet been extinguished. Berlin was on fire. A Russian horseman whipped up a horse and his steaming field kitchen bounced its way over the rubble. Our soldiers were resting on a German tank dug into the roadway, sitting on the turret, on its gun, singing, rolling cigarettes. Time for a smoke. In Berlin the battle was over.

Troops under the command of Marshal Zhukov had captured the capital of Germany.

Everything was a mixture in these streets: the happiness of people freed from captivity, the joy of our joining up with the Allies, amazing meetings. Grim-faced columns of German men leaving the city, stumbling off into captivity. The anguish of women watching them go.

The tragic fusion of victory and defeat, triumph and retribution, an end and a beginning.

In Bydgoszcz, long before that day in Berlin, Major Bystrov had confided to me on that memorable evening that he was setting himself the goal of capturing Goebbels. Goebbels and no one less. He spoke to me about it in confidence several times afterwards. I let it go in one ear and out the other. What nonsense! There we were in Poland, and where on Victory Day we, let alone Goebbels, would be was anyone's guess. In the event, on Victory Day we were in Berlin, and found Goebbels in the garden of the Reich Chancellery.

Goebbels had given instructions that after his death he, too, was to be burned to ashes. There was not enough petrol. After dousing Goebbels and his wife, who had also committed suicide, those charged with this duty fled before completing the task. A Gold Party Badge with a single-digit number that had fallen off her burnt dress lay near Magda Goebbels, as well as a gold cigarette case with a portrait of Hitler.

On 2 May, when the Berlin garrison ceased resistance, a surrender of weapons took place in the streets. German soldiers were formed into columns and marched off into captivity. In the Reich Chancellery, however, there was intermittent gunfire from SS soldiers who refused to surrender. It was in the evening of this day that Major Bystrov, along with two other officers, discovered Goebbels. It was almost beyond belief, like much that was to follow in this story.

Goebbels was carried out on the leaf of a door to Wilhelmstrasse in front of the Reich Chancellery. It somehow happened by itself that this became the apotheosis of that day. Berlin had fallen. Its Party regional leader, its commissar for the defence of Berlin, the Reich's Minister of Propaganda, Hitler's right-hand man was dead. Goebbels was still recognizable, so let the victorious warriors and the people of Berlin take a look at him. In the absence that day of Hitler, the charred body of Goebbels symbolized the collapse of the Third Reich.

The street was smoke-filled, the acrid fumes of battle had not yet cleared, the fires were still raging, not yet burned out. The Reich Chancellery building, dented by shells, pitted by shrapnel, its windows gaps with jagged glass, had nevertheless survived mainly intact. The eagle with a swastika in its talons above the main entrance was also intact. Mangled enemy vehicles had crashed into the wall of the Reich Chancellery or were scattered over the ravine of the street.

Few Berliners could get in to see anything. There were small groups of officers and soldiers. There was filming for the newsreels, and

Goebbels was surrounded by a few commanders keen to be in the picture.

I was standing to one side, and from a distance suddenly saw Major Bystrov, standing stock-still, his dark, haggard face almost unrecognizable. Leaning forward, he was staring, transfixed, at the body of Goebbels.

The whole scene, with the blackened body on its platform, in the ragged remnants of its Nazi uniform, with the yellow, noose-like tie which had somehow survived round the bare, black neck, its ends gnawed by fire and now stirring in the wind, seemed like an exhibit from history's chamber of horrors. When I later read that passage in Goebbels' diary where he gleefully records the Führer's approval of his notion of introducing a yellow star to identify Jews, I wondered if there had not been something symbolic about that yellow noose round the neck of its inventor.

Before killing himself, Goebbels slaughtered his own children, closing the circle of murder with poison and fire, the means put to so much use in the concentration camps.

The bulletin read:

On 2 May 1945 at 17.00 hours in the centre of Berlin, a few metres from the entrance to the bomb shelter of the German Reich Chancellery, Lieutenant Colonel Klimenko, Majors Bystrov and Khazin, in the presence of German Berlin residents Wilhelm Lange, chef of the Reich Chancellery, and Karl Schneider, mechanic of the Reich Chancellery garage, discovered the charred bodies of a man and a woman, the body of the man being of low stature, his right foot half bent and shorter than his left, with a charred metal prosthesis, the remnants of a uniform of the Nationalist Socialist Party, a Gold Party Badge, charred . . .

The Walther pistol found beside them had not been fired.

During the long years of the war we had passed through the ruined, burned lands of the Kalinin and Smolensk regions, of Byelorussia and Poland. We had seen Goebbels' propaganda in action: the savage devastation of the land, the death camps, the trenches full of murdered people, the 'new civilization' in which a man was his brother's executioner. The path of the war had brought us to the Reich Chancellery.

Now, many years later, I am sometimes asked, 'Wasn't it frightening to look at those dead bodies?' But that was not what I felt. I shuddered, but I was not frightened, and not only because we had seen so many terrible things in four years of war, but rather because those charred remains did not seem human: they seemed satanic.

But the dead children: that was frightening. Six children: five girls and one boy, exterminated by their parents.

The Smell of Bitter Almonds

'Whose children are these?' Major Bystrov asked Vice Admiral Voss. Bystrov had just brought Voss here, to the underground complex. Voss had been entrusted with the mission of reaching Grand Admiral Dönitz in order to hand him the supreme authority Hitler had bequeathed him, and the order to continue the war at all costs. There was to be no question of capitulation!

Together with the remnants of General Mohnke's group, which had been defending the Reich Chancellery, Voss tried to break through the encirclement in the region of Friedrichstrasse, but was captured. Bystrov drove Vice Admiral Voss through the streets of defeated Berlin. Voss represented the Navy at Hitler's headquarters. Towards them as they drove wandered dejected columns of prisoners.

Voss stared stonily through the car window the whole time. Terrible, smoking ruins. A crowd of Berliners at a camp kitchen where a Russian cook was ladling out hot soup . . . Overturned barricades, over which the car drove before crawling on through narrow alleys carved through streets blocked by fallen masonry, rubble and rubbish.

'Did you know these children?' Major Bystrov asked. Voss nodded in the affirmative and, asking permission, sank wearily into a chair. 'I saw them only yesterday. This one is Heidi,' he said, pointing to the youngest girl. Before coming here he had identified Goebbels and his wife.

Goebbels, with his retinue of journalists, had come on board the cruiser *Prinz Eugen*, commanded by Voss, in the summer of 1942. Voss owed his advancement to Goebbels. Not so long ago, only back in February when the headquarters moved to Berlin, Goebbels, his wife and Voss were invited to a family dinner party by Grand Admiral Dönitz. The conversation was diverse, and concerned the organization of the defence of Berlin. 'We talked about the need to build stronger street fortifications and to draw more young people from the Volkssturm group into defence duties. All these issues were touched on, however, only superficially; in passing, as it were.' They did not allow the intrusion of alarming thoughts to spoil their pleasant evening.

Forced by events down into the underground complex together, they met as old friends, and yesterday, before Voss left with Mohnke's group, Goebbels had said to him in parting, 'Everything is lost for us now.' Magda Goebbels added, 'We are tied here by the children. There is nowhere we can go with them now.'

Major Bystrov and Voss stood together in this dank, dreadful underground room in which the children were lying under their blankets. Voss was shocked, devastated, and sat there hunched. They were silent, each with his own thoughts. That same day Major Bystrov told me about what happened next. Voss, this seemingly completely broken man, suddenly leapt up and started running. Bystrov went after him along the corridor of the dark cellar, fearing he might disappear up a sidestreet and dive into some unknown hiding place. Bystrov caught him, however, and could see this had been an act of complete despair, pointless. Voss had never imagined he could get away.

The children were found in one of the underground rooms by Senior Lieutenant Leonid Ilyin on 3 May. They were lying in bunk beds, the girls in long nightgowns, the boy in pyjamas of light material, just as they had climbed into bed for the last time. Their faces were pink from the action of potassium cyanide. The children seemed alive and only sleeping.

Later, when Leonid Ilyin read these lines, he wrote to me,

I am that same Senior Lieutenant Ilyin. Thank you very much for remembering me . . . There was me, my soldier Sharaburov, Palkin and another soldier whose name I do not know, a Jew by nationality, who we had been given in case we needed an interpreter. At that time we were shooting, being shot at, but fortunately we were all alive. I took a loaded Walther 6.35 mm with a spare clip from a desk drawer in Goebbels' study. There were also two suitcases with documents, two suits and a watch. I have Goebbels' watch to this day. It was given to me as being of no value and I have kept it as a souvenir.

On 3 May, when I had a moment to spare, I wandered round the Reich Chancellery and food stores. Well, now that's all forgotten history . . . Well, that's everything I wanted to write. . . .

But in the room where the poisoned children lay, there was absolutely nothing apart from bedding. I asked through my interpreter why they had poisoned the children. They were not guilty of anything.

In the hospital of the Reich Chancellery there was a doctor among the medical staff, Helmut Kunz, who had been involved in killing the children. He worked in the medical department of the SS in Berlin and on 23 April, when the medical unit was dissolved, was sent to the Reich Chancellery.

He was unshaven and had sunken eyes. He was in SS uniform and spoke jerkily, sighing a lot, clasping and unclasping his hands. He was, perhaps, the only person down there in the complex who had not lost his sensitivity, his jitteriness about everything he had witnessed. He said,

Before dinner on 27 April, at eight or nine o'clock in the evening, I met Goebbels' wife in the corridor by the entrance to Hitler's bunker. She said she wanted to talk to me about a certain very important matter. She immediately added that the situation was now such that she and I would evidently have to kill her children. I gave my consent.

On 1 May he was summoned from the hospital to the Führerbunker by phone.

When I came into the bunker, I found in his study Goebbels himself, his wife and Naumann, the state secretary of the Ministry of Propaganda, talking about something.

I waited at the door of the office for about ten minutes. When Goebbels and Naumann came out, Goebbels' wife invited me into the office and stated that a decision had been taken [to kill the children] because the Führer was dead and that at 8–9 o'clock that evening the units would try to get out of the encirclement, and 'accordingly we must die. There is no other way out for us.'

During our conversation, I suggested to Goebbels' wife that she should send the children to the hospital and transfer them to the care of the Red Cross, but she disagreed with that and said it would be better for them to die.

Some twenty minutes later, while we were talking, Goebbels came back to the study and addressed the following words to me: 'Doctor, I shall be very grateful if you will help my wife put the children to death.'

I suggested to Goebbels, as I had to his wife, that he should send the children to the hospital and place them under the guardianship of the Red Cross, to which he replied: 'It is impossible to do that. They are, after all, the children of Goebbels.'

After that, Goebbels left and I stayed with his wife, who spent about an hour playing patience.

Approximately one hour later, Goebbels again returned with Schach, the deputy Gauleiter of Berlin. Schach, as I understood from their conversation, was to leave with the German Army units attempting to break through. He said goodbye to Goebbels . . .

After Schach left, Goebbels' wife stated, 'Our people are leaving now. The Russians may arrive here at any moment and obstruct us so we need to hurry with resolving this matter.' Goebbels came back to his study, and, together with his wife, I went to their apartment (in the bunker), where Goebbels' wife took a syringe filled with morphine from a cupboard in the front room and handed it to me, after which we went to the children's bedroom. At this time the children were already in bed, but not sleeping.

Goebbels' wife announced to the children, 'Children, do not be frightened. The doctor is going to give you a vaccination which is being given now to children and soldiers.' With these words, she left the room, and I was left alone in the room and proceeded to give the morphine injections. After that I again went into the front room and told Frau Goebbels that we should wait about ten minutes for the children to fall asleep, and at that time I looked at the clock. It was 20.40.

Because Kunz told her that he doubted he had the mental strength to help administer poison to the sleeping children, Magda Goebbels asked him to find Hitler's personal physician, Ludwig Stumpfegger, and send him to her.

When I returned with S. to that room next to the children's bedroom where I had left Goebbels' wife she was not there, and S. went straight to the bedroom. I stayed waiting in the next room. Four or five minutes later S. came out of the children's bedroom with Goebbels' wife and, without saying a word to me, left immediately. Goebbels' wife also said nothing to me, only cried. I went with her down to the lower floor of the bunker to Goebbels' study, where I found the latter in a highly nervous state, pacing up and down the office. Entering the office, his wife stated, 'Everything is finished with the children, now we need to think about ourselves,' to which Goebbels replied, 'Quickly. We have little time.'

Goebbels' wife told Kunz she had been given the morphine and the syringe by Stumpfegger. He did not know where she had obtained the ampoules of poison. She might have been given them by Hitler who, as we later learned, had been issuing them at the end of April.

'Kunz returned to the hospital in a very depressed state,' we were told by Werner Haase, the head of the hospital whom we interrogated after him.

He came into my room, sat on the bed and clutched his head in his hands. When I asked, 'Are Goebbels and his family dead?' he replied, 'Yes.' To my question as to whether he had been alone, Kunz replied, 'I was helped by Dr Stumpfegger.' I was not able to get anything more out of him.

Haase was asked what he knew about how Goebbels and his wife had committed suicide. He replied,

From what I was told by Hitler's first personal doctor, SS Standartenführer Stumpfegger and Dr Kunz, I know that Goebbels and his wife committed suicide on the evening of 1 May by taking a powerful poison. Which precisely I cannot say.

Vice Admiral Voss, Dr Kunz, Lange the cook, Schneider the garage mechanic, Wilhelm Eckold the head bodyguard of Goebbels, Wilhelm

Ziehm, technical administrator of the building of the Reich Chancellery, and many others identified Goebbels.

Although the body was charred, it was readily recognizable by anyone who had met Goebbels or seen him from a distance. He could have been recognized even from the caricatures of him in our Soviet press. He had a very distinctive appearance, his head disproportionately large for his puny body and noticeably squashed at the sides. He had a slanting forehead and his face narrowed markedly to his chin. He limped on his right leg, which was shorter than the left one and intoed. The right leg had not been affected by the fire and retained an orthopaedic boot with a thickened sole and prosthesis.

'On this charred body there are no visible signs of severe, fatal injuries or disease,' a medical report noted some days later. 'When examining the body, a forensic examination revealed the presence of the odour of bitter almonds and fragments of an ampoule were found in the mouth.'

When the chemical analysis results came back a conclusive verdict was given: 'Chemical analysis of the internal organs and blood established the presence of cyanide compounds. The conclusion is thus unavoidable that the death of this unknown man occurred as a result of poisoning with cyanide compounds.'

The same conclusion was reached regarding the cause of death of Magda Goebbels.

Lodging for the Night

Looking for somewhere to stay late in the evening of 3 May, we found ourselves in the Berlin outskirts. As we were walking down a dark, unfamiliar street, I suddenly heard a nightingale.

Now, when I write about it, I find it hard to explain why I found that so surprising. It had seemed that here in Berlin not only all living things, but even the stones of the city had been drawn into the war and were subject to its laws. But then, all of a sudden – a nightingale, in complete disregard of everything, was irrepressibly getting on with what nightingales get on with. After everything that had happened here, the call of the nightingale in this hushed Berlin street was an amazing reaffirmation that life goes on.

We went into a building and climbed dark stairs. We knocked and, feeling fairly awkward, went into the home of people who had just lived through the disaster of the capitulation of their city. It was a modest apartment. Its owners, an elderly couple in quilted dressing gowns, alarmed by our unexpected arrival, put two rooms at our disposal, but evidently had difficulty for a long time in getting back to sleep themselves: we heard their quiet footsteps in the corridor. I lay down on a divan, and was immersed in the stifling smell of mothballs and laurel leaves, which I had quite forgotten during the war. Four years . . . When the war began, I was studying literature at university.

There was no curtain on the window, and through it I could see pink sky, lit by the glow of the subsiding fires. After all the days of incessant fighting, the stillness was a blessing, but so unwonted it chilled your heart. Through the strain of those days, the thought that we were in Berlin kept breaking through and banishing sleep.

It was fairly light. A deer's antlers protruded from the wall opposite. There were freshly cut flowers in a vase on the table. Using a pocket torch, I read a framed saying on the wall: '*Der Himmel bewahre uns vor Regen und Wind, und vor Kameraden, die keine sind.*' May heaven protect us from wind and from rain, and from friends who are false and bring nothing but pain.

The wall was covered with photographs of a boy: here he was clambering onto a rocking horse, here lying on the beach, his head resting on the outstretched legs of a girl in a striped bathing costume. Here he was, already a soldier, standing in a new, well fitting uniform and holding a heavy combat helmet. Here he was in the group photo of a cheery bunch of soldiers. In the centre of the photo was a bottle. Someone had put a helmet on his bayonet. The caption was, '*Prosit!*' Your health!

And on the desk, under the glass top, was the sad announcement that Kurt Bremer was missing without trace on the Eastern Front.

In search of water, I wandered into the kitchen. Our hostess was sitting by the window. On her knees she had a bag of socks she had begun to darn in Hitler's Germany, and now, making do with the faint light of the dawning day, she was getting on with a job she was used to. Beer mugs lined the kitchen shelf, and at the head of the parade was a familiar porcelain lady holding out a gilded slipper and inviting someone to drink out of it.

I asked the mistress of the house whose shop it was downstairs – we had noticed it in the night as we were climbing up to the apartment – and whether it had been boarded up for a long time. She replied that it was a dry-salter's shop that she and her husband owned, and that they had closed it two months ago. 'We made a success of it by honest toil. It wasn't at all easy for us. And now, you see . . .' She sighed quietly. '*Das Geschäft macht keinen Spaß mehr.*' Business is no fun any more.

In the morning the owner of the apartment asked me whether I thought he would be able to go to a particular street today to see his dentist. I assured him I thought he would. War was one thing, but a toothache was not to be neglected. He told me that actually he did not have a toothache, but two weeks ago had made an appointment for a check-up today. Although he was not in pain, the fall of the capital of the Third Reich could hardly justify missing a dentist's appointment. He had an indomitable sense of the need to maintain equilibrium and good order, no matter what the rest of the world might get up to.

Through the window we could see the traffic at the crossroads being directed by a girl we knew. Wielding her flags, she allowed cars to pass, while simultaneously finding the time for a quick salute; she stopped service personnel who had helped themselves to Berliners' bicycles for getting around and took them off them. The commander of the front had given orders that bicycles were not to be confiscated from the townspeople. A whole mountain of misappropriated bicycles had accumulated near her on the pavement.

A soldier pushed a paint tin out of the front door opposite. He dipped a thick brush with a short handle in it, squatted down on his heels, and obliterated the enormous letters of one of Goebbels' injunctions painted in the roadway: '*Berlin bleibt deutsch.*' Berlin will remain German.

Nothing for Sure – The Petrol Canisters

It is early morning on 4 July 1945 and a rosy mist is rising over Alexanderplatz. It is chilly. In the middle of the square is what looks like a gypsy encampment: the remnants of the defeated Berlin garrison. They are sleeping in the roadway, swathed in army blankets. The wounded are sleeping on stretchers. One or two are already sitting up, huddled with a blanket covering their heads. Nurses wearing dark jackets and white headscarves are making the rounds of the wounded.

Captive soldiers are also sleeping in Unter den Linden, the street used for parades. The buildings on either side of the street are in ruins. There are yawning gaps in walls from which masonry is still falling. A cart laden with bundles of possessions clatters over the cobbles, doggedly pushed along by two women who must have come back to Berlin from the countryside. The racket invades the stupefaction of ruins and debris.

We are back in the Reich Chancellery. Who were the last people to see Hitler? Who saw him here at all, alive in the underground complex? What is known about what has happened to him?

Karl Friedrich Wilhelm Schneider, the garage mechanic who told us yesterday about sending petrol to Hitler's bunker, testifies: 'Whether Hitler was in Berlin at all until 1 May I have no idea. Personally, I did not see him here.' On 1 May, however, in the Chancellery garage he heard from Hitler's chauffeur, Erich Kempka, and from the person in charge of the garage that

Hitler had committed suicide. 'The news went round by word of mouth. Everyone was repeating it but no one really knew for sure.'

A fifty-year old man introduces himself officially as Wilhelm Lange, chef of the Führer's domestic commissariat in the Reich Chancellery and a specialist pastry cook. He tells us, 'I last saw Hitler at the beginning of April 1945 in the garden of the Reich Chancellery, where he was taking a walk with his German sheepdog which answered to the name of Blondi.'

What do you know about the fate of Hitler?

Nothing for sure. In the evening of 30 April, Hitler's dog handler, Sergeant Major Tornow, came to me in the kitchen for food for the puppies. He was upset about something and told me, 'The Führer is dead and nothing remains of his body.' There were rumours among the Reich Chancellery staff that Hitler had poisoned or shot himself and that his body had been burnt. I do not know whether or not that was true.

The technical administrator of the Reich Chancellery, Wilhelm Ziehm, tells us,

The last time I saw Hitler was at 12 noon on 29 April. I was summoned to the Führer's bunker to fix a malfunctioning ventilator. While doing the job I saw Hitler through the open door of his office.

What do you know about the fate of Hitler?

On 30 April 30 at 6 o'clock Wernicke, a plumber, and Gunner, an electrician, told us when they returned from work at the Führer's bunker that they had heard Hitler was dead. They gave no more details.

Vice Admiral Hans-Erich Voss attended meetings in the bomb shelter at which Hitler was present. He learned of Hitler's death from Goebbels. That is all we had found out by the morning of 4 May.

'Nothing for sure,' as Lange the chef had said, and even this information had to be extricated from an accumulation of other contradictory, sensational misinformation. The things that were being said! That Hitler had been flown out on a plane piloted by Hanna Reitsch three days before Berlin fell; that his 'death' had been staged, and the broadcast announcement about it was a ruse; that Hitler had been spirited away from Berlin through underground passages and was hiding in his 'impregnable' stronghold in South Tyrol.

People who were in possession of more modest, but crucial, information were so traumatized by everything they had experienced that they muddled up dates and facts, even though what they were recollecting had happened only two or three days previously. First here, then there alternative stories bubbled up and burst, each more sensational than the last. Rumours circulated that Hitler had had doubles.

To exclude these speculations definitively, one after another, took time. The search was being conducted at a furious pace: it was easy to race off on the wrong track and come to false conclusions. Complications, sometimes ridiculous, hampered the search. In Berlin, in those first days of May 1945, under very difficult conditions, it was essential to coordinate the efforts of the intelligence agents and sort through everything methodically and swiftly, to block off all the false trails and target the searching. That task was entrusted to Colonel Vasiliy Gorbushin.[1]

Again and again, metre by metre, we painstakingly examined the empty underground complex beneath the Reich Chancellery. There were overturned tables, broken typewriters, glass and paper underfoot; box-rooms and more substantial rooms, long corridors and crossings. There was damage to the concrete walls and, here and there in the corridors, pools of water. Damp, dank air. The ventilators had not worked well even when Hitler was there and now were not working at all. It was difficult to breathe and it was murky . . . Round every corner something seemed to be rustling or moving, or there was a silence you felt might at any moment be broken by gunfire from some desperate Nazi officer.

The crunching of boots on broken glass, echoing gasps from soldiers who had stormed the Reich Chancellery and now, prowling through the last residence of the German government, were coming upon crates of expensive liqueurs. They were calling out to each other as if finding their way through a forest, their torches lighting up the theatrical setting of the last hours of the Third Reich. Sometimes we heard the click of safety catches and a menacing 'Khende khokh', '*Hände hoch!*' in a heavy Russian accent, directed into the darkness where the sound of our footsteps was coming from.

It was a difficult, unpredictable situation. Above us, on the surface of Berlin, the war was over, but down here, underground, the search continued in the chaos. Our searching was tireless; we were completely focused, conscious of a tremendous responsibility, the culmination of four years of warfare. We had to find our bearings in what was, at first, the thoroughly confusing topography of the underground complex, to discover hiding places and check them. The hunt was on to find Hitler.

General Krebs had already been found, lying in the courtyard in a grey-green tunic with the epaulettes torn off. He had poisoned himself too. But as

---

1. The 'head of a SMERSH operational group': Birstein, p. 305.

to the whereabouts of Hitler, we still had 'nothing for sure'. If we proceeded from the testimony of Vice Admiral Voss, who had been told about Hitler's death by Goebbels (to whom Hitler had bequeathed the authority of Reich Chancellor); if we accepted the hypothesis of Schneider, the garage mechanic, as to what his petrol had been needed for; the missing link in the chain was someone who had actually taken part in burning the bodies, or had seen how and where it happened, or had at least heard about it in detail.

The garden of the Reich Chancellery, which subsequently was found to have been the setting for this drama, was so churned up that it was hardly going to be possible to determine where the cremation had taken place. Meanwhile, rumours abounded. Somebody had been told by somebody else that Hitler had been reduced to ashes and that Axmann, the Reichsführer of the Hitler Youth, who had participated in the Mohnke group's attempt to break out, had made off with the ashes. Axmann, at that time, had given us the slip.

If Hitler had been totally incinerated, that would confirm what dog-handler Tornow had told Lange the chef: 'The Führer is dead and nothing remains of his body.' If that was so, if there were no remains or they were never going to be found, we would never be able to show the world irrefutable evidence he was dead. Hitler's disappearance would remain a mystery and provide fertile soil for all manner of myths, something in which only his adherents could have an interest.

The information we had was now collated. We were looking for people who could clarify what had happened. Meanwhile, more and more people came trampling through the Chancellery, soldiers and commanders, staff officers and people who had flown in from Moscow, and journalists we needed to steer well clear of. They wandered through the apartments in the Reich Chancellery, came down into the underground complex looking for Hitler's rooms. As a token of their encounter with history, they carried off with them this and that as a souvenir. Everybody wanted to be here, everybody had a right to be here. Really, though, this was no time for tourists.

We were searching: in the complex, in the garden, in the building above ground, and in nearby stretches of the street. On the morning of 4 May, I had a quiet, domesticated and completely civilian man sitting in front of me, a little stoker nobody in the Reich Chancellery had noticed. As a technician, he had been sent to the Führer's bunker to mend the malfunctioning ventilator.

He had already told us that, while he was in the corridor, he had seen the bodies of the Führer and Eva Braun being taken out of Hitler's rooms, wrapped in grey blankets. She was wearing a black dress. He was not trying to persuade us of anything, just telling what he had seen. In a chorus of louder, more assertive voices the ring of truth was somehow missing. The stoker himself was so unassuming, so humble, that it was difficult to believe he could have any role to play in events of this magnitude. Vice Admiral Voss seemed far better suited to the role, only he had no direct evidence to give.

The stoker was the first German from whom I heard about Hitler's wedding. At the time, in a Berlin where the fighting and the fires had barely died down, it struck me as ridiculous beyond belief. I looked again at the humble, ordinary man who was matter-of-factly thinking through the bizarre scenes he had witnessed in the last three or four days, as if they were something from an infinitely remote past. The truth was that we had moved not just from one day to the next, but out of one epoch and into another.

I have forgotten the stoker's name. He juts out of the tome of history, an anonymous bookmark pointing us to the right page. Incredulous, inattentive, we had not taken the time to read it carefully.

Helmut Kunz, the doctor of the medical department of the SS in Berlin, was feverishly agitated. He could not get over what he had experienced. He had ended up in the Reich Chancellery almost by accident and was traumatized by his complicity in the murdering of children. The first day, everything he said revolved only around that fact. On 4 May, however, he sighed, gave a start and, mixing up the dates, began chaotically recalling the details of the last few days.

He confirmed that Hitler and Eva Braun had married by remembering he had been present when Braun told Professor Haase, the director of the Chancellery hospital, that Goebbels' children addressed her that day, as they always did, as '*Tante Braun*', Auntie Braun, and she had corrected them to 'Auntie Hitler'.

Then he remembered he had been sitting in the evening in the casino above the Führer's bunker in the company of Professor Haase, Frau Junge and Frau Christian, two of Hitler's secretaries. Eva Braun had come in and the four of them went to one of the rooms in the casino where they were served coffee. Eva told them the Führer had written a will, which had been sent out of Berlin, that he was waiting for confirmation that it had been delivered to its destination, and only then would he die. She said, 'Everybody has betrayed us, even Göring and Himmler.' She added, 'Dying will not be so difficult, because we have already tested the poison on the dog.' Dr Kunz was adamant that this conversation in the casino had taken place on the evening of 30 April, whereas, according to other sources, Hitler was already dead by then.

We were encountering conflicting accounts every step of the way, but there was one almost casual remark Kunz made that we could not ignore. He said that Goebbels' wife, telling him about Hitler's suicide, did not add anything definite about how he had done it but, 'There were rumours,' Dr Kunz told us, 'that his body was to be cremated in the garden of the Reich Chancellery.'

'Who exactly did you hear that from?' Colonel Gorbushin asked. 'I heard it from Rattenhuber, the SS Obergruppenführer responsible for security at the Führer's headquarters. He said, "The Führer has left us alone, and now we have to drag his body upstairs."'

On that day, 4 May, we had no more authoritative testimony than this information from the head of Hitler's bodyguard, communicated to us by Dr Kunz.

Documents Found Inside and Outside the Führerbunker

I am snowed under with documents. There are reports from locations where there is fighting, orders issued by the command post of Mohnke's brigade, which was defending the Reich Chancellery, radio-telegrams.

In Goebbels' rooms we find in two suitcases, besides his diaries, several screenplays sent to him by their authors; and a huge album, an anniversary gift from Nazi Party comrades for his fortieth birthday. It contains sheets of photographs, reproducing page after page of Goebbels' manuscript *The Little ABC of the National Socialist*.

It was difficult to work in the underground complex itself, where the electricity supply failed periodically, and I spent many hours analysing documents in one of the halls of the Reich Chancellery. It was the reception hall where people waited for Hitler to appear, I think, or some other. I am not sure exactly. (I had trouble working out the layout of the Reich Chancellery.) Everything seemed to have been overturned. Perhaps this was where the SS security guards had made their last stand; also, the army had passed this way, and had no reason to respect the furnishings in the grand rooms of the headquarters of Nazism.

Tables had been knocked over, glass lampshades smashed, chairs had been overturned and their seats ripped open. Everywhere were shards of glass from the windows. I still remember the special floor of this room, entirely covered by a velvety grey velour, now trampled and torn by Red Army boots. The reconnaissance squads were bringing in sackfuls of documents and dumping them on that special flooring.

In Goebbels' rooms we also found several files in a suitcase that contained Magda Goebbels' personal papers. What did she bring with her when she moved to the underground complex on 22 April from her house on Göringstrasse? There were inventories of the furnishings in the country house in Lanke, and in the castle in Schwanenwerder, which had been built by the time of the war with the Soviet Union. Everything was listed: fittings, cabinets with silver, dinner services and figurines. Nothing was overlooked: every ashtray, every cushion in the innumerable rooms, every last handkerchief of Dr Goebbels and its place in the linen cupboard, every toilet paper holder. And so from one room to the next, in the main building and the outbuildings: bedrooms, offices, children's and adjutants' bedrooms, guest rooms, halls, vestibules, stairs, corridors, terraces, servants' rooms, and cinemas. An inventory of Goebbels' wardrobe. Eighty-seven bottles of assorted wines.

There were bills detailing the cost of furnishing the castle, about which Goebbels writes enthusiastically in his diary, and sundry department store bills going back as far as 1939 and addressed to Magda Goebbels. Inventories of the children's clothing, individually for each one of them. All their dresses, coats, hats, shoes, ski suits and underwear are listed. Items that are new, and items handed down from the eldest daughter to the second in seniority, from the second to the third, and so on. And items that, for the present, were being held in reserve. A certificate awarded to her as a participant in the Olympic Games, signed by the Führer.

There was also a paper, sent to Magda Goebbels, stamped with the seal of the National Socialist German Workers' Party and signed by one of the Party leaders of the Berlin district. It contained the forecasts of a fortune-teller. He predicted in April 1942 there would be a parachute landing of Allied forces on the coast of France in early June 1942 and that fierce battles would follow. These would be at their fiercest in August 1944. In mid-June of that year, the prophecy continued, the Germans would use a new aerial weapon which would cause untold destruction, especially in England. This would lead to domestic political difficulties in Britain that would hamper the further advance of the Allies.

Fierce fighting against the invading troops would last from August until November 1944, but in early November the Allies would suffer their greatest defeat in the entire war. In April 1945, Germany would be ready to redirect all its strike force to the Eastern Front, and after fifteen months Russia would finally be conquered by Germany. Communism would be eradicated, the Jews driven out, and Russia would break down into smaller states.

In summer 1946, German submarines would be equipped with a new and terrifying weapon with the aid of which, in the course of August 1946, the remnants of the British and American fleets would be destroyed.

On one of the folders Magda Goebbels had written '*Harald als Gefangener*'. Harald as a prisoner. This refers to her eldest son, from her first marriage. Four years before Goebbels had written in his diary, 'Magda is extremely happy about the award for Harald, which can be considered a done deed' (*14 June 1941*). The file contains everything relating to him since the moment he was captured. The first sheet relates the circumstances of his capture. They are being described by a non-commissioned officer reporting to his commander. The report was forwarded to Dr Goebbels. His stepson was last seen during fighting in an African village. Then there is a letter written by Harald from his American captivity. He writes that he is being well treated. There are photographs. Harald in front of flower beds. Greetings on 'German Mothers' Day'.

This all provided atmosphere, pictures of events, but no direct clues as to what had happened to Hitler.

The Bormann folder contained an important document, a radio-telegram Bormann had sent from the Reich Chancellery shelter to his adjutant.[1]

22 April 45.
To Hummel. Obersalzberg.
  Proposed relocation overseas and south agreed.
    Reichsleiter Bormann

What did that mean?

Bormann was evidently preparing a hideaway for himself far beyond the borders of Germany. And here is how matters stood beyond the borders of his diary, which I also found was in the archive. If I had had Martin Bormann's notebook-cum-diary in front of me then, I would have read the following in the last entries:

Sunday 29 April.

A second day begins with a hurricane of gunfire. During the night of 28 April the foreign press reported Himmler's offer of surrender. Marriage of Adolf Hitler and Eva Braun. The Führer dictates his political and personal will.

The traitors Jodl, Himmler and the generals have abandoned us to the Bolsheviks!

Again a hurricane of gunfire!

1. Bormann's radio-telegrams to Munich and Obersalzberg were filed in the Council of Ministers Archive folder No. 151.

According to an enemy report, the Americans have burst into Munich! . . .
30 April 45.
    Adolf Hitler ⅄
    Eva H. ⅄

Next to their names Bormann had drawn an inverted runic cross, an emblem of death.

If we had been able to read that at the time, we would have had important confirmation that Hitler had died on 30 April, but we did not have sight of the diary. It was found in the street by reconnaissance agents of our neighbouring army and we did not get to see it. Admittedly, the peculiar circumstances in which the diary was found would probably not have allowed us then, at the preliminary stage of inspecting it, to trust it uncritically: it could have been a forgery, planted for us to find. Now, however, we can say with complete confidence that this is the genuine diary of Martin Bormann, which he dropped while trying to break through the ring of Soviet troops as a member of Mohnke's group, probably when he was fatally injured.[1]

The diary, although recording events at quite a different level, is absurdly similar to the diaries of the very stupidest German front-line soldiers, which in turn are closely similar to each other. The similarity is no sign of democratic ways but of the monstrous uniformity of thinking that Hitler counted on and Nazism cultivated.

A Long Day

Although the Reich Chancellery was only 550 metres or so from the Reichstag, it was in the zone allocated to our neighbouring 5th Assault Army, which captured it. We were not allowed to cross that dividing line, but the fighting was over and everything was a muddle. Absolutely anybody who got the chance came rushing into our army's zone, which contained the Reichstag, in order to record, 'I was here,' to sightsee, to write their name on the Reichstag, to go inside. That was true, first and foremost, of our neighbours in the 5th Army.

Certain officers in our army proved shrewder and decided to trespass on our neighbour's territory, the Reich Chancellery. I was one of them. I left my name on the Reichstag only three days later.

I actually did manage to tear myself away from the documents for a short while, and walk round the city in the company of our driver, Sergey, and

---

1. Bormann evidently poisoned himself during the escape attempt in order to avoid capture. Tr.

171

several officers. We stood at the Brandenburg Gate through which German troops had triumphantly marched when they returned from Warsaw, Brussels and Paris. Nearby, on a square piled with broken bricks, burnt metal and charred, overturned trees, the grey building of the Reichstag, not yet cool after the fire, was still smoking. Above it, above the skeleton of its dome, a red banner fluttered high in the overcast sky.

Skirting shell craters and piles of rubble, we reached the Reichstag. We climbed the pitted steps, inspected the soot-blackened pillars, stood for a while by the walls and looked at each other. A soldier was sitting asleep on the steps, leaning his bandaged head against a pillar and with a forage cap pulled over his face. A moustachioed guardsman with a bedroll over his shoulder was pensively rolling a cigarette. The large windows of the lower floor of the Reichstag were firmly boarded up with wooden panels, which were covered from top to bottom with graffiti. Sergey took out a pencil stub and, under someone's sweeping inscription of 'Where are you, dearest friend? We are in Berlin, visiting Hitler,' scrawled in a shaky hand, 'Hello to all Siberians!' After him, too emotional to speak, I added my greetings to all Muscovites.

We went inside. Our soldiers were wandering around, battered folders of documents were strewn about and there was a smell of burning. The Reichstag's documents were being used as cigarette paper.

Then we walked on through the city. The pavements were almost deserted. On pillars we saw the proclamation of the commander of the 1st Byelorussian Front to the civilian population of Berlin and the province of Brandenburg: 'At the present time no government exists in Germany . . .' In places, groups of residents were clearing the rubble, passing each other a brick at a time. Soldiers with red armbands on their sleeves were pasting up the order of the Soviet commandant of the city. A wooden arch was erected in honour of Victory in Berlin. It had a large red star set in the middle of it, and the flags of the Allies flanking it.

Vehicles were making their way through gaps where collapsed masonry had been cleared. The girls directing traffic, wearing white gloves specially issued to mark our arrival in the German capital, were energetically, tirelessly spinning round on their traffic police pedestals and enlivening Berlin's crossroads.

Looking at them brought a lump to my throat. I remembered how very recently they had been standing in foot wrappings with rifles over their shoulders, carrying out their duties on roads at the front, chilled to the marrow, hoarse, insistent. (Just try ignoring the orders of such a girl: before you knew it she would be firing that rifle at your axles.)

The infantry marched by, holding up the traffic, the metal heel plates of their heavy boots clattering on the roadway. Their banner was being carried in its cover behind the unit's commander.

Berliners stopped to read the commandant's orders and note down the food ration.

We crossed a bridge over the Spree, skirting an upside-down German truck that had inscribed on its side, 'All our wheels are turning for the war.' A woman was sitting on the bridge, her head thrown back, her legs stretched out straight in front of her, laughing her head off. I greeted her. She looked at me with unfocused, transparent eyes, nodded back in greeting, as though recognizing me, and shouted out in a guttural, crazy, voice, *'Alles kaput!'*

On 3 May 1945, a highly detailed report was compiled titled *Certificate of identification of the German Reich Minister Dr Josef Goebbels, the wife of Goebbels, and of six children.* More than ten people were involved in drawing up this document and signing it. These were people involved in the discovery, from the army's reconnaissance section, from Smersh, the political section of the corps, the medical service, and the Germans who identified the bodies. The discovery of the bodies of Goebbels and his family was made very public, which seemed only natural. On that day nobody in charge thought differently. Journalists, photographers and newsreel reporters were allowed to record everything.

In the first days of victory, people experienced what they believed was a dawning of freedom. They acted rationally and normally, but found they had been deluding themselves. They were immediately pulled up. Stalin was outraged that people had taken the initiative to make this event so public and somebody evidently got a flea in his ear. From the following day a screen of strict secrecy went up round the search for Hitler. There was to be no contact with the press or photographers, and all reports were to go directly to Stalin, bypassing the Army command.

In the first edition of my book *Berlin, May 1945*, my conscience prompted me to warn the reader that when it was described in writing, the search for Hitler would inevitably be presented as going more smoothly than it did in reality. The purposeful development of my narrative, moving from fact to fact, was bound to give the impression of a more rational, orderly and down-to-earth process than was warranted.

At that time I titled one chapter 'Without Mystification', but in fact there was no shortage of mystification, and it was very much of our own, Soviet, making. The German part of the plot was the situation surrounding the death of Hitler, while the Soviet part of the plot was woven from the customary insistence on keeping everyone and everything completely in the dark.

It was an exaggeration I was obliged to make to suggest that we were carrying out a mission we had been set. The reader would, however, have found the reality just too implausible, because in fact no mission was ever formulated. Although, actually, I was not deviating too far from the truth, because there was a mission, the final mission of the war, and it was there to be felt in the very air of Berlin. Those who were conscious of it, the 'grassroots', took the initiative themselves.

Then and there, in the first days of May 1945, in difficult conditions and with no halfway trustworthy information to go by, the mission of leading the search for Hitler was assumed in our 3rd Shock Army by Colonel Vasiliy Gorbushin. There was a need to unify the efforts of the intelligence personnel, quickly get to the bottom of everything, cut through all the nonsensical rumours and complete the task.

The search was completed in a very short period, three days of incredibly intense, dedicated effort. The electricity supply was cut, which meant there was no telling where anything was and, as if that were not enough, there was the labyrinthine geography of the shelter to cope with. Our task was to make sense of the documents found there: the official and personal papers of Hitler, Bormann and others.

We had plenty of luck, but complications, sometimes absurd, were never far away. Let me tell you about one of them. In the Reich Chancellery garden there was a dried up pond where ornamental fish used to swim but in which, during the battle for Berlin, the bodies were dumped of those killed in the bombing and shelling, or shot in the garden on Hitler's orders.

On 3 May a group of generals from the 1st Byelorussian Front head-quarters were passing through the Chancellery garden. One or other of them decided one of the bodies looked like Hitler. It was immediately pulled out of the pond and Germans were called to identify it. Their unanimous verdict was, 'Not the Führer.'

It was resolved, however, to await the arrival of a former member of staff of the Soviet embassy in Berlin who had seen Hitler before the war several times and was due to fly in from Moscow. Accordingly, a gentleman with a little moustache and his hair falling to one side of his face and wearing a pair of darned socks duly reposed for a considerable time in the vestibule of the Reich Chancellery, then in the hall, until the diplomat finally arrived and confirmed: 'Not Hitler.' Newsreel and photojournalists had meanwhile been having a field day photographing and filming the body and, proudly labelling it 'Hitler', later depositing their handiwork in the archive and the historical film library. No member of the press was allowed anywhere near the actual remains and they were not photographed.

Unsurprisingly, the false Hitler was later blithely spliced into a Soviet documentary film but, under pressure from an agitated foreign press, he was disavowed and the film withdrawn. The posthumous adventures of this unknown man did not end there, however. He spawned a whole constellation of 'doubles' whereas, in reality, Hitler never had any. Neither was the screen life of the false Hitler over. Thirty years after the ill-fated film he was again resurrected from the archive by journalists and the photo was shown on television, masquerading as the body of Hitler.

The falsehood was immediately exposed, not wholly without my involvement. For a day I was receiving phone calls from newspapers and television stations of various countries asking what they should make of the incident. A French television company urgently interviewed me in time for the evening news. The makers of the television programme responsible for all this nonsense hit back, saying on television that they had been misled by the archivists. That is how it ended that time. No doubt there will be a next time.

From the very outset, the decision to classify the discovery of Hitler's body laid the foundation for all manner of speculation that continues to this day. No attempt was made to combat it by the simple expedient of telling the truth.

What Actually Happened?

Let us return to the Reich Chancellery while the search was in progress in May 1945, with that unidentified body reposing in the great hall. A unit of our army, 79th Corps, was leaving Berlin for a new deployment and a Smersh group who had already been involved in the search went with their commander, Lieutenant Colonel Klimenko, purely out of curiosity, to take a last look at the Chancellery garden and the place where Goebbels had been found. As Klimenko later wrote to me, that was near the emergency exit from Hitler's bunker.

Now chance took a hand. Private Ivan Churakov's attention was drawn to a bomb crater three metres or so to the left of that door. The soil in it was loose and seemed to have been thrown in recently. The soldier jumped down into the crater and, from the ground which had settled under his weight, something became visible. They dug down and found the black, charred bodies of a man and a woman. They pulled them out of the crater and took a good look at them. They did not recognize the man as Hitler, and indeed he was completely unrecognizable. The analogy with the charred body of Goebbels did not occur to them, and they did not look more closely at their find. The main thing that threw them off the scent was that Klimenko had heard Hitler's body had already been found and was lying in the Reich Chancellery. That dead German in the darned socks hoodwinked them. The men filled in the crater again and left.

So the bodies of Hitler and Eva Braun were in fact discovered on 4 May, but it was not realized what they were. 'I did not report finding these bodies to anyone,' Ivan Klimenko wrote to me in one of his letters (of 9 February 1965), responding later to my questions. That could have turned out to be a fatal mistake, but fortunately the information percolated through the same day. We already had enough facts to understand whom the soldiers had dug up. Colonel Gorbushin insisted that those who had made the discovery be brought back.

In that same letter, Klimenko tells me that when he returned to his Smersh unit, he himself 'began to wonder whether those bodies we had reburied were the bodies of Hitler and Eva Braun'. This seemed all the more likely because, before leaving the Reich Chancellery, he had gone to look at the other 'Hitler' and learned he had been identified as 'not the Führer'.

Klimenko sent the soldiers back to the Reich Chancellery under the command of his deputy, Captain Deryabin. The names of those who found the bodies are immortalized in a document drawn up the following day.

Berlin. Army on active service.
Declaration
This fifth day of the month of May 1945.

I, Senior Guards Lieutenant Alexey Alexandrovich Panasov, and Privates Ivan Dmitrievich Churakov, Yevgeny Stepanovich Oleynik and Ilia Yefremovich Seroukh in Berlin, in the area of Hitler's Reich Chancellery, near the place where the bodies of Goebbels and his wife were discovered, next to Hitler's personal bomb shelter, found and recovered two bodies, one female, the other male.

The bodies are badly burned, and it is not possible to identify them without further information.

The bodies were situated in a bomb crater three metres from the entrance to Hitler's shelter and covered with a layer of earth.

Senior Guards Lieutenant (Panasov)
Private Churakov
Private Oleynik
Private Seroukh[1]

1. File 126: Identification records, vol. 2

The ground in the crater was dug over and two dead dogs found, a sheepdog and a puppy.

A further declaration was drawn up:

We have found and recovered two slaughtered dogs.

Dogs' characteristics:

1. German sheepdog (female) with dark grey fur, of large stature, having round its neck a collar in the form of a fine chain. No injuries or blood found on the body.
2. Of small stature (male), with black fur, without a collar, no injuries, bone of the upper half of the mouth punctured, blood in that area.

The bodies of the dogs were in a bomb crater 1.5 m apart under a light covering of earth.

There are grounds to believe that the killing of the dogs occurred 5–6 days ago, since there is no bad smell from the bodies and the fur is not becoming detached.

For the purpose of discovering items that might serve to confirm to whom these dogs belonged and the causes of their death, we carefully dug over and examined the soil at the place from where the bodies of the dogs were recovered. Here there were discovered:

1. Two dark-coloured glass tubes for medicine.
2. Sundry burnt sheets from typographically printed books and small scraps of paper with original handwriting.
3. A metal medallion of elliptical shape on a fine chain of beads 18–20 cm long, on the reverse side of which is an engraved inscription: 'May I be always by your side.'
4. German currency amounting to 600 marks in notes of 100 marks.
5. A metal tag of elliptical form [with the number] 31907

The bodies of the dogs and the items discovered at the place of discovery and recovery have been photographed and are stored at the Smersh counter-intelligence department of the corps, as witness the present Declaration.

> Captain Deryabin
> Senior Guards Lieutenant Panasov
> Sergeant Tsibochkin
> Privates Alabudin, Kirillov, Korshak, Gulyaev.

The dogs were readily identified. The sheepdog was 'Hitler's personal dog', as was written in another declaration. It was 'tall, with long ears'.[1]

---

1. Report of the forensic medical examination, in the same folder (File 126, vol. 2), 7 May 1945. Report of the forensic medical examination of the body of the German Führer.

It was light and windy. In the garden near the emergency exit of the bunker the soldiers stood in a circle: Churakov, Oleynik, Seroukh, Senior Lieutenant Panasov.

The wind was tugging at bits of burnt tin, wire, broken branches strewn around on the lawn.

On a grey blanket, contorted by fire, lay black, hideous human remains caked with lumps of mud.

I was there to witness that.

Without Mystification – Predictions

As dawn broke on 6 May, two bodies were heaved over the fence of the Reich Chancellery garden into a waiting truck and driven off.

That is the low cunning to which we were obliged to resort. The problem was that the 5th Assault Army, whose commander, General Berzarin, was the commandant of Berlin, was restoring order and clearing the Reich Chancellery and underground complex of all the people who had been flooding in. Sentries were posted at the entrance with orders to admit no one.

For us there was an added complication. For the intelligence services of the 5th Assault Army it remains to this day a source of enduring intolerable irritation that such a notable success was achieved on their patch not by them but by gatecrashers from our 3rd Shock Army. We were not about to leave our spoils in the hands of anybody else, abandoning the project before we had seen it through to a conclusion ourselves. So that was the ploy we resorted to: kidnapping the bodies of Hitler and Eva Braun, wrapped in sheets and, behind the backs of the sentries, spiriting them over the fence to where a truck with two large crates was waiting.

So began the posthumous adventures of Hitler's body. We had sifted through all the details of his last days to establish everything that had happened, and had confirmation and the evidence that Hitler and Eva Braun had been hastily concealed in a bomb crater.

Back then, in May 1945, we managed to codify a great deal, to compare and understand facts and get a sense of the atmosphere surrounding the events. Twenty years later, going through the Council of Ministers archival materials that preserved the details of the last days of the Third Reich, I had an opportunity again to scrutinize those events and form a more complete picture. To this day new materials and documents are coming my way. Ultimately, Hitler succeeded in concealing nothing: neither his plans, his personal degradation, nor his death.

Into Bormann's diary, into his routine registering of meetings with the Führer, receptions, the removal of some from senior positions and their replacement by others, suppers with Eva Braun, his receipt of decorations, various domestic matters, there suddenly bursts, menacingly displacing everything else, information about Soviet army groups attacking from all sides. In January the tone is still relaxed: 'In the morning the Bolsheviks went on the offensive,' and just before that we read, 'Went with my wife and children to Reichenhall to inspect the mushroom farm (champignons) of the gardener Vollmark.'

The next day:

Sunday, 14 January. Visit to Aunt Häsken . . .

Saturday, 20 January. Noon. Situation in the east becoming more and more threatening. We have left Warthegau Province. The enemy's front tank units are at Katowice . . .

Saturday, 3 February. In the morning, severe air raid on Berlin. (Damage from the bombing included the new Reich Chancellery, the hallway of Hitler's apartment, the dining room, winter garden and Party Chancellery.)

Fighting for the fords on the Oder.

The bombing has damaged the façade of the Party Chancellery.

The bombing of Dresden, the enemy advance on Weimar, an air raid on Berlin.

Second bombing of the Party Chancellery (severe).

The Russians at Köslin and Schlawe.

All this is still interspersed with the chronicling of social and political life. With every passing day, however, Bormann notes feverishly how the circle is closing in:

Deep breakthroughs in Pomerania. Tanks at Kolberg, Schlawe-Dramburg. Only one bridgehead remaining in the west. *(4 March)*

The English have entered Cologne.

The Russians are in Altdamm!!! *(8 March)*

First direct hit on the Ministry of Propaganda. *(14 March)*

Tanks in Warburg-Giessen. *(28 March)*

Guderian was dismissed, and Hitler removed Dr Dietrich from his post as Press Chief. Meanwhile,

In the afternoon tanks are at Beverungen. By night there are tanks at Herzfeld. *(March 30)*

Russian tanks at Wiener Neustadt. *(1 April)*

The Bolsheviks are at Vienna.

The Anglo-Americans are in the Thuringia region.   (*5 April*)

For three days in mid-April the same phrase explodes in Bormann's diary:

Major battles on the Oder!
Major battles on the Oder!
Major battles on the Oder!!

In February the massive fortifications on the Oder had been considered impregnable. There remained just a little more than two months before the total collapse of the Third Reich. On 24 February, celebrating the anniversary of the founding of the Nazi Party, Hitler declared,

Twenty-five years ago I proclaimed the coming victory of the movement! Today, imbued with faith in our people, I predict the ultimate victory of the German Reich!

German military experts had four weeks previously come to the conclusion that all prospect of that had gone. The Führer's predictions were buttressed, however, by Himmler's decree establishing special field courts to combat signs of failing morale. Germans suspected of insufficiently firm faith in victory faced swift, merciless retribution.

By this time Hitler himself was thinking not of victory but of salvation, pinning his faith on a miracle and, more realistically, on a falling out between the Allies. In his diary Goebbels quotes the Führer's view, expressed to him in confidence:

Our task at present is to stay standing no matter what happens. Although the crisis in the enemy camp is growing considerably, the question is whether the explosion will come while we are still at all capable of defending ourselves. That is the prerequisite for a successful conclusion of the war: the crisis must blow up the enemy camp before we are destroyed.   (*5 March 1945*)

However, Soviet troops broke through the front in Pomerania. Hitler put the blame for this on the General Staff for failing to take account of his intuitive foresight. To suppress the 'creeping disobedience' of the generals, Hitler hastily established mobile field courts, charging them with investigating all cases immediately, passing sentence, and shooting generals found guilty.

On 11 March Hitler listened with satisfaction to Goebbels' report that Colonel General Schörner, one of the few the Führer still trusted, had employed 'radical methods'. 'To raise the morale of the troops', he had hanged a considerable number of German soldiers. 'This is a good lesson that everyone will pay attention to,' Goebbels wrote in his diary, delighted by the Führer's approval. Hitler had just received a report that one of the new field courts had sentenced to death a general responsible for a bridge not being blown up, and that the general had been shot without delay.

'That at least is a ray of light,' Goebbels exclaims in his diary. 'It is only by such measures that we can save the Reich.'

On the evening of 27 March, Hitler and Goebbels take a walk in the garden of the Reich Chancellery. In Goebbels' words, 'The garden of the Reich Chancellery looks desolate. There are piles and piles of debris. The Führer's bunker is being reinforced.' They regret having missed the moment when they could have dealt with the generals by directing the blow against them rather than against Röhm, if he had not been 'a homosexual and anarchist'.

And if Röhm had had a first-rate personality without vice then, probably, on 30 June [1934] several hundred generals would have been shot instead of several hundred SA leaders.

A second call-up to the Volkssturm militia was announced and sixteen-year-olds were conscripted into the Wehrmacht. Women's battalions were formed in Berlin. 'We should place them in the second rank, then the men would lose their desire to retreat from the first rank,' Goebbels muses in his diary on 5 March.

Trains with men on leave were combed for deserters. On 7 March an order was issued that soldiers taken captive without being wounded or in the absence of evidence that they fought to the last moment, would be executed and their relatives arrested.

Massive daily air raids on Berlin by Anglo-American aircraft. (Göring, the commander-in-chief of the Luftwaffe, had assured Germans that no enemy aircraft would ever cross the border into Germany.) War from the air, with which Hitler had planned to subjugate London, Moscow and Leningrad, had come with all its mercilessness into the skies above Germany.

On 8 March 1945, Goebbels writes in his diary,

We are being bombed night and day. The damage is very severe . . . We have nothing worth mentioning to oppose the enemy's air armadas. The air war has turned the Reich into piles of rubble.

Transport was disrupted, the electricity supply was disrupted. Berlin was ablaze with fires. The postal service was no longer operating and delivery of coal was increasingly erratic. The supply of fuel had been reduced.

The food ration in Germany was catastrophically lowered, condemning the population to starvation. In mid-March, the Armaments Minister, Albert Speer, considered the war lost because the German economy could only last another four weeks.

'The problem of foreign workers is going to cause us major difficulties,' we read in the diary of the commissioner for the defence of Berlin, Josef Goebbels.

We must try to retain these workers for as long, at least, as the industry of Berlin is capable of functioning. Over and above that, we want, even if Berlin were to be encircled, for industry, at least the arms industry, to continue to operate. On the other hand, the capital of the Reich has about 100,000 workers from the east [*Ostarbeiter*]. If they fall into the hands of the Soviets, we will find within three or four days that they are fighting us as a combative Bolshevik infantry. Needless to say, we must try if necessary to isolate at least the eastern workers as quickly as possible. (*20 March*)

Hitler had promised that the outcome of this war would be the enrichment of the people of Germany, unheard-of territorial gains and world domination, but monstrous crimes had not brought victory. Everything was in ruins. A defeat was imminent that would wipe Hitler and his criminal accomplices from the face of the earth, but before that happened, Hitler would turn with murderous hatred on the German people for disappointing his hopes.

On 19 March he ordered a scorched earth policy, this time on German soil: all military, industrial, transport and communications sites and facilities, and all Germany's material resources were to be destroyed to prevent them falling into the hands of the enemy. The population was to be evacuated (but where to?). Cities taken by the enemy were to be devastated and destroyed. That the German people would thereby be deprived of their means of subsistence was of no consequence. Hitler formulated his attitude to this issue in an order he gave to Speer:

There is no need to take into consideration what the people need for a primitive continuation of life. On the contrary, it is better for us to destroy all this ourselves because the German people have shown their weakness . . . After a defeat, only inferior people remain.

In 1941, after experiencing the nightmarish December retreat from the gates of Moscow, Hitler told Goebbels that,

if he [Hitler] were to show a moment's weakness, the front would turn into a landslide and a catastrophe would be imminent that would put that suffered by Napoleon completely in the shade.

182

Paradoxically, the Führer now found the dismal scenes of the German retreat from Moscow inspiring. They fed an illusion that a mortal threat would cause an upsurge of national fervour among the Germans and, at the critical moment, when German troops were defending the capital of the Third Reich, just as their enemy had when defending Moscow, they would bring about a turning point in the war.

Goebbels, instantly picking up on the direction in which the Führer's thoughts and wishes were moving, was already describing the defence of Moscow as 'an encouraging example'.

In his diary at this time we periodically find his traditional exaltation of the Führer. In part, this rhetoric is the autosuggestion Goebbels needs in order not to fall prey to doubts about Hitler's ability to alter the course of events. 'I am amazed how firmly the Führer is taking charge.' But even the obsequious Goebbels allowed himself to criticize Hitler in his diary. At one time this is in connection with his orders: 'We issue orders in Berlin which in reality do not go down the chain of command at all, quite apart from the question of whether they could possibly be carried out.' Another time he complained that in this time of crisis Hitler cannot bring himself to make an appeal to the people on the radio. 'The Führer has now a fear of the microphone I find completely incomprehensible.' He goes on filling up the pages, one utterance cancelling out another, neutralizing it; one moment extolling Hitler, the next complaining about his lack of decisiveness.

Goebbels is dictating his diary, and has two full-time shorthand-typists employed at the Ministry of Propaganda for just that purpose. Every day he is dictating thirty, forty, fifty or more pathologically prolix pages.

Meanwhile, 'Near Berlin the Soviets have begun what is admittedly only a local, but extremely powerful, offensive' (*23 March*). The people are losing faith in the Führer and, more generally, losing hope. 'The situation is intolerable.' It has become known from a United Press report that the entire gold reserve of Germany and its art treasures (including the bust of Nefertiti) have fallen into the hands of the Americans in Thuringia. 'If I were the Führer, I would know what needs to be done now . . . There is no strong hand . . .' But what can be done? 'I always insisted that the gold and the art treasures should not be evacuated from Berlin.' On 8 April an unsuccessful attempt had been made to transfer them back from Thuringia to the capital, which Goebbels, the commissioner for the defence of Berlin, wholly irrationally supposed to be the most suitable safe place for them.

'We live in such a lunatic time that human reason is completely unhinged,' Goebbels dictates on 2 April. He, however, is the prime example of that, his reason long ago unhinged, completely subordinate to Hitler, atrophied, replaced by faith in the Führer.

'Sometimes one wonders desperately where all this is going to lead.' Goebbels, however, reassures himself: everything is in the hands of the Führer. 'I trust he will master this situation' (*8 April*).

In Goebbels' mind the outcome of the war depends ultimately less on the actual situation than on whether the Führer will manage by an effort of will to overcome everything and, like a *deus ex machina*, manifest himself an instant before catastrophe strikes.

The Führer believes . . . that this year, one way or another, there will be a turning point in the course of the war. The enemy coalition will fall apart, no matter what happens. The only question is whether it will fall apart before we are felled . . .

The situation is getting ever more trying.

The position on the fronts is like never before. We have all but lost Vienna. The enemy has made deep breakthroughs in Königsberg. The Anglo-Americans are stationed close to Brunswick and Bremen. In a nutshell, if you look at the map it is clear that the Reich is today reduced to a narrow strip.   (*9 April*)

In the concrete bunker under the Reich Chancellery, where Hitler was waiting for events to turn in his favour, Goebbels read to him and retold pages from the biography of Frederick the Great. Hitler had put considerable effort into encouraging his compatriots to see him as having a spiritual affinity with this successful king of Prussia. He had a portrait of Frederick hanging on the wall in his bunker. Now they had a further affinity through the military adversity the king had faced. At the point in the book where Frederick is facing defeat in the Seven Years War and has decided to end his life, the book's author cries out to him, 'Wait yet a little, and the days of your torments will be behind you. The sun of your good fortune is already there behind the clouds, and soon will shine upon you.' The timely arrival of news of the death of his enemy, the Russian Empress Elizabeth, brings the king deliverance from humiliating defeat.

Hitler was greatly moved and decided he would like to consult his horoscopes, which Goebbels had been holding back for several days for just this eventuality. It is curious to go back and open Goebbels' diary at the place where he is recording with exultant derision that all astrologers, mesmerists and anthroposophists have been arrested and an end put to their charlatan practices. 'How amazing, not a single fortune-teller foresaw he was going to be arrested. Not much of an advertisement for the profession . . .' (*13 June 1941*). Everything was being rationalized. Only the predictions of one person in the Reich, the Führer, were to be available to the people. In order to avoid inconsistencies, mistaken interpretations, duplication, unfavourable prophecies or, ultimately, competition, all other fortune-tellers were to be hounded mercilessly.

But that was then, on the threshold of a war with Russia which was predicted to be victorious. Now anything hinting at last-minute salvation was more than welcome.

'I have been presented with voluminous material for astrological or spiritualist propaganda, including the so-called horoscope cast for the German Republic on 9 November 1918, as well as one for the Führer. Both horoscopes correspond remarkably to the truth,' we now read in Goebbels' diary on 30 March 1945.

I can understand the Führer forbidding the performance of such phenomena outside our control. Nevertheless, it is interesting that both the Weimar Republic's horoscope and the Führer's horoscope predict an easing of our military situation in the second half of April . . . For me such astrological predictions hold no significance, but I still intend to use them for anonymous and covert propaganda, because at a critical time like this most people will clutch at any straw, however insubstantial, if it promises salvation.

Predictions offering hope were so prized that they were forwarded through Party channels to the wife of Reich Minister Goebbels, which suggests that his 'anonymous and covert' propaganda was taking off. Horoscopes were becoming convincing. In Goebbels' Berlin apartment our agents found the horoscope of his little son, Helmut, and brought it to me.

But then, the two most important horoscopes, which until recently had been kept by Himmler under lock and key in the 'scientific' department of the Gestapo, the Führer's horoscope and the horoscope of the German Republic which Hitler had called for, were brought to the bunker. With the assistance of his Reich Minister of Propaganda, Hitler was able to see for himself that both horoscopes promised military success in the second half of April 1945, after severe defeats early in the month.

A few days after this, late at night on 12 April, the news was received that President Roosevelt had died. How could that not be a portent, a historical analogy? How could it not be a turning point in Germany's destiny? 'At this moment in time, when destiny has removed from the Earth the worst war criminal of all time, the war will turn in our favour!' Such was the exclamation with which Hitler concluded his orders to the troops. In it he spoke of the new offensive by the Red Army.

We foresaw this blow, and since January of this year everything has been done to create a strong front. The enemy is being met with powerful artillery. The losses of our infantry are being replenished with countless new divisions. Amalgamated subdivisions, new formations and the Volkssturm consolidate our front. This time it is the Bolshevik who will experience the ancient destiny of Asia: he must bleed to death, and will, in front of the capital of the Reich.

This order from Hitler, dated 16 April, began to arrive at the headquarters of the troops on the evening of 15 April, and was to be sent immediately all the way down to company level.

Look out first and foremost for those few traitors, officers and soldiers who, to protect their miserable lives, will fight against us in the pay of Russians, perhaps even in German uniform. If you are ordered to retreat by someone you do not know well, he must be immediately arrested and, if necessary, rendered harmless, irrespective of his rank.

Berlin will remain German, Vienna will again be German . . .

A day later the order was published in the *Völkischer Beobachter* and other newspapers.

From the bomb shelter Goebbels spoke on the radio:

The Führer has said that this year our fortunes will change and success will again attend us . . . True genius can always foretell and predict when change is imminent. The Führer knows the exact time this will happen. Destiny has sent this man to us so that we in this time of great outer and internal ordeals may be witness to a miracle . . .

Because It's All Over

On 16 April the Red Army began its offensive. The Oder defensive line was considered impregnable by the German high command. It was here, at the Oder, they firmly believed, that the advance of the Red Army would be repulsed.

Until quite recently Hitler had been intending to institute a reorganization of the army. The itch to reorganize gave Goebbels too no rest. In his ministry he was busying himself that April with projects to reform the press and radio departments ('They need to become more flexible'), changing the staffing arrangements to ensure that the influential press chief, Dietrich, who, at Goebbels relentless insistence, had finally been sent off by Hitler 'on leave', would not be able to return to his old position for the simple reason that it would no longer be there; and thinking through harsh measures against Berlin's arts elite and 'superintellectuals'.

Career and status considerations continued to predominate among the top Nazi leaders. Sometimes this strikes even Goebbels as weird, especially if it concerns a rival.

Reich Minister Rosenberg is still opposing the dissolution of the Eastern Ministry. He is no longer calling it the Ministry of the Occupied Eastern Territories, because that would be seen as grotesque, but the 'Ministry of the East'. He wants to concentrate all our eastern policy in this ministry. I could with no less justification establish a western or southern ministry. It is complete nonsense, but Rosenberg is defending his status and refuses to accept that his ministry has long since failed.

The breakthrough of the fortifications on the Oder caused panic in Hitler's headquarters. The Berlin bureaucracy fled: the Autobahn from Berlin to Munich was choked with their motor cars and nicknamed by the Berliners the 'Reich Refugee Autobahn'. Nobody gave a second thought to the Berliners themselves.

The rumours were insistently repeated that a 'new secret weapon' would come into service on the Führer's birthday. The mass psychosis of expecting a miracle spread to all sections of the population. Someone claimed to have seen vehicles shrouded with tarpaulins, concealing the secret weapon from prying eyes. People fantasized and tried to guess its destructive power.[1] Everyone was waiting for an announcement on the radio.

On 20 April, however, the Führer's birthday, the radio was silent during the day, and silent at night, too, when shells were heard exploding as the long-range artillery of our 3rd Shock Army began firing on Berlin. The following day shells were exploding in the streets of the city. Berliners hiding in their basements could not understand why the radio had not warned them of the danger by sounding a siren.

There was neither a siren nor any announcement from the German high command when Red Army troops entered the outskirts of Berlin and the Battle of Berlin began.

After the breakthrough on the Oder, Hitler and his Headquarters prepared to move to his residence in Berchtesgaden (Obersalzberg). Orders were given to prepare to fly out.

Bormann notes in his diary:

Friday, 20 April. The Führer's birthday, but the mood, unfortunately, is anything but festive. The advance team is ordered to fly out.

1. During the Nuremberg Trials Albert Speer confirmed that Germany was considerably behind in atomic energy. 'We would have needed another one or two years to split the atom.'

In Bormann's papers, which I was going through in the now deserted underground complex and which I was next to see in the Council of Ministers Archive, there are radio-telegrams to his adjutant, Helmut von Hummel, with instructions to prepare accommodation in Berchtesgaden. On 21 April Hummel responded with his plan for locating services and departments, already partly implemented, and a request to approve it. Certain services had been moved to Berchtesgaden, as had part of Hitler's archive, one of his secretaries, and his personal doctor, Theodor Morell. (Hitler had long been unable to get by without strong stimulants and Morell was constantly by his side.)

Everything was ready for the final flight but, on 21 April, the day Soviet troops entered the outskirts of Berlin and artillery fire reached the city centre, Hitler ordered a counter-attack. On 22 April, at a regular meeting with the army, Hitler heard from the generals that his counter-attack, under the command of SS General Felix Steiner, had not taken place and that Berlin could not be expected to hold out for long. Accordingly, he should leave the capital in order to allow the troops to retreat. This was all the more necessary because it made no sense for Hitler, as the commander-in-chief, to remain encircled in Berlin. It would no longer be possible for him to command the armies from there.

Hitler's reaction was fury, hysterics, shrieking about treason and a threat to commit suicide. He halted the meeting and ordered that he should be put through on the telephone to Goebbels.

What happened then is described by Hitler's SS adjutant, Otto Günsche: 'After a few minutes Goebbels hobbled in. He was extremely agitated.' Goebbels was conducted to the Führer's office, where they talked. When Goebbels left the office, the generals and Bormann rushed to him. He said the Führer was in a state of collapse. He had never seen him in such a condition. He added, 'how frightened he was when the Führer, in a cracking voice, told him over the telephone that he should immediately move with his wife and children to the bunker with him because it was all over.'

Later, when Jodl was arrested by the Allies, he told them under interrogation,

On 22 April Goebbels asked me whether it was possible to prevent the fall of Berlin by military means. I replied that it was possible, but only if we took all our troops from the Elbe and threw them into defending Berlin. On the advice of Goebbels, I reported my views to the Führer, he agreed and instructed Keitel and me, together with headquarters, to leave Berlin and personally lead the counter-attack.

To leave the Western Front open and withdraw all forces from there to defend Berlin was now Hitler's decision. General Wenck's Twelfth Army was ordered to fight its way through to aid Berlin.

Throughout 22 April the airwaves were heavy with radio-telegrams from Bormann to Hummel. Initially there are feverish orders to prepare for the Führer's arrival in Berchtesgaden. By the end of the day, however, everything is reduced to a request in a telegram that survives in Bormann's file:

22 April 45.
From Berlin.
To Hummel, Obersalzberg.
Send immediately with today's planes as much mineral water, vegetables and apple juice as possible, and my mail.
Reichsleiter Bormann

The evacuation by air never happened. Anglo-American troops had reached Munich, which was near Berchtesgaden. Hitler could not bring himself to flee from defeated Berlin only to become a played-out pawn in the hands of the Anglo-Americans.

On 21 April Hitler had withdrawn German troops from the Elbe, opening the road to Berlin to the Americans, but they were still far away. In order to set back the hour of his death, he gave orders to blow up the barriers on the canal and flood the underground railway, which assault detachments of the Red Army, rapidly advancing towards the government district, had entered. Hitler gave that appalling order in the full knowledge that thousands of his compatriots would die as the water poured in: the wounded, women and children who had taken refuge in the underground tunnels.

His intention to remain in Berlin was seen by the generals as confirming his inability to continue to command the army.

Rumours

Berlin was abandoned by the High Command of the German Armed Forces: Grand Admiral Dönitz; Field Marshal Keitel, Chief of Staff of the High Command; Colonel General Jodl, chief of the operations staff of the High Command; and Air Force General Koller. They and their headquarters staffs departed in search of a more secure base and there was subsequently almost no contact with them.

The infantry and tank divisions of the Red Army rapidly surrounded Berlin. In heavy fighting they flattened one belt of the German defences after another and the troops rushed towards the city centre. Russian artillery shells were reaching the Reich Chancellery, and it was only the heavy concrete of his bunker that saved Hitler after a direct hit. The Chancellery's radio mast collapsed and its underground cable was damaged.

A month after the fall of Berlin, Hitler's secretary, Gertraud Junge, described those days: 'Hitler was certain the Red Army knew where he was, and he was expecting Red Army units to storm his refuge at any moment.'

No reports from the army commanders on the course of the fighting were now being received. The radio link with Obersalzberg was unreliable. It was periodically lost completely, then briefly restored. News of the fate of German cities and the situation in Berlin came mainly from Allied journalists reporting over the radio from locations where there was fighting. Rumours, each more desperate than the last, seeped down from the streets into the underground complex.

In spring 1941, as Goebbels was hatching his conspiracy against humanity, he flooded the world with rumours to sow panic, fear and despair. With diabolical glee he wrote in his diary that he was doing it 'in the name of havoc'. 'Rumours are our daily bread,' he had written then. Now the epicentre of the earthquake had moved, and was directly underneath the Reich Chancellery.

In the *Berliner Frontblatt* Goebbels urged soldiers and the Berliners not to listen to rumours. 'Rumours are used by the enemy as a weapon to paralyse our resistance and undermine our confidence. That is why at times like this we must stick only to the facts.'

At this same time, Hitler's own headquarters was reduced to extrapolating facts from the rumours on which the reports to Bormann from the local Nazi leaders were based. They found their way into his radio-telegram folder which I was analysing in the Reich Chancellery. Twenty years later, I copied detailed extracts from these reports in the archive,[1] which reflected the situation in Berlin in the days immediately before capitulation.

Reinickendorf–Wedding reports: the Borsigwalde subdistrict picked up a rumour a few hours ago that the US government has resigned. Ribbentrop is said to have flown to America, presumably for negotiations. Troops are thought to be being withdrawn from the West in order to reinforce the Eastern Front.

Other rumours:

There are Russians in basements from Gallich Boulevard to Graf von Redern Allee.

---

1. Council of Ministers Archive, folder 151.

Three vehicles: one with Russian officers, one with private soldiers, the third with an unidentified load paused in Heiligensee near the anti-aircraft gunners' barracks before driving off in the direction of Velten. The Russians talked to the local people and reportedly told them everyone should immediately take cover in basements because heavy artillery would shortly be firing. Then they shared cigarettes with the residents and told the German girls they could go out without fear because nobody would do anything to them.

It is impossible to verify these rumours since Heiligensee is in the hands of the Russians. 22 April 45. 20.00 hours.

The facts were even more dismaying than the rumours. They were contained in such communications as:

Report of Police President Gerum
22 April 45 / 14.15 hrs
Köpenick is currently wholly occupied by the enemy. The enemy is rushing across the Spree in the direction of Adlershof.

Or in messages which, more colourfully, were reporting the same thing, namely, districts that had fallen.

Wilmersdorf District, Zehlendorf.
Sector E reports:
From there a phone call was made on official business to the shelter in Struveshof. A Russian came to the telephone and demanded schnapps. The official at the shelter only managed to shout, 'The Russians are here!' 22 April 45. 06.00 hrs

Soviet tanks. Fires. A barrage of enemy artillery fire. Captured streets. People killed and injured. A lack of armaments. A request for artillery support . . . The reports of the Nazi Party district leaders characterize the hopelessness of those fighting in the streets of Berlin and the disasters experienced by the Berliners.

The leader of another district reported that the enemy had advanced along Schönhauser Allee as far as Stargarderstrasse and that there was no possibility of offering resistance in that area. He asked:

Question: what provision is there for food for the populace? People are no longer coming out of their basements, have no water and cannot cook anything.

Similar reports must have found their way to Goebbels as commissioner for the defence of Berlin and head of the Nazi Party in Berlin, but they fell on deaf ears. No notice was taken of them. In his diary there is not a shred of evidence, not a hint or word written there that would enable us to conclude that, in those days of calamity for the German people, the authors of all their misfortunes gave a moment's thought to what their nation was now going through, or felt in the least bit answerable to them.

'I and history', 'My historic mission', 'I have assumed responsibility for my people': these were words the Germans heard constantly from Hitler. 'The Führer is Germany,' Nazi propaganda drummed into their heads, using every conceivable means to bamboozle the people as it created a cult of Hitler. They were insistently told: 'The Führer does your thinking: yours is only to carry out his orders.' On 23 April, while still in Poznań, I heard on Berlin radio, 'The Führer is in the capital and calls on soldiers to defend themselves more steadfastly.'

That same day, this brief appeal appeared in the German newspapers: the last public statement by the Führer, signed on 22 April.

Remember:
Everyone who advocates, or even merely approves of, orders that weaken our resolve is a traitor! He should immediately be shot or hanged!
That applies also to orders allegedly originating from a Gauleiter, the Minister Dr Goebbels, or even in the name of the Führer.
Adolf Hitler

As the situation deteriorated, only these words, scorched by hatred, remained in Hitler's vocabulary, calling for reprisals: 'Traitor!' 'Shoot!' 'Hang!' Instant, merciless retribution awaited any German suspected of being insufficiently fanatical and imbued with blind faith in the victory of the German Army.

Goebbels' speech that day contained a summons to all soldiers, to the wounded, to the entire male population of Berlin immediately to join the ranks of the defenders of the city. He declared that anyone who failed to respond to this appeal and did not immediately go to the assembly point, at the Berlin Commissioner's Office on Johannistrasse near the Friedrichstrasse station, was a despicable swine.

Here, next to the station, and in other busy places, Nazis carried out executions to intimidate the public. I myself was confronted by the sight of a hanged German soldier in Berlin when we had just entered the city.

The commander of the SS Adolf Hitler Lifeguard Regiment, Lieutenant General Mohnke, also called on 'the men of Berlin' to join the 'Mohnke Volunteer Corps', invoking their fanaticism, 'indomitable will' and fearlessness as 'decent lads'. He, too, listed assembly points. Appeals, appeals . . . threats, executions, abuse, flattery. Assembly points . . . And all the while the scale of the disaster was escalating beyond all bounds. The city had been abandoned to its fate by the regime. No evacuation was organized. Not even the children were taken out of Berlin, which was left without bread or water.

Even at a time like this, the district leaders' reports to Bormann contain the customary spats reflecting a struggle for influence within the Nazi Party. Here is an example. Kreisleiter Koch, reporting the rapid advance of the Russians, lists areas captured, and concludes this section, 'In Friedrichsfelde the Ivans broke through to the south as far as Bielefeld.' He then moves on to another matter:

The hostile attitude of Commandant Colonel Glausen is having a very negative impact. Every notification I forward to him through my head of the local Party group he treats as trivial or absurd.

When I pointed out to him that military units had been withdrawn last night and this morning and that hundreds of soldiers had been making their way along abandoned streets to the west, he told me that they probably had all the necessary orders to do so. He assured me that Captain Baur had for a period of two hours checked their documents and had supposedly ascertained in every case that the units had orders to withdraw.

Shortly after this conversation, he gleefully telephoned to tell me with great sarcasm that last night at Friedrichshagen a Volkssturm company, without making any contact with the enemy, had gone off home. He wanted to draw my attention to the fact that under no circumstances could I allow myself to conceal this fact from higher authority. He tries to denigrate everything. Every conversation I have with him, he concludes by saying, '*Auf Wiedersehen*' [rather than the officially required, '*Heil Hitler!*']. The intonation of this greeting makes distinctly and unequivocally clear that he is glad no longer to have to obey me. From every sentence he utters it is plain that he wishes to see the Party removed.

Berlin. 22 April 1945. 13.15 hrs.

Thousands of Germans were doomed to die senselessly: soldiers and members of the Volkssturm in street fighting that could have only one outcome; the people of Berlin from shells and bombs, buried under collapsing buildings. Hitler sat in his underground complex surrounded by his immediate entourage: Eva Braun; Constanze Manziarly, who cooked the Führer's vegetarian meals; Josef Goebbels, who all his life put up with Hitler's gripes and complaints; and Martin Bormann, whom Goebbels had described in his diary on 14 June 1941, as a 'behind-the-scenes operator' hated even by the Nazi Party elite. 'Everyone who knew him found him disgusting,' Rattenhuber writes. 'He was an exceptionally brutal, sly, uncouth and selfish individual.' Bormann sat in a corner, drinking brandy and recording Hitler's every word 'for history'. What is striking is how eager the whole lot of them were to barge their way into history by fair means or foul.

Just one phrase was recalled by absolutely everybody who saw Hitler in those last days: 'What happened? What was the calibre?' These were the words with which he invariably appeared in his office doorway after the latest explosion.

When generals made it to the shelter from places where there was fighting, they found Hitler at his desk, hovering over a map with buttons on it that supposedly represented German troops. He was placing arrows on the map to indicate counter-attacks. Reporting a defeat, or that an army that existed only in Hitler's imagination had been destroyed, could cost the messenger his life. Hitler was unaware of the true state of affairs and did not want to know it. Every report of a defeat sent him into a frenzy, accusing the generals of treason and mercilessly sending them to be shot.

If the meeting went off more satisfactorily, a commander who had made his way there in the hope of getting advice or orders, was assured that a miracle was on its way and that Wenck's army was hastening to Berlin. After being awarded a medal, he would be conducted upstairs and sent back into battle.

Learning that the 56th Tank Corps, commanded by General Helmuth Weidling, had suffered a defeat and retreated from Küstrin, an infuriated Hitler ordered Weidling to be shot. When, answering the summons, he appeared in the bunker, Hitler, not understanding who was in front of him, began explaining his defence plan to the general. A major role in this fantasy was to be played by Wenck's army (which was impossible because it was surrounded by Soviet troops), and also by the corps of Weidling himself, of which there remained only a few bedraggled units no longer capable of combat. Weidling departed, expecting to be executed, but was called back and, on the whim of a tyrant, appointed commander of the defence of Berlin. In Weidling's own words, this was, under the circumstances, tantamount to a death sentence. 'It would have been better if he had shot me,' Weidling remarked as he came out of the Führer's office. He was only too aware of the hopelessness of the situation.

'His contradictory and neurotic orders completed the disorientation of the already befuddled German High Command,' Rattenhuber writes.

Rattenhuber relates that in earlier years Hitler liked to produce a dramatic effect by suddenly turning up in an active service army. His presence was usually brief. After talking to the commanders, he would show himself to the troops and immediately return to base. Rattenhuber accompanied Hitler when he took Mussolini along on a longer trip to the Eastern Front in 1941, to Brest and Uman. In Brest Hitler strutted triumphantly through the ruined fortress. That, however, was before the first painful counter-attacks.

A succession of defeats and failures on the Eastern Front, the collapse of his military and political plans, which was particularly obvious with the defeat of the German army at Stalingrad, knocked Hitler sideways and he stopped going out among the troops.

After the attempt on his life on 20 July 1944 at his headquarters in East Prussia,

Hitler became fearful and mistrustful and his innate hysteria began to progress. Now, he was literally a physical wreck. His face was a fixed mask of fear and dismay. He had the flickering eyes of a maniac. His voice was barely audible, his head shook, he was unsteady on his feet and his hands were shaking.

Treason

On 25 April the ring of encirclement closed around Berlin. That same day, Soviet and American infantrymen greeted each other at the River Elbe. Outside the walls of the Reich Chancellery people, deceived by Hitler, were being killed. In the underground complex, pinning their hopes on an imminent miracle, a couple of horoscopes and the Führer's intuition, his entourage lived in an atmosphere of intrigues, upheavals and upsets, for which there was plenty of fuel.

The news of the treason of Göring, who had left Berlin and was attempting to negotiate a separate peace with the British and Americans, eclipsed everything else that was happening on the planet for those still in the complex. On 25 April, Göring sent Hitler a message stating that, in accordance with the Führer's decree of 20 July 1941 appointing Göring his successor, and supposing that Hitler, surrounded in Berlin, lacked means of communication and was no longer able to act, he was assuming total authority in order to work 'in the interests of Germany and the German people'. The letter concluded with assurances of unconditional loyalty.

Rattenhuber, who was present at this scene, recalls,

[Hitler's] whole face became contorted. He was totally dismayed, and only after taking himself in hand, literally shrieked, 'Hermann Göring has betrayed me and the Fatherland . . . Against my instructions he has fled to Berchtesgaden and established contact with the enemy, presenting me with an insolent ultimatum that if by 9 hours 30 minutes I do not telegraph him a reply, he will take my decision to be positive.

Goebbels took up Hitler's accusations: 'Göring was always a traitor in his heart; he never understood anything, constantly did stupid things, and has ruined Germany.' Hitler ordered Bormann to arrange for the traitor to be arrested. The order was radioed to the head of Göring's bodyguard, who acted on it.

Hitler ordered his adjutant, Julius Schaub, to burn his personal papers that remained in Munich and Berchtesgaden. Schaub managed to leave in the second-last plane to take off from Gatow aerodrome.

Bormann wrote in his diary, 'Wednesday 25 April. Göring has been expelled from the Party! First massive offensive against Obersalzberg. Berlin is surrounded!'

People were well aware of the kind of person Göring, the Reich's 'second-in-command' and the only Reich marshal in German history, really was. Hans Rattenhuber, who combined the post of head of Hitler's bodyguard with the post of chief of the security service, knew everything about Hitler's comrades-in-arms that there was to know. 'I have nothing more to achieve in life: my family is provided for,' Rattenhuber quotes Göring as having said in autumn 1944. He writes of how greedily Göring enriched himself, using his power for outright theft, first in Germany itself, later in Italy, then in occupied countries. He was in charge of the project to force millions of people from the occupied territories to work as slave labourers in Germany.

Göring, the 'economic dictator of Greater Germany', often spent his time during the war in his Carinhall palace or his palace in Berchtesgaden, in the midst of treasures plundered and transported there from all over Europe. He would receive his visitors in a pink silk robe adorned with gold fastenings, and introduce them to his wife with a lion cub in her arms.

Göring continued to go out hunting as if nothing untoward was happening. What kind of hunting that was I heard in June 1945 from the head gamekeeper at Göring's hunting castle. In a forested park, where trees were planted in rows and formed straight avenues with an unobstructed view, a feeding place for deer was set up and a deer trained to come there at a certain time. The perfectly groomed Göring, in red jacket and green boots, duly arrived for the hunting, settled himself in an open car and drove down the avenue, at the end of which his target, the tame deer, was already waiting for him. He left with his victim's antlers as a hunting trophy.

Goebbels, possessed to his last moments by jealousy of his rivals in the Nazi hierarchy, kept a particularly close eye on the Führer's successor. He noted in his diary on 28 February 1945, two months before final defeat:

Fools festooned with medals and vain, perfumed fops should not be in charge of the army. They need either to transform themselves or be written off. I will not calm down and will know no peace until the Führer puts this right. He needs to transform Göring both inwardly and outwardly, or get rid of him. For example, it is a gross violation of form when the Reich's foremost military officer is poncing around in the current wartime situation wearing a silver-grey (dress) uniform. What sort of effeminacy is that in the light of current events? It is to be hoped the Führer will now be able to make a man of Göring again.

Goebbels tried in vain to persuade the Führer to replace Göring. 'Göring has now again gone off on two special trains to Obersalzberg to visit his wife' (*27 March*). Another month was to pass before Göring was at last out on his ear.

Finding himself under arrest, Göring backed away from his pretensions. Hitler sent him a radio-telegram to say his life would be spared if he renounced all his ranks and positions. A telegram duly arrived in the Führerbunker, stating that Göring had suffered a heart attack and asking Hitler to accept his resignation. The *Berliner Frontblatt* reported to the public and the army:

Reich Marshal Hermann Göring has long suffered from chronic heart disease, which has now become acute. He has accordingly asked that, at the present time which demands maximum effort, he should be relieved of the burden of leading the air force and all related duties. The Führer has granted this request.

The Führer has appointed Colonel General Ritter von Greim as the new commander-in-chief of the Air Force, simultaneously conferring on him the rank of field marshal.

The Führer yesterday received the new commander-in-chief of the Air Force in his headquarters in Berlin and discussed with him in detail the issue of bringing air units and anti-aircraft artillery into battle.   (*27 April 1945*)

The order appointing Greim could perfectly well have been telegraphed, but Hitler, who was accustomed to spectacles and parades and not accustomed to obstacles and restrictions, particularly in matters concerning his prestige, disregarding the current situation and all expediency, dooming German pilots, ordered that Greim should attend him in the bunker in encircled Berlin solely in order to be informed of his appointment.

Escorted by forty fighters, Greim flew from Rechlin and somehow managed to make it through to Gatow aerodrome, losing fighters one after another at a time when every plane and every pilot was desperately needed. Taking off in another aircraft, he left the airfield but, a few minutes later, when he was over the Brandenburg Gate, a shell ripped the bottom of the plane and Greim suffered a leg wound. His personal pilot, Hanna Reitsch, who was accompanying Greim, replaced him at the controls and landed the aircraft in the Tiergarten park.

About the sight that presented itself to them in Hitler's bunker, Reitsch gave detailed testimony to the US military authorities a few months later, on 8 October 1945. Her evidence contains unique details about the last days in the Führerbunker. It largely coincides with Rattenhuber's recollections and confirms their accuracy.

Immediately Greim and Reitsch arrived, the Führer, clutching Göring's telegram in his hand, informed them of his treachery. '"He gave me an ultimatum!" There were tears in the Führer's eyes. His head was lowered, his face deathly pale, his hands shaking . . . It was a familiar scene, *"Et tu Brute!"* full of reproaches and self-pity,' recalled Hanna Reitsch.

He then announced to the wounded Greim that he had dismissed Göring from the post of commander-in-chief of the Air Force and was appointing him in his place.

Marooned, by the whim of the Führer, in the underground complex, the wounded Greim was entirely without the means to command what remained of the air force at whose head he had now been placed. Remaining at the wounded Greim's bedside in the bomb shelter, Reitsch observed the behaviour of the leaders of the Reich over the following three days. She describes Hitler pacing around the bunker, 'waving a road map that was almost falling apart because of the sweat from his hands, and planning Wenck's campaign in front of anyone who happened to be listening to him . . . His behaviour and physical state sank lower and lower.'

The room Reitsch occupied was adjacent to Goebbels' office, around which he hobbled neurotically, cursing Göring, blaming 'that swine' for all their present troubles, and delivering great tirades to himself. To Hanna Reitsch, obliged to observe and listen to all this because the door of his office remained open, it seemed that, 'As always, he is behaving as if he is talking to legions of historians who are avidly catching and writing down his every word.' Her existing 'opinion of the affectedness of Goebbels, his superficiality and hackneyed rhetorical techniques was fully confirmed by these shenanigans'. 'Are these really the people who have been ruling our country?' she and Greim wondered in desperation.

That first evening, Hitler called Reitsch in and said, 'Each of us has a poison ampoule like this. In case danger approaches.' He handed her two ampoules, one for her and one for Greim. He added, 'Each person is responsible for having their own body destroyed so there is nothing left to identify.'

Goebbels' children, also stranded in the bunker, were told they were in a magic cave with their Uncle Führer and so they were quite safe, protected from bombs and anything nasty. Magda Goebbels, of whom Reitsch saw a lot, 'was self-controlled most of the time, but sometimes wept bitterly. She thanked God frequently that she was alive and would be able to kill her children.' She told the pilot, 'They belong to the Third Reich and to the Führer, and if both cease to exist, there is nowhere left for the children either. But you must help me. What I am most afraid of is that, when the time comes, I will not be strong enough.'

'From Hanna Reitsch's remarks we can conclude with certainty', the American investigator wrote, 'that Frau Goebbels was just one of the most convinced listeners of the "highly scientific" speeches of her own husband, and the most pronounced example of the Nazis' influence on German women.'

Hitler, in the presence of those occupying the bunker, presented Magda Goebbels with his own Gold Party Badge, in recognition of the fact that she 'embodies the truly German woman' in accordance with Nazi doctrine.

During the night of 26 April the Reich Chancellery was under severe artillery bombardment. 'The explosion of heavy shells and the crack of collapsing buildings directly above the bomb shelter put everyone under such nervous strain that in certain places sobbing could be heard through the doors.'

On 27 April a friend of Bormann's, SS Obergruppenführer Fegelein, who represented Himmler at Hitler's headquarters and was married to Eva Braun's sister, disappeared from the shelter. Hitler gave orders that he was to be found and arrested. He was captured in his Berlin apartment, wearing civilian clothing and preparing to flee. He asked his sister-in-law to intercede for him, but nothing helped. On Hitler's orders he was shot by SS men in the Reich Chancellery garden on the evening of 28 April, a few hours before Hitler's wedding.

On the night of 27 April shelling of the Reich Chancellery continued with even greater intensity. 'The accuracy of the firing amazed those below,' Reitsch said. 'Each shell seemed to land in the same place as the previous one . . . At any moment the Russians might enter, and the Führer convened a second suicide council.' There were oaths of loyalty, speeches, assurances that people would commit suicide. In conclusion, Reitsch said, 'We were told that the SS would be instructed to ensure that no traces remained.'

On 28 April it became known in the bunker from foreign telegrams that Himmler, having assumed supreme authority, had communicated through Sweden to the British and American authorities that Germany was ready to capitulate to the Western Allies.

Heinrich Himmler, Führer of the SS, Protector of the Reich, 'faithful Heinrich', 'Iron Heinrich', was a traitor. 'All the men and women were weeping and shouting in rage, fear and despair,' Reitsch related. 'Everything got mixed up in a convulsion of insanity.'

A wave of enraged hysteria swept over those present, whom Hitler had doomed to imminent death. According to Reitsch, Hitler 'was raving like a lunatic. His face was red and unrecognizable. Then he lapsed into apathy.' Shortly after that, the news arrived in the shelter that Soviet troops were advancing towards Potsdamerplatz and preparing their positions for storming the Reich Chancellery.

Hitler ordered the wounded Greim and Reitsch to return to Rechlin and immediately send all remaining aircraft to Berlin to destroy the Russians' positions. 'With air support Wenck will get through,' he again repeated. Greim's second mission was to find and arrest Himmler; to ensure he did not live to succeed the Führer. Vengefulness was still capable of galvanizing Hitler.

No matter how Greim and Reitsch tried to explain the hopelessness of this mission, Hitler dug his heels in. At the Brandenburg Gate one last Arado trainer monoplane was concealed in a shelter. In it they managed to complete a fraught journey, only to see for themselves the complete collapse of the German armed forces. A few months later an American investigator took down Hanna Reitsch's description of the flight.

The broad avenue running from the Brandenburg Gate was to serve as a runway. There was a 400 m stretch of roadway that was not cratered. We took off under a hail of bullets and, when the plane climbed to roof level, it was caught by many searchlights and shelled. The explosions tossed the plane about like a feather, but it was hit by only a few fragments of shrapnel.

Reitsch circled to a height of 20,000 feet, from which Berlin looked like a sea of fire beneath them. The extent of the destruction was immense and unbelievable. After fifty minutes they reached Rechlin, where they again landed under fire from Russian fighter planes.

'Greim gave orders to send all available planes to Berlin's assistance.' Having accomplished the first part of his mission, he had now to carry out the second: to find and arrest Himmler. To that end, they flew to Plön [in Schleswig-Holstein], where Dönitz was at that moment, to discover Himmler's whereabouts. Dönitz had no information. Then they rushed to Keitel and from him learned that Berlin could not count on Wenck: his army was surrounded by Soviet troops. Keitel had sent a message to Hitler to that effect.

Shortly afterwards they heard the news of Hitler's death and that he had appointed Dönitz as his successor. They then returned to Plön for a meeting called by the new head of the government.

Appointed commander-in-chief of the Air Force by the Führer, Greim was at the meeting when Himmler appeared in the vestibule where Reitsch was sitting. 'He had an almost playful look about him.' She stopped him and called him a traitor. There was a dialogue:

'You have betrayed your Führer and the German people in their hour of greatest need!'

'Hitler wanted to continue the fight! He wanted the shedding of still more German blood when there is no blood left to shed.'

'You talk now about German blood, Herr Reichsführer! You should have thought about that long ago, before identifying yourself with the pointless shedding of it.'

A sudden air raid interrupted the conversation.

This verbal skirmish was all that eventuated. A new Reich President was already in office, with whom Himmler initially hoped to make common cause by offering his cooperation.

At Dönitz's meeting everyone was in agreement that within a few more days further resistance would be impossible. Nevertheless, Greim flew to Field Marshal Schörner, who was in command of troops in Silesia and Czechoslovakia, to urge him to hold out, even if there was an order to surrender, to allow the German population to move west.

On the morning of 9 May, Greim and Reitsch surrendered to American forces. Two weeks later, Greim took the poison Hitler had given him. *Pravda* reported:

London, 27 May (TASS). London radio reports that General Ritter von Greim, who succeeded Göring as commander of the German Air Force, has committed suicide in a hospital in Salzburg. Greim was captured by the Allies a few days ago. He poisoned himself with potassium cyanide.

Did Hitler Have a Plan?

When researchers are examining the last days in the Reich Chancellery, they often quite rightly note the degeneration and moral monstrousness that then became so evident in Hitler, but they allow the scenes of hysteria and farce to overshadow his final plan of action.

Under the relentless pressure of the advancing armies, the feverish intentions of taking refuge in Berchtesgaden or Schleswig-Holstein, or in the South Tyrol fortress (much advocated by Goebbels), were abandoned. When the Gauleiter of Tyrol suggested an evacuation to the mountain fortress, Hitler, according to Hans Rattenhuber,

shrugged despairingly and said, 'I no longer see any point in this rushing from place to place.' The situation in Berlin in late April left us in no doubt that these were our last days. Events were unfolding more rapidly than expected.

Hitler's hope that the Allied coalition would collapse had proved vain. At the Gatow airfield Hitler's last plane still stood at the ready, and when it was destroyed, hasty preparations began to construct a runway near the Reich Chancellery. A squadron allocated for use by Hitler was set ablaze by Soviet artillery but his personal pilot remained with him.

Greim, the new commander-in-chief of the Air Force, did send planes, but not a single one made it through to Berlin. Greim had accurate information that no aircraft crossed the line of encirclement to get out of Berlin either. There was, in any case, nowhere left to evacuate to: armies were advancing from every direction.

To flee from defeated Berlin, to fall like a spent pawn into the hands of the Anglo-Americans, Hitler considered out of the question. He came up with a different plan: he would enter negotiations, from Berlin, with the British and Americans, who, he believed, should be interested in preventing the Russians from capturing the capital of Germany, and obtain some tolerable conditions for himself. He believed, however, that such negotiations would only be possible if the military situation in Berlin improved.

It was an unrealistic plan with no prospect of being implemented, but it obsessed Hitler, and if we want a full picture for history of the last days of the Third Reich, it should not be overlooked. Hitler must surely have realized that even a temporary improvement in Berlin's situation would have no major impact in the context of the catastrophic military situation of Germany. He calculated, however, that it was a political prerequisite for the negotiations on which he was pinning his last deluded hopes. That is why he kept talking so frenziedly about Wenck's army. There is no doubt that he was completely incapable of coordinating the defence of Berlin: we are talking here only about his plans.

I read in Rattenhuber's testimony, written shortly after he was captured in Berlin, that Hitler was profoundly shocked by the treachery of Göring and Himmler, not because they began negotiating with the Allies, but because they did so behind his back. Göring and Himmler betrayed Hitler and finally took the feet from him when they bypassed him.

Going through the materials in the Council of Ministers Archive, I found a letter signed by Bormann and Krebs and addressed to General Wenck. It is dated 29 April. Lost in our archive and lacking its explanatory note, it seems to me an important document that reveals Hitler's last intentions. I found it in Folder 128, in which miscellaneous documents judged to be of little interest were placed without careful scrutiny. As I have mentioned, in the preceding twenty years the archive had not been adequately sorted and systematized, but that had the fortunate side effect of allowing a degree of serendipity in the course of my researches.

And here, in this file, under the category 'Documents and items found in May in Hitler's bunker and at Goebbels' apartment in Berlin', a long list that extended from 'Certificate of Award to Goebbels, Magda, of an Olympic Badge' to 'Horoscope for Helmut Goebbels' (what future would that be promising the Reich Minister's small son?) to the uniforms of Hitler and Voss (note of identification by Rattenhuber of two caps and two tunics attached), I discovered an orphaned, unlisted sheet of paper.

22.V.45. Detained Brichzi, Josef, d.o.b. 1928, member of the Hitler Youth, apprentice electrician.

In February 1945, conscripted into the Volkssturm militia and served in an anti-tank detachment, operating in Berlin. On the night of 28 April this year. Brichzi was summoned from a barracks located on Wilhelmstrasse and, escorted by a soldier, taken to the Reich Chancellery together with a youth of approx. 16 years of age.

At the Chancellery they were brought to Bormann, who said he was entrusting them with an important mission, to cross the front line and hand to General Wenck, the commander of the Twelfth German Army, packages that Bormann would give them.

Early in the morning on 29 April Brichzi darted across the front line on a motorcycle near the Reich sports field. He was fired at but escaped the Berlin encirclement uninjured and moved towards the west because General

Wenck was believed to be in the vicinity of the village of Ferch, northwest of Potsdam.

Having reached Potsdam, Brichzi talked to soldiers of the German Army but obtained no definite information on the whereabouts of Wenck's headquarters and decided to go back to Spandau, where his uncle lived.

His uncle advised him not to carry out the mission but to report to the Soviet Military Commandant's Office and hand the documents over, which he did on 7 May 1945.

Text of the letter:

Dear General Wenck,

As can be seen from the enclosed reports, SS Reichsführer Himmler has made a proposal to the Anglo-Americans, which unconditionally hands our nation to the plutocrats.

Such a change of policy can be made only by the Führer personally, only by him!

A prerequisite for this is the prompt establishment of contact between the Wenck Army and us, in order to provide the Führer with the domestic and foreign policy freedom to conduct negotiations.

Yours, Krebs   Heil Hitler!

Head of General Headquarters Yours, M. Bormann

The Suicide Committee

In the last days of Hitler we see clearly the vicious falsity of his entire life, inspired by the desire to wield power over other people, and with the real aim of personal aggrandizement, primarily through the agency of the German people.

For as long as he had breath, he continued to kill. The courtyard of the Reich Chancellery became a place of execution, of firing squads. Hitler made his threats, but the treason spread.

According to testimony from Hitler's entourage, the commander of the Berlin Defence Area, Helmuth Weidling, asked Hitler to leave the city so it could cease fighting before it had been completely destroyed. Hitler was vanquished, crushed, dead – but even so he was determined to pull everyone else down with him. Let everything perish! 'The Allies', he declared, 'will find in Germany nothing but ruins, rats, famine and death.'

No matter how the Nazi district leaders trembled before Bormann, growing despair is increasingly open in the reports preserved in his folder. The reports become more perfunctory, more poignant: the enemy shelling is intolerable, there are heavy losses, a shortage of weapons. It is impossible to withstand the onslaught of Russian troops. Nobody took any notice.

Here, in the bomb shelter, what Reitsch called 'the Suicide Committee' had already met, but Goebbels' *Berliner Frontblatt*, dated 27 April, makes a sordid, blustering appeal to Berliners. 'Bravo, Berliners! Berlin will remain German!' It makes knowingly false promises of help to come:

Already armies are moving in to Berlin from all directions, ready to defend the capital, to inflict a conclusive defeat on the Bolsheviks and, at the last moment, change our city's destiny. The reports coming in from the outside world testify to their progress. The fighting units advancing here know how eagerly Berlin is waiting for them. They will continue to fight fanatically to rescue us. The Führer himself stands at the head of the defence of Berlin.

Let us take a look in Bormann's diary. The tone of the entry for that same day, 27 April, is completely different. It is quite unlike earlier entries, which usually consist of information and, the only evidence of emotion, exclamation marks.

Friday, 27 April

Himmler and Jodl are holding back on sending divisions to us.

We shall fight and die with our Führer – devoted to him to the grave.

Others are thinking of acting in the light of 'higher considerations', sacrificing their Führer. Phew – what swine! They have lost all sense of honour.

Our Reich Chancellery is being destroyed.

The world is now hanging by a thread.

The Allies are demanding unconditional surrender from us – that would be a betrayal of the Fatherland!

Fegelein is going to pieces; he tried to escape from Berlin dressed in civilian clothes.

People gave assurances to the Führer that they would follow him to the grave, and even made entries to that effect in their diaries, but had no intention of dying. As can be seen from Bormann's telegram to his adjutant, Hummel, he had arranged a bolthole for himself far from Germany. In short, they were preparing to act to save their own skins, but being held back by Hitler.

A foreign radio station broadcast a detailed Reuters report about Himmler's proposal of a separate peace to the British and American governments. Typed up by Gertraud Junge (enormous letters) it was handed to Hitler. His Majesty's Government emphasized once again that it could talk only about an unconditional surrender offered to all three Great Powers, between which there was the closest unanimity. This response indirectly struck a blow at his own plan.

On 29 April, following the departure of Greim, the information finally reached the Reich Chancellery that Wenck's army had been routed. Rattenhuber writes:

At that, all our hopes of rescue foundered. Our troops' attempt to break through to Berlin had proved unsuccessful. The theatricality of the situation was heightened by the fact that Hitler was receiving all these reports to the accompaniment of Russian heavy artillery shells exploding on the territory of the Reich Chancellery. That day it was terrible to look at Hitler.

Günsche, the Führer's SS adjutant, writes in his testimony,

After the breakthrough of Russian motorized units in the area of Anhalt Station and Königsplatz, the Führer became anxious to lose no time before committing suicide. It could be only a matter of a few hours before Russian tanks would suddenly appear in front of the concrete bunker.

On the night of 28 April, Hitler arranged his wedding ceremony. He had had a relationship with Eva Braun for over ten years. She had been working at the photographic studio in Munich of Heinrich Hoffman, who later became rich by having a monopoly on photographing the Führer. Together with Hoffmann, Eva accompanied Hitler, who greatly enjoyed being photographed, on propaganda trips before he seized power. Hitler installed her in his Berchtesgaden castle, and there she ruled the roost. In Berlin he lived alone: Nazi propaganda celebrated the Führer's asceticism.

Pilot Hanna Reitsch, who at that time was devoted to Hitler, observing Eva Braun in the underground complex was shocked when she saw the intimacy her Führer shared with a woman of 'such negligible mental faculties'. According to Reitsch, she was totally absorbed in grooming herself, and constantly repeated that it was essential to kill all those 'ungrateful swine' who had left the bunker because they were 'incapable of committing suicide'. In Hitler's presence she was obliging and said little. 'She did everything she could to ensure his comfort.'

Until then, the existence of Eva Braun had not been public knowledge. She was neither a wife nor an acknowledged mistress and always stayed in the shadows, at a distance. In the middle of April, however, she resolutely and unexpectedly threw caution to the winds and demonstratively appeared in the underground complex. The surmise is that this was not only in order to share a grim period with him, but finally to attain the unattainable, the thing she so agonizingly aspired to: to become truly the wife of the Führer.

Until Hitler took the decision to commit suicide, though, there was no mention of matrimony. It was only after he took that decision irrevocably that a marriage ceremony and reception were hastily arranged. This may have been Eva Braun's condition for agreeing to die with him. She paid with her life to achieve the goal of becoming the Führer's wife.

Hitler, although a Catholic by birth, persecuted the Church to prevent God from becoming a nuisance and stopping Adolf Hitler from rising to equal prominence. He will hardly have felt any obligation to atone for having 'lived in sin'. More likely he wanted to look better in the eyes of history, since his meticulously concealed relations had become obvious. This comes through in his 'personal will'. Hitler begins by explaining that he had believed he should not take on such a serious responsibility as marriage, but had now decided before dying to marry the woman who was to share his destiny. Behind these words we detect a compensation to Eva Braun for her willingness to die at his side. It would, after all, be less frightening if there were two of them, and no doubt this highly strung mystic and neuropath would also find it easier to bite the ampoule in a state of exaltation after a marriage ceremony.

When Hanna Reitsch, who had left the shelter a few hours previously, was told about the wedding she could not believe her ears. She said, 'Conditions in the bunker in those last days would have made the ceremony comical.' But take place it did: Hitler's last 'historic act'.

Outside the walls of the Reich Chancellery, German soldiers were fighting. Nearby, at Potsdamerplatz and in the underground stations, the wounded were in a state of collapse, without food or water. Hitler had thrown his last reserve into battle at the Pichelsdorf Bridge: adolescents from the Hitler Youth. German boys were sent to defend the Reich Chancellery. It was one of the most shameful acts of villainy of those days. 'The children's friend', as the propaganda represented the Führer, praised them and sent them into a senseless battle, achieving nothing more than depriving the nation of future citizens. But then Hitler did not foresee a future for Germany. He declared, 'In the event of defeat, the Germans will not deserve to live.'

'The lads are tired and no longer have the strength to take part in battles,' I read in a report addressed to Bormann on 22 April. On the same day, in another report, Reichsführer of the Hitler Youth Artur Axmann and his closest colleagues state they are planning to move to 63–64 Wilhelmstrasse, near the Reich Chancellery. He intends to deploy 40–50 members of the Hitler Youth and requests Reichsleiter Bormann's consent, which is duly forthcoming.

A report from the District of Charlottenburg–Spandau on 26 April reports the retreat of soldiers under the onslaught of Soviet units, adding: 'A Hitler Youth detachment was to hold the bridge, but proved unable to do so.' Goebbels in his *Berliner Frontblatt* on 27 April exhorts the young:

Reichsjugendführer Axmann was yesterday awarded the Golden Cross . . . Last night, the Führer in his principal apartment presented this mark of distinction to Axmann with the words, 'Without your young men, it would be impossible to continue the struggle not only here in Berlin [when we read these words of 27 April they provide circumstantial evidence that Hitler was in Berlin], but throughout the whole of Germany.' To this Axmann replied, 'They are your young men, my Führer!'

Perhaps the duped boys believed they really were defending Germany, and died while a wedding was taking place in the bunker. Or was it a wake? Certainly, death was a guest at the table, and the bride was wearing black.

The walls of the bunker were shaking from direct artillery hits. Down in the crypt it was totally macabre, Rattenhuber tell us of these hours in his manuscript:

Everyone was preoccupied with their anxieties, their search for their own way out. Some, in despair, had given up all hope of rescue and, cowering in a corner and not looking at anyone, waited for the end to come; others, instead, went to the buffet and drowned their sorrows with brandy and wine from the Führer's cellars.

SS guards patrolled slowly round the Reich Chancellery. In the garden, it was impossible to breathe because of the smoke and fumes. Berlin was burning, houses collapsing, shells exploding. Rifle fire could already be heard. Wounded people were groaning in the corridors of the shelter; there was no other place in the vicinity for them to go to.

It was in these conditions that, on the evening of 28 April, Hitler and Eva Braun were married. The formalities established by the Hitler regime were relaxed for the occasion. The bride and groom did not present, as was normally required, documents certifying their Aryan antecedents, their marriageability, their lack of a criminal record, their political reliability and a report from the police on the behaviour of the two parties. The marriage certificate notes that they requested that account should be taken of the wartime situation and the abnormal circumstances under which they were marrying, and to take on trust their verbal declarations, as well as relaxing the period of notice normally required for the ceremony to be legally valid.

The official whom Goebbels had summoned to solemnize the marriage wrote that their request was granted, and invited them only to confirm by their signatures that they were members of the Master Race and not suffering from congenital diseases.

This was followed by a wedding breakfast with champagne, attended by an intimate circle of acquaintances. Magda Goebbels, wife of the Reich Minister, was also present at the funereal wedding, Hitler having been the proxy father at her own wedding. Among the papers of Frau Goebbels there are records of a conversation with the Führer. She had been about to leave Goebbels for being unfaithful to her (this apostle of Nazi rectitude had been popularly nicknamed 'the Bullock of Babelsberg' because of his predilection for film actresses), but the Führer urged her to keep the family together. He told her that she, too, as a member of the Party, a *Parteigenossin*, had a mission in life.

The Führer presented himself to the people as an exemplary ascetic who disdained earthly joys the better to serve the nation. Magda Goebbels and her unfaithful husband similarly exemplified the ideal Nazi family of many children.

Now one piece of hypocrisy was being replaced by another. The stench of mysticism and vulgarity emanating from this wedding would have choked all but the undead. After it, Hitler dictated his will. By 4.00 a.m. it was ready. The witnesses – Goebbels, Bormann, and Generals Burgdorf and Krebs – appended their signatures.

Hitler's adjutant, Otto Günsche, testified during interrogation on 14 May 1945:

On the night of 28 April 1945 the Führer dictated his will to his secretaries Christian and Junge. The will was typed in three or four copies. On the morning of 29 April 1945 Major Johannmeier was sent with these wills to the commander of the Central Army Group, Field Marshal Schörner, to Sander, to Grand Admiral Dönitz, and to Field Marshal Kesselring.

A few days before the attack on the Soviet Union, Hitler was outlining the victorious course he anticipated the war would take and told Goebbels, who noted it in his diary, 'When we are the victors, who will question our methods?' (*15 June 1941*)

But it was defeat that came to Berlin and, evading responsibility, Hitler began his 'political testament' with the usual professions of love for the German people, declaring that he was without blame for the war that broke out.

It is untrue that I or anyone else in Germany wanted war in 1939. Those who wanted and sought it were exclusively foreign statesmen – Jews or people acting in the interests of the Jews.

At this last hour, his reflex was to blame the Jews. We have, however, only to leaf through *Mein Kampf*, a book permeated by justification of war and vengeful passion, to be persuaded that war lay at the very foundations of the doctrine of National Socialism. Its practice confirmed that unambiguously. Hitler himself goes on to give the lie to his cheap preamble in his farewell letter to the chief of staff of the Wehrmacht High Command, Field Marshal Keitel. Having brought ruin upon Germany and a catastrophic defeat upon the army, Hitler in concluding his missive insists that the goal remains unaltered: conquest for the German people of lands in the east. He enjoins the commanders of the Army, Navy and Air Force to use every means to rouse the spirit of resistance and National Socialist faith in the soldiers and to fight to the death.

In the testament he expels Göring and Himmler from the Party and appoints Admiral Dönitz president. The crowning absurdity is Hitler's formation in the testament of a government headed by Goebbels, whom he appoints Reich chancellor. For Bormann he invents the new portfolio of minister of the Party. He charges the new government and its leader, Goebbels (who, as Hitler knew perfectly well, was never going to get out of Berlin), to continue the war, to adhere to the race laws to the end, and to combat world Jewry.

Everything is just as it was when Hitler started out: the Master Race, the conquest of territorial living space, *Lebensraum*, the anti-Semitism, the waging of war.

Goebbels accepted his short-lived promotion, a reward for loyalty, as Eva accepted her wedding. He had finally beaten all his rivals and reached the pinnacle of his career.

The exploding shells shaking the concrete shelter proclaimed that these were the last hours of the Third Reich.

On the evening of 29 April, General Weidling, commander of the Berlin Defence Area, came to the Führerbunker and reported the situation: the troops were totally exhausted and the situation of the population was desperate. In his opinion, the only possible solution now was for the troops to withdraw from Berlin and break out of the encirclement. Weidling asked Hitler for permission to begin the break out.

Hitler refused.

How would such a breakthrough help? We will merely get out of one 'cauldron' into another. Do you think I want to skulk around and wait for my end to come in a peasant house or some such? It is better, in this situation, for me to remain and die here. After that they can break through if they want to.

There could, however, be no delay. Under the circumstances there was not an hour to lose.

'Even if a path from the bunker to freedom had been cleared for him, he would not have had the strength to take advantage of it,' said Hanna Reitsch later. But, completely routed, incapable of effective action, he put off the hour of his death, steadily diminishing the prospects of survival for those he was holding back.

The situation in the bunker was bizarre. Until the previous day what was required was loyally to confirm your readiness to die with the Führer. Now, after the distribution of the symbolic portfolios, it was to confirm your readiness to continue a lost war at the head of a Germany defeated and occupied by the enemy. An entrenched habit of obedience, of reverence for orders, and of imbecile automatism continued in some to function like clockwork.

On the night of 29 April Professor Haase, head of the Reich Chancellery hospital, was brought to Hitler. 'Hitler showed Haase three small glass ampoules, each in the casing of a rifle cartridge,' Rattenhuber, who was present, relates,

Hitler said the ampoules contained a lethal, instantaneous poison and that he had been given them by Dr Stumpfegger. He asked the professor how the effectiveness of the poison could be checked, and Haase replied that it could be tested on an animal, for instance, a dog. Hitler then proposed summoning Sergeant Major Tornow, who looked after his favourite dog, Blondi. When the dog was brought, Haase crushed an ampoule with pliers and poured the contents into the dog's mouth, which Tornow held open. A few seconds later the dog began to tremble and it died after thirty seconds. Hitler ordered Tornow to check later that the dog was really dead.

When we left Hitler, I asked Haase what the poison in the ampoules was and whether it guaranteed instant death. Haase replied that the ampoules contained potassium cyanide, and that it was instantly and lethally effective.

That was the last time I saw Hitler alive.

The Führer Is Dead

Gertraud Junge, Hitler's secretary, who retyped papers addressed to him, accompanied him on trips and took down his speeches in shorthand, said a month later,

On 30 April Hitler assembled Goebbels, Krebs and Bormann, but I do not know what they talked about. I was summoned to Hitler later by his valet Linge, I think. I do not remember exactly. When I went in to see Hitler, all the persons named were there, all standing. Hitler said goodbye to me and said the end had come and that everything was now over. After that I left the office and went up the stairs to the upper landing. I did not see Hitler again. This was on 30 April, between 15.15 and 15.30 hrs.

On 30 April it was reported that the Russians were within 200 metres of the main Wilhelmstrasse entrance to the Reich Chancellery. In the past this had always been besieged by journalists. (Goebbels, four years earlier, had bypassed it, secretly entering the underground complex through the emergency exit for his clandestine meeting with the Führer.) It was 3.30 p.m. Berlin time. That was the moment when the ampoule of poison came into play. A fateful time by the hands of the clock! It had been at 3.30 a.m. on 22 June 1941 that, on Hitler's orders, Germany began its war against the Soviet Union.

Death is death, and the bodyguards now carried the body out through the emergency exit of the concrete shelter to burn it, as they had been ordered to by Hitler. The doctor present in the bunker was not called.

Rattenhuber wrote later,

On the day before, Hitler called me, Linge and Günsche and told us in a barely audible voice that his body and that of Eva Braun were to be burned. 'I do not want our enemies to display my body in a panopticon.' I found this statement strange, but then I was told that on 29 April Hitler had received the news of the death of Mussolini and his mistress Clara Petacci in Milan, who had fallen into the hands of Italian partisans. Perhaps the circumstances of Mussolini's death caused Hitler to decide his body should be burned.

Much the same words were repeated to Günsche:

After my death, my body is to be burned, because I do not want my body to be displayed, exhibited later.

How events unfolded on that day, 30 April, was described by three of the surviving witnesses: Hitler's adjutant, Otto Günsche; the head of his bodyguard, Hans Rattenhuber; and his valet, Heinz Linge.[1]

Günsche: At 15.30 he was at the door of Hitler's anteroom, together with the chauffeur, Kempka, and the commander of the Führer's personal SS bodyguard, Franz Schädle.

We stood for some time without moving. The reception door was suddenly opened slightly and I heard the voice of the Führer's valet, SS Sturmbannführer Linge, who said, 'The Führer is dead.' Although I had not heard a shot, I immediately went through the anteroom to the meeting room and told the leaders there, word for word, 'The Führer is dead.'

Rattenhuber:

At this time, the territory of the Reich Chancellery was already being subjected to Russian small arms fire. I went into Hitler's anteroom and left again several times on business, as the situation was extremely tense; I considered it my duty personally to ensure that the shelter was properly protected, because at any minute we could expect the Russians to break through into the territory of the Reich Chancellery. At approximately 3–4 o'clock in the afternoon, when I went into the anteroom, I detected a strong smell of bitter almonds. (Potassium cyanide.)

His deputy, Peter Högl, told Rattenhuber that Hitler had committed suicide. The Führer's valet, Linge, came to him and confirmed it. 'My nervous tension gave way to depression, and for a time I could not recompose myself.'

Linge:

I spread a blanket on the floor . . . wrapped Hitler's body in it, and together with Bormann we transferred it to the garden.

Günsche: After he announced to those waiting in the meeting room for the end, 'The Führer is dead',

they stood up and came out with me to the anteroom, and there we saw two bodies being carried out, one was wrapped in a blanket, as was the other, but not completely . . . The Führer's feet were protruding from one blanket. I recognized them by the socks and shoes he always wore. From the other blanket feet protruded and the head of the Führer's wife was visible.

---

1. Birstein reports that during the Battle of Berlin, NKVD operatives arrested Hitler's pilot, Hans Baur; his adjutant, Otto Günsche; and his valet, Heinz Linge. 'They were held in NKVD/MVD prisons in Moscow, separately from Smersh prisoners, and brutally interrogated.' Birstein, p. 308.

Günsche helped to carry them out.

Rattenhuber:

I was shaken out of the stupor I was in by a noise and saw that from Hitler's private room, Linge, Günsche, the Führer's chauffeur Kempka, and two or three SS men, accompanied by Goebbels and Bormann, had brought out the bodies of Hitler and Eva Braun wrapped in grey blankets. Pulling myself together, I went behind them to follow on his last journey the man to whom I had devoted twelve years of my life.

Linge:

I was holding the body by the legs, and Bormann by the head. Eva Braun's body was carried by two others; it too was wrapped in a blanket.

Günsche:

Both bodies were carried out through the emergency exit of the Führer's concrete shelter into the garden.

Rattenhuber:

Having gone up the stairs, the SS officers put the bodies in a small pit near the entrance to the shelter. The constant shelling of the territory did not allow us to pay even minimal respects to Hitler and his wife. There was not even a national flag to cover their remains.

Günsche:

They were doused in petrol prepared by Reichsleiter Bormann.

Linge:

There we laid the bodies side by side at the entrance, each took a canister of petrol, and doused the bodies with it. At that time the grounds were under heavy Russian artillery and mortar fire, and we could not light the petrol with matches. Then I took cover in the entrance of the bomb shelter [i.e., the bunker], took some paper out of my pocket, lit it and handed it to Bormann. He threw the burning paper on the bodies, and the petrol ignited.

Rattenhuber:

A huge and terrible fire flared up.

Linge:

The bodies burned and turned a dark brown. We saluted and returned to the bomb shelter.

Bormann, Goebbels, Generals Krebs and Burgdorf, and Reichsjugend-führer Axmann observed, hiding from the bombardment in the shelter, crowded on the stairs of the emergency exit from the bunker.

They did not comply with Hitler's last order, to wait until the bodies had completely burned to ashes. The grounds of the Reich Chancellery were under heavy bombardment and it was dangerous to remain there.

Günsche:

After the bodies, doused with petrol, were lit, the door of the shelter was immediately closed against the heat and smoke of the fire. All present went back down to the anteroom . . . The door to the Führer's private rooms was slightly ajar, and a strong smell of bitter almonds was coming from there . . .

Hitler's death caused a sudden discharge of nervous energy in the tense atmosphere of the bunker. Cigarettes appeared, that no one would have dared to smoke while Hitler was alive. There was a grisly sense of excitement, with wine being drunk and preparations made to escape.

Rattenhuber:

The Führer was dead. Everybody in the bunker now knew that. To my surprise, the event did not have a depressing effect on everyone. Certainly, shots were heard here and there in nooks of the bunker as those who had lost all hope of being saved killed themselves. Most people, however, busied themselves with getting ready to flee.

Günsche: Even as the bodies of Hitler and Eva Braun were burning,

I made for the meeting room. The new situation was being discussed there, and the Führer's order according to which, after his death, we were to break out of Berlin in small groups. I heard that Reichsleiter Bormann wanted at all costs to try to make his way to Grand Admiral Dönitz in order to pass on to him the Führer's last thoughts before he died. I do not know what thoughts were being referred to. After that I again left that room and went into the next room to rest a little.

Shortly afterwards Günsche heard that

General Krebs had been instructed to make contact with the Russian Marshal Zhukov in order to achieve a cessation of hostilities; accordingly, the breakthrough of the Berlin garrison was postponed. After that I returned to my room and after that put myself at the disposal of the combat group of SS Brigadeführer Mohnke.

This group was formed mainly from the Führer and SS escort battalions. More hours passed as they waited for a response and anticipated an opportunity to get out of Berlin.

Bormann's diary has an entry about the death of Hitler and Eva Braun under the date 30 April 1945.

On 1 May, evidently after Krebs returned, the entry consists of just one phrase: 'Attempt to escape the encirclement!' On that the diary ends.

At 18.00 hrs the previous day, Bormann had informed Grand Admiral Dönitz by radio-telegram that the Führer had appointed him, Dönitz, as his successor instead of Göring. Dönitz, not having heard of Hitler's death, responded with effusions of devotion to the Führer and promised to come to his aid.

On 1 May at 07.40 hrs Bormann sent a top secret radio-telegram to Dönitz: the Führer's will had come into force, but an official announcement should be postponed until Bormann himself arrived to see Dönitz.

Later the same day, at 15.00 hrs, he, jointly with Goebbels, sent Dönitz a last radio-telegram reporting the death of the Führer and his appointments to the top posts.

'In the buffet corks were popping ,' Rattenhuber writes, 'as the SS men ratcheted themselves up before a desperate attempt to escape under Russian fire.'

The only people who remained were less fearful of retribution. All the others fled.

Voss:

SS Brigadeführer Mohnke, responsible for defending the area of the Reich Chancellery, saw that further resistance was useless and, in accordance with the orders of the commissioner for the defence of Berlin, assembled the remnants of his combat group, about 500 individuals. He was joined by surviving officials intending to fight their way out of the encirclement. All these people gathered by Dugout No. 3 at the Reich Chancellery . . . I was one of them.

The refusal Krebs brought back, and the words of Sokolovsky and Chuikov he reported – that, as agreed among the Allies, only unconditional surrender could be discussed – were the final catastrophe for Goebbels. He told Vice Admiral Voss that there was no point in him, with his limp and his children, even attempting to escape. He was doomed.

In fact, as I write about this now, I very much doubt he had any illusions about the possibility of an armistice. The British king had already rejected

Himmler's machinations out of hand. It was a fanatical careerist who sent Krebs to parley, purely in order to consolidate his place in history, Goebbels the second person in the Reich, Goebbels the Reich Chancellor, in case his emissaries to Dönitz proved unable to deliver the will.

He was no stranger to gestures and hypocrisy. In his will, Goebbels wrote that he was disobeying the Führer's order to leave the capital and participate in the government he had appointed only because of his desire to be at the Führer's side during these difficult days in Berlin.

In fact, however, for as long as Hitler was alive he did not allow Goebbels to leave him. When he decided on 22 April to remain in Berlin, Hitler surrounded himself with people devoted to him. It was he who, knowing Goebbels' unquestioning obedience, ordered him to move, together with his wife and children, into the bunker.

Magda Goebbels told Dr Kunz and Hanna Reitsch that she had pleaded with Hitler at this time to leave Berlin. If Hitler had agreed in a timely fashion, both they and their children would have been able to get out. She must obviously have been thinking about that. There is testimony to the effect that she asked her husband to have the children evacuated in armoured personnel vehicles, but by that time it was impracticable.

Murdering his children if defeat seemed imminent was something Goebbels had thought about a long time ago, and imposed on his obedient wife. As early as August 1943 he advised his devoted adjutant, Wilfried von Oven, of his intention. Oven wrote later that 'his thinking was directed to just one end: the effect on history.'[1]

Careerism was fundamental to Goebbels' personality. Right up until the end of his life, he fusses tirelessly, backstabbing his rivals, portraying them in a bad light to the Führer and in his diary, and extolling himself at every turn in the expectation that his monstrous diary, which reads like misbegotten self-parody, will remain a primary source on the basis of which history will award points to fanatics inflamed by their own vanity.

In the farewell letter Magda Goebbels wrote from the Führerbunker to her elder son, Harald, 'The world that will come after the Führer and National Socialism will not be worth living in, and that is why I also brought the children here. I could not bear to leave them for the life that will come after us, and a merciful God will understand me if I myself give them deliverance from it.'

And then, after describing how patiently the children had put up with the conditions in the bunker in which they were destined to die, she reports,

1. Wilfried von Oven, *Mit Goebbels bis zum Ende*, Buenos Aires: Dürer, 1950.

'Last night the Führer took off his gold badge and pinned it on me. I am proud and happy.'

Goebbels, too, in the farewell letter to his stepson, goes on about the Führer's gold badge and how it has been given to Harald's mother.

Both these letters were spirited out of encircled Berlin by Hanna Reitsch. If he had sent the letter a day later, after Hitler had signed his testament listing the appointments in his new government, Goebbels could have told Harald about his culminating moment of destiny. Everything was jumbled together in that underground complex: genuine despair and posturing, fanaticism, hypocrisy and death.

Goebbels was sometimes called the Führer's faithful dog. Well, Hitler tried out the poisonous ampoule on his beloved sheepdog, Blondi. Similarly, he kept Goebbels and his family close to him to the last, until it was too late for them to do anything about their predicament. With each successive betrayal of the Führer by his accomplices, Goebbels moved a rung up the ladder towards his ultimate ambition of becoming the second in command in the Reich. At last, on the day after Hitler's wedding, when Red Army soldiers were already in the Reichstag, Hitler awarded Goebbels the post of Reich Chancellor of a defunct empire. The pantomime continued. Goebbels accepted the top job, only a day later to follow Hitler to the grave.

Sergeant Major Tornow came one last time to chef Lange for food for the puppies. Having the day before informed the cook of the death of the Führer, he was back with a similar message. Lange told us,

He came to the Reich Chancellery kitchen at 8 or 9 on the evening of 1 May and informed me that Goebbels and his wife had killed themselves in the garden near the Führer's bunker. Sergeant Major Tornow told me no further details . . . In the evening of 1 May Sergeant Major Tornow was about to leave the Reich Chancellery and try to break through the ring of encirclement of Red Army units. Whether he managed to do so, I do not know.

Those fleeing the underground complex made their way to Wilhelmplatz, and there walked along the metro track to Friedrichstrasse. From there they needed to break through in the wake of Mohnke's combat group, but intensive artillery shelling made any mass breakthrough impossible. They broke through in groups.

Günsche:

Together with the Führer's secretaries, Frau Christian and Frau Junge, the Führer's dietitian, Fräulein Manziarly, and Bormann's secretary, Fräulein Kruger, I was to break through to the north in Mohnke's group. The breakthrough began at 22.00 hrs. Our group reached the area of Wedding railway station, where it encountered enemy resistance. After regrouping, towards noon on 2 May 45 we reached the Schultheis Brewery near the station. Among the soldiers who were there, rumours were circulating that Berlin had capitulated, and demoralization was evident among them.

The four women with us were now released by SS Brigadeführer Mohnke and immediately left the brewery. Where they went I do not know. I was taken prisoner at the Schultheis Brewery.

A group consisting of Bormann, Rattenhuber, Stumpfegger and Hitler's driver, Kempka, made their way under cover of a tank but a grenade thrown from a window hit the left side of the tank where Bormann and Stumpfegger were walking and the explosion felled both of them, according to eyewitness testimony. 'I was wounded,' Rattenhuber writes, 'and was taken prisoner by the Russians.'

Rumours that Hitler was dead leaked from the Führer's bunker to the shelter under the Reich Chancellery, which was connected to it, but the circumstances of his death were kept secret. In an attempt to keep up the myth of the Führer's greatness, his successor, Grand Admiral Dönitz, declared that Hitler had fallen, fighting at the head of the defenders of Berlin.

General Weidling, when he heard Hitler had committed suicide, considered such a demise unacceptable for a commander whose troops were still fighting. On the night of 1 May he sent representatives to parley. Early on the morning of 2 May, Weidling crossed the front line into Russian-held territory, from where he addressed an order to the Berlin garrison:

On 30 April the Führer committed suicide and thus left us, who had sworn allegiance to him, abandoned. The Führer ordered that we, the German troops, should continue to fight for Berlin, despite the fact that military supplies are exhausted and despite the general situation, which makes further resistance senseless. I order you to cease resistance immediately.

On 2 May Berlin capitulated.

When tyrants die, there is initial bewilderment: how is this possible? Can it really be that even they consist of mortal molecules? What comes next is that, if everything about the circumstances is not totally clear, their death becomes encrusted with legends. In the case of Hitler, there was plenty of opportunity for that to happen.

But it did not turn out the way Grand Admiral Dönitz had in mind. Hitler had bequeathed supreme authority to him, and he concocted what he knew to be a lie for a special announcement over the radio on 1 May 1945: Hitler had fallen in battle leading the defenders of Berlin, the capital city of the German Reich.

Neither was Hitler's end as described in a sensational book, *I Burned Hitler*, by his driver, Erich Kempka, where the shot that rings out and the crimson flowers in a vase fuse into a single emblem.

Neither was it as summarized by the British historian, Hugh Trevor-Roper in his serious study:

Whatever the explanation, Hitler achieved his last ambition. Like Alaric (who destroyed Rome in 410), buried secretly under the riverbed of Busento, the modern destroyer of mankind is now immune from discovery.[1]

Clinching the Argument

Life of a sort was going on above ground while we were still delving into the details of the last days of the Reich Chancellery. One day we stopped on the outskirts of Berlin, where several staff headquarters departments were located. Beside a house we had been instructed to occupy stood a cart laden with odds and ends and groceries, and with a red-white-green tricolour Italian flag on the front. A cow tethered to the cart waited patiently for its owners.

We went upstairs to an apartment from which music was coming. All the doors were wide open. In a large room Italians were sitting in tattered, dirty clothes, clutching big cardboard boxes on their knees and listening dreamily to the music. Their young, mop-headed musician was hammering the keys of a piano with gusto. A splendid doll, extracted from a box the same as all the others had, was sitting on the piano in front of him. On their way here, the Italians had passed a wholesale toy depot, and each had helped himself to a doll.

They noticed us and rose noisily from their seats. In reply to questions addressed to them in German, they obstinately shook their heads, not wanting to speak the language of the enemy. A cascade of gestures and exclamations washed over us. They were explaining something, putting their hands on their hearts. The musician seized the doll on the piano and presented it to me, and they all made a great noise and slapped him approvingly on the back.

---

1. Hugh Trevor-Roper, *The Last Days of Hitler*, London: Macmillan, 1947, p. 207. https://archive.org/stream/TrevorRoperHughTheLastDaysOfHitler/Trevor-Roper%20 Hugh%20-%20The%20last%20days%20of%20Hitler_djvu.txt Accessed 8 November 2017. Tr.

They left, humming and taking with them the large boxes with the dolls. Their cart was waiting for them downstairs with their luggage and the cow which was to feed its new owners on their long journey back to Italy.

'*Hitler kaput!*' they said to us by way of a farewell greeting.

He certainly was. No two ways about that.

Once More, Ampoule Fragments

The newspapers of the Allied occupation troops had already come out with a resounding headline: 'Russians Find Hitler's Body'.

Among our troops something ridiculous was going on. People were suddenly being urged to 'Hunt for Hitler'. This was a deceitful charade, a weird attempt to disguise the fact that his body had been found, a pretend search.

A declaration signed by Stalin, Roosevelt and Churchill had stated that the Allies undertook to seek out the Nazi leaders wherever they might be hiding and make them face an international court. And here the senior Nazi leader of the lot of them was, right here in Berlin, no distance at all from the Allied Control Council. So why not show them his body? Bring to it eyewitnesses of Hitler's death, both from our and their sides, and identify it? Make a joint statement and close the matter?

On 8 May, however, just as a forensic medical examination of Hitler's remains was taking place in Buch, on the northeastern outskirts of Berlin, another report appeared in the Moscow newspapers claiming that he might have landed in Argentina, or was possibly hiding with Franco in Spain. The evidence was being concealed and when, eventually, people would want to dig down and get the real facts, it would be too late: the witnesses would have dispersed or died, and even the testimony of those still alive would be unconvincing after so much time had elapsed.

Our view was that, if not at the present time, then at some point in an unclear future this conspiracy of silence would come to an end. It was bound to, so facts needed to be established now that would be unchallengeable even then. Already some of our superiors, detecting currents coming down from 'above', were looking askance at our zeal, keeping us at a distance because of their instinct of self-preservation (and perhaps something of the sort was true of Zhukov).

Quite a few people had been involved in the search and the first stage of the investigation. Now, as the secretiveness increased, almost all of them were taken out of the loop, and by the second stage, actual identification of the remains, Colonel Gorbushin's group had dwindled to just three people, including me as the interpreter.

The people doing their best to establish the truth about Hitler went about their business with a sense of heavy responsibility. They believed that the least lack of clarity about what had happened would be dangerous: it would breed legends that could only contribute to a rebirth of Nazism. Giving an unambiguous answer to the question of whether or not Hitler was alive was important also for the future of Germany.

Colonel Gorbushin decided in these difficult circumstances to obtain indisputable evidence. We were stationed in Buch, and whether in a modest house or a shed I found it difficult to say with any certainty until I later revisited the place. Sure enough, it was a small house. The remains of Goebbels, his wife and children were removed to its cellar.

Here, too, to Buch, on the orders of Colonel Gorbushin, were brought the remains of Adolf Hitler and Eva Braun.

This was a street of small, modest detached houses with a great vault of sky overhead. Young children were pedalling around furiously on their bicycles; the adults walked by, engrossed in their worries and cares, unaware of, and showing no curiosity about, what was now located here.

I was confident that within another day or two the whole world would know we had found Hitler's body. If I had known then that years later I would testify about all this in detail, I would probably have overcome my squeamishness and taken a closer look at those crudely constructed crates with their hideous, blackened remains – I had already seen them in the grounds of the Reich Chancellery – but I did not do so.

Here in Buch, when Hitler came to power, on his orders, people were subjected in the old, reputable clinics to 'racial evaluation' for the first time. In 1936 a card index of 'hereditary biological health' was introduced here, encompassing all residents of the large Berlin district of Pankow. A person's fate, his career, the right to marry, the right to life itself, all depended on what was on his index card.

And as chance would have it, this was where Hitler himself was now brought to be subjected to forensic medical examination. On 3 May, following the discovery of the bodies of Goebbels and his family, a commission of army doctors appointed by order of Lieutenant General Telegin of the Military Council of the 1st Byelorussian Front, got to work in a brick building at the clinic in which Surgical Mobile Field Hospital No. 4961 was currently housed.

Now, without needing to inform Telegin, a couple more corpses were tossed the commission's way, rather like cuckoos' eggs. The commission included eminent forensic medicine specialists and pathologists: the chief pathologist of the Red Army, Lieutenant Colonel Kraevsky; Doctors

Marants, Boguslavsky and Gulkevich. The man in charge was Medical Service Lieutenant Colonel Faust Shkaravsky, principal forensic medicine specialist of the 1st Byelorussian Front.

There was something portentous about Adolf Hitler being dissected under the watchful eye of Dr Faust. The autopsy was performed by a female doctor, Major Anna Marants, acting principal pathologist of the 1st Byelorussian Front, and it took place in Berlin–Buch on 8 May 1945.

Here is how Hitler appeared at the autopsy, as described in the official report:

The remains of the charred body of a male were delivered in a wooden crate 163 cm long, 55 cm wide and 53 cm high. A piece of knitted cloth measuring 25 x 8 cm, of a yellow colour, charred at the edges, resembling a knitted vest, was found on the body.

Given that the body has been burnt, it is difficult to judge the age, but it can be assumed that this was 50–60 years, the height is 165 cm (not an exact measurement owing to charring of tissue) . . . The body is significantly charred, exuding the odour of burnt flesh . . .

There are no visible signs of severe, lethal injuries or diseases on the body, which has been significantly affected by fire . . .

In the mouth, glass splinters were found which are parts of the walls and base of a thin-walled ampoule.

After a detailed examination, the commission concluded,

Cause of death was poisoning with cyanide compounds . . .

A test tube containing ampoule fragments found in the mouth of the corpse is attached to this certificate.

No other signs of harm that could result in death were established. Western researchers, journalists and memoirists frequently insist that Hitler shot himself: some from simple ignorance because of all the inaccurate information circulating about Hitler's death, others from a desire to embellish the circumstances of his end. It was a German Army tradition that a commander, if he committed suicide, should use a pistol. It is instructive, however, that General Krebs, who 'had the army in his bones', preferred to take poison as the more reliable method.

To us the manner in which Hitler committed suicide was immaterial, and neither were we versed in the traditions of the German Army: they were of no interest to us. The fact remains that Dr Faust Shkaravsky and his competent colleagues carried out at that time a thorough medical examination and concluded that Hitler had taken poison.

Günsche, standing outside the door, did not hear a shot but did notice a strong smell of bitter almonds when the door was slightly open. Some people, Hitler's secretary Gertraud Junge, for example, did hear a shot. She said, 'When I left Hitler's office and went up the stairs to the shelter landing, I heard two shots. I imagine the shots were fired in Hitler's office.'

Be that as it may, people decided that Hitler shot himself. Thus, Hitler's orderly, Bauer, who shortly after met the SS guard Mengershausen, told him that. Other close associates of the Führer said the same.

Was there really a shot in Hitler's room, or did those awaiting the end outside the doors imagine it? And if there was, who fired it? The testimony of the head of Hitler's bodyguard, Hans Rattenhuber, sheds light on this. He writes,

At about three or four in the afternoon, when I went into the anteroom I noticed a strong smell of bitter almonds. Högl, my deputy, told me with distress that the Führer had just committed suicide.

At that moment Linge came to me. He confirmed the news of Hitler's death, adding that he had just had to carry out the most difficult order the Führer had given him in his life.

I looked at Linge in surprise. He explained to me that just before he died, Hitler ordered him to leave the room for ten minutes, then re-enter, wait another ten minutes, and carry out the order. At this, Linge quickly went into Hitler's room and returned with a Walther pistol which he put on my desk in front of me. From its special exterior finish I recognized it as the Führer's personal pistol. It was now clear to me what Hitler's order had been.

Hitler, evidently uncertain that the poison would prove effective because of the many injections he had been having every day for a long time, ordered Linge to shoot him after he took it. Reichsjugendführer Axmann, who was present during this conversation, took Hitler's pistol and said he would hide it until better times.

Rattenhuber evidently did not know another circumstance that prompted Hitler to give that order to Linge. The problem was that, when the poison was tested on a second dog, the poisoned puppy struggled against dying for a long time and was then shot. This was established at the autopsy of the dead dogs found in the crater, although at first it was overlooked and is not mentioned in the report detailing how they were found.

The conclusion reached by the doctors was,

The manner in which the dog was killed appears to have been as follows: it was first poisoned, possibly using a small dose of cyanide compounds and then, when it had been poisoned and was in its agony, it was shot.

This may have heightened Hitler's fear, as he watched the poisoned dogs, that the poison might not work.

'Linge shot Hitler,' Rattenhuber wrote in his testimony.

I imagined that Linge's hand might have been shaking when he shot at the dead Führer and the bullet missed him. So if a shot really did ring out in Hitler's room, was it Linge who pulled the trigger? But there was no sign of a shot.

The autopsy report on Eva Braun notes a chest wound. In the first edition of my book I suggested that the bullet might have hit the dead Eva, but after the book was published I received a letter from Faust Shkaravsky drawing my attention to the fact that this was not a bullet wound. The report says, 'Evidence of a shrapnel wound to the thorax with haemothorax, damage to the lung and pericardium, six small metal fragments.'

'When and how this wound occurred I cannot say with confidence,' Shkaravsky wrote, 'but it is entirely possible that while the body was being taken out of the Führerbunker it was damaged by shrapnel from a mine or artillery shell.'

A long time later, when the State Archive of the Russian Federation declassified a large number of documents, the following evidence came to light: a year after the events I am describing, in May 1946, the Ministry of Internal Affairs organized a special expedition (code-named 'Myth'!) to the bunker in Berlin in order to collect data to support the claim about Hitler's 'disappearance'. This initiative came not from Stalin, but was born of the rivalry between two government departments: the Ministry of Internal Affairs and the Smersh Counter-intelligence Department. Witnesses were also brought to Berlin: Hitler's adjutant (Günsche), his valet (Linge), and other staff who served him who were in Russian captivity. However, no matter how much duress was applied to get them to admit that Hitler was alive, they answered as one: 'He is dead and we cannot make him alive.'

Contrary to its own mission, the expedition discovered yet another piece of evidence that Hitler had committed suicide. From the bomb crater where the burnt remains were found in May 1945, after further excavation, two detached fragments of skull bone were discovered, one of which showed signs of a bullet exit wound (the absence of part of the skull is noted in the autopsy report of 8 May 1945). This, of course, suggested Hitler had shot himself, but since it was impossible to dismiss the data from the first examination, which had established that Hitler was poisoned, an assertion appeared in print that he had simultaneously taken poison and shot himself. Many experts doubt the feasibility of performing these two actions simultaneously. The account given in the testimony of the head of Hitler's bodyguard, Rattenhuber, seemed convincing to me: Hitler, fearing the poison would be insufficiently effective, ordered his valet to shoot him after he had been poisoned, and the order had been carried out. And perhaps the 'bullet exit wound' is the missing evidence of Linge's shot. But I am not going to join this polemic. Just as then, when Hitler's remains were found, so now, in May 2007, I find the whole controversy profoundly uninteresting. What really mattered was that Hitler was dead.

Subsequently, Faust Shkaravsky confided in a letter to me that he still had a feeling of ongoing unfairness: the Commission was strictly forbidden to photograph Hitler's body, whereas the Commission was photographed in full force next to Goebbels' body strapped to the dissection table. There are also plenty of photographs taken during the investigation. But with Hitler, oh, no! Shkaravsky was not privy to the circumstances that required that prohibition.

Here again, chance played an important part. During the autopsy it was found that Hitler's dentures and teeth had come through surprisingly intact. The autopsy report includes two large non-standard sheets of paper documenting Hitler's teeth in meticulous detail. The experts removed the dentures (and lower jaw). Now the crucial task was, at all costs, to find Hitler's dentists.

The Burgundy Coloured Box

In Berlin–Buch on 8 May, the very day when the document of surrender of Germany was ratified in Karlshorst, although I did not yet know that, Colonel Gorbushin called me in and handed me a box, saying it contained Hitler's teeth and that I was answerable with my head for its safe-keeping.

It was a second-hand, burgundy red box with a soft lining and covered with satin, the kind of thing made to hold a bottle of perfume or cheap jewellery.

Now, however, what it held was the irrefutable proof that Hitler was dead, because in all the world there are no two people whose teeth are exactly alike. In forensic medicine this is held to be the fundamental anatomical item that clinches any argument about a person's identity. Moreover, this evidence could be preserved for many years to come.

The box was entrusted to me because the safe was still back with the second echelon and there was nowhere secure to put it. Why me? For the simple reason that everything connected with Hitler was being kept top secret and must not be allowed to leak out from Gorbushin's group which, as already mentioned, had dwindled by now down to just three people.

All that day, so pregnant with the sense of imminent victory, it was decidedly tiresome to be carrying a box about, and to turn cold whenever I thought of the possibility of accidentally leaving it somewhere. It burdened and oppressed me.

The situation in which I found myself was odd, unreal, especially when I look back at it now, out of the context of the war. War is itself pathological, and everything that happened during the war, everything we went through simply cannot be translated into the concepts of peacetime and does not fit into the familiar psychological categories.

Already by this time, the sense of history surrounding the fall of the Third Reich was fading. We had experienced too much. The death of its leaders and everything connected with that seemed nothing out of the ordinary.

I was not the only one feeling that way. When I was called to front head-quarters to translate Goebbels' diaries, I met up with Raya, our telegraphist, and saw her trying on a white evening dress that had belonged to Eva Braun and which had been brought to her from the underground complex of the Reich Chancellery by Senior Lieutenant Kurashov (who was in love with her). It was a long dress, reaching almost to the floor, with a plunging neckline, and Raya did not care for it. As a historic memento it was of no interest to her. Shoes from a box labelled 'Für Fr. Eva Braun' were just right and she appreciated them far more.

Towards midnight on 8 May, I was about to go to bed in the downstairs room I had been allotted in a two-storey house when I suddenly heard someone calling my name from the first floor. I hastily ran up the very steep wooden staircase. The door to the room was wide open, and Major Bystrov and Major Pichko were standing beside the radio craning their necks.

It was strange really, because we were expecting this, but when the newsreader finally came on air to announce solemnly, 'The signing of the instrument of unconditional surrender of the German armed forces . . .' we just stood there, overwhelmed.

1. We, the undersigned, acting by authority of the German High Command, hereby surrender unconditionally to the Supreme Commander, Allied Expeditionary Force and simultaneously to the Supreme High Command of the Red Army all forces on land, at sea, and in the air who are at this date under German control.
2. The German High Command will at once issue orders to all German commanders of the land, naval and air forces and all forces under the German Command to cease hostilities at 23.01 Central European Time on 8 May 1945, to remain in their places where they are located at this time, and be completely disarmed . . .

The voice of Yury Levitan resounded, 'To commemorate the victorious culmination of the Great Patriotic War . . .' We yelled something and waved our arms about in the air.

We poured out the wine in silence. I put the box on the floor and the three of us clinked glasses, deeply moved, excited but hushed as the cannonades boomed out in celebration over the airwaves from Moscow.

I went back down the steep wooden stairs to the ground floor. Suddenly it was as if something jolted me and I clutched at the banister. Never am I going to forget the feeling that electrified me at that moment.

God Almighty, is this happening to me? Is this me standing here at the moment Germany surrenders, with a box in my hands containing the indisputable remnants of Adolf Hitler?!

Many years were to pass before I stood in that place again. I wandered excitedly along the street, looking out for the house with a steep staircase where I had stood with that box in my hands and heard the news that the war was over, and where in those hours my life so freakishly intersected with the course of German history.

What is victory? You can sculpt it as Victoria, drawn by a quadriga above a triumphal arch. It can be embodied in architecture as the Propylaeum, the Brandenburg Gate . . . But what does it mean just for a person? For someone back in their own suffering homeland? For someone who has followed it here to Berlin? How can that state be articulated, that jubilant 'Aaah!' as if you are on a swing at its highest point, and everything about you is awhirl – at last, this is the end, and you are alive, and your heart sings with indescribable joy; it seems you really will get to wander once again through the streets of your home cities, to stare up at the sky, to look about you, to do so many things – now that the war is over, now that war is no more. And you are close to tears at the afflictions of the past and from bewilderment over the future you now face.

The uplifting spirit of victory, but exalted within it, and perhaps above all else, the mourning. How are you to hold on to that? How are you to reconcile the victory with all the effort it has cost, the merciless demand for self-sacrifice along the way?

Early on 9 May everything was buzzing in the village of Berlin–Buch. In anticipation of something extraordinary, some indescribable festivity and celebration to honour this long-awaited Victory Day, soldiers were already dancing, somewhere there was singing. Soldiers were walking down the village street their arms flung around each other. Girls in the army were frenziedly laundering their tunics.

The forensic medical report had noted, 'The fundamental anatomical discovery that can be used to identify this individual are the teeth, with a large number of artificial bridges, teeth, crowns and fillings.'

However, the task now facing us, of locating Hitler's dentists in the chaos of devastated Berlin, would have daunted anyone not fired up by the prospect of impudently confronting the conspiracy of silence, and buoyed up on the crest of the wave of victory. It was on 9 May, this first morning when the war was over, that we sallied forth on our quest.

A tractor was pulling an artillery piece, and on its barrel, as on the side of a truck we met, there still glowed the words, 'Berlin, here we come!' The Red Army soldiers, the guns, the cars: everything was in its place, nothing had changed, and yet, at the same time, suddenly, everything had changed.

The cannon would no longer fire, the soldiers no longer go into the attack. A long-awaited peace had descended upon the Earth and already it was not only those far-off battles on the banks of the Volga, but also those battles very near this present place, in days of an incomparable upsurge of morale, when our soldiers could not wait to get at Berlin, that today had suddenly become history.

The day before Victory Day had been warm, summer-like, even, but now the sky was overcast and the day was grey and sunless. In the Berlin suburbs, though, the gardens were flowering, the smell of lilac was in the air, and by the roadside, in grass lit up by yellow dandelions, sat two Germans – a boy and a girl, and on their young, lively faces you could read that the war was over, the nightmare and the dying was at an end, and that to be living in this world was an unbelievable blessing.

From the intact outskirts we drove back into the ruins of Berlin. In places smoke was still rising, the city's air still filled with the fumes of battle. Through the breach in a wall you would glimpse a sooty piece of red cloth, a home-made banner, one of those that the soldiers had readied on the approaches to Berlin and kept close to their hearts to be planted in the German capital.

The barricades, crushed by tank tracks, had yet to be dismantled. In places ruins not yet cool still smoked. There was rubble everywhere. The city was full of refugees from the eastern lands, but everyone who could had fled Berlin before the assault, getting away from the bombing and the impending siege. Who could we approach?

Somehow, though, the gods were with us: there is no other explanation. How else was it possible that in this tortured, vanquished city of three million souls, we found the assistant of Professor Hugo Blaschke, Hitler's dentist?

This is a subplot in its own right, but perhaps not a subplot because those develop at least to some extent in accordance with the laws of logic. This developed against all logic, an enigmatic succession of strokes of luck smoothing the path of people bent on affirming the truth.

That captured Ford 8 saloon, with our driver Sergey at the wheel, drove for many hours through the streets of Berlin that day. Here I have him, in a photo I have kept, Sergey from Siberia, a big lad who said little, lounging against the car he pulled out of a ditch. He had painted it himself, black, with its mounds and clearings on the bodywork, and now it bumped its way down barely passable streets strewn with masonry from collapsed houses, sometimes braking, sometimes roaring away and racing along highways cleared of debris.

We stopped beside a functioning hospital and asked the doctor in charge – who had looked after Hitler's teeth? He did not know. Of those who treated Hitler, the doctor could give the name only of the internationally renowned laryngologist Carl von Eicken, who headed the Charité clinic. 'Is he in Berlin?' That the doctor could not say.

The road signs attached to lamp posts had been flattened along with the lamp posts. It was impossible to navigate using our map of the city. More than once that day, pedestrians told us how to get to this or that street. The Berlin youngsters who willingly clambered into the car to show us the way had no idea of the historic adventure in which they were bit players.

Finally, our quest led us to the Charité university clinic. Its buildings had quaint, coloured stripes painted on them as camouflage against air attack. We drove to the ear, nose and throat department. Here the hospital had mainly civilian patients. It was located in a basement, where dim lamps flickered under low vaulted ceilings. Nurses in grey, with white headscarves bearing a red cross in the middle, looked exhausted as, sternly and silently, they went about their duties. Wounded patients were being carried on stretchers.

Because the wounded in this gloomy, cramped basement were non-military, the brutality of the war that had come to an end yesterday was starkly in evidence. And it was here that we found Professor von Eicken, tall, old and thin. Working in dreadful conditions, he did not leave his post in the days of danger and tragedy, did not flee from Berlin before the surrender, no matter how forcefully he was urged to, and, taking their cue from him, all the other staff stayed too. He conducted us to his clinic, also painted in camouflage colours and still empty, and there in his office we had an unhurried conversation.

Yes, he had had occasion to provide medical care to Reich Chancellor

Hitler when he had a throat ailment back in 1935. After the attempt on Hitler's life in July 1944, Eicken had again treated him because his eardrums were damaged when the bomb exploded and he had significant hearing loss. His hearing gradually returned and there had been no need to operate.

Of Hitler's personal physicians, Eicken was able to name Professor Theodor Morell. He, we knew, had been sent to Berchtesgaden, where the Führer was intending to go himself before the worsening situation obliged him to abandon the plan. The dentist in the Reich Chancellery was, Eicken believed, also Hitler's personal physician, but he did not know the man's name. That was our man.

On that single occasion I got to know Carl von Eicken in far greater depth than is possible under normal circumstances, because the circumstances in which we met were far from normal. It was as if we were at the same time having a private conversation.

'Are you the director of the ear, nose and throat clinic?' 'Quite so.' Why had he not left, not fled, not saved himself? There had, after all, been such insistent invitations. Are you not afraid to be meeting us? Yes, of course, there was his duty as a doctor, as the head of a clinic, but in the person sitting opposite me, in the eyes watching me through his spectacles, there was something else. But what? Oh, there is no mystery. I naturally follow tradition because I am German. He could have brushed it off as easily as that, but there was something more to our conversation. Yes, he had treated Hitler. A throat problem. An occupational hazard for a politician. He had treated Trotsky, too, when he arrived in 1923 and settled near Berlin.

But what tradition was this venerable old gentleman referring to in our private conversation? It was an inviolable tradition. Not that drill, that damnably alien tradition of obedience without choice. Here I was confronted by a personal, moral choice based on the genuine traditions of German culture. He had taken on the running of the clinic in 1922, and was to direct it for another five years after our meeting, until 1950. He lived ten years after that in peaceful retirement and died at the age of eighty-seven. So back then, in May 1945, he was already seventy-two. '*Er war sehr berühmt.*' He had a great reputation, his staff reminisced.

Eicken sent for someone from the dentistry department and a student arrived. He knew the name of Hitler's dentist, Dr Hugo Blaschke, and volunteered to take us to him. The student wore a light black coat, no hat, and had dark, wavy hair above a round, soft face. He was friendly and sociable, got into the car and showed us the way. We learned he was a Bulgarian, had studied in Berlin but, as the result of events in Bulgaria, had not been allowed to return there.

Soviet vehicles, flying red flags in honour of the victory, were driving through the streets in the city centre, which had just about been cleared. Germans were riding bicycles, of which there were a lot, with large baskets. A child might be sitting in the basket, or it might be stacked with belongings. The war in Berlin had been over for a week, and the sense of relief the Germans had felt for the first few days had given way to pressing concerns that now affected everyone. The number of pedestrians in the city had also increased noticeably, and they walked along the pavements with children and bundles, pushing prams and wheelbarrows laden with baggage.

We drove into the Kurfürstendamm, one of Berlin's most fashionable streets. It was in the same calamitous state as the others, but No. 213, or at least the wing of it where Dr Blaschke's private surgery was located, had survived, as if specifically to serve the needs of history. How otherwise would we have managed to find our essential witness?

At the entrance we met a man with a red ribbon in the buttonhole of his dark jacket, signal of good feelings, of welcome and solidarity with the Russians. This was unusual – at this time it was far more usual to see white, the colour of surrender. The man introduced himself as Dr Bruck.

Hearing that we were looking for Dr Blaschke, he replied that Blaschke had flown from Berlin to Berchtesgaden together with Hitler's adjutant. We went with Dr Bruck to the mezzanine and he took us into Blaschke's dental surgery. Realizing that Bruck was not going to be able to help us, Colonel Gorbushin asked if he knew of any of Blaschke's employees. 'Of course I do!' Dr Bruck exclaimed. 'You mean Käthchen? Käthe Heusermann? She is at home in her apartment right on our doorstep.' The student volunteered to go and fetch her. 'No. 39–40 Pariserstrasse, Apartment 1,' Bruck told him.

He seated us in soft armchairs in which the Nazi leaders had sat before us, as patients of Dr Blaschke. Since 1932 Blaschke had been Hitler's personal dentist. Bruck also settled himself in one of the armchairs. We learned from him that he was a dentist, used to live and work in the provinces, and that Käthe Heusermann, Dr Blaschke's assistant, had been his student and later his own assistant. That was before the Nazis seized power. Later she and her sister helped Bruck to disappear, because he was a Jew and needed to live under a false name.

A slim, tall, attractive woman in a dark blue flared coat came in. She had on a headscarf over luxuriant blonde hair. 'Käthchen,' Bruck said familiarly, 'these people are Russians. They seem to need you for something.' Even before he had finished she burst into tears. She had already suffered from encountering Russian soldiers. 'Käthchen!' Dr Bruck said in embarrassment, 'Käthchen, these people are our friends.' Bruck was considerably less tall than Käthe, but he took her hand as if she were a small child and stroked the sleeve of her coat. They had found themselves at opposite ends of the Nazi regime. She, as a member of the staff serving Hitler, was in a privileged position, while he, persecuted and living outside the law, was given support by her family, for which she might have paid a terrible price.

Looking around, Käthe saw me sitting on the sidelines. She came straight over and sat down next to me. Without a moment's hesitation we began talking to each other. Käthe Heusermann was thirty-five. She told me her fiancé was a teacher and now, as a non-commissioned officer, was somewhere in Norway and she had heard nothing from him for a long time. Dr Blaschke had invited her to be evacuated with him to Berchtesgaden, but she refused. She had been working for Blaschke since 1937, and last saw Hitler in mid-April in the Reich Chancellery when she was receiving a ration of cigarettes. With the permission of Magda Goebbels she had left the Reich Chancellery, but continued to go there for rations, which she shared with Dr Bruck.

On 2 May she had heard from strangers in Pariserstrasse that Hitler was dead and that he had been cremated. Later she told me a few details about him and the Goebbels family. It was from her I heard that Magda Goebbels had not been happily married; she complained about her husband's infidelities and had wanted to leave him, only the Führer insisted on her keeping together their exemplary German family. She quite liked Magda, or at least sympathized with her.

Back then, though, in Dr Blaschke's surgery, Colonel Gorbushin asked me to ask her whether they had Hitler's dental records. Heusermann said they had, and immediately took out a box with record cards. We watched with bated breath as she flicked through them. We glimpsed the cards of Himmler, Ley, the press chief Dietrich, Goebbels, his wife, all their children . . .

The silence was so heavy that we clearly heard in Dr Bruck's sigh, although he did not know what had brought us there, how anxious he was that everything should turn out well. The student, who by now evidently had a fair idea of what was going on, found our tense anticipation contagious and stood motionless, his head tilted a little to one side.

At last Hitler's medical card was found, and that was a start, but there were no X–rays. Heusermann suggested they might be in Blaschke's other surgery – in the Reich Chancellery itself. We said goodbye to Dr Bruck and the student and rushed back there with Käthe Heusermann.

From that day I heard no more about the Bulgarian student until, almost twenty years later, when interest was again stirred up in the question of whether Hitler was dead or alive, because the issue of statutory limitation of criminal responsibility was being debated. At that time, it was set at twenty years. I saw a portrait of this man in *Stern*. His hair was still wavy and his features soft, although naturally after so much time he had changed. I read that he was Mihail Arnaudov, who lived in Kiel, and I read his interview, which reverberated around the globe, in which he tells truthfully, if in his own way, about our visit, but then adds a fictitious account of his participation in the identification of Hitler.

He had rendered us a great service in taking us from Eicken to Blaschke's surgery, but had contributed nothing to the actual identification, because we had thanked him and then seen no more of him.

During the time the student was with us, he could easily have worked out why we so needed to track down Hitler's dentists and his dental history. But then, just when this unexpected, titillating adventure into which the young man had been plunged was approaching its culmination, the curtain had fallen and the actors were lost to view.

On the way to the Reich Chancellery, Käthe Heusermann told me she used to travel with Blaschke to Berchtesgaden, where her patient was Eva Braun. In Berlin the existence of Hitler's mistress was meticulously concealed until the very last days; there were constant statements to the effect that the Führer did not smoke, did not drink, held aloof from earthly gratifications and devoted himself only to serving the people. That was the cornerstone of all the propaganda.

We parked the car and the three of us walked in silence down the as yet uncleared, deserted Wilhelmstrasse. On a round advertising pillar there was pasted the order of the Soviet commandant of Berlin, General Berzarin, printed on orange paper.

Once more the Reich Chancellery, pockmarked by shells and bullets, blackened with soot, its walls breached in places, a long, straggling building with a single balcony, its architecture an expression of the 'single will of Germany' which, in the person of the Führer, would appear on the balcony during Nazi celebrations. Above the entrance, in bas-relief, was the Nazi emblem: a spreadeagle clutching a swastika in its talons. Within a few days this bronze had been hacked down and transported to Moscow, to the Armed Forces Museum, where it can be seen to this day. The sentry did ground his rifle, but barred our way – he had been ordered not to let anyone pass without a special permit from the commandant of Berlin.

Gorbushin whipped out his pistol and pushed the sentry aside. The man was taken aback: he would have had every right to shoot. But we needed to get in.

We opened the heavy oak door. To the right was the assembly hall: the door had been torn off its hinges, chandeliers had fallen to the floor. To the left was the gentle descent to the bomb shelter. Hitler had worked here until 21 April, when our artillery fired a volley of shells into the centre of Berlin and he moved to the Führerbunker.

We passed through the vaulted vestibule and down two flights of stairs, with one dim torch between the three of us. It was dark, deserted and spooky. In the radio studio from which Goebbels broadcast, a Red Army soldier was sleeping with his helmet slipped down over his ear. Only Käthe could find her way around in this Tomb of the Pharaohs. She led us to a boxy little room which, until recently, had been at the disposal of her boss, Dr Blaschke.

The pocket torch faintly picked out in the darkness a dentist's chair, a couch with an adjustable headrest, and a small desk. There was something on the floor. We picked it up and shone the torch on it. A photo. Käthe recognized the Führer's deceased Alsatian being taken for a walk by his adjutant. It was damp and there was a musty smell.

We searched through a box with a card index, looked in the desk and a locker. With Heusermann's help we found the X-rays of Hitler's teeth and his dental records. We were lucky, incredibly lucky, that the hurricane which had blown through the underground complex a few days ago had left this nook untouched. We found gold crowns which, according to Käthe, had been made for Hitler although, as she admitted in her memoirs written many years later, here she was slightly overdoing it: the crowns were in fact for one of the secretaries. She was understandably anxious to stay on the right side of us. Fortunately those crowns did not figure again in the investigation.

Suddenly, from the depths of the corridor, we heard, '*By the Vol-ga – a stone . . .*' It was a lonely voice. Some partying soldier was quaffing expensive wines the German generals that he had sent packing had been drinking as they sought to banish despair. The soldier must surely have been written off by his unit, while here he was consoling himself for a seventh day, sleeping, waking, drinking to the glory of Russian arms and the repose of those who never made it to the Reich Chancellery.

We left, taking with us our incredibly important finds, the most miraculous, the most wonderful of which was Käthe Heusermann herself. Through the empty underground corridors a woozy voice echoed, intoxicated by wine, victory and grief: '*Someone wai-ting alone . . .*'

No sooner had we got into the car than the engine conked out. Driver Sergey lifted the bonnet. We alighted, and found ourselves right at the

Brandenburg Gate. I pictured Nazi detachments with flaming torches marching through the six columns of the gate to the Kaiserhof Hotel, where Hitler usually stayed when in Berlin before he came to power. On the hotel balcony the puny figure of Goebbels would try to make himself seen behind the burly backs of his comrades-in-arms. Hitler would raise an arm in salute over the crowd. The torches of future conflagrations, destruction and book burnings flickered, lit by the Nazis and destined ultimately to consume them. It seemed fitting that 'torchers' was the name given in the German Army to soldiers whose job it was to set fire to towns and villages as they retreated.

We had driven on a little when suddenly the roar of guns broke the stillness that had reigned for the last few days. My heart sank instantly. What was this? Surely not war again? I did not immediately realize it was a celebratory salute! Above the hideous ruins, above the smoke and dust of battle that had yet to clear, above the grim Reichstag building and the new spring grass, tracer bullets flew skywards and the smoke-laden heavens were lit up by flashes of colour. Heavy artillery boomed, machine guns rattled, submachine guns were fired. Shrapnel clattered down on the cratered roadway. The thunder grew louder and everything around was shaking as it did in time of battle.

We returned to Buch, taking Käthe Heusermann with us. There were no lights burning in the windows of Germans: the vanquished were asleep. The victors, having celebrated all day, quietened down, but none of the wine of victory passed my lips. I just went to bed.

The Identification

Lovers of crime novels will, perhaps, be disappointed: there were no ambushes, no shots fired from round a corner, no safes were cracked. I will add, to the chagrin of those who prefer legend to the truth, that there were no cunningly disguised doubles.

I told the tale above of the origin of one would-be double. But that male corpse with his darned socks, who was so lovingly filmed for the newsreels, was no double, put in place as a decoy and to facilitate Hitler's escape, as suggested by later, romanticized accounts. It was just the body of one of the many occupants of the bunker, killed by shrapnel or shot by Hitler as the end approached, and any resemblance to the Führer was mostly the product of the over-excitability of the time.

Other 'doubles' popped up, and here is why. Colonel General Berzarin, the commandant of Berlin, promised he would nominate for the award of Hero of the Soviet Union anyone who located Hitler's corpse. As a result, half a dozen dead 'Hitlers' were dragged along to the Commandant's Office, giving rise to the tale of doubles.

At this crucial stage in our mission, luck was on our side. As always, much was down to chance. Crucial circumstances jostled side-by-side with insignificant developments but, by the same token, the insignificant sometimes proved crucial.

Käthe Heusermann might have flown to Berchtesgaden, where Hitler was assembling his attendant staff with the intention of moving there himself. Dr Blaschke had, after all, urged her to fly out with him. She had refused, because for so long she had had no letters from her fiancé, the non-commissioned officer stationed in Norway, and was afraid he would be unable to find her if she left. She told me she had also buried her dresses at a resort near Berlin to keep them safe from the bombing and fires, and was reluctant to leave them. That, too, had caused her to stay.

That is how historically insignificant circumstances did history a big favour. Käthe stayed in Berlin and, as a result, did not vanish into oblivion, did not simply disappear. She was the only available person who knew and remembered all the distinctive features of Hitler's teeth, and her contribution to identifying his remains was crucial. With Käthe Heusermann's help we obtained irrefutable evidence that Hitler was dead and were able to pass it on to our descendants.

Käthe first described Hitler's teeth from memory. It was now 10 o'clock in Berlin–Buch, the following morning, 10 May. She was being interviewed by Colonel Gorbushin and Major Bystrov, and I was translating and making notes. I asked her not to give the teeth their specialist names – incisor, canine and so on, for fear I might not correlate the German and Russian terms correctly. Instead she simply gave them numbers. The note I made is as follows:

Hitler's upper denture was a gold bridge attached to the 1st left tooth with a window crown, to the root of the 2nd left tooth, to the root of the 1st right tooth and to the 3rd right tooth with a gold crown . . .

Käthe told us:

In autumn 1944 I took part in the extraction of Hitler's sixth tooth on the left in the upper jaw. For that purpose I and Dr Blaschke travelled to his staff headquarters in the vicinity of Rastenburg [in East Prussia]. In order to remove the tooth, Dr Blaschke used a drill to saw through the gold bridge between the 4th and 5th teeth in the upper jaw to the left. At this time I was holding a mirror in Hitler's mouth and attentively observing the whole procedure.

We could compare this with the report of the medical examination of 8 May, which read, 'Bridge of upper denture on left behind premolar tooth (4) sawn vertically'. The report devotes a lot of space to a meticulous description of the other teeth. We had also X–rays that we found in Dr Blaschke's little room under the Reich Chancellery.

Most importantly, we could compare her description with the contents of the jewellery box. Käthe Heusermann examined these and confirmed that they were indeed Hitler's teeth.

She recalled this many years later for *Die Welt*. The article, like other materials from abroad, came into my hands quite by chance. Leon Nebenzahl, who translated my *Notes of a Military Translator*, showed me the magazine clipping on a visit to Moscow.

'This took place in a house near Berlin,' she writes, 'in the presence of a colonel, a major and an interpreter. "Look closely," the colonel instructed me, "and tell us what this is, if you know."'

She describes examining the teeth taken out of the box and recognizing them. 'I took the dental bridge in my hand. I looked for an unmistakeable sign. I found it immediately, took a deep breath and blurted out, "These are the teeth of Adolf Hitler." I was showered with expressions of gratitude.'

Subsequently Heusermann talked to the specialists. Their report notes that, in conversation with the principal forensic expert of the front, Medical Service Lieutenant Colonel Shkaravsky, 'which took place on 11 May 45', Citizen Heusermann, Käthe 'described in detail the condition of Hitler's teeth. Her description coincides with the anatomical features of the oral cavity of the charred unknown male on which we conducted an autopsy.' She also drew a diagram of Hitler's teeth from memory, pointing out all their specific features.

After reading the first edition of my book, Faust Shkaravsky thanked me for mentioning him and corresponded with me for many years until his death. He sent me a photographic reproduction of that diagram, which he had kept, accompanying it with an explanation:

Heusermann and I had a disagreement concerning false teeth on steel posts. During the initial examination of the teeth I registered the presence of two posts, in the 2nd left and 2nd right upper incisors. Heusermann claimed there was a third.

At the end of our preliminary conversation, Käthe Heusermann was shown Hitler's teeth and we conducted a joint inspection of them. Käthe Heusermann was right: a third post was found in the right lower canine.

This disagreement, in which Heusermann proved correct, was further proof of how precisely she knew everything about Hitler's teeth.

'All this can be confirmed by Blaschke's dental technician, Echtmann,' Käthe told us at the first interrogation. Bystrov and I went to Echtmann's apartment. In my diary I have a description of Echtmann's worn-out, listless wife (who I thought must be suffering from a thyroid disorder). She clung desperately to her husband, who was also frail and sickly.

Fritz Echtmann, dental technician, was a short, dark-haired man with a pale complexion, aged thirty-something. He had worked at Dr Blaschke's private laboratory on Kurfürstendamm since 1938, and made false teeth for Hitler. He, too, first gave a description of them from memory, and then had an opportunity to inspect them in Buch, where he, too, identified them.

This was a German starkly confronted with the death of Hitler, but Echtmann himself had been through too much, having lived with his wife and daughter in Berlin throughout the war, to be shocked by anything. He inspected Hitler's teeth calmly. When, however, he looked at Eva Braun's, he became agitated. On 11 May he said, and I wrote it down,

This way of constructing a dental bridge is my own invention. I did not make such a bridge for anyone else, and have never seen a similar way of attaching the teeth devised by anybody else. It was in the autumn of 1944. Braun rejected my first bridge because, when she opened her mouth, the gold was visible. I made a second bridge, eliminating that snag. I used a very original technique.

Many years later I saw a photograph of Fritz Echtmann in the December 1964 issue of the West German *Stern*. He had two fingers raised and had been photographed as he testified under oath to a court in Berchtesgaden that he really had identified Hitler's teeth on 11 May 1945, and could thus certify that he was dead.

The Missing Link

Back in 1945 we were, unfortunately, not aware of the testimony of two other very important witnesses of Hitler's death: Otto Günsche and Hans Rattenhuber. They were both taken prisoner in sectors allocated to our neighbouring army, but there was no staff headquarters or any centre coordinating our separate activities. Later, their testimonies ended up in the same place in the archive as our documents, but it was almost twenty years before I was able to read them. How desperately we needed, from the very outset, people who had witnessed Hitler's death, his cremation and burial.

Our investigation was already nearing its end when the Smersh agents of Lieutenant Colonel Klimenko detained a member of Hitler's SS bodyguard, Harry Mengershausen. A handsome, broad-shouldered fellow, now wearing civilian clothes, Mengershausen said he could indicate the place where the bodies were hidden, covered with earth and rubble. He pointed out the crater, not knowing that the bodies had already been removed from it.

Klimenko had displayed a lack of conscientiousness, and even gloried in his negligent attitude towards the bodies of Hitler and Eva Braun. 'Frankly,' he wrote to me, ' I wasn't that bothered, and in any case I had more urgent things to do than mess about with these corpses, especially since I'm squeamish, so I went out of my way to avoid them.' That was the reason he sent Deryabin, instead of going personally, to retrieve the bodies from the crater. Now, however, he moved with commendable alacrity. Lieutenant Colonel Klimenko, with a group of officers and men, returned with Mengershausen to the Reich Chancellery and an official report was compiled:

1945, the thirteenth day of May, Berlin
We, the undersigned . . . with the participation of identification witness Mengershausen, Harry, have this day inspected the burial site of the bodies of Reich Chancellor Adolf Hitler and his wife . . .

Inspection of the location indicated by identification witness Mengershausen established the truthfulness of his testimony . . . The testimony of identification witness Mengershausen was confirmed as true all the more because on 4 May 1945 we had removed from the crater he indicated the burnt bodies of a man and a woman and two poisoned dogs, which were identified by other identification witnesses as those of Hitler and his wife, Ifa [*sic*] Braun, his former personal secretary.

A rough survey of the location where the bodies of Hitler and his wife were discovered and photographic images of the locations indicated by identification witness Mengershausen are appended to this report.

As witness this report compiled in the city of Berlin, Reich Chancellery.

The document was signed by Lieutenant Colonel Klimenko, Senior Lieutenant Katyshev, Guards Major Gabelok, photojournalist Junior Lieutenant Kalashnikov, and Privates Oleynik, Churakov, Navash and Myalkin.

A copy of this document was mailed to me by Ivan Klimenko when he heard my book was being prepared for publication. He also wrote,

I brought this report containing Mengershausen's testimony to the army counterintelligence department, which is where I saw you.

This concluded the work of the Smersh department of the corps. Everything else was undertaken by the army and front headquarters.

Major Bystrov interrogated Mengershausen and I translated. We were sitting on logs in the courtyard. Mengershausen told us,

On 30 April I was guarding the Reich Chancellery, patrolling the corridor where the kitchen and green dining room are situated. Additionally, I was monitoring the garden because at a distance of 80 metres from the green dining room was the Führer's bomb shelter.

Patrolling the corridor and approaching the kitchen, I met someone I knew to be the Führer's orderly, Bauer, who was going to the kitchen. He told me that Hitler had shot himself in his bunker. I enquired as to the whereabouts of the Führer's wife, and Bauer told me she too was lying dead in the bunker, but he did not know whether she had poisoned or shot herself.

I talked to Bauer for only a few minutes: he was hurrying to the kitchen. In the kitchen food was being cooked for Hitler's entourage. He returned shortly afterwards to the bunker.

I did not believe Bauer's report of the death of Hitler and his wife and continued to patrol my area.

Not more than one hour after meeting Bauer, as I came out to a terrace situated 60–80 metres from the bunker, I suddenly saw the personal adjutant, Sturmbannführer Günsche, and Hitler's valet, Sturmbannführer Linge, carrying the body of Hitler from the emergency exit of the bunker and placing it 2 metres from the exit. They went back and a few minutes later brought out Eva Braun, who was dead, and whom they put in the same place. Some way from the bodies there were two twenty-kilogram cans of petrol, Günsche and Linge began to pour petrol over the bodies and set fire to them.

Major Bystrov enquired whether any of the other guards had seen the bodies of Hitler and Braun being burned. Mengershausen did not know for sure. 'Of all the security guards I was the closest to Hitler's bunker at that time.' He bent down and began to outline a map of the garden on the ground with a piece of wood.

Thus we found our missing link: somebody involved in or who had witnessed the actual cremation, who would have been so helpful in the first phase of our mission, when we were hunting Hitler. We went into the house with Mengershausen and wrote down everything he had told us.

From his post Mengershausen had been able to see only Günsche and Linge but, shielded by the bunker, hiding from the shellfire, Goebbels, Bormann and the others were observing the burning of the bodies. Nearby, a battle was raging; the Reich Chancellery was under intense bombardment. The wailing of shells, the crash of explosions throwing up columns of soil, the smashing and whistling of flying window glass. The buffeting wind disturbed the clothing on the bodies. The fire flared up and then died down as the petrol burned off. More petrol was poured over them and again ignited.

Then what did Mengershausen do? He escaped, acting on his own initiative and without waiting for new orders. 'That same day, 30 April, I changed into civilian clothing and hid in a cellar.' He was wearing a raincoat that was too short for him and obviously belonged to somebody else. His long arms protruded from the sleeves. Major Bystrov handed him a photograph of the Reich Chancellery garden. I translated, 'Tell me what you see in this photo.'

This is a photo of the emergency exit from Hitler's bomb shelter. I know this place well and can show you where the bodies of Hitler and his wife Braun were burned, and also the place where they were buried.

With one cross I am indicating on the photo where the bodies of Hitler and Braun were burned, with two crosses the place where they were buried, and with three crosses the emergency exit from Hitler's bunker.

The next time I saw that photo with Mengershausen's crosses on it was in the Council of Ministers Archive.

I was told later at front headquarters that SS officer Mengershausen, when he was taken there, told them in his written testimony that he not only watched the Führer being cremated but was also involved in it himself. What exactly that consisted of I did not hear at the time, and found nothing he had written about it among the archive documents. But then, in a manuscript written by his superior, Rattenhuber, I read,

The bodies of Hitler and Eva Braun did not burn well, and I went downstairs to arrange for more fuel to be sent. When I came back up, the bodies had already been sprinkled with a little soil. The sentry Mengershausen told me it was impossible to stand at his post because of the intolerable smell and that he, together with another SS soldier, had, on the instructions of Günsche, pushed them into a pit where Hitler's poisoned dog lay.

Going on to describe the behaviour of those in the shelter, who set about preparing to escape the moment they became aware of the Führer's death, Rattenhuber once more mentions Mengershausen.

I was startled by the cold calculation of SS guard Mengershausen, who made his way into Hitler's office and removed a gold badge from the Führer's tunic, which was draped over a chair, hoping that 'They'll pay a good price for this relic in America.'

Mengershausen's testimony was the missing link we had needed in order to produce an evidence-based reconstruction of the last hours of Hitler's life and the exact nature of his death. It was time to summarize. Reports that Hitler had been positively identified went first to front headquarters, and from there to the top.

The people involved in this investigation had a sense of great personal responsibility to obtain irrefutable evidence, recognizing only too well that a lack of clarity about Hitler's death would be harmful. It could only facilitate his intention of disappearing without a trace, turning into a myth, and thereby fuelling the fanaticism and galvanizing the Führer's adherents. Nazism was very centred on Hitler personally, and the peoples of the USSR, who had put everything they had into winning the victory over Nazism, had an inalienable right to know that the last full stop had been written in this history.

Having obtained incontrovertible evidence, I really believed that all the nonsensical rumours would be swept away and truth would prevail. I wrote a brief letter to my family, which they have preserved, to say that I had taken part in an important mission, that we would shortly be returning to Moscow, and I would see them soon.

I was sure we would be sent to Moscow with all the data and principal witnesses to the identification. I was sure that Käthe Heusermann, for her services to history, would be appreciated and rewarded. Nothing stirred. Everything stayed just as it was. Now what was going to happen?

Restaging History

Hitler – corpse or legend? We moved to Finow, a small town near Berlin, and then our Colonel Gorbushin was told specifically by Colonel Andrey Miroshnichenko,[1] that too much time was being spent on all this messing about with dead bodies and he should stop. Vasiliy Gorbushin departed for Flensburg, as a member of the Allied delegation to accept Dönitz's surrender. He entrusted to Major Bystrov the task of ensuring the safety of our 'trophies'. They were secretly moved to Finow and buried, still in their crates.

A few days later, on 18 May, a general appeared from General Head-quarters, flanked by Lieutenant General Alexander Vadis,[2] Andrey

---

1. Head of the Smersh counterintelligence section of our 3rd Shock Army.
2. Head of the Smersh counterintelligence directorate of the 1st Byelorussian Front. Birstein, pp. 306–7.

Miroshnichenko and other bigwigs from front and our army headquarters, with, we were told, instructions from Stalin to check everything relating to Hitler's death and return with a report. Miroshnichenko could have been in big trouble for failing to realize that Stalin's reluctance to make Hitler's death public, or indeed to let anyone else know about it, did not indicate that he was prepared to take the fact on trust, without having everything thoroughly verified by his personal representative. Stalin wanted to 'own' this secret all by himself.

There is a well known saying that in war a day lived is equivalent to three days in peacetime, but in those days of May 1945, even with the war over, the days were so busy and passed so rapidly they exceeded that score.

Something major was afoot. Käthe Heusermann and dental technician Fritz Echtmann had been arrested and brought in; SS bodyguard Harry Mengershausen, whom we had questioned, reappeared. A new investigation began. The whole identification and interrogation process restarted and was referred to as a 'repetition'.

In these interrogations, Käthe Heusermann and Fritz Echtmann are referred to as 'detainees'. This time, each interrogation was preceded by an official warning to me, as the interpreter, of my potential liability under Article such-and-such. At no time during the war, no matter what level I was translating for, had there been anything of that kind. This was new. In part, no doubt, it reflected the special burden of responsibility I bore in the interrogation, but it reflected no less the coming of a new, postwar era. During the war there had been more trust and less formality but, of course, a full seventeen days had elapsed since victory had been celebrated in Berlin.

The general studied everything, asked questions and listened attentively. He did not sign the records, but during breaks their text was forwarded verbatim to General Headquarters over the government's special high-security communication lines. The records were signed by the assembled top brass and, in front of my eyes, I witnessed the brazen falsification of history. Anyone reading those documents would suppose Miroshnichenko was the leading figure in the investigation, the man who made history. It was straightforward fraud. Gorbushin is nowhere in the records. The historian commentators, bless them, are unaware that he had been sent off to Flensburg as a member of the Allied Commission.

At the end of the second day, this terribly senior investigation reached its climax. Picture the scene: a small town, the gentle light of evening, and a strange procession on its way to the city outskirts. There, in sparse woodland, during the curfew to ensure no snoopy spy among the local townsfolk should witness the deed, the crates containing the remains brought from Buch had been committed to the earth and a covert 24-hour guard deployed. Now Major Bystrov again walks ahead, showing the way. Behind him, the general, the Supreme Government Inspector, so to speak. Next, the military. Next, Hitler's dentists Heusermann and Echtmann. Next the Führer's bodyguard, Mengershausen, then some others.

Hardly speaking among ourselves, we walk slowly, oppressed by knowledge of what is imminent, our approaching confrontation of the mystery that always surrounds death. Finally we enter the woodland. The crates have already been exhumed.

Another report is compiled. All present, the Germans as well as the Soviet military (except for the general), sign. This report, compiled in the presence of his nuncio, is for Stalin himself.

The materials discovered by the investigation, the irrefutable proof of Hitler's death, namely his jaw and his denture, are readied before my eyes to be sent to front headquarters and thence, presumably, to Moscow with the general, who departs shortly afterwards.

Judging by the documents, soon after the general left Finow, there was an influx to 'the heights' of top secret information 'concerning the discovery of Hitler's body'. The Council of Ministers Archive preserves a 'Note via the top-security line', sent by Lieutenant General Vadis to Beria and Abakumov on 23 May 1945,[1] detailing the circumstances of the discovery of the bodies of Hitler and Eva Braun; the testimony of Kunz and Schneider, the former having heard about Hitler's suicide from Goebbels, while the latter reported the request for petrol; the interrogations of Günsche and Linge confirming the fact of the suicide and burning of the bodies; and the identification of Hitler's teeth by Fritz Echtmann and Käthe Heusermann. And the note from Beria to Comrade Stalin and to Comrade Molotov, passing on the information. Everyone was very busy, but what would Stalin do? Would he announce the discovery?

Next, Colonel Gorbushin was summoned to Moscow to report on Hitler to Stalin. Gorbushin had just returned from Flensburg. When he returned from Moscow, he told Bystrov and myself he had been ordered not to leave his hotel room and to await a call from Stalin, which never came. Instead, he was summoned by Abakumov, who said,

Comrade Stalin has familiarized himself with the entire course of events and the documents relating to the discovery of Hitler, and he has no questions. He

---

1. http://feldgrau.info/other/6484-statya-r-belforda-gitler-trup-ili-legenda. Accessed 23 December 2017.

considers the matter closed. At the same time, Comrade Stalin said, 'But we shall not make this public. The capitalist encirclement continues.'

Vasiliy Gorbushin told me and Bystrov now to forget what he had said.

'Hitler – Corpse or Legend?' Such was the title of an article by Ronald Belford, circulated on 25 May 1945 by Reuters,[1] and that was precisely the question we confronted. 'The examination of these human remains', Reuters' reporter wrote, 'is the culmination of a strenuous week-long search in the ruins of Berlin.' It was a culmination, however, that never happened. What happened instead was a cover-up.

A tyrant is always a mystery and that is his strength. Everything emanating from him is imbued with a secret significance hidden from the eyes of his subjects. Stalin's pragmatic motivations are easier to work out, but not sufficient to explain why he would conceal such an important historical fact. The answer is largely hidden away in his inscrutable personality, in his ambiguous attitude towards Hitler, in the way he measured himself against certain analogous situations in which Hitler found himself, in the devastating sense of loss he may have experienced with the death of the hated, alluring enemy he had spent the days and nights of the war opposing, and in Stalin's many psychological complexes. These depths I will not attempt to plumb.

The foreign enemy and, no less, the domestic enemy, were an essential component of the system Stalin created. He loathed the idea of detente, and there would be less pressure for it if Hitler was still alive and secretly hiding somewhere. If Hitler was alive, Nazism was not yet vanquished and the world was still in danger. Stalin saw that as tactically important in the imminent discussions with the Allies about the nature of the postwar world. So in Potsdam, when he was asked whether anything was known about Hitler, he was evasive. With a knack for dealing unceremoniously with inconvenient facts that by rights belonged to history and hence to the people, Stalin sat on the truth.

History abhors the arbitrary removal from its narrative of this or that particular event, no matter what the motivation. It is a great theatre producer, and trying to correct its productions only spoils them.

Was Stalin wise? Was there some advantage he derived from keeping his secret? Hardly. The political and moral damage, however, was immense. At the end of the war, and for some time after it, the approval rating (as people would say nowadays) of the Red Army throughout the world was extremely

---

1. R. Belford's article: 'Hitler – a Corpse or a Legend?', in V. K. Vinogradov, J. F. Pogonyi and N. V. Teptzov, *Hitler's Death*, London: Chaucer Press, 2005, p. 277.

high. If, when Stalin was asked about Hitler at the Potsdam Conference, he had announced he was ready to provide proof that Hitler had been found, imagine the impact! A total triumph for Stalin! For the Red Army! And his work at the conference would have benefited from that far more than it did from galvanizing a corpse. But I wonder now, as I write, whether Stalin was already sensing a growing tension between himself and his Allies, and concealing a truth that was their common achievement was perhaps his first move in the approaching Cold War. So he threw that question at 'played-out' Zhukov: 'Well, where is Hitler?'

When I was demobilized and, five months later, left Germany for good, as it then seemed, the Allies continued to work, trying to reach a definite conclusion. In late October and early November (by which time I was already back in Moscow), they were trying to bring together all the loose ends and appealed to the Soviet side for assistance. On 31 October, as a goodwill gesture, the record of the interrogation of Hanna Reitsch was sent by US intelligence to Major General Sidnev,[1] Following that, on 1 November, Brigadier General Ford sent a circular to Brigadier General Conrad (USA), Major General Sidnev (USSR) and Colonel Poulu (France), proposing that the next meeting of the Intelligence Committee should discuss the various claims about Hitler's death.

First paragraph of that text: 'The only conclusive proof of Hitler's death would be the finding and definite identification of the body.'

It was, however, just this conclusive proof that was being denied, concealed both from the Allies and from Russians themselves. Brigadier General Ford continues, 'In the absence of this proof, the only positive proof consists of the detailed accounts of particular witnesses who were either acquainted with his intentions or were eyewitnesses to his fate.'

As we have seen, there really was no shortage of such witnesses. Analysing the testimony of those witnesses who fell into the hands of the Allies, and the information that had leaked from our side, the British intelligence officer summarizes:

It is impossible to suppose that the accounts of the various eyewitnesses are a fabricated story. They were all too busy planning their own escapes to . . . have any inclination to memorize a fictional charade that they would maintain for five months in isolation from each other under detailed and persistent cross-examination.

---

1. Alexey Sidnev, deputy head of the Smersh directorate of the 1st Byelorussian Front. Birstein, p. 304

However, the evidence about the last days and death of Hitler is 'not yet complete', and Brigadier General Ford appeals to his colleagues on the quadripartite Intelligence Committee for information about the whereabouts of, and a request to be allowed to interrogate, Günsche and Rattenhuber (who are in captivity 'according to the Russian communiqué of 7 May'), Traudl Junge (Gertraud but called Gertruda in our records) and Hans Baur, Hitler's personal pilot, who had been seriously injured and, according to unconfirmed reports, was in hospital, again in the Russian sector.

At the end of this message to his colleagues is the most important point:

A rumour came from the Russian side that a body had been found that was identified, or was believed to have been identified, as Hitler's body from the teeth. Could they perhaps report the results of that investigation to establish the extent to which that can be relied on?

There was no response.

Evidently it had not proved possible to conceal the facts completely, and perhaps nobody had tried all that hard. The main thing was to keep everybody guessing. 'Nothing for sure.' 'Hitler vanished without trace'. That provided a foundation for legends and myths about him: just what Hitler wanted. A romantic aura was created around his image, while the truth that we knew was simple and prosaic. But it was the truth.

Hitler wanted to remain an enigma, to become myth, a new phoenix ready to be reborn in someone else's lunatic dreams of power and violence.

The End of the War

Back then, in May 1945, I supposed our adventure was over and that I would soon be home. I did go home, but not soon by any means, only on 10 October 1945, four years to the day after I had gone off to the war. During those first postwar months I was again to encounter the documents from the Reich Chancellery. First, at front headquarters I was instructed to translate the Goebbels diaries, but things did not work out. There was nothing of operational value in his old diaries, and the historical value of documents from a war now ended, as I have said, declined rapidly. I was sent off back to Stendal, where the headquarters of our 3rd Shock Army was stationed.

The German town of Stendal was my last stop in a war that had lasted four years and that, no doubt, is why I so remember it. We moved there when the demarcation line was drawn on the map of Germany and Stendal, though situated to the west of Berlin, fell within the Russian zone. The Americans had been there in the morning, and we moved in at noon.

The city was intact and vibrant with life. We settled in a quiet street with detached houses covered in vines. From early morning middle-aged German housewives were busy in the orchards by the houses. Their hair in old-fashioned buns and the low hems of their skirts made them resemble their peers to the east.

German children played in the square, and never ceased to amaze us: they never cried and did not make a lot of noise when they were playing at war. In the square, old women dressed in black sat all day long on a bench. They had probably been brought together long ago by widowhood, and would not have been very young even at the time of the First World War. Sometimes they began to gossip excitedly about something, trying to outdo each other as they wagged fingers in black cotton gloves.

From time to time a black hearse would appear, drawn slowly, smoothly, contemplatively by two horses. What we knew about horses was that they were used for pulling artillery or galloped with a courier in the saddle, or died in battle, or were eaten. There had been none available for other purposes for years.

These black, gleaming, well-fed horses wearing a solemn funeral caparison and a fluffy pom-pom above their withers, with a black-clad driver wearing a bowler hat, sitting on the box of the glazed and lacquered hearse, were the custodians of the majesty and sacramental nature of death, of the death that is called 'natural'. Not death in battle, or from wounds, or the agonies of captivity, but the death of someone who has passed away 'naturally', the kind of death that used to happen so long ago that we had forgotten during the war that it was possible.

In the evening, always at the same hour, a column of German prisoners of war returned. It turned off into our street through a dark archway, separating it from another street that led down to the market square.

All day the soldiers were taken off somewhere to work, and in the evening, at the exact same hour, they returned. You could hear them coming even before their first rank appeared under the archway. Tired, sweaty, hungry, they sang as they marched, and their singing reached our street before they marched down it. They sang in tune, like a good male voice choir, something of their own, something German, and they passed us in an orderly column.

The housewives peered out of open windows. Lying on embroidered cushions placed on the sills for that purpose, they were resting at the end of their day's housework. Downstairs, by their front doors, the old men sat in chairs they had brought out, casting long, faint shadows on the pavement. Listening to the men marching, they rocked slowly in time to the song, and their shadows, etiolated by the late hour, also rocked a little.

But overall everything was so calm, not agitated. It was as if those presently marching into the street had no connection with those who lived on it. The appearance of the prisoners took me aback every time. Even later, when there was no singing because they had been forbidden to sing, they marched in line, silently, down our street, their steel-shod boots clacking rhythmically, to where they would be under guard by sentries. I stared at them transfixed. They were a living part of a war that was taking revenge on them for their defeat.

The town was intact, but there were ruins on the outskirts. By the time we got to Stendal, however, the ruins were no longer redolent with drama. The war in Germany had been over for two months, and the ruins already looked dilapidated. The inferno of war, it transpired, becomes extinct immediately the all-clear is sounded. You, a tiny ember, are still hissing and smouldering and flaring up, but it has gone out, and the flames of war no longer tint the now cold ruins. By now they only merit a paragraph as the property in the town is inventorized, an essential part of its variety.

These ruins are the town's contribution to the past and its new starting point.

At the front, I did find myself talking to captured German soldiers whose psychology was wholly permeated by Nazism, but they were the exception. Much more commonly, the soldiers were just ordinary human beings bizarrely at odds with the monstrous monolith of which they had been a part until half an hour ago. That was distressing. In Stendal, up close, I found many of the town's residents likeable, and the creature known as 'a Nazi' was nowhere to be found.

This was a strange period, without war, in a foreign, largely incomprehensible world that did not need you to come and organize it, because it was not you who were going to be living there. Shortly before I left Stendal, wandering through the streets one evening, I found myself in the town's park. On the overgrown paths, a courting couple might be glimpsed in the distance, before disappearing and again leaving the park deserted. There was a brook with a little bridge over it. In the stagnant water matted with algae, the elongated leaves of a willow had clumped together. They were glued also to a moss-covered stone.

Along the bank the grass was swaying on long stems. A handful of sparrows flew up out of it. On the other side of the bridge I could see, where the pond weed had not taken over, the water moving on its way to somewhere. I gazed at it helplessly, surprised by a kind of awakening, having up till that moment been separated off by the war from that water, that grass, from everything that was not war.

Now it was August and the fourth month without war. In Stendal the headquarters of my army was accommodated in houses whose windows looked out to a highway. A barrier placed across the street was supposed to keep out the civilian population.

A retired railway official scuttled resolutely across the highway and burst through the screen of bushes that separated it from our street. He had come from wherever he had been temporarily resettled with his family. In a worn suit and wearing a bowler hat, wiry and tense, he came on some pretext into his house, which we had occupied, hoping by turning up to avert destruction and chaos. His carpets, rolled up and sewn into covers, stood in the corners of the rooms, but in the humid twilight, moths were in the air. The glass cabinet with his delicate porcelain coffee cups, which we used when cleaning our teeth, now had empty spaces on its shelves, and the cups were to be found in the bathroom perched precariously on the edge of the wash-hand basin, from where it was only too easy inadvertently to send them crashing to the tile floor. The house's small garden was sadly and plaintively offering up its fruits.

Not far away, on the bridge or by the market square late at night, it did happen that a soldier would stop a lone passer-by and say, 'Yer watch! Gerrit off,' but by now marauding was being punished.

An ex-typist for the Gestapo, as dark-skinned as an Indian, her back as slender as a boy's, with a black fringe of straight hair, in a short, fluttering skirt, climbed lightly and impudently over the fence, ready to make herself useful or make herself scarce, and walked along 'our' street with an arch spring in her step, showing off gleaming legs and dangling a broad-brimmed raspberry red hat by its elastic. (Hats were still fashionable.) She walked bouncily along, audaciously intending to treat someone with apples from her bag, evidently wanting to dispose them favourably towards her. This seemed not to be an insurmountable challenge, if the tall, handsome soldier sent here to headquarters from a Lithuanian division, in view of the acute need for translators, was anything to go by. This risk-taking young fellow was, in defiance of all regulations, smitten by the diabolical Gestapo girl. On the other side of the wooden fence, the typist's fit, handsome young husband was waiting for her. Climbing back over the fence in the same manner as before, she quickly rejoined him and they went off back to their uneasy, and to us incomprehensible, life.

Hungry refugees sat all day on the ground in the square by the town hall. Victorious soldiers, growing languid in the hot sun, hung round the necks of stray dogs long ropes of precious pearls recovered from a bombed jewellery shop during the advance, and were drowsily amused, watching as these strange, weightless collars dangling on the dogs' chests and, when they ran, flapping up in front of their muzzles, goaded them. The dogs rushed around crazily until the thread broke and the pearls scattered over the roadway. Then the dogs went back to the soldiers and waited patiently to be thrown something to eat, and wandered around with strands of thread, strung with pearls, caught in their fur.

A truck driver I barely knew, having only ever been driven once or twice in his truck, hailed me in the street: 'Comrade Lieutenant, wait!' He handed me a letter and asked me to read it when I had a moment. It was a written proposal of marriage. He promised me a good life, on the basis of a house in Sochi which he co-owned with his sister. The letter brimmed with confidence that I would respond positively, but he was not in the least downhearted or offended when I did not. From then on, though, when we met we would stop and chat like friends, not mentioning the letter but with a sense of having a connection, because we knew about something that had happened, and also knew something about each other that nobody else knew.

He was still wearing the tunic of the rank-and-file front-line driver, but these days of peace had given him new confidence: very soon he would again be behind the wheel in a holiday area and, moreover, in the midst of all the devastation, owning half a house on the fashionable Black Sea coast. He was probably mentally asking me, 'How many of us men have survived, and how many of you women are going to be looking for a man back there in Russia?' – and aware of his immeasurably stronger negotiating position. 'Not every woman is going to get one. The wretched war has done you quite some disservice.' Or perhaps he was genuinely taking pity on me in what he took to be my unenviable circumstances by offering his candidacy.

When a sergeant happened to come by one day with a camera my suitor yelled, 'Oy! Take a photo!' He inscribed on the back of the photo, which showed the two of us standing together, words of parting that had become almost traditional in the war: 'If not I, at least my picture is always with you.'

An elderly, nondescript looking lieutenant (on our travels all he ever did was issue us our monthly allowance), had until very recently been shy and self-effacing, presumably burdened by a sense of the insignificance, and even oddity, of his position as an accountant in the headquarters of an army on active service. But now he opened up and lost his inferiority complex. A roadside incident had helped. On the highway, a huge

Studebaker truck that was hurtling towards a pedestrian, him, suddenly braked. As was not uncommon now on the roads, a huge black driver jumped down from the cabin to greet him. He grabbed his puny form in his arms, pressed him ardently to his bosom, expressing his admiration for the Red Army, and delightedly tossed the accountant, along with his briefcase, up in the air. Having endured the initial terror and survived (he did not crash down on to the concrete of the highway), the diffident accountant suddenly had a blinding revelation of the part he had played in the heroic events of the war.

We unrolled the old carpets smelling of mothballs and rolled up and sewn into their covers, and spread them on the floor. Perhaps we wanted to live the way the people who were here before we came had lived, to have a taste of their comfortable German way of life. Or perhaps we were in a hurry: when would life again be so comfortable and seemingly carefree?

The old plush armchair, the standard lamp with its faded grey silk lampshade, the cabinet with the porcelain ... A place for everything and everything in its place. And the moths circling, businesslike, in the humid evenings just above the carpets. And completely covering the end of the house, the crimson leaves of the twining vine. And in the evenings the old wrought iron lantern will be lit. What could be better? And yet, something is missing. There is no sense of being at home. Something is not right. There's no living in a house where there's no master. This is no more than a billet. In places we had been put up in at the front, even in dugouts, we had felt far more at home, far more carefree, more relaxed and secure. The owner's wife is working away in the tiny garden where one kind of fruit succeeds another. On the porch the owner's ginger-haired mongrel, Trudi, is slumbering. The owner brings her something to eat in a paper poke, the dog gulps it down, whimpers, quietly licks its owner's hands, runs after him, wagging its erect tail, following him as far as the dense barrier of shrubbery stretching along the boulevard. Until recently, no one, neither the owner nor his dog, would have dared to push their way through those bushes.

Before disappearing into them, her master firmly orders Trudi to turn back (the dogs here are amazingly well behaved), and she trots back to the house with her tail between her legs. The owner, holding his bowler hat firmly on his head, disappears into the bushes. Then the dog, after looking all around, nervously wagging her tail, heads for the kitchen of the victors.

Bystrov was greatly impressed by Germany, by its roads, and particularly by the way the town merged unnoticeably with the countryside and how the countryside, with its stone buildings, merged with the town. 'This is where socialism should really have been built,' he told me in confidence. 'It should have been started here, not in Russia.' In Rathenow, from where we later moved to Stendal, we had lived in the gloomy mansion of the owner of a factory that made cases for spectacles. For some reason Bystrov particularly took to that house. It had a grand staircase up to the first floor and a chandelier in the hall. He seemed so downcast when he said there was absolutely no possibility he could ever have anything to compare with it. I felt nothing remotely like that regret. I was, of course, much younger than him, and what had I in common with the respectable owner of the house, who on Sundays invariably took his ease on a chaise longue on the balcony?

Bystrov changed. Little by little, it has to be admitted, he forgot Klavochka, which is forgivable given that their romance had lasted for only the one evening of their acquaintance, when our army was being given a send-off. What a succession of massive events and alarums were to follow.

In Rathenow Bystrov had a modest lyrical interlude, a light, amusing romance with a pretty German woman, the local hairdresser. It was so uncomplicated, so irresponsible, and had an added dash of danger, because it could have done serious damage to his career. I think he looked back fondly on his amorous escapade. It is no small matter how we see ourselves afterwards, remembering, and now Bystrov could remember himself as a fine, gallant gentleman, with none of the churlishness of a victor, with little posies of flowers, sneaking out through a window at night, completely unseen, in violation of a strict prohibition of intimacy with German women, overcoming the conditioning of servile obedience and fear, seizing a moment of freedom, and feeling almost European.

But that, too, passed and Bystrov changed again. I do not think I knew anyone as inwardly restless as he was. He worried feverishly about what direction his life should take now, what choices he should make, whether he should go back to his previous studies as a biologist or stay in the army. There was some obscure, disquieting obstacle to his returning to his old career. He could not speak about it with his usual directness, something remained unsaid. He also lamented the loss of a loyal, discriminating counsellor in his mother-in-law, who had died before the war. He evidently had been guilty of some pre-war misdeed in respect of one of his colleagues and wondered whether now, in what seemed like the purer atmosphere after the war, he would be welcomed back by his fellow biologists. It troubled him.

At first he wondered about staying in the army. An observant person, he asked me, 'Do you see the type of commander they want now?' He saw for himself that promotion was coming to those who made relentless, harsh demands on their subordinates over even the most trifling detail. He understood that he himself needed to change, to change his completely inappropriate manner when dealing with his subordinates. Having given a task to a private, he would often ask, 'Right then, sport, sure you've got that?' He tended to be indulgent, over-lenient, too understanding of the other person's situation, and was inclined to cover up if they got something wrong.

He began trying to break himself in, to act a part, to adapt to the stereotype of the successful officer. Instead of his easy-going, and often affectionate, term of address ('sport'), he now became relentlessly demanding and obnoxious. Soon, however, realizing he was a round peg in a square hole, that he did not belong in the army and would never go far, Bystrov gave up the idea and tried to go back to being his old self. That, however, proved impossible. You cannot violate your true self without leaving a wound.

There was only one thing left, and that was to go back to biology. He was soon acting with his characteristic purposefulness, still unable to imagine living without setting himself targets and achieving them.

If the refugees are sitting on the ground by the town hall; if at the customary lunchtime, between twelve and one o'clock in the afternoon, the Germans, closing their stores and shops and offices, greet each other when they meet in the street with, *"Mahlzeit!"*; if in the atelier a dress is being sewn for the wife of the Burgomeister to attend the opening of the local theatre; if Trudi, dishevelled, going feral, is torn between her master and the foreigners' kitchen, breaks free and, jangling on her collar the highest Nazi military and paramilitary award, the 'Knight's Cross of the Iron Cross with Oak Leaves', and a medal 'For Participation in the Winter Campaign in the East', rushes to greet her master and he, squeezing through the green hedge, with some effort replaces the bowler hat on his head, totally ignoring Trudi's satanic decorations and responds with his customary strictness to her greetings and walks unabashed into the house, leading his wife – if all this happens, then truly the war is over.

In the evening, through the open window of a nearby house come the tones of Alexander Vertinsky, a captured record. That, instead of a low whistle, is the signal for a secret assignation with R.

Even before Vertinsky has finished the song, a captured 8 mm film projector for home use is switched on. 'Wait till you see this!' The projector clatters and on a white pillowcase hung on the wall as a screen a little mouse starts running round a pantry in pursuit of a sausage hanging from a hook.

'Funny?' 'Uh-huh.' But it isn't the least bit funny. I translate the subtitles, but my viewing is being blocked by a sorrow rising from the bottom of my heart. Something is leaving us, evaporating. A beastly German cat puts an end to the beastly German mouse that nibbled a beastly German sausage . . .

What is happening to us? Where are we? We are being dragged out to the provinces of a victory. We are now two trains on a narrow-gauge track. One lets the other pass, not yet knowing which route to follow into the chasm of days ahead, not exchanging whistles, deaf to each other.

How shall we honour this victory? How shall we honour the life it has given us, which we have yet to know? That tumultuous sense of living that bubbled up with victory, is receding.

Life without enchantment. During the war nobody expected any, but in the war nobody was ordinary. No one. The ordinariness followed almost immediately, in a foreign, vanquished land, with the hatefulness of occupation.

And that wonderful sense of being alive: is it possible now or was it taken away with them by those who perished? Perhaps, too, victory itself is only a short period of festivity followed by a persistent sense of disquieting responsibility.

While we were in occupation of Stendal there swept out of the darkness of the Nazis' concentration camps the Eternal Chancer, an obligatory character that follows in the wake of wars and cataclysms. In Stendal he appeared in the guise of an adroit, nimble gentleman with a narrow-brimmed hat and a face moulded from grey, heat-resistant clay, on which the dots of eyes, the crosses of nostrils, and the line of his lips had been etched.

Declaring he was a former political prisoner, he lost no time in setting himself up nicely. He moved into the Schwarzer Adler (Black Eagle) Hotel and cornered the legal owner. His eye had alighted on this well-kept hostelry because its owner, who had vanished without trace, had been a prominent Nazi in the town, which now enabled this type, whose first name was Hans and whose surname I have forgotten, to carry out, covertly and with impunity, an expropriation. The abandoned co-owner, a small, rounded woman, now spent her inactive days in an obscure corner of her restaurant in the guise of an employee, and in reality under house (restaurant) arrest. The old staff were fired and their replacements kept a close eye on her. The chef, a concentration camp chum of Hans, was a hunchbacked strongman with a cheery, red, roguish face who could cook dishes unimaginable for that time, in total disregard of norms and the strict ration limits.

A theatre opened in Stendal and a dreamy actress with luxuriant ash-blonde hair crooned something pre-Nazi. From the screens, Marika Rökk, 'The Woman of My Dreams', in a chinchilla fur coat, raked over old coals by hymning the blandishments of the high life. 'Ex-prisoner' Hans sent out a team of women he hired near Potsdam to find champignons. German boys walked with their arms round German girls as if we were simply not there. At the time-honoured hour, the Germans, locking up their *Geschäfts* and offices, dispersed for lunch, calling *"Mahlzeit!"* to their acquaintances. Ramming their spades into the ground, the road workers stood in trenches in the street, unwrapped their packed lunches brought from home, and ate the stale bread of poverty.

An interpreter was constantly in demand, if not for anything of great importance. It was an odd life, as if you were imagining it. There was nothing here for Bystrov to do. A car he had captured was being repaired in a German garage and he was planning to drive back home in it. He was expecting at any moment to be given the signal that would allow him to leave. There was already a distance between us. It was like approaching your destination in a train when the food for the journey has been eaten, everybody has told their personal stories to everybody else, the cases have been put out in the aisle and scarves are already on necks. The temporary community that has come together on the journey is falling apart. Everybody is on their own, separately thinking about what they have to do next, about the excitement of imminent reunions.

But the train has come to a stop and is waiting for the green signal to allow it to pull into the station. The delay is irksome, and the remoteness of everyone and the emptiness that has appeared is a pain, and everyone is now irrevocably only looking out for themselves.

But now, out of the Black Eagle, from the fraternity of questionable ex-prisoners, the sturdy, ruddy faced hunchback is bringing across the highway a roast suckling pig, standing on all fours in a dish. The dish is being steadied by the owner himself, the Eternal Chancer. The pig, with a tomato stuck in its jaws, with carrots and green branches stuck in its back, is placed at the head of a farewell banquet. Major Bystrov is leaving.

Later Bystrov did come to see me once or twice in Moscow. He had a new position. He told me about his problems over moving from Omsk. I passed on a request from Klavochka to see him and he agreed to meet her at my apartment. I will never forget that evening, Klavochka in an attractive black silk dress with a square neckline and heavily embroidered with beading, patiently getting colder and colder in our chilly apartment, still under the impact of how much in love with her he had been and his proposal. Waiting for him to come at any moment, whereupon everything would work out well. He stood her up.

It seems to me that in the candlelight on that day in wartime so long ago, by the stove in Bydgoszcz, when he confided to me his plan to capture Goebbels, he began to dissolve, and was dissolving the whole time from then on, until he became a phantom and ultimately disappeared, leaving a trace in the form of Klavochka's sequins, and a profound, sad puzzlement in her heart.

But, for now, we are still in Stendal. People are gradually leaving. Bystrov has gone, driving off in his car. The headquarters courier, Zhenya Gavrilov, looks at me with plaintive courtesy. In Poznań I had witnessed what at first had seemed no more than a harmless flirtation with Zosia, a local girl, and their inconsolable separation washed with his tears. The memory of that happiness only grew more intense in his sorrowful separation, until his heart was filled with despair. He passed his days now in a state of stupefaction, all his old initiative gone. Victory had not been the harbinger of a reunion with his beloved. While the war was going on, he had been able to hitch-hike back, with the kindly permission of Colonel Gorbushin, once or twice to Poznań. Now, as day by day ever more stringent conditions were being imposed on us, there was little chance of that, and marrying foreigners had been prohibited. He lost the will to live. Puffy, red eyelids corroded by tears reluctantly opened a slit, to reveal dull eyes which not so long ago had been quick and covetous.

Did it happen at the front that a soldier cried on leaving a village and bidding farewell to a girl he had fallen in love with? Hardly. In war men are warlike. Victory is the time for love, and that is why Gavrilov is crying now.

'And you? After all, we agreed.' 'Well, what about you?' 'My grandmother used to say, "Victory is a disaster. Look what it's done for us."' 'She said that?' 'She was talking about something different. We will honour our Victory.' 'We shall.'

'On 9 May, when they let off the fireworks, no matter where we are, we will think about each other. That is forever. The first glass on 9 May I will always, in my mind, drink to you.' 'And I to you.'

'You have important work ahead of you. I know you will cope with it. How much we have been through. That cannot just disappear. I believe in you. You will write, I know, and you will not have to make anything up. You will write everything just the way it was.'

When we were still in the Baltic States, we came across a single domino piece, a double two. I broke it, gave half to him and kept half myself. These jokey halves seemed to be a pledge nobody else knew about of our secret oneness, or rather, and this was no joke, two talismans, which people so need at the front. Six months later, when R. was in Moscow, and through the years when he dropped in as he was passing through, he would 'present' his half of the double-two as a sign of faithfulness to our memory of the past.

I do not know what missions his native land sent him out on with my talisman in his pocket. He rose in his career through the ranks, and perhaps this modest little fragment reminded him of a time when he was pure, aloof and brave, like a free man. I keep my half of the double-two in a jewellery box with my medals.

Eventually a lorry took me from Stendal to front headquarters, to which I had been ordered to report for demobilization. We drove through Berlin and saw an American patrol, soldiers in khaki overalls strolling confidently down the street arm-in-arm with young German women.

Our truck sped another forty kilometres along Hitler's famous autobahns. The driver, that same driver, my would-be 'intended', looked at me without a hint of ruefulness. Keeping his left hand on the steering wheel, he offered me a pack of American cigarettes a black driver had presented to him. 'Help yourself, Comrade Lieutenant!' Only I was a non-smoker.

He delivered me to my destination in Potsdam, front headquarters, lowered the side of the truck and carried a big heavy radio into the hotel. It was a parting gift to me from our army unit.

'At home they'll be preparing the dough for me, distilling the schnapps!' he exclaimed euphorically, anticipating the welcome he would soon also be enjoying. 'All the best for your life in peacetime,' he said. He shook my hand firmly, and with that last handshake all my ties were broken. For four years I had not been my own person, I had been one of a community in the thick of a war and suddenly . . . I was out, completely alone. It was something I had forgotten or perhaps never known, something stupefying, just very bewildering.

On my own now, in those bewildered days in Potsdam, I slope in perplexity past gardens barely touched by yellow and crimson rust that screen the detached houses and the concealed, muted liveliness within them. I meet almost nobody coming the other way. It is a warm autumn. Lakes, mist above them, a haze that envelops and engulfs the feverish, nagging pain of parting.

What lies ahead? What is going to happen? I have no profession, only the unrelenting obligation I have, for some reason, taken on myself: to write. And is it an obligation? More likely, it is an alarming, doomed destiny. It is so little, but at the same time too much for my impending life, when I will be completely alone with everything that happened, everything yet to happen, with my secrets and my faltering faith in the logic of ordinary life and its fragmented routine.

In May we were still full of marvellous hopes for our peacetime future. On the threshold of victory, and for a brief moment after it, we all imagined a renewed world of real living, with much more freedom and much less mistrust than before. Our people, who had so selflessly displayed their best qualities in the war, could surely, we believed, count on the trust of their rulers. Had not the children of 'enemies of the people', and those 'enemies' themselves, to the extent that they were released from the prisons – priests, the supposedly 'wealthy' peasants who had been purged, the thieves – all risen up to defend the Motherland? Had they not given their lives?

In line with these awakened hopes, for a time excited 'news' spread, and Bystrov shared it with me, that some freedom of initiative would be allowed, like under the New Economic Policy of the 1920s, as the quickest way of healing the gaping wounds left by the war. Or that now we would be allowed to go on holiday abroad. In a word, we were thrilled and excited by the prospect of new uplands.

I do not remember why I was travelling somewhere with Bystrov when we got stuck and were sitting by the roadside on overturned empty cans, waiting for a vehicle to be going our way. We got to talking about the future, because I, too, had applied for demobilization. Bystrov, forgetting the failure of the 'creative' days he had allowed me for writing stories, told me with solemn confidence and hope, 'There were three of us at every stage of this Hitler saga. Of those three, you are the only one who can write about it. It is your duty.' He had taken care to keep copies of records not known to the rest of the world, and had also given copies to me. He had supplemented his private collection with invaluable photographs, and these he shared as well.

Five months had now passed without war. Little news reached us from Moscow, and it was beginning to look as if the future would not differ much from the patterns established in the years preceding the war. But if, in the midst of the war, our pre-war life had seemed alluring, vivid and varied, somehow now it had dulled. Some of those who were older than me, and had already had jobs in the past, now decided life had been better during the war. That was true primarily of the officers, although similar sentiments were to be found among the rank and file, who had found the front exhilarating.

In the war, they found, there had been more freedom, more room to breathe; there was not the same suspicion and persecution, not the same danger lurking round every corner, and the goal for which you might have to give your life was necessary, was righteous, not just a lot of hot air and speculation. It was clear, indubitable and palpable. Staking your life on that, a person could feel like a human being, a hero – something you had been deprived of before the war.

In Potsdam, Raya the telegraphist and I sat, taking our farewell of each other in an autumnal garden. It was the quiet hour before sunset. The German owner of the house climbed a stepladder he had placed by a fruit tree and carefully picked the apples with a gloved hand. Everything was right, as if a deep peace had descended on the Earth. Only not in my heart.

The demobilization paperwork might have been completed but it was not possible just to go home. Demobbed troops besieged the trains and battled for a place in them, clung to the roofs of the carriages. We heard it could be months before things settled down. Everyone was in the grip of a furious urge to get back home. Every day of delay counted as a disaster. Yells and guffaws from those who had climbed in, or clung on, or clambered up; singing, wanton recklessness. 'We are back from the war!' proclaimed posters along the carriage. 'Welcome us!' 'We won!' 'Back from Berlin!' It was only later, when people actually were back home, moving away from all that, settling down to peacetime living, that they began to feel nostalgia for the war and you would hear, as contagious as a yawn, the officers joking, 'Oh, for an hour of that damnable war again!' as they remembered, or now imagined, their finest hour.

Meanwhile I was wilting in this demoralizing wait to get away. There was nothing I could do, except live in hope that someone would do me a favour. For the present, I was accommodated in the officers' hotel – a vast building with wide corridors and spacious rooms which, until recently, had been an almshouse. Where were the old ladies who had inhabited it living now?

In the room I had been allocated there were traces of its recent occupant: under a glass dome was a little ivory church with a crucifix in it, crosses on a rosary made of mother-of-pearl or wooden beads. Soon these objects of devotion were joined by a prominently displayed white enamel colander. It belonged to Tanya, the girl now sharing with me. I was leaving but she had just arrived in Germany, having served the whole war in the army, but seeing it through to the end in the USSR.

Her large, happy, hospitable family had all been killed in Stalingrad, with the exception of her mother, who lived on among the ashes, a prey to deprivation and loneliness. Tanya, womanly and gentle, was full of positive feelings about life and of constructive intentions. Once she had a job in Germany she intended to bring her mother over. She wanted to have children and, to that end, to marry a good man, never doubting that she would soon meet one here. The colander, purchased or otherwise acquired, was the first step in realizing that life, and the therapeutic news about it flew by mail back to Stalingrad to her mother who had lost everyone and everything, including her kitchen utensils that were completely irreplaceable in our devastated country, and in the midst of which she had spent her life, taking care of her family. Tanya had nothing other than the colander to show for the present, but she had made a start. Her calmness, her warmth, her very basic human aspirations and attractive, womanly appearance made it easy to like her.

There she was, waiting to be appointed to a job, while I was waiting to be sent home, and neither of us had anything to do. We walked through the outskirts of Potsdam in the warm autumn haze of the lakes. How still it was here, and beautiful. The German gardens were preparing for their winter rest: we had no inkling on those walks of the terrible winter about to befall the Germans in their unheated homes.

Living in Potsdam at that moment, I knew nothing of Cecilienhof, where just over two months previously a conference of the Allies had taken place. I knew nothing of the Garrison Church to which, when he came to power, Hitler immediately repaired, wearing a tailcoat, to pose for journalists at the grave of Frederick the Great. I did not even know about Sanssouci, the palace of that emperor in Potsdam, which had suffered during the war. If I had, I would in any case have had no interest in it, because the only thing I wanted was to go home. That gentle, healing autumn, Tanya and I wandered by the shores of the lakes, in the park, along the streets past the hedges in front of the houses, and a sense of joie de vivre was born in my heart. It was not that keen, animal sense of being alive that could transfix you for a moment at the front, but a different, quiet feeling, consoling, life-affirming.

We did not stray far from headquarters, and one day I was sent for to report immediately to the aerodrome. I cannot remember now who the kind person was who had taken the trouble to help me. Perhaps it was just the headquarters commandant, for whom I was a burden. It is a pity, though, that I do not remember. It can have been no simple matter to get me a place on Marshal Zhukov's cargo plane. It was going to take off even though it was not 'flying' weather and Moscow would not give permission for it to land. The aerodrome there was closed because of the bad weather.

In order not to overload what was, after all, a cargo aircraft, I was ordered to, and did without regret, leave behind the radio receiver, the official 'valuable parting gift' awarded me by my military unit. A car hastily transported me, and Tanya who came to see me off, to the aerodrome. It was a gloomy, overcast day. A few sturdy, surly chaps in leather coats, Zhukov's aircrew, were standing by the plane. In Poznań Zhukov's aircrew had often dropped in to have tea or a meal with us, but theirs had not been a cargo plane. These were pilots I did not know. One of them silently jabbed a finger at the leather case hanging from a strap over my shoulder with a complete set of Vertinsky's records, an unofficial gift when the radio centre was dismantled. 'The aircraft is already overloaded,' the others chimed in. I obediently took it off and transferred the strap to Tanya's shoulder, rescuing only my favourite record.

Whether they were genuinely concerned about overloading the plane, or whether they just thought it was bad luck to have a woman on board, especially in bad weather, I do not know. Perhaps they hoped that, reluctant to part with my booty, I would refuse to fly. At all events, if they were wanting to get rid of this unwelcome passenger, they may have had a point, because I was to give them a hard time on the flight. Then, though, I had no such thoughts in my head and just wanted to make sure they took me with them. My cardboard suitcase, my rucksack, and the box with the doll presented to me by the Italians in the already far-off days of May were grudgingly lifted into the plane. I said goodbye to Tanya and, through her, to everything that had happened or would happen here. I had nobody else to say goodbye to as I bade what I thankfully supposed to be my last farewell to Germany.

It was the first time in my life I had been in a plane. The propellers thundered and I never noticed the aircraft leaving the ground. I was immediately distracted and captivated by the indescribable sight of Berlin beneath us. However devastated it might have appeared from the ground, from above this vast, immense, dead city was a truly monstrous sight. Blackened grey hulks of city blocks, buildings that looked like opened boxes. Our allies' air forces had bombed the city night and day, systematically wrecking building after building, and appeared to have contrived to drop a bomb in every last one.

And then Berlin, which a moment before had been so close beneath us, was out of sight. The plane gained altitude and the ground, disappearing from under my feet, suddenly lurched towards me. I do not know what that was or how to convey it. It felt as if the force of gravity had suddenly caught up with an inept runaway. I was plunged into a depth of despair such as I had never experienced during the war. I can't do this, I can't! Throw me out, let me get back down to the ground!

The Douglas cargo aircraft had two bench-like metal seats solidly attached opposite each other to the sides of the aircraft. Not including me, there were four passengers, all pilots. They took off their leather coats, turned a suitcase on its end, and were soon furiously playing cards. The plane was empty: there was no cargo. The light cardboard box with my doll in it skated up and down its empty floor. I didn't care. There I was, all my insignia jangling, with my officer's belt and shoulder straps, as helpless as a kitten and very miserable. The airmen solicitously laid me on an iron bench, magnanimously spread their coats under me and assured me I would feel better lying down.

And no doubt I should have felt better, lying behind their calm, warm backs, but we were tossed around the sky, jerked sideways, and fell precipitously down into some celestial underworld. It was, after all, not flying weather and the aerodrome in Moscow had been closed for a reason. But no prohibitions or weather forecasts deter the aircrews of Marshal Zhukov who was, for some reason, returning them urgently to Moscow. And so I came, however remotely, into contact of a sort with the commander-in-chief who, by commanding them to fly, enabled me to be taken along with them. I little dreamed at the time that I would meet the marshal himself twenty years on. That, too, would be in autumn.

We did, despite the weather, land on the Leningrad Highway, which was where the aerodrome was at the time. I set foot unsteadily on the soil of my home town, of my own street. But had I returned? Even today I feel I have not exhausted everything that needs to be said about what I experienced in the war. Such close personal contact with history is something infinite, because there are so many different facets. From the distance of all these years they sometimes reveal themselves more distinctly, and the reality of what happened is all the more poignant.

Käthe Heusermann

It had been in the second half of May 1945 that I was summoned from Finow to front headquarters to translate those diaries of Goebbels we had found. In the same room a special container was being made for sending Hitler's teeth to Moscow. They were evidently being taken back by the general Stalin had sent to check that the body we had found really was that of Hitler.

The notebooks of Goebbels' diaries that we had found came to an end on 8 July 1941. I found translating it slow work because his handwriting was difficult to decipher. Headquarters decided the diaries were of no immediate operational interest, my work came to a halt, and then it was time to return to my army. I knew, however, that Käthe Heusermann was still somewhere here at front headquarters and wanted to see her. Finding her proved very straightforward: she was only one stair landing away. There was a sentry posted there, who told me which door I needed. Käthe was very pleased to see me. Fritz Echtmann was there with her. He had lost weight, although that might have seemed impossible, given how thin he had been already.

He was not well and Käthe, worried, was trying to look after him. She asked quietly whether I might be able to get more suitable food for him. I did, of course, mention his condition and interceded, but whether it did any good I have no idea. Throughout the war no attention at all had been paid to that kind of ailment.

Käthe came to life in my presence, probably feeling a bit more secure. She raised her foot and deftly prodded the window frame with the toe of her shoe. To her delight the window yielded and opened wide, giving us a breath of fresh air. Perhaps until now she had not been allowed to open it. Käthe and I went out and down into the garden. The sentry did not react.

I liked everything about her: the lightness with which she walked on high heels, her voice, her womanly stoicism even in her present unclear situation. Käthe was just somebody people liked, I sensed; she was a splendid person. For many years she had supported Dr Bruck. Käthe got food vouchers for him in the Reich Chancellery. Helping a Jew was very dangerous for anyone, but for Käthe Heusermann who, with Dr Blaschke, attended Hitler and was in and out of the Reich Chancellery, in Berchtesgaden, and at the Führer's headquarters in East Prussia, it could, as Dr Bruck pointed out to me, have been fatal. Käthe herself never once spoke about that. We talked eagerly about all our problems as women, which needed urgent attention now that peace had come. 'I'll take you to my hairdresser,' she said, 'as soon as I get home.'

She did not get back home, and after that meeting at front headquarters I heard no more about her for twenty years.

I was working myself into the ground in the Council of Ministers' secret archive. Getting into it at all came as a great shock and I had nearly given up. For many years it seemed hopeless. The answer was always the same: there is no access to these materials and no exceptions are likely to be made. On the crest of a wave of national pride, however, as the twentieth anniversary of victory approached, a miracle occurred and the doors opened before me. It was September 1964 and I was allowed to work in the archive for twenty days.

A document retrieved from the depths of bygone times often has an increased impact, and here we had official materials, notes, records and protocols, some of which bore my signature as a military interpreter, some that were in my own handwriting on inferior wartime paper, yellowed with the patina of time. And then there were documents I was seeing for the first time. Taken together they were a significant, eloquent, authentic component of those events.

Again I saw before me those files, folders, bundles of letters, diaries, and also the final notebook of Goebbels' diary. There were Soviet documents and records that nobody had looked at since 1945. It was my destiny to make sense of them. My appetite for work, while I was digging through them for *Berlin, May 1945*, was way above normal.

A few words about documents in general. There can be all sorts: aggressive, reticent, biased, or candid and naive, but often in their nakedness the words have an aesthetic dimension. For me they reanimated what I had experienced, threw bridges back to the past, and armed my memory.

This morning, too, Vladimir Ivanovich put a new pile of folders on my table. The one on top seemed rather thin. I pulled it over and opened it. Inside were delivery notes for items the staff at front headquarters were sending to the Smersh directorate in Moscow: a table lamp, an adding machine, a stapler with instructions in German and my translation. I was about to close this irrelevant folder and move it aside when I mechanically turned over another sheet. It was like an electric shock. Two of Hitler's tunics and his cap were being sent to the directorate, along with two other seemingly inanimate items: K. Heusermann and F. Echtmann.

I just sat there dejected, switched off. What the hell was I doing here anyway? I would stand on my head to prove, to clarify, to persuade, but no matter what digging I might do, the unyielding inhumanity would be there to stop me. Here was the proof. At that time there was no way I could bring it to the surface. I just had to live with it, another secret.

I was so jealous of my working hours in the archive: there was no telling, perhaps they had already put a time limit on them and would suddenly announce, 'We've let you work here but that's enough,' but I continued to sit there, my enthusiasm wilting in the face of total wretchedness. It was not because I am so brave, it was because of the sheer intolerableness of the situation; there in that top secret folder was my own name. It was unendurable. I scrubbed it out.

The foreign press was excitedly debating what should be done as the twentieth anniversary of the end of the war approached. Under the statute of limitations then in force, a criminal who had not been charged with his crime within twenty years could not be held legally liable for it. So was Hitler still alive? How would the law play out in his case if he suddenly showed up? It was at this moment that the sensational 'admission' by Mihail Arnaudov, the Bulgarian who had accompanied us to the surgery of Dr Blaschke, became public knowledge. He claimed to reporters to have identified Hitler's teeth, but became muddled over details. In fact, however, Arnaudov had already been exposed: 'The False Witness' was the damning caption under his photograph in the press. He had, nevertheless, done us a great service. Almost simultaneously, a photo of Fritz Echtmann appeared in *Stern* in 1964. He is photographed taking the oath in the Berchtesgaden court where he confirmed that he identified Hitler's teeth and could therefore certify that he was dead.

The name of Heusermann cropped up too. I received a clipping from *Die Welt* in which she recalled our first interrogation in Buch on 10 May 1945, when she definitively recognized Hitler's teeth, and how we showered her with thanks.

So they were both alive. But what had happened to them? Perhaps they had quietly been used as dental experts. Perhaps among our top bureaucrats there was one who could boast that his false teeth were as good as Hitler's. Who could tell?

After many more years there chanced to come into my hands some pages of Käthe Heusermann's memoirs. These had not been published: they were in typescript and with sentences inserted in places in her own handwriting. Poorly photographed, at times indecipherable, there was nevertheless enough that was legible to tell me about the outrageous, monstrous injustice she had suffered in Moscow. After rendering a uniquely important service to history, Heusermann was held as a dangerous criminal first in the Lubyanka, then in Lefortovo Prison in solitary confinement for six years!

In Lefortovo, finding the isolation intolerable, she rebelled and loudly demanded some company at least. A woman was moved into her cell: a cousin of Hitler (who had never met him). She and Käthe did not get along well and she again found herself alone.

'In August 1951 I was finally charged: by my voluntary participation in Hitler's dental treatment I had helped the bourgeois German state to prolong the war. While attending to Hitler's teeth I could have killed him with a bottle of water and thereby done the world a favour.' What are we to make of this? Was it lunacy, barbarism? Was it the shameful silencing of a witness? Or a bit of all three together?

I was sentenced to ten years in severe regime labour camps, less the six and a half years I had spent in solitary confinement. I signed, accepting the sentence, and was glad to be sent to a 'corrective' forced labour camp along with other women who were my fellows in misfortune, finally getting out of that stone dungeon in Moscow. In December 1951, along with three other German women and several men, I was despatched in a cattle truck to Siberia.

Falling between such stone idols as Stalin, Zhukov and Hitler, who attract all the limelight of history, silently, inconspicuously a human life was crushed.

In the camp in Taishet [700 km northwest of Irkutsk], lacking the strength to fulfil the labour quota, Heusermann was put on penal rations. She received no parcels because her relatives knew nothing about her. She would have died of starvation had it not been for another prisoner who became her lifelong friend, a Carpathian Jew, as Käthe calls her, who spoke German. This woman was able to meet the quota and, earning a little money, had a few rubles to spend when the mobile food store came round. She shared her food with Käthe and, when released before her, memorized the addresses of her relatives. She let them know about her and Käthe began receiving parcels.

Käthe Heusermann was in prison for ten years. The end of her camp term coincided with a visit to the USSR by Chancellor Konrad Adenauer, who reached an agreement with Khrushchev about returning German prisoners to Germany. Then came the end of her sentence, transfer between prisons, arrival at Moscow's Bykovo Airport. After all the nightmare she had lived through, accommodation was provided in a well-furnished house near Moscow with a garden and a library of German books. According to Heusermann this was where Field Marshal Paulus 'served' his sentence. Now she was leaving, there were amazing courtesies – after all her torment, a fascinating sightseeing bus trip round Moscow: the Kremlin, the University and, above all, the Moscow Metro 'with its artistically designed stations'. She specially liked Mayakovsky station. All that was in the run-up to her departure by train for Germany. 'And then we were off, in sleeping compartments with white bedlinen and silk lampshades, to Berlin.'

Alas, her fiancé or husband, returning from Norway and not receiving news or even knowing if she was alive, waited five years before marrying and raising a young family. Käthe was forty-five when she returned.

In these notes Käthe writes that she had a good life in Düsseldorf. For a while she worked in a dental practice, then retired with an enhanced pension. Her Carpathian Jewish friend came to stay with her in Düsseldorf every year. Happily, she did at least live another forty years after her release, a free woman. I learned she was alive from documentary film-makers who wanted to interview us as witnesses to Hitler's death for some anniversary.

An Australian film director who made a film titled *The Berlin Wall* suddenly stopped shooting and, evidently thinking something over, said to me, 'How would it be for you to meet up with Heusermann?' Startled by the unexpectedness of the suggestion, I bristled: 'Why? What could I say to her?' I had been spared, but had evidently myself come within a whisker of her fate.

I know that if we had not found Käthe, Stalin's plan would most likely have been successful and Hitler, as Stalin wanted, would have remained a myth and a mystery. Without Heusermann it would probably have been impossible to refute his version of events. But what a scandalous price was paid, without our knowing it, for achieving our goal. What suffering we unwittingly doomed Käthe Heusermann to endure. That burden of guilt will never leave me.

Shortly before her death, Käthe and I were reunited, if only on the screen, filmed separately for a German film, each of us with her role in Berlin in those days of May 1945.

In 2000 the State Archive of the Russian Federation presented an exhibition of newly declassified documents under the title, 'The Agony of the Third Reich: Retribution'. For me personally this event proved momentous. There were many interesting and important documents on display, including some I had never seen before.

The organizers gave me a catalogue of the exhibition inscribed 'To Yelena Moiseyevna Rzhevskaya, without whom this exhibition, and many other things besides, would simply have been impossible.' That was flattering, of course, but I cannot sufficiently express my gratitude to the organizers for just one document they found. It is listed in the catalogue together with many others.

November 1951.

F. Echtmann, K. Heusermann, H. Mengershausen, H. Rattenhuber and O. Voss are condemned by resolution of a Special Council of the Ministry of Internal Affairs as 'witnesses of Hitler's death'.

That document is the last full stop in the saga of the death of Hitler. Here we see it publicly admitted, and the names of the people who suffered as witnesses to it. International jurisprudence had been unaware of the possibility of such a crime, but it was evidently found needful and this shameful case devised in order the better to keep a secret Stalin found expedient.

5 Talking to Zhukov: Moscow, 1965

My mother called me to the phone one morning at nine o'clock. Not usually renowned for the acuity of her hearing, she added unexpectedly, 'Sounds like an army person.'

'Yelena Moiseyevna? This is Zhukov.'

The voice was ebullient but without military affectation. I found that straightforward 'Zhukov', not bolstered by his title and risking confusion with the many other less distinguished Zhukovs who shared his name, very winning.

'Good morning, Georgiy Konstantinovich,' hoping I had got his patronymic right because I had never before had occasion to use it.

'I would like to meet you. Can you come tomorrow at 1600?' I did not hear the time clearly. 'At four in the afternoon,' he repeated, making allowances for a non-army person on the other end of the line.

'I can.'

He was writing my address down. I started giving directions: it was a building behind an iron fence. 'They will find it!' he interrupted me. 'Write it in your notebook: tomorrow at 1600 hours.'

Hearing that I was meeting Zhukov the next day, Viktor Nekrasov became very excited. 'I'm coming with you! I'll pretend to be your secretary. Everything about this is interesting: what Zhukov is going to talk to you about, or the way he kicks me out of the car.'

In the evening I called Anna Mirkina at Novosti Press Agency (who was editing Zhukov's memoirs). On his instructions she had contacted me in advance. When she heard I was planning to take Nekrasov with me she was very alarmed.

'That is out of the question! For all my admiration of Nekrasov, it is out of the question! You must understand, this is very serious, Zhukov is traumatized, he is not meeting anyone. Every new person he meets is another trauma. You must understand . . . I am telling you this in confidence: he is under surveillance as someone who knows all the secrets. He is an elderly man, sixty-nine years old. He is a difficult person.'

The next day, it was 2 November, about twenty minutes before the agreed time, the phone rang and a pleasant female voice said, 'I'm phoning on Georgiy Konstantinovich's instructions. The car will be with you in fifteen minutes' time. The number plate is 34–27.'

When I went down I found a big, black, unusual looking car with a yellow headlight under the radiator, parked by the pavement outside our fence. The driver opened the door and looked out. 'We've just gone off to look for you.' At this the people he had referred to as 'we' came back: a little girl and an elderly lady with a kindly, round face, very modestly dressed in a dark spring raincoat and with a coloured woollen headscarf.

We shook hands and the woman introduced herself: Klavdiya Yevgenievna. She introduced the little girl: 'And this is Masha, Georgiy Konstantinovich's daughter.'

The old black ZIS ('Stalin used to be driven around in one of these,' the driver told me on the return trip) moved off. In its worn interior, the many kilometres it had covered creaked and groaned and clattered, and I had the feeling that I was not just driving down Leningrad Prospekt to the ring road, but deep into the past, turning back the clock of history.

The driver I was sitting next to was a small man in a shabby blue raincoat and a khaki-coloured felt hat with a thin ribbon round the crown and a broad unbent brim, the edges of which hung down in places, giving it a dilapidated look. The only evidence that this was a former member of the armed forces was that his civilian-style trousers were sewn from cavalry twill, and the foot on the accelerator was in a battered black half-boot. He was subdued. There was none of the assertiveness or temperament usual in people of his profession. He seemed very intense, and there was something quite touching about him, as if he were a craftsman, or just in the wrong job. That was not far from the truth: he used to be the driver of the minister of defence, but now drove the ex-minister's wife from their *dacha* to her job and his daughter to school and music lessons.

The little girl was fresh-faced, grey-eyed, and Masha seemed just the right name for her. It was clear she had her new front teeth, and they seemed large, as if waiting for her to grow into them. Masha was in second grade and attending a special school for English language on Kutuzovsky Prospekt. It was only a twenty-five minute drive from the *dacha*. 'All the same, the air is clean,' the elderly lady said in defence of living out there.

I thought I detected a certain reserve in the way she talked to Masha, and at first took her for a nanny, when in fact she was Zhukov's mother-in-law. For her, though, Masha was primarily 'Georgiy Konstantinovich's daughter', and only after that her granddaughter.

I was pleasantly surprised by the modest, likeable people surrounding Marshal Zhukov. There was no sense of superiority. I don't know what I had been expecting. In this untaxing company I was approaching the goal of my journey.

I had never seen Zhukov at the front during the war, but just his name, and even more, his appearance at the front, promised reliability, steadfastness in any critical situation, and in battle – victory. I remember one time we had intercepted some German mail. I was going through the sack of unsent soldiers' letters. There was despair in them as they hastened to say goodbye to their families: Zhukov had turned up on their sector of the front.

During the war nothing could tarnish the heroic image of Marshal Zhukov, although even then, and particularly after the war ended, I heard a lot about his rudeness, his cruelty, and outbursts of often unjustified rage. I heard he was callous about the cost in lives. I was not entirely without prejudice towards him myself. Mark Gallai, a Hero of the Soviet Union and the first pilot to shoot down a German aircraft over Moscow, told me, 'If it had not been for Rokossovsky, we would never have known a different style of command was possible, but this does not mean Zhukov was anything other than a really big commander, and we owe more to him than to anyone else.'

We came off the ring road to a metalled forest road which ended at a green wooden gate in a high, sheer fence. The driver got out to open the gate. It seemed odd that there was nobody on the gate: no watchman, no security. A short distance away Zhukov, in a black leather coat, was strolling along the front of a two-storey house with imposing columns. He came over to me, said hello, and added, 'There, we never did meet back then,' referring to the 1st Byelorussian Front in Berlin.

It was hardly surprising, the distance between me, a translator at the headquarters of one of the armies making up the front, and him, its commander, was just too great.

In the hallway he helped me out of my coat, himself threw off his light leather coat, and we entered a vast hall, ceremoniously flooded with light from a huge crystal chandelier, although the daylight would have been quite sufficient.

'Well, where should we sit?'

The fact that Marshal Zhukov was in civilian clothes made our meeting seem unofficial, but that it was taking place in such a grand setting made it less easy for a visitor to feel there was nothing official about it. The design was that of a grand, official hall, with fine, large windows that brought the garden up to the house. Everything was enormous: the table in the centre of the hall, end-on to the entrance doors and stretching away into the interior of the room; the convex buffet installed in an extremely broad niche on the wall opposite the windows; the sheer size of the carpet. Everything here belonged to those far-off days when we were the victors. Of the fashions of later years there was not a trace.

Zhukov was straightforward, natural and attentive, although there was still some awkwardness and formality (on my part). It was disorientating for me that Marshal Zhukov was in civilian clothes: that was something I took time to adjust to. In my imagination he was always in military uniform. As time passed, however, the tone became more cordial and relaxed.

Zhukov himself and the atmosphere of his house, his enforced removal from the course of events, his loneliness, his vulnerability to his much loved, playful little daughter: I took in so much during the hours of our meeting that, when I returned home, I sat until late into the night writing it all down in my notebook. The main thing, though, was the rather challenging conversation we had.

For our first few minutes together eight-year-old Masha was present, which made everything unforced and homely. Zhukov then sent her off to have her dinner, and said he had read my book. That was what he called it, although what he had seen was only my manuscript retyped on to a duplicator. He had been given a copy by Novosti, who had signed a contract with me for the translation rights. By this time the book, *Berlin, May 1945*, had been translated and published only in Italy, but German, Finnish, and Polish translations were being prepared. In Russia it had not been published as a book: there was only a magazine publication, which he had not seen.

He touched on his own memories of the Berlin campaign, asked me about my army service, and enquired about the archives I had worked in. Finally he got round to his real concern. Here I can quote Zhukov verbatim, because I recorded his words in my notebook. Marshal Zhukov said,

I did not know Hitler had been found, but now I have read about it in your book and believe it, even though there are no references to archives, which would be customary. I have faith in you, though, and in your conscience as a writer. I am writing my memoirs and have just now got as far as Berlin. Now I have to decide how I am to write about this.

He was speaking unhurriedly, flatly, contemplatively.

I did not know that. If I now write that I did not know, it will be taken to mean that Hitler was not found, and politically that would be the wrong thing to do. That would play into the hands of the Nazis.

After a pause, he said, 'How is it possible that I did not know that?'

We were sitting at a round coffee table. The deputy of Josef Stalin, the supreme commander-in-chief; the hero of famous battles; the illustrious marshal who had accepted the surrender of Germany in Berlin and reviewed the Victory Parade of our troops on Red Square in Moscow was asking a rank-and-file translator why he did not know something it was inconceivable under any circumstances that he should not have known. Where in the world, in what other country could such marvels and phantasmagorias occur?

It was not a question I had seen coming, but I knew what strict secrecy had surrounded everything connected with the discovery of Hitler, and that it was reported by order of Stalin directly to him, bypassing the army command; bypassing, as I now learned, even Marshal Zhukov.

I said, 'That is something you would need to have asked Stalin.' That might have sounded insolent, and I did not want to repeat it word for word in my account, so I altered it slightly to, 'Why that was so, is something only Stalin could explain.'

Zhukov immediately rejected that. 'Under any circumstances, I should have been informed of this. I was, after all, Stalin's deputy.'

I had, of course, no clear and convincing answer to that. Having come into possession of such an important historical fact, and perhaps not yet sure what use to make of it, Stalin had instinctively turned it into a secret. Perhaps his decisions were affected, as I wrote, by the difficulty and volatility of the relationship between these two men. It shows us Zhukov as someone whose directness was innate, something Stalin valued, but for just as long as the war continued.

Stalin had no sense of responsibility to the historical record, to the people living in the USSR, or the world. Reality was reality only to the extent that it suited his pragmatic ends, otherwise, as far as he was concerned, it simply did not exist. He evidently had no intention of letting go of such a crucial piece of information as that Hitler's body had been found and the matter closed. What if he decided he did not want it closed?

'If this had gone through NKVD channels, then Beria would have been in on the informing of Stalin. He said nothing,' Zhukov reasoned, sincerely believing, it seemed to me, that that proved Beria could not have known.

At that moment I did not recall that, in the Council of Ministers Archive there was a document proving that Beria did know. Checking a few days later through what I had copied out, I again came across it. There is a detailed note sent via the government communications network, addressed to Beria and dated 23 May 1945.

'Serov was there too, in Berlin. He still lives in the same building as I do, on Granovsky Street. I asked him. He does not know.'

General Serov who in May 1945 was Beria's deputy, did know, if not then, then somewhat later. There are documents to prove it. But it continued to be a secret kept from Zhukov.

'I wanted to ask you,' Marshal Zhukov said, still in the same even, although now not so meditative, tone, 'to help me out with a few things here.' And then, with heavy emphasis, ponderously, 'Since what I write in my book will decide the fate of yours . . .'

He sat back in his armchair and crossed his legs, and suddenly there was that heavy, menacing jaw familiar to the whole country from his old portraits.

'If I write that I know nothing about this, you will not be believed.'

He said that more brutally than I am managing to convey here, because it is not only a matter of the words, but of the way they were delivered, a matter of his posture, and that suddenly so prominent chin. He was not asking (although that was the word he had used), but compelling, not appealing but forcing compliance, which should be all the more zealous for being done under duress. There was a strained pause. Allowing it to drag on for a time, Zhukov asked, 'Do you have extracts copied from documents? Do you still have them?'

'To the extent that I have used them,' I said dryly, clamming up. My prejudice had returned.

'And you have nothing else left?'

'Bits and pieces from Goebbels' diaries.'

'Photographs?'

'I have none. There are some in my book – in the Italian edition.'

He was not interested in published photographs.

What he was asking me was extremely modest, and I would have been more than willing to assist him, but that tone stopped me in my tracks. The trust that was in the course of being established had been violated, and after that the conversation limped along. I found it offensive to seem to be helping him out of fear for my book. By that time it had already been translated and the facts published in it had been acknowledged to be indisputable. I had written only about what the main identification witnesses, Hitler's dental technician and his dentist's assistant had publicly stated: that they had identified Hitler's dead body from his teeth. That was exactly what I had written, and it confirmed that we had found Hitler. This testimony, the photograph of Echtmann in the court under oath, their reminiscences had all been published in the West.

'Oh, they write all sorts of stuff over there,' Zhukov grunted. But after that he repeated that he entirely believed me, having read my book, and had no doubt Hitler had been found.

Zhukov did not smoke and neither did I, so there would have been no way to discharge the tension in our conversation had it not been for Masha. She ran in from the garden, without taking off her coat and bringing in a lapdog in her arms. She sat down at our table, pulling a chair closer, put the dog in her lap and started tickling it.

'Stop it,' Zhukov said. She ignored his command and we carried on talking. Zhukov again told Masha to stop. 'You can see how dirty she is.'

Her father had told her twice to put the dog down: Masha continued imperturbably to do as she pleased. And he, before whom everybody had quailed – both on our own side and the enemy's; he to whom everyone from generals to soldiers unquestioningly submitted; he, with his reputation for ruthlessness and a will of steel, was powerless to get a vivacious eight-year-old girl to do as she was told. That truly proved a more intractable proposition than commanding the obedience of an army of many millions.

Shortly after the birth of his daughter, Zhukov's public life had ground to a halt, and the only living evidence that time was passing was this little person growing into her life. His wife went off to work in the teeming city and he was left here. We can imagine, without exaggeration, that in his isolation he raised this daughter born so late to him, tending the small, life-enhancing shoot of her life. His daughter helped him, unaware of how much she was doing. She was now the most important person in his present mini-garrison, which had formerly been so vast. Masha sat with us for some time more, still occupying herself with the dog, and then went off.

'I don't suppose you have that document I sent to Stalin?' he asked. At the very beginning of our conversation I had mentioned there was a document in the archive where he informed Stalin of the discovery of the bodies of Goebbels and his family. It had been sent to Stalin over the signatures of Marshal Zhukov and General Telegin (as a member of the military council of the front).

'That I do have.' Still offended by the tone he had adopted earlier, I answered curtly and reluctantly. As I write this now, I can see that I was being insensitive, not fully taking in a situation that was complicated and abnormal. Marshal Zhukov was appealing to me for documents he needed for his work and to which he had no access, even though some of them bore his signature. That was something that would be painful even for a person whose self-esteem was not so vulnerable. Nevertheless, Zhukov behaved straightforwardly and naturally. He asked me all about the archive I had worked in. I think I forgot to tell him the reason there were no references to the archive in my book was because the documents had not been declassified and, in any case, at that time I had not even known the name of the archive.

Zhukov guessed it was probably the archive of the Council of Ministers, but said there was also a Kremlin archive. His comments about that were based on impressions from further back. 'There are serious files in there, about important matters, and some that are curious, or even a bit spicy,' he added with a smile, which made his face suddenly fresh and youthful. He asked some more questions about me and my service in the army.

'I was there, in the Reich Chancellery, in the garden, on the day it was captured. And for a second time on 4 May. They did not let me down there,' he said, with an honesty that compares favourably with that of other authors of memoirs. 'Down there was not without risk.' Yes, in the underground complex isolated shots did ring out.

'In the garden I saw that round, what would you call it . . .?'

'Hitler's bunker?'

'That's it.'

'It was probably then they reported to you that Goebbels and his wife had been found near the exit. I'm going by the message you signed and sent to Stalin about it.'

He remembered receiving the report about Goebbels. 'It was reported to me, on 2 May, I think, or on the 1st, that a certain number of tanks had broken out of the Berlin encirclement in a particular direction. I ordered that they should be pursued. I believed Hitler might be escaping with those tanks.'

He also remembered that a few days later he had a report that Hitler's jaw had been found. I told him these were distorted rumours about what had actually happened. There was no separate finding of a jaw. The forensic medical examination established at the autopsy of Hitler that the main evidence for identifying the body was surviving jaws and dentures, and that was the route the identification process took.

'We, at any rate, were waiting very eagerly for an official announcement, and some people were even hoping to be made a Hero of the Soviet Union, which General Berzarin, the commandant of Berlin, had promised to arrange for the first person to find Hitler.'

'That was nothing to award that title for,' Georgiy Konstantinovich grunted. And that was fair. The search had not taken place under fire, no one had given their life. In part it was luck, but more important was the genuine success and determination of a few people to gather comprehensive evidence for the investigation; and that we managed to do despite the obstacles put in our way. But then the discovery of Hitler's body was turned into an undisclosable secret by order of Stalin. It was only many years later that I was able to make that secret public, at first as part of my book *Spring in a Greatcoat.*

Back then, though, in May 1945, the newspapers of the Allied occupation troops came out with headlines, 'Russians Find Hitler's Body', 'Heroic Search in Ruins of Burning Berlin Crowned with Success'. This was put out by Reuters, but in the absence of confirmation by our press, they abandoned it, perhaps believing they must have been misled by their informants. Who, after all, would keep quiet about a success like that?

I said that, back then, there was a feeling that front headquarters did not seem to be showing any great interest in the hunt. Zhukov did not disagree. Indeed, indirectly, he confirmed it by saying he had been informed about 'the jaw' being found. For some reason that had not prompted him to demand that he be fully informed about everything.

When, in besieged Berlin on the night of 30 April, the Chief of the General Staff of the German Army, General Krebs, appeared with a request for an armistice and a written message from Goebbels about the suicide of Hitler, this was reported to Marshal Zhukov and he called Stalin. In his book he gave this, already mentioned, account of the conversation:

I reported the message received about Hitler's suicide . . . I asked for his instructions.

J. V. Stalin replied, 'The game's up for the scum! Pity we couldn't have taken him alive. Where's Hitler's body?'

'As reported by General Krebs, Hitler's body was burned on a bonfire.'

'Tell Sokolovsky,' the supreme commander said, 'to conduct no negotiations except on unconditional surrender, neither with Krebs nor with other Hitlerites. If nothing out of the ordinary happens, do not call until morning. I want to rest a bit before the [May Day] parade.' For some reason, no instructions to investigate the circumstances of Hitler's suicide or to obtain confirmation of it followed. Neither were there any later.

It was only after everything had been completed and the main German participants in the identification and the 'material evidence' had been sent to Moscow that the supreme commander-in-chief asked Marshal Zhukov, 'Where is Hitler?' Zhukov did not have the answer. If that question had been addressed to him earlier, he would, of course, have demanded the information from all the services under his command and would have been aware of what was happening. As no questions followed, he may erroneously have believed that the supreme commander-in-chief was satisfied with that first report of Hitler's suicide, and that that was the end of the matter.

TASS reports began appearing in our newspapers that Hitler might have landed in Argentina dressed as a woman, or might be hiding with Franco. The question of whether he was alive or had committed suicide, let alone whether he had been found, was removed from the military sphere to the sphere of international politics, and Zhukov might have stood back deliberately, taking the view that this was outside his remit. In May 1945 Marshal Zhukov was snowed under by the sheer volume of urgent matters needing his attention in the changed situation, many of them quite new to him. There was a massive redefinition of his responsibilities because, not only was he the commander-in-chief of the Soviet occupation forces, he was also commander-in-chief of the Soviet military administration. This meant he was expected to oversee every sphere, from the diplomatic, military and political to the economic. A new day had dawned, bringing complex new problems and concerns and relegating the defeated Führer to one of yesterday's worries. That, at least, is how I imagine the situation. Information about the course of the investigation was going directly to Stalin, and I was able to explain exactly how that had come about.

So why did Stalin ask him in July, 'Where is Hitler?', when the investigation had long been completed? That Stalin could conceal the truth about Hitler from him was an absurdity that Zhukov did not want to consider. He would have preferred to believe that Stalin did not know either, and it was that belief he wanted to bolster by talking to me. That was his main question, and my explanation differed from what he wanted to hear. Nevertheless, he felt obliged to repeat that he believed me implicitly and now no longer doubted that Hitler had been found. An already fraught situation was, however, made worse by another circumstance, and he let me know that he now faced a dilemma. After the victory in Berlin, at a press conference of Soviet and foreign correspondents he responded to a question by saying that we knew nothing about Hitler's whereabouts. If he confirmed now, twenty years later, that Hitler had by then been found, he would put himself in an intolerably false position. To appear on the world stage, however, with the admission that Stalin had hoodwinked him and concealed the discovery of Hitler's body would, I think, have struck him as no less intolerable.

Asking about Hitler, had Stalin been lording it over him? Who, if not Zhukov, should have known of the achievement of his troops who had captured Berlin: that they had discovered and identified Hitler's body? So why not goad the celebrated 'Stalin's military commander' with a question he was incapable of answering? Stalin was no longer dependent on Zhukov: the war was over, and he was preparing to despatch him from Moscow.

That is what I thought then, but as I write about it now, I wonder whether Stalin had a more pragmatic reason for asking that question. It was the eve of the Potsdam Conference, where he would have to fight his corner in drawing up the postwar world order. Perhaps the reason for his question was to check whether the cloak of secrecy he had thrown over the fact that Hitler was dead might have proved imperfect and that information might have leaked out in the army.

The fact that Zhukov did not know would have satisfied Stalin on that point. He needed to galvanize the corpse of Hitler. Hitler still alive guaranteed the continuation of tension and danger without which Soviet politics could not function at home or in the world at large. It seems to me that now I am closer to clarifying why Stalin behaved as he did. Back then I did not delve any further into all the murkiness, and proposed two explanations.

One Zhukov had rejected and cast aside. 'To the other he did not object: he saw a certain amount of sense in it,' I wrote. Now here is something curious. I have been asked a lot of questions about this account, both by readers, journalists and historians, but no one has ever asked, 'What was the "certain sense" Zhukov saw?'

The second hypothesis I put forward was as follows:

Maybe Stalin wanted to keep the world in a state of tension. Remember the TASS report in the newspapers at that time that Hitler had landed in Argentina dressed as a woman. Later the claims he was hiding with Franco. That felt like kite-flying, a probing of the possibility of striking at Franco.

Zhukov 'did not object'. He 'saw a certain amount of sense in it.' He remained silent, consenting.

Our conversation ranged broadly. I sensed that Zhukov felt a need to speak out about important things, things he would not retract. The content of the conversation, the degree of openness with which Zhukov talked to me, a person he was meeting for the first time, amazed me. Perhaps he was anticipating that a time would come when I would write about our conversation. When I think back, it seems to me that is the explanation.

Zhukov described Stalin's personality very trenchantly and boldly (which, even twenty-one years later, made the censor very, very cross), but without prejudice. He had nothing but contempt for Khrushchev's caricature of Stalin as conducting military operations around the globe. Zhukov said that at the beginning of the war Stalin really did not know anything. His only military experience was of the Civil War. 'But he got the right idea after Stalingrad.'

I asked Zhukov if Stalin had any personal charm. He said, 'No,' and shook his head emphatically. 'Quite the reverse. He was intimidating. Do you know the kind of eyes, what kind of expression he had? Scornful. He could sometimes be in a good mood, but that was unusual. If he had scored some success in international affairs, or military, then he might even sing, sometimes. He was not without a sense of humour, but rarely showed it. People went to him as if they were going to something dreadful. Yes, when he summoned people, they went as if in dread.'

'But without him, it would have been difficult in the war . . . He was strong-willed.' I am quoting Zhukov verbatim.

The situation really was desperate. You yourself have no idea how desperate. We had absolutely nothing, 'no steel, no powder'. And yet, it came from somewhere. It was taken from virtually anywhere. It was like a miracle.

Here he cited the example of Stalin's harsh, menacing, relentless insistence (we were talking about the issue of tank production), and I could feel that Zhukov had been impressed. But then he got round to talking about how Stalin had annihilated the most talented military commanders. 'We entered the war as an army without a head. There was no one. Of course, that is something for which he can never be forgiven.' Losing his measured tone, he began talking emphatically about documents Khrushchev had given him to read.

I read them in 1957. Khrushchev showed me them. Yezhov presented him with a list of people to be shot and Stalin signed it, and with him Molotov, Voroshilov and Kaganovich. Without trial. He did not even summon them, talk to them. Uborevich, Yakir . . .

'Yakir wrote him a letter,' he said vehemently, abandoning the measured tone,

It is unbearable to read that letter. That he is devoted to the revolution . . . Unbearable. Heart-rending . . .

In Zhukov's voice you could hear the shock at what he learned, when he saw and read these things with his own eyes.

'Admittedly, Hitler tricked Stalin,' he said, meaning that the Germans had forged and planted documents 'incriminating' Tukhachevsky of collaborating with them. 'But how could he not summon him, not talk to him? Not listen to what he had to say? That was unforgivable!'

'A giant of military thought,' he called Mikhail Tukhachevsky in his memoirs. 'A star of the first magnitude in the pleiad of our Motherland's military leaders.'

I spoke again about lawlessness and its tragic consequences for the country. Zhukov agreed. I could sense he had been deeply affected by the Twentieth Party Congress.

Years later I made the acquaintance of Alexander Buchin, who had been Zhukov's driver at the front. He visited me at home. He told me about visiting Zhukov in hospital after his heart attack. Buchin lamented, 'What's this, Georgiy Konstantinovich? What's all this about?' Zhukov replied tersely, 'It's about 1937, 1947, 1957 . . .'

In 1937 he had been denounced. The storm clouds had been gathering over his head. Arrest and disappearance seemed imminent. During the war Zhukov served Stalin faithfully as a soldier, recalcitrant but reliable, more capable than anyone else. After the war Stalin needed yes-men and Zhukov was unsuited to the role. He belonged to a different breed, and so began his fall from favour. But, remembering that time of war, he could not reconcile himself to the thought that Stalin had kept him in the dark, deliberately tricking him. It was a situation worthy of Shakespeare. 'I was very close to Stalin.'

But was Stalin close to him? Probably, when he asked him over the phone, 'Are you sure we can hold Moscow?' and waited for the fateful answer to come back. No doubt then he was exceedingly close. And when from time to time he threw Zhukov into the heat of battle when the situation was at its most desperate and most critical, no doubt then he waited sleeplessly by the phone to hear from him.

'I was very close to him, closer than anyone else, until the end of 1946 when we fell out.' That was when he was dismissed from the post of commander-in-chief of the army, so as not to detract from the aura surrounding the Generalissimo, and despatched to command the Odessa military district.

A new bout of persecution came in 1947, with Zhukov removed from the Central Committee of the CPSU and, shortly afterwards, transferred from Odessa to command the interior, also second-rank, Urals military district.

Beria and Abakumov rummaged through everything in his office; they cracked his safe. All they found was operational maps from the war or something else of that kind – all played out, out of date, stuff he should have handed in, except that for Zhukov it was not out of date.

This was a time when the generals who had worked under him were being arrested, including Telegin, staff and people who had served him personally. A 'Zhukov anti-Soviet conspiracy' was being concocted. His driver, Buchin, was also arrested. 'Stalin saved me. Beria and Abakumov wanted me destroyed,' Zhukov repeated, and it seemed to me that with his trusting nature he really believed their actions could not possibly have been agreed by Stalin. He touched in our conversation on the dysfunctional state Stalin was in after the war. I asked if Stalin had been ill.

After the war, maybe. He was traumatized by the war. He told me himself in 1947 [I wonder whether he was mistaken about the year, when he had already said they fell out in 1946], 'I am the most unhappy of men. I'm afraid of my own shadow.' The war traumatized him. Beria harassed and scared him. Told him some kind of agent had crossed the border on a mission to kill him.

'To show Stalin what a good job he was doing of protecting him and keeping him safe?' I asked. 'To strengthen his position?' Zhukov confirmed that was the aim: 'When doing it he always acted through somebody else. Not himself. Mostly it was through Malenkov.'

Zhukov had once been in a car with Stalin.

The car windows were like this. [He indicated the thickness of the glass with his fingers, about 10 cm.] Stalin's chief bodyguard sat in front. Stalin told me to sit in the back seat. I was surprised. That was how we drove: Vlasik, the chief bodyguard, was in front, behind him was Stalin, and behind Stalin there was me. I asked Vlasik afterwards why he had told me to sit there. 'He always arranges it like that, so that, if they're firing from in front, they'll get me, and if from behind, they'll hit you.'

After Stalin's death in 1953, Marshal Zhukov was appointed deputy minister and then minister of defence of the USSR. He was a member of the Party Central Committee Praesidium and again in the kind of job his abilities merited. But then in 1957, while he was on an official visit to Yugoslavia, the Central Committee Praesidium decided behind his back to get rid of Marshal Zhukov, this time once and for all, by stripping him of all his positions and completely removing him from all state, Party and public engagements. Portraits of Marshal Zhukov were torn down, and his name and photographs disappeared from the history of the Second World War.

Zhukov's years of banishment began. He devoted himself to working on his memoirs. Did he realize the snooping was still going on, even though this period was called 'The Thaw'? This document is dated 1963:

Top secret. Committee of State Security of the Council of Ministers of the USSR, 27 May 1963, No. 1447c, Moscow. To Comrade N. S. Khrushchev.

I report to you certain information recently received concerning the mood of former Minister of Defence G. K. Zhukov.

In . . . a conversation about the publication *The History of the Great Patriotic War* Zhukov said: '. . . this is rewritten history. I consider that in this respect the description of history given by the German generals, although it too is perverse, is nevertheless more honest; they write more truthfully. *The History of the Great Patriotic War*, though, is completely untruthful.

'This is not history as it was but history as it has been written . . . It corresponds to the spirit of the present time: who is to be glorified, who is to be kept quiet about . . . And what matters most is what it is silent about . . . I do not know when it will be possible to bring this to light, but I am writing everything as it was. I have already got around a thousand pages behind me . . .'

According to information in our possession, Zhukov is intending to go to the south in the autumn with his family to one of the Ministry of Defence sanatoria. At that time we shall take measures to acquaint ourselves with the part of his memoirs he has written.

Vladimir Semichastny, Chairman of the KGB

Zhukov said again that he was writing now about the Berlin operation. 'I make reference to you there,' he said. 'to *The End of Hitler* . . .' He halted, smiling and trying to remember the continuation of the rather contrived title Novosti had given my book for foreign distribution: *The End of Hitler, Without Myth or Mystification*.

I looked at my watch. 'I've overstayed my time. You must be tired.' He did not want me to leave, however; I could see there were still things he wanted to discuss. We sat and talked some more. He asked if I would give him that document (a copy, of course) of his report to Stalin about the discovery of Goebbels' body. I promised I would.

When I got up to leave, I told him I was flattered that he found my work interesting and would willingly give him all the help I could, but not because the fate of my book might depend on it. I would look through the documents

I had to see if there was anything else that might be useful to him. I felt I also had to mention that mistakes had crept into documents signed by him during those unsettled, turbulent days and I could point them out to him. Zhukov readily accepted my offer. He said, repeating what he had said in the first minutes of our meeting, 'Well, so now we have met. That is all the same something more . . .'

This remark, repeated at the beginning and end of our meeting (that the fact that our meeting was 'something more' than acquaintance only through reading a book), was the only comment in the course of the entire conversation that was vague and open-ended, and that made it eloquent and somehow on a different level from all the rest.

We went down to the car. A last handshake with Marshal Zhukov and the car moved off.

In November 1965, when I saw Georgiy Konstantinovich, he was finishing his long-term project and still in good health, strong, not yet ground down by editors, censors, commissions of the Central Committee and the sundry overseers, overt and covert, of his manuscript who were to keep him under siege. He had as yet no idea of just how much he would have to put up with to steer the book through to publication. He completed his *Reminiscences and Reflections* in 1965, but no sooner were the first steps taken to have it published than it was blocked.

In the presence of my friend Zoya Mikosha, who was in charge of the photograph section of his book at the publisher's and visited him on business matters in hospital, Zhukov told the editor, 'This book is absolutely vital for me.' He furiously rejected the advice proffered to appeal to the then minister of defence, Andrey Grechko.

Novosti Publishers asked me for a translated copy of my book, which had been published in Italy before it appeared in the USSR, to give to him in hospital. I could not imagine why Zhukov would want the book in Italian but it was explained to me that, for the first time in many years, it included a photograph of him. There had been a complete ban on publishing them. The publisher had prepared a selection of photographs for the Italian edition, all of which were passed by the Soviet censorship, and that made their publication official. They included his photograph, and that was important to him. It is just the way things were in those days.

This proved to be the first photograph of Marshal Zhukov since he fell into disfavour eight years previously that the Soviet censorship had approved for publication abroad, even if no such liberties were allowed to be taken within the USSR. My book, *Berlin, May 1945*, was about the assault on Berlin, the search for and discovery of Hitler. I inscribed it, 'Esteemed Georgiy Konstantinovich, Please accept this book about events that are wholly associated with your name.'

When he reappeared from his 'banishment' for the first time in eight years, in the praesidium of a solemn commemoration on 9 May 1965 of the twentieth anniversary of victory, the hall greeted him with a tumultuous ovation. That evening he attended a banquet at our House of Writers. Khrushchev, his persecutor-in-chief, had been deposed and it seemed that Zhukov's exile was at an end.

Evidently, however, the warmth of his reception at that commemoration had not gone down well with the 'authorities'. Bent on depriving Zhukov of fame during his lifetime, the regime learned its lesson and was less impulsive when it came to celebrating the anniversary of the Bolshevik revolution on 7 November 1965. Zhukov was expecting an invitation, but it did not come. Nothing, it seemed, had changed. One more blow, for which he was not prepared. He was offended and wounded. His heart, which in the past had borne many burdens less petty than this, reacted badly and he suffered a heart attack.

Just six days before that heart attack, I had my meeting with him. I was probably the last person outside his family to see him so healthy and buoyant, at the best moment in his life for many years, as he was finishing his memoirs. Working on them again, he relived the war; he was happy in his family life and, it seemed to me, had hopes of returning to a role in the functioning of the state.

The merciless years of 1966, 1967 and 1968 passed and it was now the beginning of 1969. Zhukov had taken a battering and was seriously ill. 'This book is absolutely vital for me.' To this day I find the tragic resonance of that remark deeply painful.

Subjected to cuts, and with insertions and additions imposed on it, with its emphasis altered, the book finally appeared, but it was only in 1989, fifteen years after Zhukov's death, that *Memories and Reflections* began for the first time to appear in a version that was faithful to his manuscript.[1] The text had restored to it, and printed in italics, what had been excised. The appearance of this edition came as a surprise to me and was profoundly gratifying.

In it Zhukov mentions the press conference of June 1945 (which he had anxiously discussed with me). As if to explain why he replied at that time that nothing was known about Hitler's whereabouts, he writes that he had

---

1. The first edition in 1969 had over 100 pages missing. The cuts were restored in the tenth edition, published in 1989.

wondered whether, after the victory, Hitler had not 'scuttled off' somewhere, and said so at the press conference. Somewhat later (in fact, twenty years later), 'we began to receive additional information confirming that Hitler had committed suicide'. After that statement come the following lines, cut out during his lifetime but now restored and italicized: *'How the investigation was conducted is described in exhaustive detail by Yelena Rzhevskaya in her book,* The End of Hitler, Without Myth or Mystification, *Novosti Press Agency, Moscow, 1965. I can add nothing to what Ye. Rzhevskaya writes.'*

I had good reason to be moved. His decision to refer to my book and support it in his memoirs was generous. It did not cut out the circumstances Zhukov found embarrassing. To his own detriment he asserted what he had decided was true. But the Soviet guard dogs had pulled it out, and more than twenty years had to pass before it finally saw the light of day.

Zhukov, Hitler, Stalin. In that moment in time, in Berlin in May 1945, they all come together, and the future analyst of Stalin's personality will not ignore this episode and will try to work out the answers to the riddles Stalin poses. Why did he conceal the fact that Hitler's body had been discovered and turn it into 'the secret of the century'? Why did he keep it from Zhukov? And why did Zhukov not pay the search for Hitler the attention it surely merited?

I am writing about things that I know, of historic events I remember as a participant and witness, and in the search for answers I have tried to trace why the conspiracy of silence began and how it was implemented. Fate decreed that I should have a role in preventing Hitler from successfully carrying through his final vanishing act, of becoming 'the stuff of legend' the more potently to rouse the passions of those thinking as he did, both at the time and in later days.

It took time for me to overcome obstacles that seemed insurmountable even after Stalin's death and to make public this secret of the century. I managed not to allow Stalin's dark, enigmatic plan to take root, concealing from the world that Hitler's body had been discovered by the Red Army. The way was long.

When, twenty-one years after my meeting with Zhukov, I was preparing a documentary account of it for publication, I had just two notebooks to retype and one or two things to add. But although this was 1986, the censors were totally against allowing the piece to be published: the Party was not going to yield on its stance. Grigoriy Baklanov, then editor-in-chief of *Znamya*, has written in his memoirs about how much effort he had to put into wresting this story out of the censors' clutches and publishing it. They were particularly incensed by my report of Zhukov's harsh remarks about

Stalin. 'Just look at the picture of Stalin she is presenting!' they squealed.

On 20 June 1974, I opened the newspaper in the morning and saw Zhukov's portrait framed in black. An unspoken, half-clandestine invitation to bid him farewell.

I decided to go with my friend, Lyalya Hanelli. At the front she too had been an army interpreter. During the disastrous retreat of our troops in the south in the summer of 1942, intelligence she obtained in the mountains at a critical moment saved a division from catastrophe. From her house on Kalyaevskaya Street we set off through quiet, uncelebrated backstreets, across old, grassy Moscow courtyards as touchingly homely and unpretentious as their grass. They were in an improbably good state of preservation and there was a little functioning church tucked away in one of them. Overshadowed by soulless new buildings, they were still unexpectedly alive and perfectly adapted to drinking tea together, having a good gossip, a doze, or reading quietly on your own; to everything that makes life good and natural and unforced.

You walk through one courtyard, then another, each with its own character, and you gaze around enchanted by some places you have never seen before despite having lived in Moscow for so much of your life. At the same time, you are sadly saying goodbye to them, because in the blinking of an eye they will vanish without trace and be replaced by some new development.

And perhaps you are so acutely, so painfully drawn to them and cling to them because you are on your way to say farewell to someone who has gone now to a very different place, and you are chilled by a sense of the unfathomable, of desolation, of a misery not of this world.

We finally emerge from an archway on to the street somewhere near Commune Square and the National Soviet Army Club. The streets, however, have been cordoned off by ranks of police to stop us going any further. 'The public will be admitted from 10.00 to 18.00', but that was only in the newspaper, and admitted the public are in the sense that 'representatives of the workers' are being bussed in, unloaded, formed up in columns, and the columns are marching with orders not to allow unauthorized mourners into their carefully selected ranks. The unauthorized mourners, however, intend to work their way in. The column is instructed to form up in threes. We are not wanted. They attempt to elbow us out: 'Stop trying to worm your way in.' This column has been brought in all the way from Tushino. 'And who are you with, then?' We are not with anyone, but they are not going to get rid of us that easily. We make our way along the column, all the way to the front.

'Where have you turned up from?' the vanguard of the Tushino marchers demand as they turn us away. 'From the 1st Byelorussian Front,' I reply. Only the 1st Byelorussian Front which, under the command of renowned military commander Georgiy Zhukov, stormed and captured Berlin. My answer means little to these recently sprouted officials of district-level activism.

I appeal to the young police officer to let through two women who fought, it is fair to say, under the command of Zhukov. That gets us nowhere. We take up position to one side of the column, and are promptly removed by the police cordon that is here to ensure that nothing happens spontaneously, on personal initiative, uncontrolled, anarchic; nothing at the dictate of a human heart, only at the dictate of the Soviet authorities, officially, in accordance with instructions.

That quiet, consoling, melancholy mood that had been building up on our way here through the courtyards fades and dies, to be replaced by a growing sense of protest and outrage. What sort of way is this Russia has of bidding farewell to its greatest generals! Tsar Paul I failed to honour the dying Suvorov, and sought to quash, by his neglect, the passionate impulse of the people to show their respect. He failed. Great crowds of sorrowing people saw Suvorov to his grave.

This time the government has taken a firmer grip on the amount of honour to be allowed Marshal Zhukov, who had fallen into its disfavour, and the carefully composed columns have been arranged to file past his coffin between 10.00 and 18.00 hours on the same day as the announcement of his death and the funeral arrangements. Not everyone will have had time to open their newspaper that morning, to decide what to do, to get time off work. And to make sure this is exactly what happens, the petty-minded 'competent authorities' get busy, to ensure there is no outpouring of emotion. 'Zhukov? Great was he? Don't ask me.'

For all that, what has been decided buckles under the pressure of the 'unorganized' like Lyalya and me, who flood here to pay our last respects and augment the ranks of the officially approved. War veterans with medal ribbon bars on their chests, free-thinking young and not-so-young people. Bypassing our column, the stewards let through some other endless one. Thousands and thousands of people stand waiting patiently, only worried that we may not fit into the brief period allotted for the lying in state. It is a pity there are no pictures of these people, no pictures of their faces. There is no filming.

The sun is hot. Slowly, step by a step, we move past the newsstands, where the deliberately downbeat tone of today's newspapers on the subject of Zhukov is suddenly rudely disrupted by a headline in *Komsomolskaya Pravda* that shouts: 'Suvorov, Kutuzov, Zhukov!' We go past a photo in the newspaper of Zhukov with his youngest daughter, Masha, long plaits, a frank, marvellous face.

We are shuffling about in the shade of trees by the tuberculosis hospital on Bozhedomka, and in the depths, between the cast-iron bars of the railing, we can see a sorrowful-looking Dostoevsky. Next to me is a young man who is travelling with his family and only passing through Moscow. He has left his wife and child at the station to rush here, and with every passing half hour becomes sadder as he loses hope of reaching the coffin before his train leaves.

In over three hours we have come about one kilometre and finally emerged on to Commune Square. The Museum of the Armed Forces is not far away now. I came to the museum once before, shortly after Zhukov and his wife had visited it. Neither in the Hall of Victory nor in the other halls of the museum was there a single photograph of Marshal Zhukov. Forget him! There never was a great military leader called Zhukov, the embodiment of Russia's victory! Banished for years from all state or public office, he lived in isolation behind a high wooden fence in an official *dacha*.

We were nearly there when the column was diverted to move slowly round Yekaterininsky Boulevard, extending our route. Having circled round the boulevard, we set foot on to the pavement, finally almost at the National Soviet Army Club where the coffin lay. Out of the open doors of a new army hotel adjoining the club, brisk, energetic bearers appeared carrying trays of rissoles and mountains of sliced bread, crates of bottled water and basins of hot sausages. Exhausted people stampeded to drink and sate themselves with the raging gluttony that besets them at wakes and in war. In an instant all was chaos, as if some theatre director had given the signal to sweep away the solemn mood called for by the moment. Coins clattered, empty cardboard cups were thrown to the ground. Those left behind with the hawkers ran back to the column, with their mouths full and excitedly clutching their rissoles.

And then, from above, peals of thunder roared and the skies opened. The rain poured down with such unbelievable force that the money-changing in the temple was instantly washed out. Coloured umbrellas unfurled above the heads of the crowd in their bright summer clothes. Lyalya and I had not thought to bring any, so, unprotected against the wrath of heaven, with an élan born of desperation, we rushed forward to one side of the column, jumping the queue. We were so soaked from head to foot it seemed unlikely we would survive the day. Nobody stopped us. We ran a hundred metres and no one prevented us from squeezing into the soggy mass of people and with them getting inside the National Soviet Army Club.

There was a smell of pine branches, the smell of official funerals, with numerous wreaths leaned against the walls. The chandeliers were swathed in black crepe. The banisters of the staircase were draped with black and red cloth that reached down to the steps.

We went up a little and then were stuck for a long time at the second flight of stairs. The water was running down from our hair, from our clothes which clung to us, and squelched in our shoes, but through the windows we could see a column of thousands of people standing in the teeming rain, not dispersing. Some shielded their heads with umbrellas, newspapers, jackets, but the majority had no protection from the rain. They waited. No one was going to see and remember them standing there. There were no cameramen to film them.

The rain was lashing, bucketing down, bubbling on the asphalt. Peals of thunder. Only the intrusion of the elements was worthy of the grandeur of this funeral.

We entered the Hall of the Red Banner. The coffin was covered in flowers. At its head were three furled red banners with black strips fastened to their shafts. At Zhukov's feet, a red cloth sloped down to the floor, covered in his numerous decorations. A little to one side were rows of chairs for his daughters, family and friends. His beloved wife was not by the coffin, however, having died after a long, painful illness. He survived her by six months.

How lonely that coffin looked, even from a distance. We passed slowly. No stopping, whether to take a breath or give expression to the emotion engulfing you. On a high catafalque Marshal Zhukov lay with a typical expression on his face, his lips tightly closed. Only the lowered eyelids set him apart from all earthly things. There was no sign of frailty or senility. Death had given back to him the earlier, imperious face so familiar from his portraits. The elderly man walking beside me was weeping and muttered, 'What a shame! That was a real man! What a shame!'

After leaving the hall Lyalya and I paused on the landing. We were not ready just to leave immediately. People were coming down the stairs past us, those who had been through the war with Zhukov, and those who were born after it. Their faces showed how moved they were. An old air force lieutenant colonel in a worn, sodden tunic was sobbing as he came down the stairs, leaning heavily on a walking stick, his false leg creaking. Lyalya and I were soaked through but, as at the front, didn't expect even to catch a cold. Outside the window, quietening, the peals of thunder were moving away.

In 1944 a German general was captured in the Carpathians, and Lyalya asked him, 'How does the German command assess the actions of the 4th Ukrainian Front?' 'We are not alarmed by the actions of the 4th Ukrainian,' the general replied. 'We are alarmed by the inaction of Zhukov.' They were alarmed by what he might be planning while invisible to them.

Lyalya and I spent over four hours with the thousands and thousands of people in the streets and the Soviet Army Club, bidding farewell to Marshal Zhukov. It was the same amount of time as my meeting with him had lasted, and for me this day of mourning was a silent continuation of that day and brought me closer to Zhukov.

That very night Zhukov's body was cremated. I heard about it on the radio. For me there was something intolerable about their haste to rid themselves of this man they had long ago worn down and who was now dead, but to whose face death had suddenly returned its old expression. They wanted him reduced to ashes, to dust, to nothingness.

The procession moves towards the centre of Moscow. At the House of Unions the urn is transferred to a gun carriage. Accompanied by a military escort, the funeral procession advances to Red Square, over whose stones the hooves of a white stallion had once clattered victoriously.

Here it was, the day so long awaited and unforgettable! I was summoned to his *dacha* by the supreme commander-in-chief. He asked if I had forgotten how to ride a horse. I answered, 'I have not.'

'Well, here's what,' said J. V. Stalin. 'It is for you to inspect the Victory Parade. Rokossovsky will be in charge of the arrangements.'

I replied 'Thank you for such an honour, but will it not be better for you to inspect the parade? You are the supreme commander-in-chief. It is your right and obligation to inspect the parade.'

J. V. Stalin said, 'I'm too old to be inspecting parades. You do it, you are younger.' [Zhukov was forty-eight.]

At three minutes to ten I was on horseback at the Spassky Gate.

It was drizzling. Not yet visible from the square, Zhukov shook the raindrops off his cap. Rokossovsky commanded, 'Parade, atten-shun!' and at the tenth stroke of the clock on Spassky Tower, Marshal Zhukov rode on a white horse on to Red Square.

Then he stood on the podium of the mausoleum next to Stalin and they were photographed side by side at that historic moment. The photographer was cameraman Yevgeny Khaldei. At an exhibition of his work in 1973 he took me to this photo and told me he had visited Zhukov to give him photographs. Holding this picture in his hands, Zhukov recalled he had wanted to brush the rain off the peak of his cap, but looked at Stalin and changed his mind. Stalin was standing patiently and immobile in the rain.

What was going on under the wet cap in the mind of the leader and supreme commander-in-chief? Zhukov himself did not go in for that kind of mind-reading, and in his simplicity did not realize that Stalin, with a very different personality, was trying with great concern to read his mind. Stalin had been closely watching the victor on his white stallion. 'I'm too old to be inspecting parades.' (He had hardly been a noted horseman when younger.) Zhukov had capered to the jubilant roar of the approving square, to the breath-taking strains of Glinka's patriotic 'Glory to Russia!', and the cream of the army that had won the war, those who had survived, watched him, enraptured, in their new dress uniforms – valorous marshals, generals, majors and rank-and-file soldiers. Enraptured by him, by Zhukov. How could Stalin not be jealous, not be anxious that Zhukov, this commander with his energy, his glory, his willpower, his organizing ability, and his army might be planning something?

And so the rain poured down on Zhukov at the great hour of victory, and the sun of good fortune never again shone on him from behind the thunderclouds.

He had lived twenty-nine years after the war ended. Of those, he worked to the full extent of his abilities and stature for perhaps five. Even when he reminded the world so loudly of himself with the publication of his memoirs, he was never during his lifetime given the official recognition of his importance and achievements that was his due. And now his lightweight ashes were being borne across the renowned square on the shameless shoulders of the likes of Brezhnev, Suslov, and Grechko.

Zhukov had not asked for the Kremlin's funeral rites; all he wanted was to be laid to rest in the ground. But what did his personal wishes matter? This was what political expediency required.[1]

Zhukov will go down in history as the victorious defender of Moscow and the vast expanses of the Motherland, but his native land expressed its gratitude by grudging him even a grave plot, awarding him instead, for his eternal rest, a slot in the Kremlin wall.

For the last time he manifested himself to Red Square as a handful of dust, Marshal Zhukov, who, at the supreme moment of his destiny had entered it on a white stallion whose hooves struck sparks from its cobbles.

---

1. Many years later Mikhail Pilikhin, a cousin of Zhukov, told me he had been present during a telephone conversation in which Brezhnev promised Zhukov he could be buried in the ground.

6 Things Lyuba is too Young to Remember

Talking to my Granddaughter, Moscow, January 2006

You want to understand what it felt like being in Hitler's last headquarters in the underground complex of the Reich Chancellery at the time of the fall of Berlin.

If I had not had behind me a long history of following the front line to Hitler's Chancellery, I would have felt deprived. The assault and defeat of Berlin cannot be understood properly outside the context of the war as a whole and of everything we experienced. I travelled from Moscow with the army, and cherish the memory of that. The first I saw of the front was in February 1942 at Rzhev, and I feel that Rzhev was really the city where I began to have a destiny. It was here I first encountered war. A crippled, burned land, misery and selflessness, cruelty and compassion; soldiers with the great simplicity of their courage; village women bearing the terrible burden of caring for children in the front line of fire. The astonishing magnanimity and self-sacrifice of people, when the turning of the tide of war was still so far away, filled my heart with pain and will remain with me forever. The historic events I was involved in during the last days of the war in Berlin might have been expected to overshadow all those other front-line impressions for me, but my most moving experience was those days of lowering skies in the environs of Rzhev.

Rzhev has a special place in the immense map of the war. Not only was the city occupied for seventeen months, but for almost all that time there was unrelenting, bitter fighting there, on the approaches to Moscow. In their orders, the Germans called Rzhev 'the springboard for a decisive second leap to Moscow'. The Rzhev salient, which German orders referred to as 'a dagger pointed at Moscow', was a real threat to the capital. When the situation turned against the Germans, Hitler's order said that to surrender Rzhev would be to open the road to Berlin to the Russians.

Rzhev, tormented by occupation, brutality, hunger, bombardment and bombing, a city the opposing armies battled for relentlessly, saw some of the bloodiest fighting in the war. The tragedy of Rzhev confronted us starkly when we re-entered it in 1943.

You talked one time about the changing 'soul' of the war.

When you say 'soul', you immediately hint at something elusive, and what I was referring to was the deep, spiritual aspect of war as it revealed itself at different stages. Rzhev, standing at a junction of railways and major highways, at a crossroads in the war and in people's destinies, illustrated that dramatically. The dedication of the army and the whole nation at that point, when it was not yet being rewarded with victory, was especially eloquent testimony to the indomitable spirit of that tragic time.

The year 1943 was a turning point in the war. Our army was fighting its way to the west, and coming across everything that the war had swallowed up during the period of defeats: our prisoners, the occupation. We were clearly not prepared for what we found. During that time of retreat, our army had left an unarmed and defenceless population to the mercy of the enemy. We should have been the ones with the sense of guilt, but instead, as we liberated those lands, the returning liberators came not with any consciousness of their guilt towards the population but as if to judge them. As if people who had lived perhaps two, perhaps three years under German occupation had not needed somehow to feed themselves, to keep their children from starving to death, and had therefore no option but to do a certain amount of work, perhaps performing compulsory labour with German assault rifles pointing at them, clearing the roads of snow, for example. Yet in spite of that, it seemed that everyone was guilty of something, singled out for something of that kind, and under suspicion.

Our military doctrine disregarded the concept of the prisoner of war. No matter how hopeless your situation might have been, to be taken prisoner was officially considered treasonable, even if a doomed million-strong army had fought to the last after being surrounded. War has not only heroes but also martyrs, and these were our prisoners of war. Our people felt sorry for them. They could see how brutally the Germans treated them, how they perished in captivity. When prisoners were being herded back behind enemy lines, women would take bread or a potato from their children and risk their lives (because the Germans would open fire on them) to go out to the road and try to pass something to eat to the prisoners.

Our soldiers and commanders, liberated from captivity, were subjected to the humiliation of blatant distrust and abuse and found themselves once more behind barbed wire. I have heard many of them say they found that worse than German captivity, because there their tormentors were at least the enemy. And who can claim this did not contribute to so many supposedly 'displaced persons' being Soviet soldiers who had not committed any crimes towards their homeland, but feared persecution if they returned.

The mistrust and inhuman treatment of those who had suffered the torments of captivity and living under German occupation damaged not only those victims, but undermined and warped people's innate sense of justice and compassion. The pressure was so great that it suppressed natural morality and could come to be regarded as something self-evident: 'Well, I wasn't behind enemy lines, so I am pure; but you were, so you are tainted.' People began to be divided into the pure and the impure.

I wrote and spoke out about this issue many years ago, but only recently read in a newspaper that in 1954, when Marshal Zhukov became minister of defence, he set up and chaired a special commission that proposed a change in the law, so that there would be no discrimination against former prisoners of war, general compensation, and removal from the personal questionnaire ex-soldiers had to fill in of the question asking if they had been a prisoner. The Party leaders of the USSR, with Khrushchev at their head, rejected the proposal. Right up until the fiftieth anniversary of the end of the war, the stigma of people who had suffered in this way was, criminally, retained.

How many years have passed, and still there is more to be said about the war . . .

You are right. It is difficult to convey the truth about the war, and anyone who succeeds is fortunate. How many decades have passed and now here we are, we and our descendants, alive at the same time, and everyone's life is fragile and finite. But never has a whole succession of generations warned so directly, with such awareness, 'We are about to pass on . . .' These are the people who fought in the war and, facing their inevitable end, each of them feels all the more acutely that they are part of a great epic. Anyone who aspires to tell the tale of what they experienced is conscious that, if it is not done now, then when will it be? There is an extreme anxiety to do what has to be done while there is still time, not to leave this life with things unsaid. But it is not easy to convey the truth about the war.

Why should that be so?

What I mean is the hard-won truth of a work of literature. A good intention to write the truth is no guarantee that it will be achieved. Truth about character, the portrait of a period, of its events, is broader, more significant and more all-encompassing than the facts alone. Truth calls for hard work involving the soul and talent. Sometimes it needs to come through inspiration, because it is an act of grace. So, it is fortunate if you are able to comprehend, assimilate and give that artistic expression. Artistic truth cannot be dependent on the current climate or expedient, and its influence comes from everything that goes into it: the nobility and pain, talent, intelligence, courage, and the limpid and mournful poetry of life. From its mistakes, too. That is when the truth can speak to us readers, enlighten and elevate us. And it develops the talent of the writer, too – it is creatively contagious, and that is why all through your life you pursue the bluebird.

Just now, rereading your conversation with Zhukov, I was struck by his words, 'I trust your conscience as a writer.' I was brought up short: not 'your account as an eyewitness', not 'you as a researcher of the archives', but 'your conscience as a writer'. That chimes with what you say about getting to a truth that is more profound than a conscientious, direct relation of the facts: to an artistic truth.

I think what he most likely meant was the moral responsibility of the person writing.

He had already suffered during his years in disfavour from all sorts of writers; what would have made him think he could trust the profession as such? No, he was referring to your own, personal talent. The military leader who led us to victory was the first to recognize your secret, your gift of trustworthiness.

What sort of a gift is that? It's more of a burden.

Because you carry it as a responsibility. But Berlin, May 1945 *is not only a documentary account of the death and identification of Hitler. Look at the subtle brushstrokes and details which, perhaps, nobody else would have spotted, with which you paint the portrait of those days? Modern historians draw on you to reconstruct them.*

And your Rzhev, a cycle of novellas and stories giving a unique evocation of the people's war! Everything seems to be happening right here and now, before our eyes, even though I had not been born at that time.

It is a kind of alternative memory, not memoirs but a constant presence of past experience in me. Even now, many decades later, it sometimes prods me very forcefully. The pre-war years, the war and everything that came after it have not just been swallowed up in the mire of life. Landmarks. They are not equal in how long they lasted or how significant they were, they differ in their spirit, their meaning, their content and what they teach us; some of them are interrelated while others diverge or merge, but there is an interaction, a debate going on as we strive to find our bearings in reality. It is a great shame that human life is so short – from a distance and in the depths some things are more clearly visible.

The sense of affliction is precious, it enlightens us. What it anchors in memory is sometimes not the great, momentous events. It makes its own unaccountable selections. That is probably true for all of us.

But does affliction not turn to hatred of those who have caused it?

It does. And how! I was asked on Swedish television, 'How have you been able to overcome hatred for Germans, knowing only too well at first hand all the evil their army perpetrated on the territory of your homeland?'

What did you say?

My answer was never going to be anything conventional. An army interpreter is in a peculiar position in the avalanche of war. I had not only to know about what was happening to the enemy behind the front line that divided us, to recognize telltale signs of what they might be planning and how they were preparing to implement it, to make sense of intercepted orders, letters and diaries, but also to be in direct contact with Germans at the very moment catastrophe struck them, when one of them had just been seized in battle, or kidnapped by our scouts from a lookout post – when he was a 'squealer'. Whether he was dumbstruck with shock, dejected, or stoical and trying to suppress his dismay – he was always vulnerable and unhappy.

The enemy in captivity. I found that contact a hard, trying experience. With rare exceptions it was difficult to feel that the person presently in front of you was a Nazi. Ejected from the sinister community he had shortly before belonged to, he did not conform to the notion the word 'Nazi' conjured up for us. But nobody could understand what he was saying, and the language barrier cut him off from the possibility of being seen as anything other than 'the enemy'.

Between the German prisoner and his opponents, in whose power he now found himself, I was a kind of connective tissue. His eyes followed me anxiously; I could see he was frightened. The hatred I felt for the armed enemy bringing death, brutal violence and devastation, receded. A sense of acute pity interceded for this prisoner – a victim of the Nazis' lunatic war.

The gift of compassion. Without it there would probably be no gift of trustworthiness.

I am not sure I would call the feeling compassion. I called it involvement.

That is a very important word for you. Tell me what involvement is?

I participated in a multi-part documentary, *The World at War*, made by Thames Television. I saw several of the episodes and wrote about them.

And then there was one about the occupation of Holland by the Nazi army. On the screen is a close-up of a man who was in the Resistance. When he was still just a very young lad, he heard the Jews were being deported from Amsterdam and went to the station.

There was a goods wagon already there. They were brought, under escort. Armed German soldiers with assault rifles and dogs had cordoned them off. What could I do, on my own, unarmed?

'But I had seen that!' he said emphatically. 'I had seen it.' And, he said, if he had seen it he was involved in it. He felt complicit, and became actively involved in the Resistance.

So, what about me? God only knows the things I have seen. Perhaps if I wrote about that I would get the horror out of my system. But what would that leave?

7 Things We Should Never Forget

Talking to Lyuba, Moscow, March 2006

Now, with the passing of so many years, it is difficult for me to get a clear understanding myself of why, when the war came crashing down upon us, I decided to go to the front. I had not been brainwashed, I did not read the newspapers, I had no dreams of heroism. I had no illusions on that score, but probably something had been building up in me. Spain, of course; Spain was a landmark. For the first time in our lives, and the last time before the war, the Spanish Civil War united us in solidarity with the Western intelligentsia who were prepared to stand up against fascism. The environment in which I spent my youth also readied me for signing up, despite the fact that in practical terms I was totally unqualified: I was not sporty and have never learned to shoot, having bunked off military training classes. There was a sort of shooting gallery in the basement of our institute and, in the spirit of the times, some girls visited it. They were really keen to do a parachute jump and get the badge: I was too scared even to try jumping off the parachute tower in Gorky Park. The practical side of the military training was, as it were, one thing, while a readiness to go to war was something separate, and seems to have been what mattered most. Whether I would actually be any use there was something I never asked myself. A desire to play a part in our common destiny was something I think many people who signed up felt.

But did you not at first work in an arms factory?

In No. 2 Clock Factory, which was immediately switched, under the mobilization plan, to manufacturing cartridge cases. My job at the lathe was to chisel the burr off the blanks. 'Lathe Operator, Class 3' is how I was described in my work record book. There is nothing following that: after the war I was out of luck as a job-seeker, at least as an employee.

Point Five in my CV ('Nationality: Jewish'), told against me.

You write that at the beginning of the war it was difficult for a girl not liable for military service, let alone one with no relevant peacetime skills, to get to the front. In the end, though, you did train as a military translator and interpreter and went off to the war. I simply can't imagine what it must have been like for you, a young girl, under conditions that would have been hard for a man. Svetlana Alexiyevich has written about 'the unwomanly face of war'. Do you think she is right?

The face of war is unwomanly, I agree, but neither is it manly. The face of war is just the face of war. Can one really find any point of comparison between war and ordinary human life? The way people behave in the circumstances of war are out of the ordinary, unimaginable, as a result of the dictates and the demands it makes on a person's physical and mental endurance. In fact, at the front people tended never to fall ill, and even chronic ailments often retreated and ceased to be troublesome. In my own experience, I caught a slight cold during the winter in Stavropol-on-Volga while I was wearing a summer forage cap, canvas boots that were no good for keeping your feet warm, and staying in an unheated room; but for just over three years after that, when I was continuously at the front, I was never ill at all, although the circumstances and conditions I was working in would have seemed guaranteed to make you ill. But that was only by peacetime standards.

Of course, life at the front is particularly difficult for a woman with her natural differences from men, and there is no need to go into further detail about that. Women can also be subjected to sexual harassment, although most of the time relations were on a comradely level. The Germans had no women right at the front: no typists, no nurses, no female cooks or laundressess. Not one. Only at a very remote airfield might you happen to find a female German telephonist.

The army at Rzhev in which I began my service was commanded by General Lelyushenko. 'The Soldier General', he was called out of earshot, always at the front line, with one foot in a jeep and the other on the ground. He could not abide women in the army, and for some reason called them 'flatheads' and bawled out a divisional commander he heard was keeping a woman. 'Catching flatheads, are we?' Everybody quailed before that reproach. At that very trying period in the war, moral standards in Lelyushenko's army were markedly strict. But that only meant that emotions, which in any case no one was expected to show, were even more furtive. In war, when any hour might prove your last, feelings were intense and not even an army commander could abolish them.

After the war, when our army had reunions, Colonel Kozyryonok, the military prosecutor, told me there had not been a single military crime committed in our army by a young woman. They were significantly more reliable than men. The Germans might be on the outskirts of a village, but the telephone operator would not leave her post until given the order. The prosecutor was less complimentary about men. 'If men could have got away from the front by becoming pregnant,' he said laughingly, 'we would have had an epidemic of desertion on those grounds.' One girl was, in fact, court martialled for desertion after she ran away to another unit to which her boyfriend had been transferred.

Her time to love coincided with the war, and no doubt she was judged without pity, bearing the full brunt of martial law. All that sort of thing was hair-raising.

In war a man can dedicate himself wholeheartedly to warfare, but a woman continues to live to a much greater degree with her emotions. I think a woman living at the front is always in conflict with war (even if she doesn't know it) and that it violates her emotions.

Is there such a thing as a woman's view of war? What does it reveal?

I wouldn't presume to say whether there is a women's view that reveals something new, because that is what I write about. Someone less involved could probably be more objective. It might be simpler to talk about the general attitude of women towards war. Nowadays they are unanimously against it. Women do not accept war in any guise: it brings death and violence and they oppose it. As far as the Second World War is concerned, there is no evidence of a specifically women's view of it in the literature.

We might well ask women who were young girls then, rushing headlong to the front without a clue as to what might be awaiting them, why, having found out and faced mortal danger, why when they were wounded and lying in hospital, they could not wait to get back to the front line, despite having every opportunity to stay in relative safety. Why today is it far more difficult to find a woman who will decry her years at the front and say her youth was ruined, than to find one who will say those were the best years of her life? Why? If we take their answers we will be get a sense of women's views about what we rightly call the Patriotic War.

Did anything at the front remind you of the fact that you were Jewish?

On the very first night I arrived there, I found that our army was trapped in a pocket. From periodical reports we gathered the neck was widening at one moment, but contracting the next and might at any moment be closed completely. At the time I reached the front our neighbouring 39th Army was totally surrounded. Facing the risk of being taken prisoner, you could hardly forget the answer to Point Five. I did not yet have any comrades I could turn to; I was an unknown quantity to those I needed to escape with. Everything was rather wobbly. When I was eventually issued my own TT pistol I felt a whole lot more secure.

You were not taught to shoot on the course for translators . . .

That's right. General Biyazi who was in charge of the course assured us we would be taught to shoot at the front, but that did not happen. I was given a loaded pistol and shown what to press. I had no expectation of going into battle, but at least I would be able to deal with myself.

What about the people you came into contact with. Did it matter that you were Jewish?

That did not affect me at all. What got you accepted was something different. They needed an interpreter, and now it turned out the interpreter was a woman. I was the only woman among a lot of men and it was awkward for them, too. They couldn't swear in front of a woman, which meant they could hardly speak. I was deployed in an army that had retreated all the way from the USSR border. These people had been through a lot together, and then along comes some Muscovite, some student. They needed to be very tolerant. I was not one of them.

I had a Bible in my backpack, which I had seen for the first time in my life in the possession of my friend. Her mother worked in the Party publishing house and among her anti-religious armaments was a Bible published, for some reason, by the Seventh-Day Adventists. At the end of the course we went to General Staff Headquarters in Moscow to be assigned and I spent a couple of nights with Vika Malt. Noticing I was interested, Vika gave me the book with the thoroughly atheistic inscription, 'Good luck, Lena. Vikukha.' At the front I sat down one day to read the Bible still, of course, a bit disorientated. We had a major from the Border Guards assigned to us for a time. He had a pleasing, open expression. Someone pointed me out to him. 'She reads the Bible.' 'And why not?' he said. 'A very fine work of literature.' That took the heat out of the incident.

At the front I made notes, not systematically though, in fits and starts. That was looked askance at, too, at first, because keeping a diary or making notes was not allowed. I was well aware people would get curious and peep into it, so I wrote in the notebook, 'Comrade Captain Borisov, are you not ashamed to be reading someone else's diary?' One day when I opened it, I found scrawled in large letters, 'Should I be?' I still have that notebook, complete with its obtrusive comment. After that I was left in peace, accepted, and in any case they appreciated my interpreting. I found I could do the job well. As time passed the attitude towards me became friendly.

You said once that, working as an interpreter, you found being a woman had its advantages.

I think in some ways it had. One prisoner told me that meeting a woman in such circumstances seemed like a good omen, a sign of mercy. The prisoners asked for help: one told me his wife had 'a child on its way' and asked me to let her know through the Red Cross that he was alive and in captivity; he did not know we were unconnected with the Red Cross. If I was on my own with a prisoner, which was usually the case, it was less like an interrogation than a conversation. And I had successes. Sometimes it was remembered I ought to have security and a soldier was assigned. On one occasion an officer who had come down to the dugout heard the guard snoring and grabbed a sheath knife lying on the table in front of me.

'What's this knife doing there?' he asked.

'It's for sharpening my pencil.'

Did you find it difficult to play the role of interrogator?

I was helped in a way by a pilot who had been shot down and who had been strafing women. I asked him why he had been firing at them when he could see they were just women working in the fields. The plane had been flying very low, directly above them.

And he replied, '*Ich habe meinen Spass daran.*'

He did it just for fun. That made me shudder. It was the first time I had encountered a real Nazi, an enemy.

I felt sorry for the first prisoners. That was upsetting. The middle-aged German, the same age as my father, who was trying to remember the Russian word for melon and was feeling cold in the shed and asked for a blanket. Or handsome Thiel, with his university education. They were bewildered and feeling wretched. It is probably impossible to convey the feeling, to reproduce it artificially. What comes closest is perhaps the notes I jotted down in my notebook. I included them later in my book, *Near Approaches*.

On the course for military translators, skipping the firing practice and anything military, we did in an odd, unconventional way, as if from the wrong end, get drawn into the war, immediately coming into contact with the enemy, his German language, his pass and record book – the *Soldbuch* – his regulations and commands, his personal letters (how those Germans tormented us with their letters!), his intricate Gothic script, his military terms we found it so difficult to learn. And to enable us to master the language as such, children's reading books and stilted dialogues: '*Wo warst du, Otto?*' 'Where have you been, Otto?' 'Oh Karl, I had a lovely boat trip on the lake.' And Heine: '*Mein Liebchen, was willst du mehr?*' And our role-play interrogations, when we took it in turns to be the German prisoner and then the Soviet commander interrogating him.

And then, when we were about to go off to the front, charged up, if very hastily, with the German language, I felt my heart contract with fear that, when I met an actual prisoner, I might suddenly have to witness him being subjected to cruelty and violence.

On my first morning at the front, in a lull between two frenzied bombings, I came out of a peasant hut to see a sleigh being drawn along the street bearing a wounded prisoner. I followed it, fascinated, and it soon stopped. I caught up when the driver had just got off and was thinking something over. I drew myself up and asked loudly, 'Are you taking him to be shot?' assuming that must be the case. The elderly, moustachioed driver scowled at me over his shoulder and said rattily, 'We don't shoot prisoners,' and went off behind the hut to relieve himself.

Then I excitedly asked the German lying in the sledge where he came from, and heard his listless response, 'Oh, whatever next!' The wounded man was not in the mood for polite conversation. I walked back, grateful to the old driver for the lesson he had taught me with his contemptuous scowl. At the time, I wrote down in my notebook, 'This war will be won by those who show magnanimity,' hoping that we would be those winners.

However, our strong and, for the time being successful, adversary had long ago rejected the concept of greatness of heart. What mattered was only strength and brutality. The world was increasingly divided into the conquerors and the conquered, with no gradations in between. What place did that leave for greatness of heart? Increasingly what was being inculcated, and accepted, was that against victorious strength and brutality we should pitch our own strength, hardware, and brutality.

The army in which you found yourself had retreated all the way from the frontier and become charged with hatred of the enemy, but you too saw a lot of dreadful, inhuman sights, and your experiences were soon the equal of theirs.

The Rzhev concentration camp was monstrous. The living and the dead were lying side by side on the ground. The Germans derided their prisoners: they would bring frozen potatoes and scatter them on the ground; the half-dead prisoners would crawl to get them, and the guards would lash them with whips. In the middle of the camp a gallows operated tirelessly.

Advancing westward, we walked over trenches full of bodies. Trenches. In addition to the large, well-known concentration camps, there were so many local camps. In the camps the bodies were dumped in pits and had a light covering of soil thrown over them, and when our armies were advancing, the Germans started digging them up and burning the bodies to cover their tracks. They rarely had time to finish the job.

Burned villages. There were dedicated arsonists, 'torchers' in the German units. Hitler's order for scorched earth when they retreated, that was Nazism in action. Destruction of the land, destruction of the people. When we entered a village there was no longer a village, just embers and ashes. Out of a ravine, or some dugout they had put together, an old, exhausted man would emerge, women, a child barely alive. Yes, that made you feel hatred.

But I can say, looking back now after so many years, my humane feelings were not eradicated. It was hard, but something I had brought from my childhood, that had grown stronger when I was a young student, my – and I am not going to shrink from using the word – my internationalism, stayed with me. In the institute where I studied there was not and could not have been any discrimination along racial or national lines, and after many years, when we reminisced about one of our fellow students, we often could not remember what his or her nationality had been. There was then, there really was, an amazing sense of national fraternity and unity, and it is unforgivable that it has been perverted and destroyed. It will be a long time yet before we recover from the consequences of that.

Your youth was identified with the amazing, unique Moscow Institute of Philosophy, Literature and History that existed for seven years and was closed down at the outbreak of war and merged with Moscow State University. You have written wonderfully evocative words about it, which echo in the heart of anyone who has been touched by the sense of community in colleges and special schools or even dreamed of it.

I was looking to explain to myself what it was about the institute that remains so indelibly alive in all of us who studied there: a generation cut across and crippled by the war, that endured such terrible losses and upheavals.

What was it about IPLH? Just pronouncing those initials aloud is a signal, they radiate something. Unacquainted people, when they discover they both came from IPLH, immediately feel they have something in common. Is it because that is where we spent our youth? Of course, but that is not the whole story. Or perhaps the IPLH legend is just an illusion, albeit a long-lasting one. But if it is, then it is one of those about which a clever English writer said that an illusion is one of the most important facts of life.

It seems to me that IPLH is a code yet to be decoded. IPLH was something new, somebody's secret plan and intention, something that for a brief moment seemed to be possible, a brief twinkling of light in that succession of brutal years. And something more: IPLH was the spirit of a time whose very passing was history. We could feel that, and it fostered a passion for life in us.

The phenomenon that was the 1930s was a surge of covertly accumulated culture, but already a reckoning was near, the executioners were biding their time. IPLH was part of that brief break in the clouds, and of the mayhem that was to come. This was a coming together of students with great potential, broad interests and aspirations: future philosophers, major literary specialists, critics, historians, literary translators, journalists, experts on world culture, folklorists, linguists, publishers and editors who did so much for our country's culture in those difficult times. For those alumni of IPLH who became writers, the war was tremendously important, as it was for me.

At that time IPLH brought together the thirst of students for knowledge in the humanities with an ardent desire on the part of its amazingly distinguished professors and dazzling young academics to impart it to them.

It would be a mistake to suppose all those who graduated from IPLH were like-minded people. No, for me some were close to my values while others were not; but when we marked the fortieth anniversary of the day the Germany attacked the USSR, the reunion of graduates of IPLH was held in a state of joyful emotion; we were glad in all sincerity to see each other, without raking over old grudges, and deeply moved. We assembled by the old familiar building in Rostokino Street and filled Lecture Theatre 15. Neither in what was said, nor in the atmosphere of the reunion were there any reproaches or embittered reminders of misdeeds dating back to the bad old days. It was a friendly, sincere, open-hearted occasion.

And how was that possible? The answer is probably contained in the code, but perhaps it was also because this generation had not had an easy life. It was weighed down with the ballast of blunders and hopes, darkness and insights; it was seduced, persecuted and, who can say, perhaps redeemed.

Even before the war you were conscious of the spirit of the times. Misha Molochko spoke about the mission of your generation and the coming war against fascism. What effect did the USSR's pact with Hitler have on you?

Immediately after the signing of the pact we were very disturbed and upset by it. Perhaps we even felt humiliated. The IPLH students from then on invariably referred to the Germans as 'our implacable friends'.

That year I met a girl in the street who had been a fellow student of my elder brother and now worked as a translator in the People's Commissariat for Foreign Affairs. She told me in confidence that translators who were Jewish were no longer being sent abroad on assignments and were beginning to be fired from the Commissariat. I thought to myself that seemed to be taking fraternization with the Germans too far, and in any case, why were we choosing to lose face and trying to curry favour with the Nazis?

A few years ago, when a journalist asked when I thought the Stalinist state had adopted a policy of anti-semitism, and persecution and repression of other peoples of the USSR, I suddenly remembered that conversation in the street so many years before, and I replied, 'Since the signing of the Molotov–Ribbentrop Pact. They had only to start . . .'

At the institute, the board with its name in Russian and French was taken down and replaced with one in Russian and German. I remember an episode when the general discontent in the institute did surface. As part of the cultural events accompanying the pact and the exchanging of art, an old German film was dug out and delivered to IPLH. Word went round that the reel was very interesting and had been banned until recently. Lecture Theatre 15 was full to the rafters. A white screen had been erected over the stage. The reel had no sound so an accompanist was needed and a student, Lev Bezymensky, was identified as suitable and dragged up to the stage. To start with, he dutifully accompanied the images on the screen with neutral melodies, but suddenly took off, and when Siegfried mounted his horse, the piano belted out the Cossack, 'Lads, Saddle up the Horses!' After that there was no holding Lev, scene after scene! Brünnhilde's appearance on a cliff high above the Rhine was accompanied by 'To the Cliff Came Loveliest Katyusha.' How the audience responded! They fell about laughing, guffawing, giving vent to their pent-up emotions.

On one occasion, after the fall of France, I saw seven or eight portly, respectable, self-satisfied Germans at the circus talking loudly and animatedly among themselves during the interval. I remember the wave of animosity that swept over me.

But the German language I loved. I was drawn to it, and was fortunate enough to have lessons for a year with a wonderful teacher, formerly the governess of Pyotr Stolypin's children. From her I heard: '*Sie haben eine Gabe für die deutsche Sprache.*' You have a gift for German. That was unforgettable. Alas, she died in the spring of that year, but I did not drop German. I enrolled in parallel with my school lessons on an extramural course at the Moscow State Pedagogical Institute of Foreign Languages. I joined a circle conducted by the widow of Karl Liebknecht.

And earlier than that, before I was even at school, my grandfather would recite Heine to me by heart.

You wrote about your grandfather and this German teacher in Punctuation Marks, *a novella about the 1930s. Today, talking to you about the book you are finishing, I am getting ever deeper insight into all you have written, into your memory, learning something about my own ancestors and the spirit of those times. So, for you young people destined to fight this war, the threat of hostilities did not seem to have receded after the pact was signed?*

Perhaps to some extent it receded in time, but we were well aware war was inevitable. It was obvious. Already in *Mein Kampf* Hitler had written that he was not just interested in restoring Germany to its 1914 borders, but in conquering lands to the east. Russia must cease to exist and be repopulated by Germans. The fate of its population would depend on the extent to which slaves were required to cultivate these lands. After Russia, if his plan was successful, there would be no holding him. All of Europe was to be under the heel of Germany.

Why did the war start so catastrophically for us?

If we are going to talk about the beginning of the war, we have to go back to 1937–8 and Stalin's terror. It is difficult to believe the extent to which the Red Army was vandalized. Of five marshals, three were liquidated. Almost without exception the commanders of armies, divisions, and even regiments were shot. When the trials began in Moscow, Hitler and Goebbels, who were constantly listening to radio reports, at first decided Stalin was murdering Jews, and were only puzzled that Litvinov had not yet been done away with.

'Crisis in Russia and constant arrests. Now Stalin is going after the Red Army,' Goebbels wrote on 3 February 1937. 'The killings in Russia have the whole world agog. There is talk of an extremely serious crisis of Bolshevism. Voroshilov has issued an order to the army, singing the same old song about Trotskyites. Does anybody still believe all that? Russia is very long-suffering' (*5 June 1937*). Finally Goebbels – Goebbels of all people! – comes to a conclusion he will repeat many times: 'Stalin is mentally ill' (*10 July*), he is destroying his own army!

How could Goebbels not rejoice at the news? 'Since Stalin is himself shooting his generals, we will not have to.' (This is in the entry for 15 March 1940, when Goebbels already had his eye on war.)

Shortly before the war, the newsreels showed footage of the last manoeuvres conducted by Tukhachevsky. They showed a tank–air assault for the first time. It makes an impressive spectacle, and was observed by military attachés and other foreign experts, among whom was General Guderian. After Tukhachevsky's arrest, his theory, introducing new methods of warfare, was labelled as 'wrecking' and banned. Tank corps were disbanded and the tanks dispersed to army groupings. As the war developed, mechanized and tank corps and tank armies had to be reconstituted. The generals of the Wehrmacht, meanwhile, were assiduously adopting new methods, not a few of which had been demonstrated during Tukhachevsky's exercises.

Stalin's support enabled Germany to ratchet up its aggression in the West, but boomeranged back on the USSR. Hitler exploited the neutrality of the USSR to assault the Western countries with all his military might. He did not, however, place much reliance on the long-term stability of that neutrality and, just three months after concluding the non-aggression pact with Russia, announced to his generals on 23 November 1939, 'We shall be able to attack Russia only after we are free in the West.' With Russia obsessively on his mind, he was eager to achieve his goals in the West.

On 10 May 1940 Hitler moved against France. 136 German divisions were opposed to 135 French, British and Belgian divisions. Although the latter had the same number of tanks as the Germans, together with the powerful defences of the Maginot Line and the Belgian forts, the German Army with its dive bombers, massed introduction of tanks into battles, with its parachuting of troops, brought an entirely new dimension to its offensive which stunned and crushed the enemy. After six weeks, France surrendered.

The surrounded British troops, barely able to resist the onslaught of the German tank armies, especially of Guderian's tanks, held Dunkirk and evacuated from the coast across the Channel to England, evading destruction. This was a proud and tragic time when the British showed their fortitude, but what do we Russians know about it? Shamefully little or nothing at all. What do we know about Britain which, deprived of its defeated allies, stood fast and alone in the war against Nazism?

Goebbels, like Hitler, underestimated the resilience of the British and their refusal to acknowledge the defeat they had suffered. The next phase was to be Hitler's 'Operation Sea Lion', the invasion of the British Isles, but then the Führer took a decision not even his closest colleagues expected. The plan to invade the British Isles was abandoned and the immediate military priority became the drive to the east, an attack on Soviet Russia.

Why did Hitler decide to attack us before he had finished the war with Britain?

The war we unwisely embarked on against Finland flaunted very convincingly the weakness of the Soviet army after Stalin's depredations. I heard the view that these events were directly connected expressed by Marshal Zhukov.

I even think now that the war might have been avoided and history could have taken a very different turn. After invading Russia on 22 June 1941, Hitler told Goebbels it had not been an easy decision to make, and perhaps it was just as well, he said, that the German intelligence service had not given him an accurate picture, because otherwise he might not have dared to do it. And if Stalin had not so trashed the Red Army? If it had not acquitted itself so dismally in the Finnish campaign?

Stalin set the army up. In reality we were defeated. The whole of 1941 was one long defeat. During that first phase of the war more than 3 million Russians were taken prisoner, and that is only according to German data. Those are the ones who were brought to the Nazi camps and put on lists of names, but how many never got that far, killed by the cold, by starvation, by Nazi brutality, executed. That is an enormous number of losses, despite the most amazing self-sacrifice. It is like an unbelievable force of nature, something very humbling.

I was very sensitive to the life of the people during the war. I had so much contact with the population and ordinary soldiers. Just the way they lived their lives was therapeutic. It helped to straighten everything out after the depravity of the later 1930s.

We really were liberators, of the whole world, when we arrived in Poland, and further on when people were coming out of the concentration camps to us: Jews herded there from other countries to be exterminated, the last few who had survived; and the French prisoners of war, and the British, the slave labourers, from every imaginable country, like that Belgian. I realized then that I was taking part not only in Russia's Patriotic War, but in a Second World War.

Many years later, Martin Smith, a British film-maker, sought me out in Moscow and I gave a long interview for the *World at War* documentary series. This was for the last episode, and I talked about the discovery and identification of Hitler's body. Six months or so later, I found myself in London. We landed just as Princess Anne was getting married to her horse-riding companion. In the hotel lobby, while we were registering, the newlyweds and those accompanying them escaped from the television cameras into the palace and, at some moment when I was distracted, getting my key from the receptionist at the desk, something completely different appeared on the screen, which riveted my attention. It was a black-and-white chronicle of the war. Dunkirk, tragic shots . . .

This was another episode from the *World at War* series. In the summer it premiered simultaneously in seven countries, and every week, on Tuesdays, the episodes were shown in Britain. A week later, in the evening when the next two episodes were being shown, the streets of London were empty.

The war at sea. A real chronicle of the war. I had barely heard anything about all this, but now, to be actually seeing it . . .

At my request, the organizers of our trip contacted Thames Television, and we were immediately invited to the studio. We were a whole group of journalists. A beautiful woman in a velvet jacket, light, vivacious, Martin Smith's assistant (he himself, she explained, was currently with his wife, who was giving birth) – read out a message on his behalf: 'We welcome . . .' I heard my name.

She invited us all up to the stage. We stood there with our glasses filled with wine, toasted our friendly meeting in the studio, and were photographed. The film for which I had been interviewed was not yet ready, so we were shown the 'Dutch episode'.

A large part of the film consisted of black-and-white newsreel shots. Only three scenes were close-ups, in succession. They had been shot on colour film, which was not available during the war. They were from the present. The first speaker had been the mayor of Amsterdam at the time the Germans invaded. He was summoned by the occupiers' Burgomeister who asked, 'Do you have Jews in the municipality?' He replied, 'No, we have no Jews here.' 'In doing that I was guilty of my first betrayal,' he says, looking intently at the black-and-white past, or rather, inside himself. 'I allowed myself to accept their differentiation of human beings.'

Then on the screen there is a simple Jewish woman, with a big, expressive face. When she was being taken to the ghetto with her two children, a baby and a three-year-old, and her sick brother, the German who came for them was crying. 'I never saw another German soldier cry.' She could have kept quiet about that. She had lived through just too much monstrous brutality: her baby and brother died in the ghetto, but it was clear how important it was to her to mention that soldier. Perhaps there had only been one, but one there had been.

The newsreel scenes took us through the city of those times; something important was changing, brewing. The last straw was the deportation of the Jews. Again, a third, last close–up: an ordinary sort of man, unremarkable, burly, almost portly, with a short haircut. 'I went to the station. A freight train was already there. They were brought, under guard. Armed German soldiers with assault rifles and dogs surrounded them. What could I do on my own, without a gun? But I saw it,' he says angrily, with a shudder, clenching his fists. 'I saw it.'

I think we mentioned him in our first conversation. What mattered very much to me was that he could have looked at that and not seen it. But he did see it, and what he felt was that, if he had seen it, he was complicit in it, and guilty of it and responsible for it. And at that he, eighteen years old at the time, became actively involved in the Resistance.

The film does not show, and there is probably no footage of it in the documentary film archive, a general strike by the Dutch dockers in protest at the deportation of their Jewish fellow citizens. The film does not show the statue of a docker, erected after the war in the square into which the Jews were herded. Neither does it show the monument to the leaders of this strike who were shot by the Germans. It electrified the country and the Dutch Resistance dates from that time. The director addressed not only the facts, but more the profound personal morality in individual people in those historical circumstances. When the lights came on, the very various members of the audience were red-eyed. Those people spoke so sincerely from the screen, as if at confession, as if talking to their own souls. What responsibility they feel for the time to which they belong, and for the mark they personally have left on it.

Personal responsibility for the time to which you belong. That is what you call involvement. And finally, after having been kept separate for so many years from your contemporaries, your fellows in the fight against Nazism, you saw them for the first time then, in London, on the screen in a television studio, and were deeply moved. This is another 'meeting on the Elbe', and profoundly touching.

After watching the film, as we left the television studio, we were each given a copy of the photo showing us on stage with our glasses of wine. Outside, in the studio's showcase window, under a bright banner heading reading, 'Our guests today . . .' was the same photograph, greatly enlarged. So we ourselves entered the life of the city. It was not at all the London we had pictured from Dickens, shrouded in fog, prim, with gentlemen in top hats. This was a multi-cultural city with a picturesque mixture of races; it was both a financial centre and the home of hippies and miniskirts.

We were staying on bustling, commercial Oxford Street. Here, in the dense, diverse flow of people, modish, colourful gypsy skirts mingled with more formal attire, or suddenly you might see a long fur coat on a young man, or a man's formal shirt revealing a bare young chest. There might appear a walking advertisement, like a round poster-covered pillar that had come to life, in which some hapless fellow had been squeezed headlong; or a hereditary professional beggar in a Scottish kilt, playing the bagpipes; or a posse of students suddenly pouring out of a bus and miming on a street corner a scene depicting the atrocities perpetrated by the Pinochet regime in Chile and appealing for protest.

Then a group of willowy Krishna devotees, in gauze robes completely unsuited to the season, with rings in their noses and partly shaven heads might fill the street with melodic chanting, moving along in line and leaping in the air to the accompaniment of a tin-whistle band.

Gazing wide-eyed at this colourful theatre of city life, I could not get out of my head that other, black-and-white, newsreel of a London on which German bombs were falling, which faced invasion by Hitler's troops, and was covered in barricades, ready to fight and die on them.

The London Underground at night. For a full six years, just like in Moscow at the beginning of the war, little children were sleeping on the tracks. Anxious adults, the invariable accordion, and in the morning, on the pavement next to offices destroyed by air raids during the night, here and there a table and stools carried out, a secretary tapping away at her typewriter under a banner reading, 'Still here. Still alive.'

Through a street strewn with the rubble of bombed buildings, the royal family pick their way to Madame Tussaud's museum of waxworks, which has been damaged during the night's bombing. Again the air raid sirens wailing, the three little pigs singing 'We're not afraid of the big, bad wolf!' in a popular cartoon that was screened in the USSR, before the war came to us, too.

Churchill perched on a barricade, his great bulk looming above its top tier. His voice is heard: 'If the British Empire and its Commonwealth last for a thousand years, men will still say . . .'

On the screen we see Dunkirk. Defeat. British ships, besieged by fleeing soldiers, overloaded, listing, casting off. Soldiers too late to get on board swim desperately, furiously out from the coast after them. On the shore behind them there are only dead bodies, but the ships sail further and further out to sea.

An Englishman sitting by the television screen finishes the sentence before Churchill:

'. . . this was their finest hour.' It is a very famous speech.

'. . . will still say,' Churchill concludes resolutely, 'this was their finest hour.'

The ships sail further away, to the coast of England, and there is no catching up with them. On the abandoned shore the wind rakes sand until the bodies of the fallen are motionless mounds. In the sea, soldiers drown.

Yes, that was Britain's heroic, tragic, finest hour. I was filled with admiration as I saw for the first time the dignity and fortitude with which Britain, standing alone, confronted Nazi Germany, when almost the whole of continental Europe was under occupation or, in alliance with the Germans, had been dragged into the war, and imminent invasion by Germany was a real threat which receded only with Hitler's attack on the USSR in June 1941.

I had a glimpse, if only through the lens of a film camera, of what lay beyond the lands our soldiers liberated. And I saw so clearly, and with such deep emotion, something I thought I already knew, and did, only in a more abstract way than I had realized: the Red Army saved the world. Our Patriotic War was the central event of the Second World War, and it rescued the Western countries with their self-sacrificing Resistance movements and this great island.

That means we rescued London and Big Ben, the British Museum, the graveyard for much-loved faithful pet dogs, Hyde Park with its Rotten Row trampled by horses' hooves, the concert halls, the famous pubs, department stores and scattering of market stalls, Westminster Abbey and the slab under your feet enjoining you to 'Remember Winston Churchill.' (He is not buried under that stone but in the modest graveyard of his ancestral estate, as he himself willed.) Yes, we saved London, with all its problems, modern, bursting with life, with its own destiny and all its culture.

I took all that very much to heart and have never forgotten it. That too is part of the sense of involvement.

In Distant Thunder *you can feel this sense of involvement, the joyfulness of the liberators, but in* Berlin, May 1945, *after the victory salvos, after the rejoicing, there is immediately a sense of the bitterness of victory. What was that? Where did it come from?*

Bitterness is inseparable from victory. Victory brings to the surface our mourning for the dead, our sorrow at all we have been through. It engenders a tremendous sense of answerability for the future. And then, there is the need to return to civilian life, which seems already to have moved so far away from us. That bitterness brought enlightenment, but it could also bring despondency and crush people.

While I was in Poznań, I complained I was stuck there just as my army was marching through Germany and the assault on Berlin was nearing. In fact, though, fate had done me a favour. Already in Poznań, I heard someone phoning from a neighbouring division to ask what to do about two soldiers who had raped a German woman. Colonel Latyshev's response was immediate and uncompromising: they must be shot in front of the ranks. This was in conformity with our peacetime laws, which prescribed the death penalty for gang rape. That was the only possibility, completely unambiguous. A stop had to be put to unacceptable behaviour. Stuck in Poznań, however, the colonel was behind the times. As the Red Army advanced through Germany, rape was being condoned.

When a million-strong army came from its own land that had been violated by war on to the territory of its hated enemy ('Take a good look:

this is fucking Germany'), it was probably inevitable that there would be atrocities, but in those circumstances the failure to punish turned effectively into incitement.

Do you think it could have been stopped? Or was it impossible to contain such a charge of hatred and vengefulness?

I appeared in a film about those events and I said: yes, German women suffered for what their men had done; but when individual acts were not punished, all hell broke loose. Where attempts were made to stop it, they were successful. It was within the power of the Red Army command to prevent it.

The character this took on during the time I was in Poznań I heard about from German women themselves. For me, rape is the worst crime of all. It robs women not only of their future but also of their past: memories of love and intimacy can come to seem repulsive. What happened was a genocide of love.

I felt this as a wound. I loved our fighting army in all its anguish and will never repudiate that feeling. It was an army that made unbelievable sacrifices and liberated Europe. The rapes were the army defiling itself.

But, all the same, victory must have felt sweet.

It did. Our victory was a tremendous achievement. But Stalin's toast on the occasion of the victory, which we heard over the radio, left a permanently bitter taste. He failed to acknowledge, fulsomely, the courage, self-sacrifice and valour shown by our citizens: he praised only the endurance they had shown in the war. And even that mealy-mouthed praise he gave exclusively to the Russian people, isolating it and raising it up above the other nationalities of the USSR. People hung on every word uttered by The Leader, and that was how this toast was interpreted: Hosannah to the Russian People! The consequences were only too predictable in a country like ours. That precious sense of unity, of solidarity in a war to defend our Motherland without thinking twice about our race or nationality, was destroyed. Something mendacious was imposed: Big Brother Russia, relative to whom all the other nationalities and republics were junior. And that was as much as we got in place of that all-important sense and belief that we were all compatriots. It was bad news for everyone, including the Russians. What built up from that time has expressed itself in our days as an undisguised, sometimes highly aggressive, urge towards separatism, which is a threat to Russia.

You write that the situation was already changing in the postwar months while you were still in Germany, but nevertheless there was still some hope, an expectation of certain freedoms. Were those hopes completely dashed when you got back home?

After demobilization I returned home to Moscow in October 1945. I wrote a story not that long ago, *Hearth and Home*, about how difficult it was going back to this new old life I had lost touch with. Here I will only say that I so wanted, so much needed to hear a human voice addressing the living and the dead, addressing everything we had been through in the war. Instead the newspapers and radio only went back to banging on about targets Stalin had set for the output of pig iron and steel, the new five-year plan, and how people were no more than the cogs to fulfil it.

The very next Victory Day holiday, 9 May, Stalin turned into an ordinary working day, which is what it remained until the twentieth anniversary of victory when, with Stalin no longer around, it again became a day of major celebration.

Even the little signs of special respect for those who had been awarded medals were revoked, like free travel on public transport and other minor privileges. In short, in the minds of all those who had contributed to victory, what they had brought to the tragic battle for the country's survival was belittled. The victory belonged to the state, not to the peoples of the USSR.

The big question was, where is Hitler? He was the personification of Nazism and if, after all the horrors of the war he had caused, he was alive and kicking, as Soviet propaganda claimed, what kind of victory was it anyway? It spread apathy among the population.

It is unquestionable that the discovery of Hitler's body was an important historical fact, knowledge owed to our people and to history. Stalin, who had first set up our country for defeat by the enemy at the beginning of the war, Stalin, who concealed the truth about Hitler and turned his death into a state secret, cheated our people of their victory.

You mention in Berlin, May 1945 *that Major Bystrov very much wanted the discovery of Hitler's body made public and charged you with writing about it. Did he try to share the secret with anyone else?*

When Bystrov and I were interrogating Käthe Heusermann once more before leaving Buch, Bystrov allowed the *Pravda* correspondent to sit in on the questioning. Martyn Merzhanov and the writer Boris Gorbatov had been reporting from Berlin on the storming of the Reichstag. Merzhanov sat there, and although Bystrov warned me not to translate, he did, of course, realize what was being discussed. Later, back in Moscow, he invited me to his home and introduced me to Klimenko, who was also visiting him. Merzhanov told me he had written to the Central Committee asking for authorization to publish a story about the identification of Hitler in *Pravda*, based on what he had gathered while present at our interrogation. Georgiy Alexandrov, Secretary of the Central Committee for Propaganda, told him,

'The Politburo were agog reading your report,' but Stalin noted on it, 'Is this making him out to be a hero?', meaning Hitler and the fact that he had stayed in Berlin to the end.

Many years later, Martyn Merzhanov, with whom I had maintained friendly relations, phoned and asked, 'Yelena, can you help me? I'm going through my Berlin notebooks and I've got a note, "Tell Boris! Hitler's teeth are with Kagan." Who was Kagan?'

Well, yes, who was Kagan? After all this time nobody else would be likely to know.

Lyuba, Kagan was me! And all the reports and documents, of course, are signed with my name. When I began to get into print, Rzhev was the memory closest to my heart. My first stories were about that, and as there has been a conspiracy of silence about it in the history of the Patriotic War and it had been left without a voice, I took 'Rzhevskaya' as my pen name, and that has been my name for the past forty-five years.

The first stories I wrote were about the war around Rzhev. Quick verbal sketches in my notebook, scraps of dialogue, reflections while we were on the move, later proved, to a greater or lesser degree, to be the raw material, or the prompt, for stories. It happened that the tone of the writing in a notebook somehow evolved of its own accord. I still sometimes glance in one, something jumps out, opens up to me. Even a soldier's naughty word, caught and written down in a notebook, is terribly affecting.

The person conducting my seminar at the Gorky Literary Institute approved of my writing and advised me to get it published. I worked up a cycle of stories, 'At Rzhev', and took it to a magazine. They gave it back to me: 'Your stories are sad. They are about everyday details of war which are probably not really worth describing. People are tired of the war.' And that was the end for me of writing about the war for a long time. I was not aware of how deeply this topic was embedded in me. I felt I had written as well as I could.

You returned to Moscow bearing the burden of feeling you had a duty to history and already knowing you had the vocation of a writer, but you were really very young by today's standards – just twenty-five. You had yet to graduate from the Literary Institute, to find your own voice, and on top of all that to resolve some difficult issues of where to live and how to earn a living.

Lyuba, I won't go into all the ups and downs of the twenty years that passed before the first publication of *Berlin*, when I managed to tell the whole truth about the death of Hitler and the discovery of his body, and to back up my eyewitness account with documents. That is for another book, which I intend to write. I want to write about it with all the details of life at that time in reminiscences that will be a continuation of *Hearth and Home*. It was a long, difficult journey.

Yes, I had a mission to make public the secret of the century, that we had found Hitler's body. The way it turned out, none of the people caught up in those historic events was present at every stage of them except me, because you cannot get by without an interpreter. And none of the other participants had ever taken up the pen, or had any intention of doing so. People pinned their hopes on me to write about it because after I was demobilized I would be going to study at the Literary Institute. I myself had no intention of leaving these things hidden away, and my silence weighed heavily on me, but these facts had been classified a state secret and the price for disclosing them would have been seven to fifteen years' imprisonment. Quite a long time. I had to watch history being distorted without saying anything, confiding only in close friends.

In 1948 the arrests started again. They affected people close to us. The sense of vulnerability was aggravated by my sense of having no rights and being unable to get a job on account of Point Five. Nothing – four years of active service in the army, medals – was considered in your favour. And worse was to come.

Do you remember, Lyuba, that visual aid, the skeleton with inventory number 4417 who migrated together with the Russian Red Cross' evening course up and down Malaya Bronnaya, turning up one moment in the food hall of a grocer's shop and the next on the stage of the Jewish Theatre? Next to us evening students, two elderly ladies were talking loudly to each other on the stage and clicking away on their abacuses. Backstage the scene-shifters were moving things around. The theatre was preparing for the start of the season.

At the start of the war, in summer 1941?

Yes. But some quite different memories are also associated with that stage for me: taking our farewell of Solomon Mikhoels.[1] One dark, dank night in January 1948, I was waiting with my husband, Isaak Kramov, among a silent, dejected crowd who did not believe the story about a 'road accident'. We were waiting for the coffin to be brought. It did not appear.

When I was very little, I lived on Tverskoy Boulevard in a building facing Malaya Bronnaya Street, and this nook of Moscow, with the colourful posters of the Jewish Theatre and the boulevard, bordered on my domain. That terrible evening it was tainted for me forever by something ominous and repulsive. In the towns and villages abandoned by the retreating

1. The artistic director of the Jewish Theatre, and chairman of the Jewish Anti-Fascist Committee during the war. Tr.

Germans I remember the tragic face of Mikhoels in the role of King Lear, the duplicated photographs slapped on fences, stuck on wires, as the image of the Jew who must be exterminated. Now it had happened.

The following day the coffin was placed on the stage of the Jewish Theatre. We said goodbye to Mikhoels, along with a stream of people who walked past the coffin, crushed by our loss and this appalling sign of trouble brewing, from which there was no escape.

How could you live and write in a time like that?

You cannot live in constant fear: it just doesn't happen. The contact between people, and love and friendship were more intense. We were close friends with some wonderful people. Despite all the hardships of daily life, we had such a creative atmosphere at home.

I was afraid of forgetting things about those events in Berlin, of letting them slip if I put everything off, so I began to write shortly after returning to Moscow, drawing on some entries in the notebook from that time. After Stalin's death, in 1954, I took the manuscript to *Znamya*, which specializes in prose about the army. Because of the subject matter, the manuscript was sent for permission to publish to the Foreign Ministry. It was returned with their resolution: 'At your discretion': that is, they were not banning it. The editor, Vadim Kozhevnikov, was, however, highly circumspect in matters of discretion. He said to the editorial staff who were rooting for the manuscript, 'This has never been written about before. Why should we be the first? And anyway, who is she?' I was just someone off the street.

The manuscript was, nevertheless, published in *Znamya* (No. 2, 1955). It contained all the details of the suicides of Hitler and Goebbels, the discovery of Goebbels' charred remains and those of his six children, murdered by their parents. They also kept in the testimony about the documents found in Hitler's bunker and the main find: the diaries of Goebbels. There was the story of the removal and burning of Hitler's body, and his burial there and then in the Reich Chancellery garden in a crater. In fact, everything except that we had found Hitler in that crater and identified him.

In other words, they left it hanging in the air whether this was fact or speculation. How did you manage to get round that ban?

That happened in 1961, in my book *Spring in a Greatcoat*, and in a fairly roundabout manner. After the war, I was drawn to impressions of life in peacetime. I wrote novellas that were far removed from my own biography, about life without the war, although interlayered with it.

The Soviet Writer publishing house was intending to publish a book consisting of two of my novellas, which I had already largely been paid for. It didn't come off. Of course, I was very upset, but it was not the first or last time that a setback, providing it was not fatal, turned out to be all for the good. The publishing house had not forgotten the fee already paid and, two years later, suggested I should update the book. The writers Isaak Kramov and Boris Slutsky suggested I should slip in the Rzhev stories. So it was that in 1961 a book was published, titled *Spring in a Greatcoat* and containing stories about the war which had been lying around for fifteen years. They were warmly received, and that encouraged me to return to writing prose about the war. In addition, however, the book included my uncensored documentary account of how we found Hitler's body. I put back in everything that had been taken out by *Znamya*: that is, everything about finding and identifying Hitler. Happily the censors paid no attention to the additions, because basically the text had already been published. And that is how, for the first time, the fact was made known that the Red Army had found Hitler's body, although I had no documents to back that up, except for the one copy Ivan Klimenko had sent me.

Having that publication behind me was very helpful when I was trying to get permission to work in the Council of Ministers Archive. The Writers' Union supported my application. I appealed to publishing houses and the Communist Party Central Committee, referring to the fact that I had been a participant in these events, that I was a writer who had already written about them, and that I now needed documentation for more in-depth and reliable work. For a long time it all seemed hopeless. The answer was always the same: 'There is no access to these materials and no exceptions are likely to be made.' But on the crest of the wave of national pride as the twentieth anniversary of victory approached, a miracle occurred and the doors of the secret archive opened before me. It was September 1964, and I got to work in the archive for twenty days.

At that time I did not know the name of the archive. During my conversation with Zhukov, he speculated that it was the Council of Ministers Archive, and he was right. Now that the documents are beginning to be published and the secrecy relaxed, we finally know which archive it was.

For me, the encounter with these documents was overwhelming. The intention had clearly been to leave them to moulder, silently covering up the mystery, and now it was my job to bring them out into the light, come hell or high water.

Here were our notes, documents, reports; and German orders, dispatches, letters, diaries, the folders I had worked through in the Reich Chancellery. There was much, too, that I now held in my hand for the first time. I plunged into the work, and made many amazing discoveries. For example, the testimony of Lieutenant General Rattenhuber, written under interrogation by the Ministry of Internal Affairs at General Staff Headquarters in Moscow; the testimony of Hitler's adjutant, Otto Günsche; or a document revealing Hitler's last plan, his gamble on a split between the Allies.

All the documents I did already know were also unique: the document about the discovery of Hitler's body, the materials about our identification of it, and so on. In Western newspapers they were writing, and some information about it reached us, that the world still did not know the truth about Hitler's fate. A shiver ran down my spine: 'But I do, and I have the ability to describe it.' It was all in my hands.

For twenty days I worked in the archive, and in just four months, with alacrity untypical of me, I wrote *Berlin, May 1945*. I was very conscious that I needed to get it finished in time for publication in the anniversary May 1965 issue of *Znamya*, which meant I needed to submit it in March. The publication in *Znamya*, under the title 'Berlin Pages', was followed by my book *Berlin, May 1945*. All the official items, documents, reports, diaries and letters reprinted in the book, both from the Soviet side and from the German, were being published for the first time.

What sort of reception did the book get?

A completed book, for as long as it has life, plays a role in its author's destiny and can bestow unexpected gifts on him or her. It brought me my meeting with Marshal Zhukov. It caused a sensation in the USSR and internationally. In our country twelve editions of *Berlin* have appeared, the latest only in 2006, and in total over 1,500,000 copies have been sold. It has been translated and published in over twenty countries and serialized in newspapers in Poland, Finland, Switzerland, Yugoslavia and Hungary; in Italy four issues of the magazine *Tempo* had my portrait on the cover.

The historians took an interest. Most notably, Lev Bezymensky corresponded with and interviewed the participants of the history I described, worked on the topic, and in 1968 published his book *The End of a Legend*.

When your book was being published, was there any niggling from censors about the documents?

Mostly over Goebbels. In the diary he allows himself unflattering remarks about the Soviet people, and gets the date of the Germans crossing the Dnieper wrong – he says it was on the second day of the war, but our historians say we held out longer than that. In the first days after the attack on the USSR Goebbels in his diary is a bit 'put out', as I expressed it, because the British sank the *Bismarck*.

Goebbels' diary is of recurring interest for you. It was only in the mid-1990s that you put it behind you by writing Goebbels: A Portrait Based on the Diary.

Even in the hectic days in the bunker, in the feverish sorting through of documents that might give us a clue to the main issue of where Hitler was, it was obvious to me that this was probably our most important find, only there was just no time to spend even an hour or two reading it, because it plainly had no relevance to tracking down Hitler. It dealt only with the years before the war and the first weeks of the invasion of the USSR. At that moment we had more pressing concerns. Then front headquarters went off the notion of translating the diaries.

I was even afraid that they might have been lost, but when I encountered the last notebook in the archive I was persuaded that they were safe in our archives. As I said, my publishing of extracts from this last notebook alerted German historians to the whereabouts of these volumes of the diary, and eventually, in the late 1980s, the Munich Institute for Contemporary History published the handwritten diaries of Goebbels in four volumes. More than half of that publication was the notebooks we discovered back then in Goebbels' office in the Führerbunker.

The institute invited me to conduct a seminar and presented me with these four thick volumes. I was writing a novella at the time and did not suppose I would be immersing myself in studying them. It seemed that all this was an old story and it was time to say goodbye to it, even though I was bound to it by personal involvement and by things that remained unsaid.

However, circumstances in the world, and especially in our country, encouraged and obliged me to return to them. I was amazed how Goebbels exposes his real self in the diaries. It would hardly be possible to describe the kind of politician Nazism brought to prominence more graphically than he did himself: a fanatic and mountebank, careerist and criminal, one of those wretched individuals to whose will the German people surrendered themselves, condemning themselves to the insanity of war.

The diary dissipates the mystical haze which those who write about Nazism periodically try to envelop it in and reveals it as a criminal political conspiracy. Something that seemed impossible happened to Germany: ridiculous individuals seized power.

The diary enables us to trace the alterations in Goebbels' personality, to picture more clearly the genesis of Nazism with its cult of violence, its cult of the Führer, Hitler's fatal seductiveness and how totally destructive he was for everyone.

In this difficult and laborious work on the portrait of Goebbels, in which you helped with the translation, I was very aware of the need to stress to the reader the danger of pernicious phenomena which, with the connivance of the state, encourage the proliferation of nationalistic forces in our country, forces that threaten Russia with self-destruction.

You know, when you and I were working on Goebbels' diaries, I was not fully aware of how topical they were, the pressing need for the didactic pathos of your book. It seemed all that was already a thing of the past and could never happen again. I was wrong.

Goebbels and the discovery of Hitler's remains are documentary topics to which you returned from a sense of responsibility to history. You personally are drawn more to the first period of the war, the time of a self-sacrificing people's war and of Rzhev, to which you became so attached. You wrote your novellas, February, Winding Roads *and* Raking the Embers *about that, and your collection of stories,* Near Approaches, *an unexpectedly modern montage of fragments. You once let slip something. You said, 'I have never really returned from the war.' What you experienced has never let you go. You went off to the war as a young student, Lena Kagan, and came back as the writer, Yelena Rzhevskaya. Rzhev was your destiny, both in the war and in your writing. I see nothing coincidental in that. In one of his conversations with you, Yury Dikov called Rzhev 'the conscience of the war'. That is so akin to the pain that motivates you.*

As I have said, I started out in 1946 with stories about Rzhev. Then I wrote about life in peacetime, roaming far from my own experiences into literary fiction. But what I had lived through would not let go. The last time I wrote about material quite detached from my life was when I submitted a story to *Novy mir* in 1961.

Since then what I have written has been not so much autobiographical as based on my own experiences. That was not what I first set out to do, but I found that my life was so full of impressions (as probably everybody's is) that it squeezed out the adventitious, the borrowings, and that it was better to transfigure experience into prose unfettered by biography.

From a distance the war seemed to become more allusive, more visual. For many years I was pigeon-holed as writing what we call 'war literature'. That is not entirely accurate because I do not write about pitched battles; I write about the world in wartime, about life in wartime.

In some ways it is harder and in others easier to write about the war. It is harder because much about war is monotonous, starting with people's clothing. But it is easier because the plot is self-propelling. The war itself is the plot.

But you write wonderful prose about life before the war in Punctuation Marks; *and about returning from the war. And you have promised to continue your novella,* Hearth and Home. *You looked even further back, into the history of your family and your ancestors in the cycle* Byways of Memory. *It is so enchanting, about how life is precious in itself, and there is no need for a plot.*

Well, now I have been trying these last years to write about what affects me, what I have taken to heart, what stirs, enchants or torments me, to write without inhibition, without thinking about plot and character, and certainly not about whether something belongs to one genre or another. That is actually closest to autobiography, not necessarily in terms of facts although, if they do creep in, then in the context of everything associated with them that nourishes the soul, and memory, and emotion.

Perhaps, though, plot is a presumption, even a deception. Life itself in all its interrelatedness is the plot. Language is the self-propelling force behind prose.

I feel I should thank fate for my presence in all the unbelievable happenings of my many decades, and for being able to take advantage of the fortunate opportunity of wandering back through my life, looking more closely at some things, thinking them through, loving them more or repudiating them. Yet as I do that, I do not have the feeling of being transported back to the past, but of staying firmly in the here and now. The present is only an extension of our past, without which it would be completely surreal.

Epilogue

by Lyuba Summ,
Yelena Rzhevskaya's Granddaughter

The main thrust of Yelena Rzhevskaya's book as initially conceived was that Hitler's corpse was found and identified by Soviet intelligence operatives in May 1945, but Stalin classified the information. In 1965, when *Berlin, May 1945* was published in Russia, one state secret spawned another. All right, Hitler's body had been discovered and identified, but there must be no mention of that having been turned into a state secret. Before Gorbachev's *perestroika* it was impossible to publish the conversation with Marshal Zhukov. That story, and the frank discussion of Stalin's personal decision to conceal the discovery of Hitler's body from his own citizens and the Allies, and the analysis of the causes and consequences of that decision are among the main additions to the original text.

Vladimir Kozlov has revealed that in 1964 it was decided to create a special archive dedicated to the victory over Germany. It was in this nascent archive that Rzhevskaya worked.[1] All archives were administered by the KGB, and its minders would allow no identification of the archival materials she had used in the book.[2] Kozlov also describes Operation Myth in detail, which entailed trying (in vain) to force captured German witnesses to assert that the Führer was still alive and had disappeared. Rzhevskaya reconstructed the last days in the bunker and Hitler's suicide using the testimony of Günsche, Linge, Baur and others, but did not know in 1965 that these records had been compiled as part of Operation Myth. When she

---

1. Vladimir Kozlov, *Gde Gitler? Povtornoe rassledovanie NKVD-MVD SSSR obstoiatel'stv ischeznoveniia Adol'fa Gitlera*. Moscow: Modest Kolerov i Tri kvadrata, 2002.
2. In 2007, preparing her book for translation, Rzhevskaya added references for the archive files. The archive she had worked in has been closed and part of it transferred to the State Archive of the Russian Federation. In 2014 I found these materials among the Molotov Papers, six substantial volumes which duplicate the Stalin Papers. The internal numbering of the folders is retained.

did, she was again unable to disclose this mystery about a mystery.[1] It is an aspect she specifically worked on for this edition.

Memoirs of a Wartime Interpreter further differs from *Berlin, May 1945* in including as many documents from Rzhevskaya's personal archive as space would allow, and three chapters about the earlier years of the war in Russia and Poland.[2] My grandmother was insistent that 'The storming and taking of Berlin cannot be properly understood outside the context of the war as a whole and of everything we experienced.' As the years passed, she increasingly attached importance to the human dimension of the war. That is why this volume tells us not about battles, not only about the search for and identification of Hitler, but also about Matryona Nilovna, the indomitable mother in Zaimishche; about the sad story of a Belgian soldier and a Polish prostitute; and about Käthe Heusermann, a dentist's assistant who identified Hitler and was rewarded with ten years in Soviet prisons.

Rzhevskaya featured Käthe Heusermann sympathetically in her memoirs from the outset, but knew nothing of Käthe's transportation to Moscow until 1964, and learned of her subsequent fate only in 1996 thanks to Lev Bezymensky, when a copy of the typewritten pages of her memoirs found their way into Rzhevskaya's archive. Excerpts from those memoirs are included here for the first time.

My grandmother wanted to do more for Käthe's memory, and when *Memoirs of a Wartime Interpreter* was already being translated into different languages, she asked me to search the Internet to find out more about Käthe's later life and locate her relatives. That is how I obtained the memoirs of Theodor Bruck, the Jewish dentist, recorded by his granddaughter. These reveal the full extent of the efforts Käthe made to keep him safe.

In 2015, Zvezda, a Russian television channel, made a film about the discovery and identification of Hitler's body and the role Yelena had played. For the first time the facts of Käthe Heusermann's fate were made public on Russian television. Then, in summer 2016, Nina Belyaeva came to Moscow from Paris, intending to shoot a documentary about the finding of Hitler but, after hearing this story, decided instead to relate the fate of Käthe and

---

1. Rzhevskaya heard about Operation Myth back in the 1960s. An editor at a publishing house whom she knew from her days at the Institute of Philosophy, Literature and History showed her the manuscript of a book by a Soviet participant in the operation. The book was not passed for publication.
2. Sadly, Major Boris Bystrov did not live see the book published. He returned to academic life after the war and died in 1963. Rzhevskaya's archive contains illuminating letters from Faust Shkaravsky (1897–1975), and postcards and letters from Ivan Isaevich Klimenko (1914–98), as well as later interviews. Having worked in counterintelligence until 1970, Klimenko finally allowed himself to speak freely.

the relationship between the two women, their meeting on the day the war ended, and their hopes for life in peacetime.

By this time my grandmother no longer had the strength to participate in filming and it fell to me to read on her behalf from her books and diaries. Nina Belyaeva managed to find Käthe's eighty-year old niece. That is how her film ends: I in grandmother's apartment in Moscow and Käthe's niece in her own home read in turn from Käthe's reminiscences of prison, her sentence, the journey to Siberia, the hard labour camp and her return. At one remove, Yelena and Käthe finally met in us and told the story to its end.

The film was shown on French television in spring 2017, and on 25 April Nina Belyaeva sent me a link to download it.[1] I found it in my mailbox a few hours after my grandmother passed away.

---

1. The film, *The Death of Hitler: The History of a State Secret* (in French), can be viewed at https://www.youtube.com/watch?v = XcDCtElYTT4.